THE POLITICS OF MULTINATIONAL STATES

The Politics of Multinational States

Edited by

Don MacIver
Senior Lecturer in Politics
Staffordshire University

First published in Great Britain 1999 by
MACMILLAN PRESS LTD
Houndmills, Basingstoke, Hampshire RG21 6XS and London
Companies and representatives throughout the world

A catalogue record for this book is available from the British Library.

ISBN 0–333–65319–X

 First published in the United States of America 1999 by
ST. MARTIN'S PRESS, INC.,
Scholarly and Reference Division,
175 Fifth Avenue, New York, N.Y. 10010

ISBN 0–312–17487–X

Library of Congress Cataloging-in-Publication Data
The politics of multinational states / edited by D.N. MacIver.
p. cm.
Includes bibliographical references and index.
ISBN 0–312–17487–X (cloth)
1. Ethnic groups—Political activity.   2. Ethnicity—Political
aspects.   3. Multiculturalism.   4. Pluralism (Social sciences)
I. MacIver, D. N., 1940–
JF1061.P65 1997
323.1—dc21   97–5323
                                                             CIP

This book is printed on paper suitable for recycling and made from fully managed and
sustained forest sources.

10   9   8   7   6   5   4   3   2   1
08   07   06   05   04   03   02   01   00   99

Printed and bound in Great Britain by
Antony Rowe Ltd, Chippenham, Wiltshire

This book is for my mother

Contents

Tables and Figures

TABLES

FIGURES

The Contributors

Christopher Bennett is at the School of Slavonic and East European Studies. He was born in Yugoslavia and has worked both there and in Britain as a journalist and historian. He is author of *Yugoslavia's Bloody Collapse*.

Peter Duncan is head of the Politics section at the School of Slavonic and East European Studies. He has researched and published extensively on culture, ethnicity and politics in Russia.

John Fitzmaurice is a political advisor to the European Parliament and lives in Brussels. He is author of *The Politics and Government of Belgium*, now in its second edition.

John Gibbons is a lecturer in politics at Manchester Metropolitan University and has written a number of papers and articles on Spanish politics.

Karen Henderson is a lecturer in politics at Leicester University and has researched and published on both Czechoslovakia and its successor states.

Michael Keating is Professor of Political Science at the University of Western Ontario. He is author of *State and Regional Nationalism* and *Nations Against the State*.

Don MacIver is a lecturer in Politics at Staffordshire University and has written a number of papers on nationalism and on Canadian politics.

Fida Nasrallah is at the Centre for Lebanese Studies in Oxford and has published a number of articles on politics in Lebanon.

Vernon Hewitt is lecturer in politics at Bristol University and author of a number of articles and books on India.

Jonathan Steinberg is at Trinity Hall, Cambridge, and is a well-established student of Swiss society. He is author of *Why Switzerland?* now in its second edition.

Preface

The much remarked resurgence of ethnic nationalism since the 1960s has revealed the extent to which many supposed nation states are in fact multinational states. It has also produced a considerable interest amongst scholars in national and ethnic conflict within states. Much of this work has been concerned with ethnic minorities, regional peripheries and separatist movements. Ethnic conflict, however, is not only a problem for minorities and peripheries but also for the centre and for government.

Multinational states present a variety of problems of interest to scholars in a range of disciplines. For political scientists in particular ethnic pluralism has significant implications for the political integration, the government and the viability of states. Multinational states, incorporating major ethnic, language or religious differences, tend to have fragmented political cultures, which may produce strong and competing identities. These may be expressed in loyalty to particular regions or ethnic groups, commitment to distinctive symbols, traditions and institutions and sometimes in resurgent nationalism. Such pluralities are likely to produce divided communities with conflicting orientations to politics and disputed standards of legitimacy which may lead to serious civil conflict or even political disintegration.

In such conditions, however, it may be difficult on occasions to achieve consensus or to govern through the institutions and processes of 'normal' politics, especially as conflict may arise over the constitution, composition of government, recruitment to the public service and official language policy, not to mention the prioritisation of groups and regions in the allocation of resources.

This book is concerned with the particular problems which the composition and structure of multinational states present for their government and for their ability to adapt and persist in circumstances of ethnic conflict. It focuses on the politics and government of multinational states and will examine some of the distinctive features, the specific outcomes and the range of experience which may be encountered in governing multinational states.

The book includes studies of ethnic politics in ten multinational states by a group of political scientists who have specialist knowledge and experience of those specific countries. It is intended to make a coherent study, providing comparable information on each country and an examination of the responses of governments to the problems of ethnic pluralism. The contributors have worked diligently to produce what was asked of them and they have each presented their own analysis and conclusions. The credit for whatever merits the work may have thus belongs to them, although responsibility for any shortcomings in the coherence and completeness of the work as a whole remain with myself.

The completion of this work has involved the cooperation and support of many to whom I am considerably indebted. I am grateful to the contributors for carrying out the tasks I asked them to undertake and especially those who completed their contributions on time and promptly returned their corrected proofs. I wish to thank colleagues at Staffordshire University for reading parts of the manuscript and particularly Emma Clarence, Graeme Herd, David Morrice, Michael Stephen and Trevor Taylor for their comments on the introduction and some of the chapters. Others helped in other ways, particularly Sheila Berrisford who typed some of the manuscript. I have a particular debt to Geof Bridgewood of the Design and Print Unit at Staffordshire University for his indispensable advice and assistance in preparing camera ready copy. Finally, I have to thank Sunder Katwala, Karen Brazier and staff at Macmillan for their support during the preparation of the book.

Don MacIver

Introduction

States and Ethnic Pluralism

Don MacIver

This book addresses the politics of ethnic pluralism and examines the distinctive features, the range of experience and some of the specific problems of ethnic relations in multinational states. The catastrophic ethnic conflicts of the 1990s have highlighted these problems but this should not obscure the fact that some form of ethnic pluralism is a feature of the majority of states. Ethnic pluralism complicates both the domestic and international problems of states and ethnic conflict can make them unmanageable and destabilising. A well informed understanding of ethnic pluralism and its implications for the internal politics and political stability of states may in itself be a contribution to the maintenance of stable political order within and amongst states.

Ethnic pluralism generally arises because the boundaries of ethnic groups and the boundaries of states do not coincide. The boundaries of states are relatively rigid and only change as a result of very exceptional external pressures or cataclysmic conflicts. The boundaries of ethnic groups may be more fluid and frequently cut across the boundaries of states. Ethnic groups generally have older pedigrees and often receive very much greater loyalty than states. They may be the focus of an alternative national identity and loyalty to that associated with the state and officially sponsored by it. Moreover, ethnic groups are persistent and resilient and can be forceful in the expression of their identities, interests and demands, which are a recurrent source of political and even armed conflict within states. The legitimacy and integrity of states may be challenged by the demands of ethnic groups for recognition, autonomy or independence.

Ethnic groups become politically engaged to redress perceived injustices. They usually seek political power in order to maximise their control over their own affairs. Their claims, sometimes based on the principles of self-determination and articulated in the the rhetoric of popular sovereignty, may challenge the legitimacy and integrity of the state. Democratic self-determination based on national identity is the fundamental principle of the nation state and has become almost the only acceptable basis for the legitimate exercise of political power and authority in modern states. In societies with a homogeneous or a dominant culture and a high level of agreement about national identity, the basis of legitimacy is likely to be undisputed. Where these conditions are lacking and there is uncertainty or conflict about national identity, agreement about political legitimacy may be difficult to establish or simply unattainable. Then not only the foundations of legitimate political authority but the whole framework of political organisation are likely to be contested.

STATES AND ETHNIC GROUPS

Nationalism and Political Order

The argument that people should determine their own government and that the most appropriate basis for this is nationality or national identity was presented most succinctly by John Stuart Mill. There was "a *prima facie* case", he wrote, that a national group should be united "under the same government and a government to themselves apart".[1] This was an idea that had been evolving in western Europe, especially in England for nearly two hundred years, when Mill wrote. His demand that, if a people were free to do anything they should be free to choose their own form of government, was a culmination as much as a beginning in political thought. The strength of liberal ideas in the late nineteenth and early twentieth centuries, the influence of Anglo-American Liberal internationalism and the powerful advocacy of Lloyd George and Woodrow Wilson then ensured that this idea became well established in the political thought and practice of international relations, though not so much of international law. Thus the nation state became dominant form of political organisation throughout the world in modern times.

   The idea of the nation state pre-dates the term, which only came into use after the first world war, and is therefore a relatively recent addition to the vocabulary of politics. It is intended to indicate the coincidence of the nation and the state and thus represents the fulfilment of the liberal idea of the nation as a self determining group of people. The term, however, was a misnomer even as it was invented, a statement of political aspiration rather than reality. It is also problematic since its practical meaning is in many respects confusing, being applied by some conventions to all states, whatever their ethnic and national composition. Moreover, the concept itself is ambiguous and simply begs the question of what is the nation that constitutes the nation state.

There are two concepts of the nation in general use in the history and political science literature. First, there is the cultural concept of the nation in which the nation is defined as an ethnic community with a distinctive culture usually expressed in a language peculiar to its members. The nation in this sense is an organic entity with an existence of its own, the bearer and repository of the traditions and experience of a community. The nation defines its members who inherit and transmit its culture and values. This view of the nation was first proposed by Herder in the eighteenth century and, although it has appeared in a number of different versions, it has been the dominant view of the nation in European thought since then. This view has always appealed to conservatives and romantics who have seen the nation as a self-sufficient organism which forms the "natural" basis for the state.

Second, there is the civic concept of the nation in which the nation is defined in terms of citizenship through membership in a civil society with distinctive civil institutions, associations, values and interests. In this sense the nation is an association with a common history and a collective personality whose continued existence is an act of will expressed in the consent and participation of its members. The nation, therefore, is defined by its members who renew it every generation and may permit the entry of new groups to citizenship. This liberal view of the nation evolved in England in the seventeenth and eighteenth centuries and came to maturity in the French revolution, when it was given its dynamic character and universal appeal by the Jacobins. It was strongly resisted by the traditional states of Europe, who saw its democratic ethos as a threat to their traditional authority. It became more influential with increasing democratisation, however, and is crucial to understanding the relationship between nation and state in the modern world.

Nevertheless, the idea of the nation was captured by statesmen who exploited it for their own purposes and interests, using it as the principal instrument of state building in the nineteenth and twentieth centuries. They manipulated and invented national traditions' to secure and legitimise their regimes amongst a newly mobilised population, creating national communications, comprehensive social welfare programmes, education systems and fostering national cultures to provide a basis for identity, loyalty and integration. Instead of the nation being the basis of the state, the state became the basis of the nation. Thus the state became the state nation (or national state) claiming to be the nation state, a political community in which the state exploited the sentiments of national identity as a basis of cohesion and integration.

The nation state may, therefore, be considered a variant of the state in which nationalism or national identity is one of the principal sources of legitimacy and integration. It is a political community with three major capabilities. These are first, that it is able to exercise a monopoly of political authority and legitimate force within its territory; second, that it has a government which is an effective centre of decision making, able to significantly influence the determination of goals and the allocation of resources in society; and third, that it operates as a focus for political identity, loyalty and support amongst its population. These capabilities may be described as coercive, instrumental and identitive and when functioning effectively, they are normally assumed to be mutually reinforcing. One of the problems facing many contemporary states, however, is that they face challenges to the exercise of these capabilities which impair their ability to function as coherent and effective political communities.

Challenges to the State

These challenges to the state have placed it under increasing pressure which has eroded its position as the dominant form of political organisation in the world. There is now growing acceptance of the view that the state as we have known it is in decline. It is argued that the state has lost its sovereign independence. Its ability to maintain the integrity and security of its borders has been impaired by the technical advancement of strategic weapon systems and the spread of international terrorism. The growth of supranational institutions, especially in Western Europe, has effectively reduced the state's control of policy and decision making in its own territory. As a consequence of the proliferation of international organisations, multinational corporations, transnational interest groups and a range of other non-state actors, the world economy has penetrated the state's domestic economy, enabling regional and local institutions and non-central governments to play an increasingly important role on their own behalf, making transactions with other actors, including corporations, non-central governments and even states. Thus they encroach on the formerly exclusive role of the state, further reducing its significance as the primary actor in international economic relations.

These changes in the structure and composition of international society have altered the environment in which the state operates. While such external changes do affect the behaviour of states and the role of states relative to other actors in the world order, they do not necessarily challenge their legal status or continued existence. There is one development, however, which does present a significant challenge to some states and could threaten their persistence in their existing form.

This challenge comes from the mobilisation of ethnic nationalist movements some of whose demands can be met only by restructuring or even dissolving existing states. There are about 185 states in the world today but thousands of ethnic groups. Few states are ethnically homogeneous; some include two or more major ethnic groups; most include significant ethnic minorities. Many states have ethnically distinct regions with their own cultural identities which in some cases are politically active, with substantial popular support for autonomy or independence. Where regions believe themselves to be distinctive relative to others, local identities are more likely to be cemented and the commitment of local interests sustained. Even regions without a distinct ethnic base may have the social and political cohesion to articulate their particular interests effectively within the state and even beyond, as the experience of Canadian provinces demonstrates. Territorial and ethno-regional groups may compete with the state and seek to share or take over its support, legitimacy or decision making powers. The existence of such disaffected, discontented or simply distinctive groups and regions within a state may not immediately threaten the state, but it may indicate some failure of political integration and an incomplete acceptance of the state amongst a section of the population. The mobilisation of ethnic minority and ethno-regional nationalism challenges the political authority of the state and reveals shortcomings in its cohesion and legitimacy which threaten its stability and integrity.

The state, therefore is having to respond to both external and internal pressures for change. The globalisation of the world economy and the changing framework of international security have reduced dependence on the state and facilitated a revival of ethnicity and regionalism. This in turn has encouraged the expression of ethno-regional identities and generated powerful fissiparous forces which have fuelled conflict within states. While the decline of the state as a political actor, however, is a function of its changing role in international society and particularly its diminishing capability as an effective centre of power and decision, ethno-national and ethno-regional movements may threaten the survival of the state as a coherent political

community. This could have significant implications for political order and
stability in all parts of the world.

Ethnicity and ethnic mobilisation

Increases in ethnic group activity have been noted by social scientists since
the 1960s. This apparent resurgence in ethnic activity, however, may equally
be regarded as the continuation of a trend which has been proceeding through
most of the twentieth century and may be expected to continue. It began
with the collapse of the Central European empires, and continued through
the inter-war years, the period of decolonisation, the 'ethnic revival' in the
West, the end of the Cold War and the uneven development of the state system
in the Third World. Ethnic groups are at various stages of political
development, including hundreds that have not become politically mobilised,
leaving considerable potential for further expansion of ethnic awareness and
ethnic activity.

Ethnicity is a complex social identity made up of a wide range of
distinctive characteristics blended together in a unique combination. These
may include physical characteristics such as stature, skin colour or hair type,
socio-cultural characteristics such as language, religion or ideology and
behavioural characteristics such as style, ritual or traditional customs. In
addition all ethnic groups appear to claim an exclusive tradition made up of
a myth of origin, a common history and a shared socio-political experience
as well as a number of other properties. The particular combination of these
various characteristics then defines an ethnic group and distinguishes it from
other groups, especially those in spatial and social proximity to it.

How ethnic groups come to be formed is not entirely clear, but there are
two principal schools of thought on the issue. The primordialists maintain
that ethnic identities are deeply rooted in a specific matrix of genetic, historical
and social origins whose unique development determines the nature of a
particular ethnic group. According to this view ethnic groups are in some
sense natural formations. On the other hand the modernists or rationalists
argue that ethnic identities are socially constructed by group elites from
various available components, some of which are simply invented, in a
particular social context, with particular purposes in mind. According to this
ethnic groups are purposively formed in order to serve the consciously
determined interests of their members who adhere to them because they derive
certain benefits from doing so. Both these propositions offer valuable insights
into the nature of ethnic groups, but both are to some extent declaratory and

incomplete. Many groups do have a long history and close internal ties which invest their claims with an aura of authenticity. On the other hand, many ethnic groups especially in advanced and modernising societies appear to behave like special interest groups. It may be reasonably maintained that all ethnic groups have been formed at some time for some purpose and continue to be re-invented until they cease to yield benefits to their members.

While each individual ethnic group is unique, ethnic groups may be classified in a number of different, though not necessarily exclusive categories. First there are ethno-national groups, sometimes desribed as 'nations without a state', which have highly developed identities, are effectively mobilised and usually demand collective rights or considerable autonomy within their host state. Ethno-regional groups are an important variant of these with the additional property of claiming a defined territory of their own, such as the Catalans, the Quebecois and the Scots. Transnational groups such as the Kurds, occupying territory in several contiguous states but denied a state of their own, are a further variant within this category. Secondly, there are national minorities which which may identify with a nearby nation state and receive its patronage and support such as Hungarian minorities in Slovakia or Russian minorities in successor states of the Soviet Union. Thirdly, there are ethnic minorities, such as the Druzes in Lebanon, Indians in East Africa and Blacks in the United States who do not enjoy the patronage of a kindred state and may be too small or insufficiently mobilised to exercise significant power, but nonetheless demand rights and recognition within their state. Fourthly, there are immigrant ethnic minorities such as Turks in Germany, Afro-Caribbeans in Britain and Hispanics in the United States who have settled in their host country for two or three generations and seek to integrate into its civil society and enjoy full rights of citizenship but face problems of harassment, discrimination and racism. Fifthly, there are aboriginal groups, such as Indians (First Nations) in Canada, Sami in Finland or Maori in New Zealand, who wish to protect and maintain their traditional culture and way of life in face of the alien and frequently unsympathetic values of the culture around them. Sixthly, there are ethnic lobbies, based on diffuse ethnic communities which uphold their identity through ethnic associations and community newsletters, such as the Jews and the Irish in the United States, who seek to deploy their economic and voting power to influence government policy or to promote causes valued by the group.

Every group in each of these categories is defined by its ethnicity and all are engaged to some extent in some form of ethnic political activity. The process by which ethnic groups become poltically engaged and mobilised and maintain a programme of political action especially in conditions of adversity is an important contribution to understanding how they function. This process varies widely but always involves a particular relationship between identity, motivation and political activity

The fundamental property of ethnic groups is their identity. Identity exists for both individual members and for the group. It consists of two components, consciousness of being part of the group and the perception and recognition of this by others. Some ethnic groups coexist happily and productively with their neighbours, but many groups, particularly minorities and historically subordinate groups experience various forms of adverse treatment including exclusion, discrimination and oppression which produces a sense of grievance. This sense of grievance or rights denied is likely to inspire demands by the group for better treatment which endows the group with motivation and a propensity for action. Effective mobilisation, however, also depends on the extent of support for the stated objectives and the chosen strategies and on the solidarity, leadership and cohesion of the group.

Mobilisation of the group is a critical stage in its political development. Political mobilisation transforms both the internal dynamics of the group and its outlook and relations with society and the state. It increases both awareness within the group of its distinctive identity and interests and the possibility of conflict with the larger society and the government. Such conflict is frequently of low intensity, limited to verbal advocacy, constitutional action and public demonstrations of political support for specific demands and usually capable of being peacefully resolved. But conflict can easily intensify, resulting in damage to property, disruption of society and loss of life in riots, terror and civil war. The quality of ethnic relations and the development of ethnic conflict is thus affected by a number of complex factors including the structure of pluralism, the extent to which the state acknowledges the claims of groups and the political context of ethnic relations within the state.

PLURALISM, IDENTITY AND THE STATE

Varieties of Ethnic Pluralism

Although the most striking feature of multinational states is their variety, there are certain recurring features and patterns in the structure, types and management of pluralism, the analysis of which may yield an enhanced insight into the nature of communal conflict. Both comparative and case by case analysis illuminate the experience of different conditions of ethnic pluralism and contribute to a more complete understanding of the problems of governing multinational states. Such analysis may not in itself resolve problems but it adds to the information available for doing so.

Three kinds of structure of pluralism in multinational states may be identified, which probably cover most of the states in the international system. The first of these, dominant pluralism, is characterised by one dominant majority group or culture and a large number of minority groups as in India and Russia, in both of which there is a wide range of minority demands. In the second type, bipolar pluralism, there are two distinct groups, each of which may be identified with a particular territory, and perhaps one or two minority groups, as in Belgium and former Czechoslovakia. The third kind of structure is complex pluralism in which there are more than two major or primary groups and possibly several minority groups. Former Yugoslavia is the most complex example of such a structure but a number of others, such as Switzerland and Lebanon, may be also be considered in this category. A fourth category, ethnoregionalism, includes states which incorporate a number of distinct regions which differ significantly in terms of language, religion, culture or the traditions of their civil society and which may have been historically independent or to some extent politically autonomous. Britain, Canada and Spain could be considered representative of this type of multinational state. In many cases these structures are legacies of imperialism or residues of past nation building efforts and may incorporate a heritage of suspicion and resentment which may add to the bitterness of ethnic rivalry and conflict. While these categories are distinct in themselves problems may sometimes arise in assigning states to categories.

The factors underlying ethnic identity and conflict in plural societies are usually complex but language and religion, recur frequently. Language is the most frequent basis of division and conflict within multinational states Even where it is not the only or the main source of group identity, it may be a major cause of conflict between groups. The demand of minorities to use their own language equally in work, education and public administration is part of the drive for equal opportunities as well as identity and self-respect. Where a language has been historically subordinated or deliberately marginalised, the establishment of its cliam to public recognition may be associated with prolonged conflict, as in Belgium. Language divides and separates groups in a variety of ways, some of which are paradoxical and perverse. In Yugoslavia and North India, for example, the languages spoken by most of the population have a common vocabulary and grammatical structure facilitating speech communication, but written communication is impeded because the alphabets and scripts are different. On the other hand, significant language differences in Switzerland are accommodated and do not become a source of communal conflict, while the experience of Northern Ireland demonstrates that even the use of a common language does not prevent communal conflict.

If language is the most common cause of division, religion is the most fervent and the most likely to lead to social violence as witnessed in India and Lebanon. Where there are religious differences there is always the potential for mistrust, cultural misunderstanding, unwitting offence and passionate conflict as is demonstrated in Northern Ireland. In Switzerland religious differences cut across language differences and are politically more significant, but few societies manage religious divisions more effectively. In Canada, where the political significance of religion has subsided, religious differences have been an important line of social conflict in the past. Religious affiliation may still define the boundaries of cultures and provide powerful identities for both individuals and communities even where religious practice and confessional commitment have themselves declined or virtually disappeared as in the former Yugoslavia. Religion, like language, is more likely to be a cause of social conflict if it is linked to other, especially economic and political, divisions such as class. In societies otherwise divided such as Belgium and Spain, however, a common religion has not provided a basis of social integration. For all its potency, therefore, religion does not always divide, but it is not a reliable social bond.

In any particular case in any structural category ethnic populations may be territorially concentrated thus adding a regional dimension to ethnic relations. In some cases language may have a territorial dimension which divides societies regionally as has been the case in Canada and increasingly in Belgium. In others, where regional differences become important for economic or other reasons, language may develop more salience as in Catalonia and the successor states of Czechoslovakia.

Variations in the structures and bases of pluralism are matched by variations in its management. There are states where a number of different ethnic, language or religious groups have coexisted peacefully for long periods, managing their differences through a variety of powersharing arrangements, as was the case in Lebanon and continues to be in Switzerland. Switzerland is generally regarded as a successful multinational state, despite the movement for Jura separatism, while Lebanon disintegrated in a bitter and bloody civil war which makes the reconstruction of a national community even now very difficult. The crucial factor in the management of ethnic relations is the mutual recognition of group rights and the equitable sharing of power between groups. The most dramatic and widely known case of breakdown and failure is Yugoslavia. Both Canada and Yugoslavia have responded to the stresses of ethnic and regional conflict by devolving ever more power and competence from the federation to the provinces and republics, which in the latter case at least severely undermined the capability of the federation and probably contributed to its demise, while in the latter it may have provided a basis for its salvation. On the other hand, Britain and Spain have adopted very different responses to the challenges of regional diversity and its political demands.

The variety of patterns of ethnic pluralism is an indication of the complex and contingent nature of political issues in multinational states. Multinational states are usually characterised by fragmented political cultures, social pluralism and 'deep diversity'.[2] They probably incorporate major ethnic, language or religious differences that sometimes reinforce but frequently cut across socio-economic cleavages. There may be strong identification with particular regions or ethnic groups, possibly expressed in commitment to distinctive symbols, traditions and institutions and sometimes in resurgent nationalism. Older and well established states may have had more time and opportunity to develop satisfactory procedures of conflict management and resolution, but they still do not escape the divisive effects of renascent ethnic and regional identities. Thus ethnic pluralism has significant implications not only for the social cohesion and political integration of states but also for the structures and processes of their government.

Plural Identities and Political Theory

Despite its complexity and potential political significance, the issue of ethnicity and ethnic pluralism has been generally neglected by political theorists. While both liberal and Marxist-Leninist theory recognise the right of national self-determination in principle, liberal and Marxist theorists and statesmen have been extremely parsimonious in acknowledging these rights for ethnic groups within states. Liberals have always given priority to the claims of individuals and Marxists to the to the claims of class above those of ethnic groups. Indeed both for different reasons have regarded ethnicity as atavistic and reactionary, an historical aberration which would disappear with advancing modernisation. Today the validity of this view is difficult to sustain and, after decades of neglect, western political theory has begun to address the issue of collective rights and particularly the claims of cultural minorities in plural societies. Many political theorists now acknowledge that the existence of such pluralities can produce divided communities with conflicting orientations to politics which may lead to disputed standards of legitimacy, serious civil conflict or even the disintegration of states as in Lebanon and Yugoslavia. This kind of experience would probably be regarded by John Stuart Mill as confirming his theory of multinational states. Mill took the view that it would be virtually impossible to maintain liberal democratic government or political unity within a multinational or polyethnic state. The common public opinion, the exposure to similar influences, the shared goals, the unity of purpose and leadership which Mill thought necessary to the proper functioning of free institutions would be lacking. This would be compounded by the existence of widespread mistrust and suspicion, divided leadership and possibly even significant differences over fundamental values. In such a situation simple conflicts of interest would be turned into issues of principle and matters of right on which there could be no accommodation or compromise. This could be avoided if minorities were prepared to assimilate, which would in any case be to their advantage as it would give them access to a largter cultural and political system with greater opportunities for their members.[3] It seems that Mill's model was not the nation state but the state nation whose official nationalism provided a sort of canopy for the cultural and political socialisation of all its members, however diverse their origins.

Mill's view was directly challenged by Lord Acton, whose famous paper on *Nationality* was conceived as a fundamental criticism of Mill's theory. Acton argued that any state which identifies itself with a particular idea or section, be it nation or class, tends to become absolute and unable to tolerate dissent. Thus, while the nation state (or the state nation) absolutises the 'popular' will, the values of particular communities tend to be marginalised or simply disregarded. Contrary to Mill, Acton thought that multinational states provided a promising framework for the success of pluralist liberal democratic institutions. The conflicting interests and divergent loyalties in multinational states would act as a focus and inspiration to particular communities and form a bulwark against the absolutist tendenceies of central government. Acton believed that the ideal society and the ideal state would include several national or ethnic communities each of which would be to some extent self-governing.[4] He apparently did not consider the possibility that such a state could disintegrate into a number of separate absolutisms.

Acton's view was shared to some extent by Otto Bauer, the Austrian thinker who was at the centre of a school of thought which tried to explain ethnicity and nationalism and bring them into a political framework. Bauer's views were based on a more fully developed theoretical foundation, a lifetime of direct experience and a very much larger body of empirical data gained from a long period of research. Bauer's approach did not condemn nationalism or attempt to marginalise it, but affirmed it as one of the great forces of history. Bauer, however, regarded ethnicity and national identity as essentially a cultural phenomena which should be protected within the state by measures of autonomy and self-regulation. Together with Karl Renner, Max Adler and others Bauer developed a political and administrative scheme for this purpose based on the idea that national identity should be treated as a personal rather than a collective or group attribute and that states should provide a system of support to enable members of all ethnic groups to gain access to public life.[5] For a multinational state to succeed on these principles, Bauer was acutely aware that the rights of individuals and ethnic communities would have to be guaranteed and national identity as far as possible depoliticised.

Mill did not deny that individuals are influenced by the groups and communities in which they live, but argued that a political society which developed around rival or conflicting communities was not likely be a succesful democracy. Liberals in the tradition of Mill see political society as a collection of free and rational individuals guided in their behaviour by their own interests and obligations and the search for a good life. Liberals reject the idea of 'political society as a community because, among other things, it leads to the systematic denial of basic liberties and may allow the oppressive use of ... force'.[6] Acton and Bauer offer rather different views of political society and the relation of individuals to it. Acton argues that as a matter of preference and Bauer as a matter of circumstance individuals do not relate to society simply as individuals but through the communities in which they live.

A more thorough version of this view is offered by communitarians who argue that it is not just as a matter of preference or circumstance that people belong to communities or groups. It is inevitable in the nature of human social relations that people exist in communities which not only influence their outlook and behaviour but actually determine who and what they are; the communities they belong to are 'not relationships they choose ... but a constituent part of their identity.'[7] People, therefore, are not isolated individuals; moreover, the communities to which they belong play a crucial part in creating them and their needs, preferences and consequent demands. In dealing with issues of social and cultural diversity, therefore, it may be desirable not only to take account of communities, but to give priority to communities. The vital role of the community in shaping the individual means that the purposes of individuals are part of a common good that can only be validated by and within the community and its system of values. There is no political principle which gives universal validity to any political purpose and political purposes generally do not have any necessary validity outside the community which supports them and is affected by them. Thus the purposes and prevailing values of a society should not be imposed on one of its minority communities. Minorities may wish and be entitled to protect their own core values.

One of the implications of this is that, while it is necessary in the interests of social justice that all groups in society should be treated equally, it may be desirable in some conditions to treat certain particular groups differently. This is important to some ethnic, regional and minority groups who wish to protect their own culture and resist the assimilative pressures of a larger society or dominant culture. Such groups seek the opportunity to maintain a minority language, a distinctive civil society, a traditional way of life or even a combination of these. They may demand recognition for the distinctiveness of their community culture and seek some special treatment, such as a privileged status or a measure of local, sectional or functional autonomy or in some cases full territorial self-government, to enable them to protect it. These kinds of demands are more likely in multinational states, where they are likely to create difficulty for political authorities. Attempts to concede special treatment to any group is likely to produce a reaction, either negative or imitative or both, among other groups. It may also meet objection from the majority population who may feel that separate or different treatment can not be equal. On the other hand, such concessions may be the only way to avoid seething discontent, serious domestic conflict or even the breakup of the state.

While it is true that the social structure and ethnic composition of multinational states frequently presents them with particularly intractable problems of government, there is also considerable evidence that social pluralism need not be an obstacle to the development and maintenance of stable national polities. Indeed many states have been able to persist and succeed despite having fragmented political cultures (eg., Switzerland and Canada), while others adapt or change to accommodate plural identities (eg., Belgium and Spain). Thus the development of a national political community with an integrated identity and regime loyalty may be compatible with the existence of active ethnic and regional sub-cultures. In such conditions, however, it may be difficult on occasions to achieve consensus or to govern through the institutions and processes of 'normal' politics. There is likely to be conflict over the constitution, composition of government, recruitment to the public service and official language policy, not to mention the prioritisation of groups and regions in the allocation of resources. Today such problems have become widespread and the growing tendency of ethno-national groups to mobilise in support of their demands has made them increasingly visible. Moreover, recent events in several parts of the world have highlighted the serious and savage consequences of political failure in resolving the problems of ethnic relations in multinational states.

Ethnic Relations

The mobilisation of ethnic groups is the process by which they become involved in political action. It represents the transformation of the group from a primarily cultural community, in which some issues may be from time to time politicised, to a political one, in which its leaders are politically engaged on a permanent basis to to secure its interests. Ethnic groups seek to preserve their culture and way of life, to gain or protect special privileges such as ethnic language education, to enhance their social and economic prospects and to secure political power for their communities. The political activity they engage in depends on many factors, including the objectives of the group, the strategies chosen to pursue them and the political context of inter-group relations. The political context influences the objectives and strategies selected by groups and is possibly, therefore, the factor which most directly affects the quality of ethnic relations.

The political context is a function of the political culture and the decision making regime. The political culture is itself a complex factor determined by the prevailing ideology, social values and the legacy of the past, particularly as they affect attitudes to ethnic relations, the conditions of social competition and the expectations of groups. A heritage of repression or systematic disadvantage, for example, may leave a legacy of mistrust which is not conducive to good ethnic relations at either the personal or community levels and may impair efforts by both ethnic groups and governments to improve them. As they affect ethnic relations, political cultures may be characterised as ranging from hegemonic-assimilationist to pluralist-communitarian, the latter being moretolerant of ethnic diversity.

The decision making regime is a function of the structure of government and the distribution of power in society as they affect decisions which impinge on the interests and relationships of ethnic groups. Decision making regimes range from democratic to autocratic but mostly occur between these polarities. Democratic decision making permits participation by all parties, consultation on disputes and agreed implementation of solutions. Autocratic decision making is characterised by unequal participation, lack of consultation and imposed solutions.

Decision making regime

Democratic   Autocratic

	Liberal	Authoritarian
Political culture: *attidudes to ethnic diversity* **Hegemonic-** *Assimilationist*	Liberal	Authoritarian
P l u r a l i s t - *Communitarian*	Multicultural	Populist/ Mobilising

Fig 0.1. The Political Environment of Ethnic Relations

The political context as a product of the relationship between the decision making regime and the political culture is represented in the diagram in figure 0.1. According to this there are four categories of political environment, multicultural, liberal, authoritarian and populist/mobilising, which should be regarded as ideal types. Authoritarian environments are probably characterised by a prescriptive ideology, a hegemonic or assimilative attitude to minorities, a centralised government with power concentrated in a narrowly based elite. These conditions are unlikely to tolerate the expression of diversity or to encourage wide participation in decision making. In liberal and multicultural environments, on the other hand, there is likely to be more political competition, a more decentralised structure of government and a relatively wide dispersal of power in society, although liberal environments are more assimilationist and multicultural ones give more positive recognition of minority identities. Both, however, are more likely to provide opportunities for resolving conflicts, accommodating differences and developing inter-group relations than authoritarian systems. Liberal and multicultural societies are likely to have more resources and capabilities for accommodating the pressures and demands of ethnic pluralism. In these conditions ethnic relations are more open, robust and possibly more resilient than in authoritarian systems in which they are likely to be both more rigid and more brittle. In populist or mobilising systems, especially in weakly integrated societies engaged in reformist or nation building projects, ethnic plralism may be tolerated of necessity or even celebrated, but the regime itself is likely to be narrowly based and relatively autocratic. While this may permit recognition of ethnic diversity in society, it provides little scope for consultation or participation in the making or implementation of decisions on ethnic issues.

Ethnic relations in multinational states thus develop within a framework determined by three complex factors, the structure of ethnic pluralism, social acknowledgement of ethnic diversity and the political context of relations between groups. Within this framework ethnic groups formulate objectives and strategies and develop their relations with the rest of society and the state. This framework shapes the outlook of all types of ethnic groups, the opportunities available to them as well as their behaviour and political demands. The demands of most types of ethnic groups can be accommodated by the state without threatening its stability or integrity, enabling them to become incorporated into an integrated civil society. While this depends to some extent on the response of the state, it also depends on the political behaviour and demands of the group, which are likely to be most implacable amongst ethno-national groups. Ethno-national groups tend to develop very intense communal or regional identities that encourage a sense of separateness from the rest of society and may bring them into direct conflict with the state. They may challenge the legitimacy of the state in certain domains of policy that affect their interests. Such separatist attitudes thus complicate the accommodation of ethno-national demands and makes the resolution of ethnic conflict more difficult.

IDENTITY AND SEPARATISM

Separatism

The demands of ethno-nationalist movements are not uniform or consistent and are sometimes ambivalent, but they may be classified in three groups.

First, there are demands which are mainly output oriented, that is they are concerned to win specific benefits from the political system, such as increased expenditure on regional projects, rather than change the system itself. Second, there are demands which are regime oriented, that is for significant changes in the structure and organisation of the state such as demands for powersharing or more participative decision-making arrangements. Third, there are demands which are community oriented, that is for fundamental changes in the definition of the political community and its relation to the state. The demands of self-government, secessionist and irredentist movements are thus community oriented.

In polyethnic and multi-national societies the articulation of society, and particularly of minority groups and regions, in relation to the state has two dimensions, identity and legitimacy which define the level of political integration of the state. These are represented in the diagram (Figure 0.2). Identity is an expression of the preferred identity of individuals and communities, that is, the relative strength of minority or regional as opposed to official 'national' identity. In many multi-national states people prefer to identify themselves with ethnic minorities or regions, for example, as Quebecois or Catalans or Scots rather than the official nation, as Canadians, Spanish or British. Legitimacy is an expression of the attitudes of people and

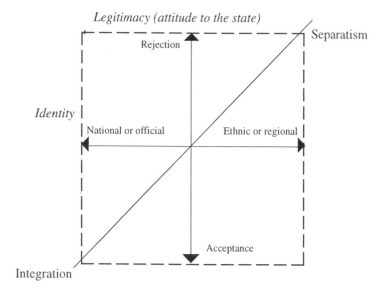

Figure 0.2. Separatism

communities to the state, that is their acceptance or rejection of the existing national state and its role in their lives as opposed to a preference for allocating some or more of its functions to a regional government. These two dimensions provide an index of national integration within the state and, conversely, of the strength of ethno-nationalist demands. separatist attitudes and the liklihood of secession.

Some states have relatively low levels of national integration, due to competing identities, and low levels of legitimacy, due to incomplete acceptance amongst minority or regional populations. This is frequently expressed as a strong ethnic or regional identity combined with an ambivalent view of the state. The dimensions of this attitude are presented as the diagonal line in the diagram. This line plots the range of attitudes from support for the state to a preference for regional autonomy (through devolution or federalism) or secession. The demands of ethno-national groups are not necessarily for secession or independence, but their conception of their own identity emphasises their separateness, while their rhetoric makes frequent use of the vocabulary of national identity. National separatism, therefore, is a term which effectively describes the ideology and demands of all ethno-nationalist movements. National separatism may also be viewed as a political process in which the relationship between an ethno-national community and the state develops and it may be understood in terms of the socio-political and environmental conditions which initiate and shape its development.

Social conditions include the ethnic composition and distribution of the population, the cultural homogeneity and solidarity of minority groups, the social and economic relationship between ethnic groups and the extent to which any minority group regards itself as a distinct society or a political community, including the strength of support for that view within the group. While ethno-national groups may be generally agreed about their identity, they may be divided about its expression and their ultimate political aspirations. Environmental conditions include several factors, but three are of particular significance: first, the territory of the separatist group and its location in relation to the state; secondly, the quality of the physical and natural environment, in particular whether it has the resources to sustain economic autonomy; thirdly, other states, which may offer encouragement or support to a separatist movement, even to the point of secession, as the European Union did in the case of Croatia. Indeed, the presence of favourable social and environmental conditions enhances the possibility of separatism leading to secession.

Minority and regional ethnic nationalism may reveal shortcomings in the legitimacy and cohesion of the nation state, especially amongst minority populations and regions. In doing so it raises two further issues concerning the capability of the state: first, that the extent and effectiveness of political integration in polyethnic and multi-national societies has been overestimated; second, that confidence in the capacity of states to respond effectively to the challenge of ethnic nationalism by the manipulation of economic resources has been misplaced. The question then is whether states (or at least some states) can persist in face of these challenges by seeking to accommodate the demands of ethnonationalists. Separatist demands for autonomy or independence are the most severe expression of these challenges to the state.

Secession

Separatism does not involve the break-up of the state whereas secession does. In a society or a regional sub-culture with distinct traditions, culture and civil and social institutions a sense of separate identity develops easily and provides the foundations for separatist political attitudes, but not necessarily for secession. Secession occurs when a territory and its people break away from a state and establish a new politically independent society with a government of its own and a claim to statehood. To accomplish an act of secession, however, a society needs to have control of certain resources without which it would probably not be possible to sustain political independence. Mainly for these reasons successful secessions have been very rare through most of the twentieth century and Bangladesh was the only new state formed by secession from 1945 until 1990, when Eritrea became independent.

Some regions or ethno-regional groups may have certain coercive, instrumental and identitive resources which they may be able to deploy in support of their separatist demands. Coercive resources are primarily autonomous institutions for maintaining authority, control and security in the form of a legal administration, courts, police and military forces. Instrumental resources are economic, technological, administrative and human resources and the ability to utilize them effectively for the provision and delivery of public services. Identitive resources are values, symbols, traditions, religious and cultural institutions which endow the group or region with social and political coherence. A secession movement in a society with deep and politically active internal cleavages, for example on religion (eg., Ireland 1920-21) or clan loyalty (eg., Somaliland post 1992), may find its cohesion reduced and its prospects of success damaged.

The crucial part of the process of secession is the transfer of these resources, especially the identitive resources, from the existing political system to the group and their internalization within the group. The internalization of such resources in regions or groups not only strengthens groups themselves politically, but may place additional stress on the political system, thus making secession more practical and more probable. This would suggest that some containment responses to ethno-territorial disaffection, especially the expansion of political autonomy in the form of home rule or devolution, may be counterproductive because the enhanced opportunity they provide for the internalization of integrative assets may actually increase the possibility of secession.

Secession may gain more support, especially in the international community, if the claims of the seceeding community can be supported by a convincing moral case. Such a case can be made if the community and its people were incorporated into the state by force (Georgia or Estonia in the Soviet Union, Eritrea in Ethiopia); or if the region and its people are being oppressed, exploited or economically disadvantaged by the state (Biafra, Bangladesh); or if the state or the central government consistently ignore the terms on which the state or the union was originally agreed, a claim sometimes made by Quebec and Scottish nationalists; or if the region has an historic experience of separate statehood which its people wish to restore (Norway in 1905, Poland in 1919, possibly Scotland). If such a moral case can be made, the claims of separatists are more likely to meet a sympathetic response within as well as beyond the state.

The internalization of integrative resources, particularly of identitive and instrumental capabilities, in regions or groups endangers the integrity of the state. The secession of Norway from Sweden in 1905 is instructive on this point. The establishment of a home rule constitution for Norway made it possible to internalize coercive, instrumental and identitive resources, weakening the integrative capability of the union and the legitimacy of Swedish rule, while boosting a rising Norwegian nationalism based on the revival of a proud if distant heritage. The increasing internalisation of integrative resources, notably national identity, political autonomy and control of economic resources accelerated the secession of Norway as the union simply became an obstacle to its further development. The final separation, following a non-violent uprising, was almost a formality. Similarly, the extensive autonomy and control of resources demanded and gained by the republics of former Yugoslavia during the 1970s and 1980s made it very much more difficult to defend the federation against the rising particularist nationalisms of Serbs, Slovenes and Croats in the 1990s.

State Responses to Separatism

States do not usually look with equanimity on ethnonationalist and separatist movements, especially when their objective is secession. The United States government prosecuted one of the most destructive civil wars in history to maintain the union and in more recent years other states such as Nigeria have suppressed ethnoregional secession movements after extensive and costly civil wars. There is thus ample evidence that all states are prepared to use deadly force to protect their integrity. Even if they are not threatened with imminent disintegration states may face fundamental ethnic demands affecting the nature and structure of their regimes. On the other hand, some states, particularly liberal democracies, have greater resources, capabilities and skills to deploy in such situations and are more likely than authotitarian states to resolve them without the use of deadly force. In former Yugoslavia, ethnic demands were latterly community oriented with direct implications for the political and territorial integrity of the state itself, whereas in other cases, such as the Belgium or Canada, demands have been more regime and output oriented, though not necessarily any less intractable.

Some ethno-regional groups claim to be resisting oppression or annexation, but the more usual complaint of ethnic and regional minorities is that the state is remote and indifferent to their cultural concerns and special needs. What ethno-territorial groups generally seek is greater control over their own affairs in the belief that they can apply their own resources more efficiently in pursuit of their own interests. Ethnic and regional groups, therefore, tend to define their needs and their differences with the state in cultural and political terms, in the expectation that this will strengthen the legitimacy of their claims to special treatment or autonomy.

The state and central government, however, are more likely to define ethnic and regional problems in economic and administrative terms, assuming that they can contain the issues within parameters that they can control. To the extent that ethno-regional discontents are generated by the unsatisfactory performance of regional economies and the insensitive administration of minorities and regional societies, this is reasonable. Governments have responded to these challenges in fairly consistent ways. They have tried to define their purposes more clearly, sometimes making concessions to special cultural demands and regional economic needs. They have tried to improve the effectiveness of their services by increasing consultation and participation in decision making. They have tried to relieve the pressure on government structures by various devices of functional and territorial devolution. Such reforms are presented as an expansion of regional autonomy and new contributions to more effective government. In reality they are more likely to represent an effort to accommodate regional demands to the interests of central administration and to bring regional elites more within the control of central government.

Attempts to deal with minorities and regional problems in this way ultimately place the state in a dilemma. From the point of view of the state, the object of increasing regional autonomy is to broaden the area of consent and secure the integrity of the state. Economic development, however, requires more central control of resources to ensure the success of regional policies. From the viewpoint of the region on the other hand, the expansion of autonomy is meant to provide greater local control of decision making. Regional economic problems are seen as the result of the repeated failures of central government, the redemption of which must involve less rather than more central control of resources. Thus, while some of the benefits of state intervention may be eagerly sought by the regions, the state itself may be resented. The dilemma of the state is that concessions to regional demands must mean yielding central powers to the regions, which might be seen as endangering the integrity of the state. On the other hand, witholding concessions may intensify regional identity, fuel separatist sentiments and reduce the legitimacy of the state in the regions.

It is possible to resolve this dilemma by the moderation of regional demands, modification of the constitutional regime, political repression or the breakup of the state. The breakup of the state is not always an objective of nationalist groups and is not necessarily in their interest. Ethno-nationalist movements, however, sometimes employ community oriented separatist rhetoric in pursuit of output and regime oriented demands, a stratgy which can misfire as in the case of the Slovaks in former Czechoslovakia. Many ethnic demands, except on the part of a few extremists, are not for political independence, but for recognition of a cultural identity and the provision of the political, economic and administrative framework to sustain a distinct cultural community. If this is generally acknowledged to be the case, the problem facing states may be more tractable and solutions which could preserve the integrity of states, while satisfying the aspirations of minority and regional groups, may be more readily found. Such solutions involve the institutionalisation of political arrangements which recognise cultural diversity and facilitate the accommodation of plural identities. Today the procedure of the plebiscite or referendum, followed by secession or federalisation is increasingly faoured by ethno-regional separatist groups, such as those in Quebec and Scotland.

RESOLVING ETHNIC CONFLICT

Inter-group and ethnic conflict is a recurring feature of the politics and international relations of multinational states. The liberal expectation that the problem of ethnic minorities would disappear within the framework of the nation state has been disappointed. Even in Europe, with a long experience of cultural pluralism, there are few examples of truly successful multiethnic states. Attempts to resolve ethnic conflicts have been made by a number of methods such as genocide (Armenians in Turkey, Jews in Germany, Hutu in Burundi), forced population transfers (Chechens and Crimea Tartars in the USSR), boundary changes, including annexation (Sudetenland, Moldova), partition (India, Ireland) and plebiscite, (Saar) and assimilation of minorities (a widespread practice in most states). In these cases the solutions have been intended to be conclusive and, with the exception of plebescites and some cases of assimilation, have involved imposed solutions with little or no consultation or collaboration.

The alternative to a conclusive solution to ethnic conflicts is to manage or regulate ethnic relations within a framework of territorial or communal autonomy based on the principles of federalism and consociationalism The recent resurgence of ethnic and ethno-regional nationalism has renewed interest in these posibilities and in the general problem of maintaining the state in multinational societies. Federalism and consociationalism are essentially power sharing arrangements which enable two or more groups to avoid direct conflict and cooperate within the same state. They avoid domination by the majority, protect the rights of minorities and enable diverse groups to protect their own cultures and ways of life. By creating a measure of self government they may provide greater sensitivity to the demands of local and particular groups and reduce discontent by adjusting policy to their needs. Such systems of shared rule are intended to facilitate political integration and stability in polyethnic societies thus maintaining the integrity of the state while satisfying both the interests and ethno-territorial aspirations of some groups within it.

Federalism is probably the better known of these power sharing devices. The theory of federalism is that sovereignty is vested in the people who delegate powers to federal and provincial governments. It is based on the idea that government powers may be divided so as to create jurisdictions which, in Wheare's words, are 'coordinate but independent'.[8] In Elazar's alternative formulation, the federal division of power creates a condition of 'self rule and shared rule'[9]. What both these formulations suggest is that regional and provincial governments have clear jurisdictions and the powers and resources to deal with the issues and meet the demands which legitimately arise within these jurisdictions. This means that there is a presumption of a high profile role for the regional government through which it provides political and policy leadership in designated areas for its own territorial community, leaving the central government to deal only with matters that are of common interest to the federation as a whole. Thus federalists point out that, by sharing power and providing a clear role for both levels of government federal systems can accommodate differences and problems which could not be surmounted in a unitary system.

Many states have adopted federalism as a solution to the problems of ethno-territorial pluralism. To be wholly successful, however, federal systems should meet certain conditions. There should be a clear allocation of powers, a universally accepted appellate authority, such as a constitutional court, a shared economic regime and common market. There should also be clear territorial boundaries which can, as far as possible, enable ethnic communities to preserve their own identities and enjoy some measure of political security within a cultural 'homeland'. With all this it is still important that the powers allocated to the regional or provincial authorities should meet the needs of the regional community

Whether federalism really can provide an adequate framework for integration and maintenance of polyethnic societies is, however, problematic. In Canada, for example, it is under considerable strain, while in Yugoslavia and Czechoslovakia it broke down completely. The Soviet model of federalism was developed specifically to deal with problems of ethnic and national pluralism, but it had many structural anomalies and weaknesses, notably the powers which could be exercised by the centre through the Communist Party. There have been many attempts to create federations in anglo-phone post-colonial societies, but with the outstanding exception of India, they have mostly failed. On the other hand, there are many variations on the federal theme, different ways of allocating jurisdictions and structuring the federal constitution. Thus some federations like India are relatively centralised while others, like Canada, with extensive provincial autonomy, are highly decentralised. A form of asymmetrical federalism has been proposed for Canada which would allocate greater powers to Quebec, but this has not been accepted by the other provinces. Cantonisation on the Swiss model allows partition of the state into very small self-governing units with extensive jurisdictions and a wide measure of autonomy.

Various forms of regional autonomy have been canvassed from time to time and a number of experiments have been attempted, including the constitutional autonomies in Spain and the newly developed system of communal federalism in Belgium. A system of quasi-federal regional government or devolution operated in Northern Ireland from 1922 to 1972, when it was suspended by the British parliament. A similar form of legislative and executive devolution, sometimes described as Home Rule has been proposed for Scotland and Wales and is on the political agenda again, following a change of government in the United Kingdom. One objection to devolution as a form of territorial government is that it may limit the effective political and administrative jurisdiction of the central government but not provide the legislative freedom and the control of economic resources which regional groups demand. Thus a devolved regional government may be unable to establish its domestic independence with sufficient credibility to allay suspicion of the central government. This is only likely to increase rather than reduce popular discontent and perceptions of government failure. In these circumstances it may be difficult to inhibit demands for increased regional powers and continued advocacy of secession.

Federalism is a form of institutionalised power sharing which is appropriate where ethnic and cultural groups are territorially concentrated and separate, but not all cases of ethnic pluralism have such a clear territorial dimension. In such cases a form of non-territorial communal power sharing or consociationalism may be more appropriate. Where there are religious, cultural, linguistic or ethnic divisions on the basis of which political communities form, the political system may be structured on the basis of voluntarily segregated communities using established cultural institutions and elites for the conduct of inter-communal activities, politics and government. Such consociational arrangements have tended to develop gradually and almost informally before becoming institutionalized. Their institutionalization, sometimes formal and legal, brings them close to federalism. This is the case in Switzerland where highly complex ethnic, linguistic and religious divisions are accommodated in a system which has elements of both consociationalism and federalism.

There may have been early experience of consociational politics in Canada and possibly Switzerland in the nineteenth century and, indeed, there may be elements of consociational politics in all democratic societies. But it is usually accepted that modern consociational principles were first developed and formulated in the Netherlands and Belgium, although it has also been suggested that these principles developed under the British system of colonial rule. According to their most notable exponent there are four basic and essential principles.[10] First, each group has protection and autonomy in respect of its core values, that is the matters that are of most precious and intimate concern to it. Second, each group has a veto on decisions that affect such matters. Third, representation in government institutions, including the legislature and the bureaucracy, allocation of expenditure and the distribution of public goods must be proportional to communal populations. Fourth, governments should normally be based on inter-communal coalitions. These principles are the distinctive features of consociationalism and also conditions for building confidence and achieving political success in consociational systems. Further conditions are that there must be goodwill and trust between communities (for example that one does not seek to dominate or betray the other) and trust between leaders and, of course, between leaders and their own communities. A further distinctive feature of consociational systems is that groups remain voluntarily segregated and their leaders make agreements and settle differences in a process of elite accommodation.

Both federal and consociational systems would appear to offer a better chance of success in conditions of ethnic pluralism than unitary systems, which are more likely to permit the dominance of majority ethnic groups. In such cases 'one man one vote' ceases in and by itself to be a completely satisfactory principle of just rule with inevitable and possibly unsustainable stress on the political system. The most notable point about federalism and consociationalism is that they offer a greater opportunity for the effective diffusion of power in polyethnic societies than alternative arrangements. The significance of this cannot be underestimated, since the political expression of ethnic, as opposed to state and imperial nationalism, is likely to remain a major feature of contemporary politics, posing a recurring threat to the stability and integrity of states. Finally, as the protection of ethnic and cultural identities becomes more of an end in itself, federalism and consociationalism offer the opportunity to provide political equity within parameters that are familiar to and potentially manageable by democratic politicians.

CONCLUSION

While the demands of regional and ethnic minority groups puts more pressure on the state, the state is itself increasingly expected to provide order, justice, economic development and social welfare to its heterogenous populations. This places increasing strain on the distributive and administrative capabilities and the economic resources of the state. These mounting demands on the state occur in a period when increasing permeability and interdependence have created conditions and forces which have eroded its position and it is no longer expected to be the sole provider of its own security and less able to behave as a wholly independent actor in the international economy. Indeed, sub-state units such as regions and provinces have themselves become increasingly active in the international economy. Some have sought to convert this to a basis for autonomy or limited independence in a new international environment. Hence proposals such as Quebec separatists' 'sovereignty association' and the Scottish nationalists' 'independence within the European Community'. It is possible that such ideas may provide an alternative way of reconciling the tensions between the diminishing capabilities of the state and the raised expectations of ethnic minorities and regions, but it leaves the problem of the state unresolved.

The nation state has been the dominant form of political organisation in the modern world. Most states, however, are ethnically heterogeneous and the claims of minorities are a perennial issue and a recurrent source of conflict both within and between states while the problem of accommodating ethnic and regional identities threatens the cohesion of particular states, On the other hand, while ethno-national and ethno-regional movements may threaten the cohesion and stability of some states, the view that they threaten the state irself possibly arises from an oversimplification of the nature of nationalism. Nationalism is rarely simple and its significance has to be assessed in each particular case. The relationship between nationalism and the state is a complex one, but vital to an understanding of both. Nationalism has had a central part in the development of the modern state, especially its transition from the absolutist and imperial forms to the nation state. Nationalism may yet again influence the development of the state into the twenty-first century as it faces new pressures for change, from without and within. Thus nationalism does not necessarily threaten the persistence of the state as a form of political organisation, but it may challenge the continuance of some states in their existing form.

The source of this challenge is the dynamism of nationalism itself and the shortcomings of past nation building efforts by statesmen. Nationalism is an aspiration and a demand for self-rule by the people defining themselves as the nation with the object of bringing the nation and the state ultimately into concurrence. Where such concurrence does not exist, nationalism creates strain, instability and breakdown in political systems, as is already clear from the experience of several states. The Soviet Union simply imploded under nationalist pressures and in the successor states, including Russia, considerable tensions remain. In Czechoslovakia, Lebanon and Yugoslavia the stresses of communal and ethnic conflict led to the disintegration of the state and only in Czechoslovakia was this process accomplished peacefully. In Yugoslavia and Lebanon the state collapsed in catastrophic violence which was only pacified by large scale international intervention and in parts of former Yugoslavia the restoration of political stability remains problematic. In both Belgium and Spain the peaceful management of ethnic pluralism has led to extensive reconstruction of the constitutional arrangements of the state. In Britain, Canada and India communal and ethno-national demands have brought the state under varying degrees of pressure which have forced these demands to the top of the political agenda. Even in well ordered and peaceful Switzerland there have been marginal adjustments to the constitutional structure to accommodate the demands of Jura separatists. The demands of ethnic and regional groups may have a significant impact on public policy, complicating the tasks of managing the economy and delivering social services. In some states, such as Belgium, Canada, Lebanon and Spain, even foreign policy, traditionally the ultimate preserve of high politics, has to be sensitive to and take account of the demands, aspirations and external associations of minority and regional groups.

THE CASE STUDIES

These problems of governing multinational states are discussed in more detail in the following case studies which are grouped into four categories according to the classification presented on page 9. Thus Part 1 considers India and Russia as two cases of dominant pluralism. In chapter 1 Vernon Hewitt argues that secularism is one of the central principles of the Indian political system and that the state can accommodate ethnic differences so long as these are rooted in linguistic, caste and economic class differences. Social change, however, has shifted the basis of ethnic differences to a more explicitly religious basis which directly challenges the ethos of the state. The rise of Hindu fundamentalism, particularly its expression by the BJP, has exposed both the internal diversity of Hinduism and the ambivalence of Hindu dominance, opening an unpredictable avenue of development in Indian politics. In Russia the dominance of ethnic Russians is not significantly diminished by their ideological, regional, economic and class divisions. In chapter 2 Peter Duncan finds that the resurgence of nationalism in Russia after the fall of communism has led to increased tension between Russians and ethnic minorities on the one hand and between the government and the autonomous republics and regions on the other, even those republics in which the titular ethnic group is not itself a majority. With a few exceptions, notably Chechnia, however, separatism and demands for secession have not been a major problem for the regime, because the titular ethnic groups constitute a majority in only a few of the autonomous republics.

The experience of the two cases considered in Part 2 suggests that bipolar pluralism may be inherently unstable because one of the communities has been historically privileged and the other correspondingly disadvantaged. When changes in economic and political circumstances have made such inequalities unsustainable, the communities have tended to become estranged leading to a restructuring or a breakup of the state. In chapter 3 John Fitzmaurice examines the development of relations between the ethnolinguistic communities in Belgium, the shortcomings of consociationalism and the gradual federalisation of the state. He explains the complexities of the Belgian federal model and the disaffection with politics that has resulted from the prolonged process of accommodation. In chapter 4 Karen Henderson finds that the failure of Czechoslovakia was probably due to a marked imbalance of power between the Czech and Slovak communities which meant that the politics of the country was always dominated by Czech interests. The collapse of communism and the rise of nationalism led to a confronatation between elites rather than peoples which was difficult to resolve in a system which had long been elite dominated and had little experience of popular participation in high politics.

Part 3 includes three studies of complex pluralism which illustrate the very great difficulties of maintaining political unity and social peace in such conditions. Switzerland has been the most successful of these cases, but Lebanon and Yugoslavia also enjoyed long periods of prosperity and peace before dissolving into civil war. In contrast to the Swiss experience, however, there were a number of contested concepts of Lebanese society, while attempts to construct an overarching Lebanese identity were not wholly successful. In chapter 5 Fida Nasralla discusses the issue of Lebanese identity, the cleavages and conflicts in Lebanese society and the factors contributing to the breakdown of the Lebanese state. She then assesses the efforts to build a new Lebanese republic on consociational principles similar to those of its predecessor. In chapter 6 Jonathan Steinberg explains the success of the Swiss model which, he maintains, is rooted in shared values and attitudes and a strong sense of place. Essential to its success is the structure of Swiss federalism, especially the extensive autonomy of the cantons and communes which permits various groups to withdraw into their own enclaves while working together in the wider community. By thus sustaining a range of local, regional, ethno-linguistic and religious identities within the umbrella of Swiss nationality, they are able to accommodate their sometimes profound differences. In Yugoslavia, by contrast, the conflicting goals of Serb and Croat nationalists, the frictions between them and the smaller nations, the rivalry of the republics and the manoeuvrings of political elites created conditions which reduced the prospects that this society could persist. Of all ethnic plural societies, Yugoslavia, with its bewildering diversity and intricate structures, was probably the most complex, both in its composition and political organisation. In chapter 7 Christopher Bennett shows how mistrust, suspicion and fear eventually broke into open conflict which, partly due to the weaknesses of Yugoslav federalism, led directly to the breakup of the state and the collapse of the Yugoslav experiment.

Part 4 considers three cases of ethno-regionalism which illustrate the diversity of structures included in this category of ethnic pluralism. In chapter 8 Michael Keating examines the regime of territorial politics which was established in the United Kingdom and shows how it came under increasing strain following the growth of nationalism within the peripheral states. He then assesses the growing consensus on home rule in Scotland and Wales in the light of the confused response of central government which, he concludes, are symptoms of a deep identity crisis. In chapter 9 Don MacIver traces the sources of ethnic conflict and regionalism in Canada, showing how these have centred on the French-English divide and the rise of separatism in Quebec. He explains how the difficulties of accommodating the divergent interests of Canadian politics have been complicated by the reluctance of other regions and groups to make political and constitutional adjustments that would satisfy Quebec. In chapter 10 John Gibbons outlines the historical basis of cultural and regional diversity in Spain and the system of regional autonomy in the Spanish constitution. He discusses the working of the Spanish system, the incorporation of ethno-regional institutions into the decision-making process of the Spanish state and the emergence of inter-regional policy networks on a range of issues including the external relations of the nationalities.

These studies demonstrate that ethnic pluralism occurs in many types of state and that the conflicting demands of ethnic groups can add considerably to the stress on their political systems. While states make a wide variety of responses to ethnic demands, failure to accommodate them can lead to intolerable strain and even to political breakdown. Politicians, therefore, can not safely underestimate the strength and determination of mobilised ethnic groups. Once ethnic demands become a factor in the politics of a state they can not be ignored, but must be carefully and delicately managed. Old states are no more immune to the demands of ethnic groups than new ones and democratic states no more than authoritarian ones, although well established democracies are more likely to be able to deal with them.

NOTES

1   J.S. Mill, *Utilitarianism, Liberty and Representative Government*, London, J.M. Dent and Sons, 1948, pp.360-61.

2   This term has been borrowed from the Canadian philosopher, Charles Taylor, although it is possibly not used in precisely the same sense as in the original text. See Charles Taylor, *Reconciling the Solitudes*, Montreal and Ottawa, McGill-Queens University Press, 1993, p.183.

3   J.S. Mill, *op. cit.*, pp.359-66.

4   Lord Acton, *Essays on Freedom and Power*, New York, Meridian Books, 1962, pp.141-70.

5   Ephraim Nimni, *Marxism and Nationalism*, Pluto Press, 1991, pp.119-95.

6   John Rawls, *A Theory of Justice*, Oxford, The Clarendon Press, 1972, p.146.

7   Michael Sandel, *Liberalism and the Limits of Justice*, Cambridge, Cambridge University Press, 1982, p.179.

8   K.C. Wheare, *Federal Government*, Oxford, Oxford University Press, 1963.

9   D.J. Elazar, *American Federalism: a View from the States*, New York, Thomas Crowell, 1972.

10 A. Lijpart, *Democracy in Plural Societies*, New Haven and London, Yale University Press, 1977

Part One

Dominant Pluralism

1 India

The State, Ethnicity and Nationalism

Vernon Hewitt

The degree of social pluralism in India is by any account extraordinary. To the European observer, the multiplicity of differing – and often competing – identities within the Republic of India seem more appropriately described by concepts such as 'Empire' or 'Civilisational Areas' rather than the more familiar and monolithic idioms of state and nation.[1] India consists of an area measuring 3, 287, 263 square km, with a population somewhat in excess of 900 million persons. The Indian constitution recognises no less than 19 regional languages, (which themselves break down into over 250 regionally distinct dialects). In turn these languages lend themselves to many differing and interrelated scripts. In terms of religious and confessional identities, India contains numerous communities, from the Hindus (who constitute over 83 per cent of the population), to Indian Muslims (11 per cent), Sikhs (just over 2 per cent) and further minorities such as Jains, Buddhists and Parses.

While separate in terms of confessional practices, these discrete communities nonetheless share specific and wider cultural points of reference: Sikhism draws upon Hinduism, while Buddhism began as a radical reform movement against specific aspects of Hindu practice.[2] Even Islam, entering the sub-continent around the time of the 12th century AD from the north-west, came in a particularly mystical and saintly form, understandable to a native population used to Hindu and Buddhist practices. In many respects, religious conversions have taken place within the Indian sub-continent because of, and not inspite of, cultural affinities, although such conversions have acted to change and differentiate broader cultural outlines.[3] Subsequent

Islamic practices significantly interacted with local Hindu beliefs and customs, for example, especially with regard to Shi'ite practices. The categories of language and religion are further divided – or regrouped – through the pervasive influence of caste and *jati* identities. Caste has become a notoriously difficult concept to define in practice, especially concerning its relevance to politics.[4] As is well known, the term is a Portuguese one, relating only indirectly to the four varnas – or colours – which account for the creation of Brahmins, Kshatriyas, Vaishyas and Shudras from the body of the God Brahma in Hindu mythology. Caste is also a misleading term if used as a guide to *jati* – often translated as a sub-caste group within a specific locality or village. It is within the *jati* group that social practices such as marriage, dietary regulations and ritual enforcement take place. There are well in excess of 2,500 jati groups throughout India, and these only loosely correspond to wider caste categories. Caste categories also overlap significantly with dominant linguistic groups.

Caste has further political significance. Not only does it structure social interaction and group identity, it also correlates broadly to economic well being. The emergence of a caste based society coincided – and rationalised – a specific economic division of labour. Although religious in origin, and clearly associated with the coming of Hinduism, caste has a pronounced economic dimension that remains influential within non-Hindu minorities. Specific professions became ranked hierarchically through an index of polluting and non-polluting tasks, with menial agricultural and labouring jobs becoming the preserve of the Shudras, the clerical and administrative jobs those of the Brahmins. Kshatriyas provided kingship and warriors. Low caste Hindus, those below the twice-born category, have both low status within the caste system as well as few economic and social assets. Upper caste Hindus, such as Khasatriyas and Brahmins are not only high in status, but are still more likely to command economic and political power than lower caste members. The concept of the dominant caste, devised by Srinivas,[5] describes the political clout of landowning castes, socially dominant in specific regions and districts.

The creation of a large number of Harijans, (previously called untouchables, and known amongst themselves increasingly as Dalits), as a reserve of manual labour excluded from the hierarchy of the varnas altogether because of their excess pollution, adds a further layer to the structure of Indian society. While many Dalits converted to Christianity, Buddhism and Islam in protest of the doctrinal links between Hinduism and untouchability, (or were themselves forcibly converted) they were to retain the economic and social stigmatism associated with Hindu Dalits. Other social identities exist, such as various tribal and indigenous peoples, referred to as a *Advasis*, which make up significant percentages of the population in the South, North and North East. Religious practices here are generally animist, although some degree of hinduisation has taken place, wherein local saints and gods have become accommodated within the Hindu pantheon. Like the Dalits, Advasis are amongst the poorest of India's population.

Superimposed across these differences of language, religion, and caste are the broader, more illusive categories of regionalism. One of the most enduring geographical distinctions made throughout the sub-continent separates 'hill' people from the people of the 'plains'. Although generally refering to the Gangetic plains of Northern India, the polarisation of 'hills versus plains' is reproduced in the eastern and western Ghat (or hill) areas, as well as in the North-East and North-West of India. The distinction takes on a racial dimension when it is maintained that most hill peoples are non-Aryans – remnents of indigenous races who were displaced from the plains by subsequent Aryan invasions from the north west, beginning about 1000 BC. Physically isolated from the cultural and religious innovations of the invaders, hill peoples remained separate from the developments within hinduism (such as the evolution of caste), and from the economic and political influences of subsequent sub-continental empires.

Further differences also reinforce the regional distinctions in India between north and south: between the Hindi speaking, Brahmanically dominated north Indian plain and the southern, shudra dominated tamil speakers. Reinforced by cultural and dietary differences (wheat, chappti eaters of the north versus rice eaters of the south), the North-South distinction is further illustrated by differences in political culture (with north Indian politics being especially violent and caste ridden), and significant differences in electoral support at the time of national elections. Often the southern states have supported one party, while the north has supported another. At the state level, many states have voted in their own regional based party.

How, economically and politically, has the Indian state managed to deal with such social complexity? More critically, how has such a degree of social pluralism sustained a democratic and *secular* system of government, in which until recently, one party has remained politically dominant? How has the style of Indian state intervention into society affected and to some extent directed the nature of social change and generated specific types of 'new' social identity? This chapter will explore how Nehru's approach to nationalism changed in the 1950s, and how subsequent nationalist policy changed under his daughter. The argument presented here is that the Indian state's ability to deal with ethnicity has significantly diminished over time, not just because

of institutional decline and political incompetence, but because of a change
in the nature of ethnicity itself.

TERMS AND METHODS

Jawahalal Nehru's articulation of Indian nationalism was essentially 'modern',
stressing the importance of a scientific and rational culture. 'Little' traditions
of social identity were not just 'sub-nationalist', they were feudal, inimical
to the project of state formation. Indigenous challenges to the nationalist
project, from religious identities such as the various Hindu reformists, and
specific Muslim parties in the 1930s were labelled 'obscurantist'; in India an
early euphemism for 'ethnicity' was 'communal' – a religious conception of
group rights. Under Nehru's pervasive acceptance of Westernisation, India's
'dominant discourse of ethnicity [was] loaded in favour of those who
propagate[d] the monotheistic creed of a single unified nation'.[6]
    To Nehru, religion in India was not a 'positive identifier', it was stigma.
If properly confined to the private, it could be a source of individual strength,
if brought out into the public, it was merely the mark of a backward polity.
Nehru's belief in secularism was premised, self-consciously, on the European
experience wherein religions, and religious symbolism, had ceased to have
any civic authority. The monolithic imprint of the territorial state was, to
Nehru then, a monolithic secular nationalism. While some degree of
compromise was necessary in the early years of independence, and while
this new civic nationalism drew selectively upon a whole series of regional,
linguistic, and cultural symbolism, it would ultimately brook no religious
resistance. Moreover, it would strive to weld linguistic, regional and cultural
differences into one seamless collective identity.
    For a while this commitment to a monolithic nationalism seemed to work,
yet it soon became apparent that the belief that ethnicity was capable of
being absorbed by nationalism soon gave way to the realisation that ethnicity
had a dynamic all of its own. Throughout the post colonial world, the tenacity
of ethnic identities questioned the simplistic dichotomy made between
nationalism and ethnicity. Modernisation did not eliminate ethnicity at all:
on the contrary, it appeared to spawn differing types of ethnic identities,
which in the context of a wider nationalism, attempted to assert their
differences, and their rights to be treated differently.
In recognition of what one author has referred to as the 'ethnic upsurge',
ethnicity is now rightly perceived in the same way that nationalism was
before it – something that is deeply instrumental and political, an active

process of identification. Gone is the emphasis on primordiality, the belief that ethnicity was given and timeless. Ethnicity is now 'a question of attitudes, perceptions and sentiments that are necessarily fleeting and immutable, varying with the particular situation of the subject. As the individual's situation changes, so will (their) group identification .... [Such a view] makes it possible for ethnicity to be used instrumentally to further individual or collective interests.'[7]

This new emphasis on ethnicity as a type of 'cultural collectivity', using a variety of devices such as language, 'collective memories', religious practices and customs, or even a specific set of institutions, perceives ethnicity as a conscious tool or social strategy to further specific political demands. Such arguments acknowledge the instrumentality of ethnicity and recognises that they are not in themselves static, they continue to define and redefine themselves in line with broader political and economic issues. While often an act of imagination as opposed to outright invention, and structured to some extent by what is historically feasible[8] the fluidity of ethnicity is, paradoxically, one of its key characteristics: 'ethnicity has to be a fluid concept, contextual, situational and relational'. [9]

The given trajectory of an ethnic claim depends largely upon the flexibility of a set of institutions and a given nationalist ideology. In outline, a given set of ethnic demands may initially be couched in terms of what the state structure concedes as 'legitimate' (a linguistic state, political recognition as an economically disadvantaged group, as will be discussed below in the Indian case). Demands may change however, they may widen or deepen (a state for a religious group of community, special laws for a community exempting them from certain impositions by the state), and the ethnic group itself may change or fracture, with one side announcing that 'they' are the 'real' Assamese, or more 'truly' representative of Kashmiri opinion. Furthermore, ethnic identifiers change and alter in response to state repression or to state accommodation.

ETHNICITY AND NATIONALISM IN INDIA

In attempting to understand the changing basis of ethnic identities in India, it is obvious from the onset that ethnicity cannot, in each and every case, be equated with subversion and secession. It is part of the cultural fabric of the nation-state itself. Moreover, it is tied intimately with the concept of representation and election. It should come as no surprise that ethnicity has come to prominence in the context of nation building and democratic practice.

Any attempt to separate 'ethnicity' in South Asia from the socio-economic compulsions of nation building, is fundamentally flawed. As one writer has put it:

The 'national question' has become the ethnic question, or rather the two issues are appearing simultaneously and partly merging, thus presenting social scientists [sic] with a demanding task, and probably a need to reconsider some conventional wisdom's concerning nation building.[10]

Following on from the ideas raised in the works of Reetze and Hettne, this chapter accepts the argument that ethnicity is a discrete social identity, consciously formed in the context of a pre-existing state structure and a given 'official' nationalism. Often it is in opposition to 'official' nationalism that ethnic categories become reordered and politically active, triggered either by discriminatory economic or social policy or some other palpable sense of historical grievance. Yet in the case of India, the degree of opposition is usually conditional. Ethnic identities need not, in themselves, challenge the state. Such identities often seek redress on quite specific, 'tailor-made' issues. If access to the state is denied or in some sense frustrated, ethnic identities can seek out-right secession, seeking to convert themselves into a ready-made nation claiming statehood with international recognition. Yet such extremes are not often desired by ethnic leaderships, and are often the end result of a failure to reach some political accommodation within a given state structure itself.

The historical peculiarities of the Indian state as set up by the British, and the nature of India's ruling elite – situated within the institutions of the Indian National Congress party – gave India an enormous capacity to direct and order state-society relations and to merge the identities of caste, language, and culture into a relatively clear notion of the Indian citizen with guaranteed rights and obligations. One of the main explanations for such a success was the apparent commitment by India's elite to secularism, federalism, and parliamentary democracy. Given such a high level of social pluralism, secularism provided the necessary framework to retain the unity of the Indian state, and to give the Indian state the capacities to accommodate a series of linguistic and culturally based ethnic challenges.

As India approached the 1970s however, this inbuilt capacity to govern became seriously eroded, in part through the very successes of the democratisation of the Indian political system, and the nature of state economic management, which successfully targeted aid and assistance to 'differing' communities, on the basis of relative economic backwardness. Yet since such economic categories were not in themselves free of wider cultural or religious categories, such economic management increased perceptions of social differentiation even as it successfully corrected historical economic injustices.

By the 1980s the state came to face a whole new series of 'ethnic' challenges, explicitly based upon a religious discourse, and far beyond the institutional capacity of the state to manage. The two most critical examples are those of Punjab and the state of Jammu and Kashmir. Accounting for the decline in the Indian states' capacity to manage a pluralistic society involves understanding the nature of institutional change since the 1960s, as well as comprehending the change in India's political elite following the rise of Indira Gandhi from 1969. It will be argued that one of the main explanations behind the current waves of religious ethnic 'revivalism' lies in dynamics of Hindu culture as it has emerged from the 19th century, and the apparent success of other non-Hindu minorities to have economically benefited from secular politics. The change in the basis of ethnic identities, from linguistic to religious, confronts Indian secularism with a most serious crisis.[11]

INDIAN NATIONALISM AND THE IDEOLOGY OF SECULARISM

From 1947 onwards, India's ruling elite attempted to construct a territorially defined homogenous Indian nationalism, while accommodating India's high level of social pluralism. This brought them face to face with issues such as language, religion and culture. The fulcrum in which India's territorial and civic nationalism was to be forged was ideological – the clear links between liberalism and democracy and the Congress moderates of the early 20th century, and their clear commitment to secularism. Only in the context of a secular Republic, it was argued, could India guarantee the rights of individual representation. The separation of citizenship from confessional identities, was radical in the Indian context because confessional identities had been used by the colonial power to invest communities with political rights. So-called communal awards, which recognised discrete religious communities and awarded them separate electorates, often hedged with complex weightage, to protect them from brute majoritarianism, was seen by the Indian National Congress as a characteristic of imperial 'divide and rule'. It ignored cultural continuities between religious groups as much as it ignored doctrinal divisions within them. With specific reference to colonial Lucknow, Oldenburg sums up such a policy very neatly when she argues

The British ignored the complex affinities that cut across religious and cultural lines. For political reasons they chose to see society as simple aggregations of Hindus and Muslims, and accorded representation on official bodies likewise. In time, when local representatives began to understand the implications of a religious and vertical division of the polity, this straight forward division of the polity generated communal constituencies.[12]

Central to Nehru's conception of modernity and democracy was a universal and uniform notion of citizenship as the necessary condition for economic and social emancipation. Congress opposed communal awards and sought to bring together India's various elites on the basis of a secular, civic territorial nationalism. In this endeavour it opposed both the British conception of India's 'natural' political divisions (i.e. the primacy of religion) and the demands of the Muslim League for the division of the British Indian Empire into two states, one Hindu the other Muslim. For Congress, such a view was feudal and backward. Despite the reality of partition, the Congress remained committed to secularism, despite the fact that the overwhelming majority of Indians were Hindus.

Thus the Indian state was neutral to religious appeals for political or social preference. In theory at least, the Indian citizens stood before the authority of the state as equal. While the state did not ignore the importance of religious symbolism – or indeed religious sensitivity – at the height of the Nehru period it over-rode them through common codes (or future commitments to such codes) imposed upon the territory of India in matters such as marriage, criminal law, and taxes. No where was this commitment more apparent than in the adoption of English law and its displacement of traditional practices.[13]

The Indian constitution contained a directive principle which compelled the Indian state, at some future date, to 'secure to the citizens a uniform civil code throughout the territory of India'. In 1955-6, the Indian Parliament (the Lok Sabha) passed a series of bills known collectively as the 'Hindu Code' , which completed the displacement of dhamasastra, or 'traditional' law, and reformed Hindu practices related to family and domestic matters, separating issues such as marriage, inheritance etc. from any specific religious overtones. The fact that the state even attempted to change the social customs of the majority was seen as evidence of its commitment to a secular polity. The political impartiality of secularism was seen as the greatest guarantor of minority rights. Secularism constrained the social identity of minorities to forego the use of religious symbolism to claim exclusive rights and to define themselves as minorities on some other basis.

While claims of political exclusiveness could not be made within India in terms of religion, language provided a flexible basis for the incorporation of social movements into nation building on the basis of claiming special ethno-linguistic identities. Throughout the 1950s, the old multi-lingual provinces of the British period were redivided to correspond with linguistic groups, and as a concession to powerful regional groups demanding such action from the centre. Although Congress was committed to making Hindi the national language, a political compromise ensured that India evolved a three language formula: Hindi, English and one of the other recognised national languages of India. The Indian state proved capable of recognising the primacy of differing language groups by equalising recognition, and by providing translation and other multi-linguistic solutions in public buildings.

Other identities were also 'legitimated' within the constitutional language of the state itself. Marc Galanter notes that

'The constitution of India authorises the government to provide special benefits and preferences to previously disadvantaged sections of the population.'[14]

The identity of such disadvantaged groups is recognised on the basis of social need and economic 'backwardness'. Given the association between such groups and other sets of social identity, especially that of caste noted above, various disputes have arisen over specific claims, and the overall consequences of such positive discrimination. Nonetheless, despite various agitation's for inclusion into such groups, India's political elite were able to deliver such policies and to significantly advance the well being of Indian 'minorities' who successfully claimed a history of economic exclusion and discrimination.[15]

THE MANAGEMENT OF SOCIAL PLURALISM

While condemning the workings of the colonial state, modern nationalism aspired to control a modified form of it. By the time of the Government of India Act 1935, the framework of the modern Indian state, democratic and federal, was complete. The structure of the state remained intact even after Independence, with 70 per cent of India's 1950 constitution being carried over from the 1935 Government of India Act. The only significant change that took place involved the abolition of communal awards. Because of the primacy of secularism, principles of positive discrimination (or the principles of over-representing disadvantaged groups through reserved seats) were introduced on strict economic criteria: scheduled castes and tribes, and 'other backward castes' were given privileged access to the state. Such policies were codified into the constitution, and various institutions, the Finance Commission, the Backward Caste Commission, etc., were set up to monitor such policies.

While recognising itself as a 'unitary state', India would eventually devolve significant powers to twenty-five state units. This institutional legacy is important in understanding how the Indian federal constitution facilitated the flexibility of Indian nationalism to deal with regional and linguistic challenges. Powers included financial arrangements, primary legislation in matters of health and education policy, and powers in agricultural matters on land reform and taxation. The Indian prime minister, through the office of an indirectly elected national president (who replaced the British Monarch as head of state shortly after independence), appointed governors to each state, to ensure that popularly elected Chief Ministers executed their responsibilities in accordance with the constitution. If governors believed that this was not the case, the Indian constitution empowered them to submit a report to the President (in effect, given India's Westminster style system of government, the prime minister) authorising the state government in question to be removed, and for the state to be directly administered by the centre until such a time as a new government could be formed.[16] Where the ability – or indeed the willingness – of the state to accommodate regional forces has been breached, India's national elite made widespread use of the army and the paramilitary to 'restore' the accepted political process and the accepted cultural and nationalist symbols of power. Breaches occurred when political parties came to power in the states committed to carrying out 'anti-nationalist' forces, policies that sought to establish religious power, or when political and popular movements sought to secede from the Union.

So called President's Rule, otherwise known as article 356, (a direct replica of Governor's Rule from the 1935 Act) has not surprisingly been one of the most controversial issues in centre-state relations since Independence. Governors also had powers to refer legislation passed by state assemblies to the Indian President, or indeed the Supreme Court of India, to ensure that such legislation was in itself constitutional, or in keeping with all Indian legislation. Such a device, if abused, could cause considerable delays in implementation, especially if the state government in question was of a different political complexion than the national government in New Delhi.

Yet such centralising caveats within the Indian federal system, strengthened after Partition through the fear of national disintegration, did not necessarily stand in the way of India's democratic and federal development. In terms of political accountability, Nehru survived long enough as India's first Prime Minister (1952–1964) to establish the principles of cabinet and parliamentary responsibility. With regard to the national President, Nehru established a working basis on which the potential powers of the President – implied through the powers to issue ordinances and to dismiss the Prime Minister – were tied clearly to the same conventions that governed the relationship between British prime ministers and the Monarchy. Nehru is credited with preventing presidential power – the modern governor-generals and viceroys of India – from reducing parliamentary government to the whims of the executive. Federalism in India recognised the imperatives of the nation-state project, while at the same moving towards a compromising with the regional diversity of linguistic states.

Economic powers were not irrelevant to the cultural interests of regionally defined states. Having adopted a commitment to economic planning, the Indian state created a series of institutions in which regional plan outlines and economic objectives could be brought to the attention of a powerful Planning Commission, based in New Delhi and under the control of the Prime Minister's Secretariat. The National Development Council, as well as experiments in zonal councils and regularly held meetings of state Chief Ministers and Governors, created the conduits under which development policies were formulated and implemented.[17] In the realm of education, Sheth comments that 'the use of ... regional language as the language of administration in a state, and as the medium of instruction in schools is by now an established policy. It has been followed, although not uniformly, in almost all the states of the Indian union'.[18]

THE POLITICAL DYNAMICS OF CONGRESS INDIA

The Indian state's commitments to secularism and to democracy were successfully implemented because of the strength and institutional integrity of India's premier political institution, the Indian National Congress. With a clearly organised party and legislative wing, and with power devolved within the national party organisation to local, state based elites, the Congress gave the federal ideals of the constitution tensile strength to move and accommodate a huge variety of social identities. Surprisingly, the degree of India's social pluralism did not immediately generate a multi-party system. Until 1977, the Congress won the national elections with convincing majorities. Until 1967, it dominated state elections as well. Other political parties were small, regionally based, and likely to be reabsorbed by the Congress itself. The Left wing parties, including the two Marxist parties, were regionally based, even though they lay claim to a national ideology of secularism and state power.

The explanation for Congress' success lies in the social differentiation at the basis of each state Congress party, and the crucial autonomy between

Congress state parties and the national Congress leadership. Congress Chief Ministers, the elected 'prime ministers' of their respective states, had ample scope to mediate and accommodate specific interests: interests that might well be in opposition to Congress government's in other parts of India. Manor has calculated that throughout the 1960s, Indian political voting was informed – determined in fact – by as little as 1/6th of the population: members of an influential political elite, nationalist in conviction, members of the dominant caste groups in the regions and of the local vernaculars, and committed to election as an expression of their political power. Such an elite – regionally diverse – ensured that the Congress reflected the degree of social pluralism within each state.

For example, in the 1960s, the Congress state government of Uttar Pradesh in Northern India was conscious of the importance of Muslim votes and the need to construct coalitions inclusive of Muslim interests. While such interests could not be expressed in terms of a confessional identity, they could be expressed in terms of social backwardness, economic hardship, and the defence of culture (such as the protection and propagation of Urdu and the development of the Urdu press). Such strategies, practised by astute Congress chief ministers, ensured that a key minority had access to the state and to the redistribution of state wealth. In the state of Gujarat, Congress success in securing state power for itself relied upon something known popularly as the "Kham' strategy: an acronym for a rainbow coalition of Khastriyas (high caste Hindus), Hariyans (Dalits), Advasis (tribals) and Muslims. This need to accommodate broad political support in order to win election was replicated in each state. Given India's regional diversity, the electoral significance of minorities, and the need to accommodate coalitions of differing minorities became crucial for winning national and state elections.

THE DECLINE OF THE CONGRESS SYSTEM

The reasons for the early absence of any serious ethnic movements claiming secession thus appear obvious: a secular polity within which linguistic identities could co-exist with apparent equal legitimacy within the territorial state, a much more clearly defined and institutional federal structure, and a well knit national party that was not uprooted by partition. 'Ethnicity' was not absent during this period, it was present in a series of linguistic and cultural movements which were easily accommodated within the structures of the Indian state. Yet it would be wrong to assert that the workings of this system have not produced their own problems, or that India has not faced the risk – or indeed the threat – of secession or violent opposition from subsequent ethnic challenges. Although throughout the 1950s and the 1960s India's political institutions continued to respond to rapid social change, some sections and regions attempted to assert religious claims for preferential – or differential – treatment within the Indian political system: primarily the Akali Dal party, associated with the political aspirations of the Sikhs of the Punjab, tribal groups situated in India's troubled North-East, and the Kashmir Muslims of the valley districts of the state of Jammu and Kashmir.

These identities were different from those that characterised the earlier period of Indian independence. Sheth states clearly that

> Unlike in the late fifties and the early sixties, when cultural identities were linguistically defined, today ... religion, rather than language has become the epitome of the culture of the people.[19]

Such an explicit use of religion confronted the Indian state with a dilemma. More critically, such challenges did not respond to the old remedies of greater political devolution within the framework of the Indian constitution, or greater economic access to state resources. On the basis of religious exclusiveness, new ethnic groups sought to establish the right to deal with themselves according to their faith, a right which invariably determined how they were to deal with people of other religious groups as well.

How do we account for this shift in the basis of ethnicity? In the 1970s and 1980s, the mediation of mass voting by elites – Manor's one sixth – became more problematic as the elite itself began to change and dissipate through socio-economic and educational change. People became much more assertive of their political rights, and national and state leaders found it increasingly harder to convince people to but their faith blindly behind one party. Moreover, Congress too began to change as the giants of the independence movement died or retired. It seemed increasingly irrelevant to an impatient Indian electorate, to stress the role Congress had played in freeing the state from the British. What mattered was economic performance and the speed and depth of social reform. As the association between the freedom struggle and Congress weakened, so to did the direct association between the Congress and Indian nationalism.

As India's political system matured, the electorate became increasingly volatile in its political loyalties: voting for different political parties at different levels of the Indian federal system. While returning the national Congress government to power in New Delhi, the electorate grew more circumspect in voting for Congress at the state level, and increasingly voted in a local or regional party closer to their immediate political and cultural aspirations. The main watershed is the 1967 elections, in which the Congress majority at the centre was reduced from 358 to 279, and in which Congress lost eight state governments, an unprecedented outcome.

The rise of new social groups throughout India, with more strident and urgent agendas, brought non-Congress state governments to power, despite the weakness and instability of such parties. Although Congress governments were subsequently restored to power, mainly through defection or bouts of President's Rule, the unquestioned association between Congress and government had been breached. Yet significantly – and of great political importance for the future of India's political system as a whole – the opposition parties proved incapable of replicating between themselves, either in coalition or indeed party merger – the all inclusive nature of the Congress party at the time of Nehru. As such they were excluded from taking national power in any form other than a weak coalition or party merger.

This further deepening of the Indian political system – the democratisation of the Congress vote banks itself – coincided with the political centralisation within the Congress party and the politics of Mrs Gandhi, Nehru's daughter, during the turbulent years from 1967 until 1984. This was one of India's most troubled and difficult periods. In large part, Indira Gandhi sought to re-establish Congress dominance through centralising the system, breaking down the autonomy of the state Congress parties (which involved reducing the powers of the Chief Ministers) and stressing the socialist credentials of her party. She did this in the belief that the explanation for the Congress defeats of 1967 lay in the degree of accommodation reached with state leaders, and the fact that such autonomy was now getting in the way of national aspirations. She sought, in many respects, to stress the homogenous nationalist agenda of her father's earlier years. In doing so, she consciously began to 'close down' the very political spaces in which India's social diversity had been successfully compromised with the necessary requirements of the territorial state.

Indira Gandhi's tenure as prime minister can be divided into two distinct phases. The first, beginning in 1967, but not really developing until the Congress split of 1969, can be labelled a socialist phase. During this time Mrs Gandhi sought to restore the electoral fortunes of the Congress by appealing directly to the poor, free of local state party machines and independent Chief Ministers. Throughout the Congress party, election gave way to the principle of nomination. The high tide mark of this phase is her celebrated *Garibi Hatao* (abolish poverty) campaign of 1971 which gave her party a two-thirds majority in the national parliament, the Lok Sabha, and returned many state Congress parties to power as well.

The success of her socialist strategy was marred by the Emergency of 1975-77, in which she appeared to abandon any commitment to parliamentary democracy at all. It was during her socialist period that Indira Gandhi perfected the style of interfering into the workings of non-Congress state governments, using the powers of the governor's to dismiss them from office. Other styles of intervention involved engineering divisions within non-Congress parties by encouraging factionalism – a case exemplified in the centre's dealings with Punjab – and bribing MLA's to defect to the local Congress party, wherein they could name their office. Indira Gandhi even began a process wherein independent state Congress governments were dismissed: especially if they appeared to be politically successful. The fear here was that independent Congress Chief Minister's might well establish an independent power base from which to challenge the Prime Minister.

The second phase – and from the perspective of religiously based ethnic separatism – the most important – concerns what has been called her 'Hindu' phase. On her return to national power in 1980, following the collapse of India's first non-Congress national government, Indira Gandhi appeared convinced that, if socialism could not provide an enduring basis for national power, or if a socialist programme was too difficult to implement, then perhaps Hinduism, or some variant of Hinduism, could be used to manage the Indian political system. Despite the confusion and complexities of Hinduism and its links with the political world, (to be discussed below) Indira Gandhi undertook a cynical manipulation of religious symbolism. The consequences for Indian secularism have been profound in that Indira Gandhi's second phase brought into political significance the role of Hindu chauvinist parties and extremists, which imperilled the position of India's minorities, especially the Muslims, and threatened to create a profound identity crisis for Indian nationalism, especially concerning the nature and viability of secularism.

Indira Gandhi's appeal to Hinduism, muted as it was, and articulated for primarily electoral purposes, was to have several unintended consequences for the Indian polity. What made such a strategy successful electorally – at least in the short term – was that, for complex reasons quite separate from Indira Gandhi's political ambition, the Hindus of India were becoming increasingly assertive in terms of their religious identities vis-a-vis religious minorities themselves. One reason for this is structural and concerned the change in the relative economic positions of differing non-Hindu groups within India, such as the Muslims and the Sikhs. At the time of partition, Muslims who remained in India after partition were usually poor. By the mid

1980s, the Muslim position had changed significantly. Enriched through a process of savings and work, positive discrimination by both central and state governments, and in most cases substantive financial remittances from family members working in the Gulf states, Muslims began to invest some of their new wealth in the public construction of Mosques, and in important Muslim festivals. Their decision to invest in outward symbols of a religious nature is in turn partly explained by a broader perspective of a resurgent Islam.

Within a society in which poverty is erroneously perceived as the failure to win political backing, (or a process of 'robbing Peter to pay Paul') the apparent growth in the well being of the Muslims created ill feeling amongst poor Hindus, who in turn became vulnerable themselves to the politically overtures of Hindu chauvanist parties, such as the Shiv Sena, a militant party well represented in the Western state of Maharashtra, and the Bharatiya Janata Party, India's premier Hindu party, well represented in the North. Both of these political parties, albiet through slightly different styles, stressed a link between Congress, secularism and so-called Muslim appeasement. Many of these chauvanist parties (dubbed 'communal' in the language of Indian elections) were established in the 1920s and '30s, linked to Hindu revivalism.[20] Some, like Shiv Sena, were well linked to political violence and the use of terrorism against non-Hindu minorities. By the 1980s, the political leadership of the Hindu parties were articulating the apparent belief amongst Hindus in India that since minorities have been better able to deliver blocks of votes, political parties have pandered to their whims against the interest of the majority.[21]

Such language disguised the significant economic divisions within the Hindu majority, as well broader cultural divisions (see below) and stressed secularism as a form of Muslim appeasement. More seriously, Hindu reformism self consciously stressed the syncretic basis of Hindu culture, and with the possible exception of Muslims, claimed to be the cultural basis of Sikhism, Buddhism and many other religious minorities. Political parties found themselves responding to political sensitivities they had in themselves partly created. In an attempt to retain or to win power, the Congress, under Mrs Gandhi and later her son, Rajiv Gandhi, tried to deploy the language of religious minority rights *simultaneously* within the idiom of Hindu chauvinism, indeed even on occasion to deliberately create anxiety within the minorities about the fears of Hindu domination. Such a fine balancing act, in which Indira Gandhi and the now renamed Congress-I would act as the swing gate of religiously defined minority and majority opinion, was in effect a recipe for disaster, the result being that religion became paramount to a political process that was once secular.

THE PUNJABI CRISIS: THE FAILURE IN ETHNIC COMPROMISE

In outline at least, and despite broader historical issues which cannot be dealt with here in any depth, the immediate genesis of the Punjab crisis of the mid 1980s dates back to the Anandpur Sahib resolution, apparently agreed by the Akali Dal party in October 1973.[22] Although a number of versions are known to exist, the resolution articulates Sikh grievances against the Central government in economic and social policy terms. Punjab is a wealthy state, the self-proclaimed 'bread basket' of India, and yet much of this wealth has apparently gone elsewhere. The Anandpur resolution calls for greater powers of financial autonomy, by which the Punjabi state government can retain more of the state's wealth, and ensure that such wealth is put to use within the state's own plan outlines. The Akali Dal's submission to the Sarkaria Commission, a Commission of Enquiry set up my Mrs Gandhi to discuss possible changes to centre-state relations in the 1970s, dealt almost exclusively with economic and financial issues.[23] Other issues of concern to the Sikh community concerned attempts to reduce their presence within the Indian Army (in which they had been traditionally over-represented), and river disputes between Punjab and the state of Haryana.

The link between the Anandpur resolution and Akali grievances over the fate of the Sikhs as a religious minority within India is controversial. Akali demands for the creation of a Punjabi speaking state, articulated throughout the 1950s, was conceded in 1966, but took into a Punjabi speaking state a large number of Hindus. Some authors have argued that it was an attempt by the Sikh leadership to disguise a religious demand under the rubric of linguistic autonomy. Some Sikhs had, in the 1940s, argued that the partition of the sub-continent into Muslim and Hindu majority areas opened the way for the creation of an independent Sikh state – so-called Khalistan – but a majority of Sikh political opinion remained committed to Indian nationalism and the politics of the Congress, exemplified by Nehru.

The Anandpur Sahib resolution made reference to the Sikh's need to defend their traditional cultures, and to retain the autonomy of their traditional religious sites and to continue the financial management of Gudwaras (primarily Amristar). Such demands could easily have been accommodated within the framework of Indian federalism as devised by Nehru, and at various stages appeared to be on the point of solution. That they were not, and that they were allowed to become issues of increasing irritation, is indicative of the refusal of the Congress leadership in the 1970s to brook any political compromise, as well as important changes going on within the secular outlook of India's wider nationalist elite. Hindu revivalist movements, active in stressing the similarities between Hinduism and Sikhism were beginning to alarm Sikhs, afraid that their traditions and cultures would be in some senses reclaimed. For this reason alone, Sikhs were more strident, and, in the early 1970s, perhaps more conscious of their religious identity than at any time since the 1940s.

Indira Gandhi's intervention into the politics of the Akali Dal became virtually continuous after 1971. In the context of competitive elections, and in circumstances in which Sikhs were as likely to vote for the Congress-I as they were for the Akali party, the Congress-I sought to engineer radical Sikh militants into positions of political prominance, especially those associated with Sikh student politics, to mobilise Sikhs who were willing to work within the framework of the Indian constitution and to retain access to state power. By encouraging the militants, and portraying the Akali Dal as a party of ethnic extremism, the central government also succeeded in alarming Hindu opinion. The political associations between Indira Gandhi and Sant Bhindranwale, the Sikh militant, involving both financial and logistical support, has now been clearly established, as have links between the Sikh militants and the Pakistanis. Once Bhindrenwale had started a general terrorist campaign, from his base within the Golden Temple, Indira Gandhi distanced herself from him and finally used the Indian army to retake control of the Temple.[24]

Such action – the infamous Operation Blue Star in 1984 – shocked Sikh opinion, in that the Indian Government was seen to desecrate their holiest shrine. The anger, coupled with a clear historical grievance in which the Sikhs were portrayed as a loyal community betrayed by Delhi, led ultimately to the assassination of Indira Gandhi in New Delhi in October 1984 to 'avenge' Sikh honour. The subsequent mass killings of Sikhs in the aftermath of Indira Gandhi's death, which implemented senior Congress politicians, completed a process in which religious images and definitions of communities, had moved centre stage. Subsequent attempts by the central government to desegregate religious communities along economic or sectional lines (jat Sikhs, poor hindus etc.) become difficult in the wider context in which religiously inspired 'outrages' – the storming of a temple, the killing of a leader – have become part of a communities psyche. The restoration of the political process in the Punjab, apparent since 1994, is testament to the economic rewards open to Sikhs should they accept New Delhi's primacy. Exhausted by the militants, and financially ruined through lost business revenue, moderate Sikhs were able to ignore militant pressure and accept some form of accommodation, a process which culminated in the return of an Akali Dal government in 1993. It not clear that this solution is permanent.

KASHMIR: REGIONALISM AND RELIGION COMBINED?

Since 1989, the Indian state of Jammu and Kashmir has witnessed an extraordinary degree of political and social violence, aimed primarily at New Delhi. As a result, many of the Kashmiri Pandits (Hindus) have fled their homeland, and a majority of the Muslim population in the Srinagar and Valley districts have been caught in a bloody war of attrition between various militant groups (representing a variety of foreign, ideological and political positions) and the Indian Army. It has been estimated that since the crisis developed in 1989, between seven and twelve thousand people have been killed, ten thousand have been placed in detention, and well over $ 4 billion dollars worth of damage has been caused to homes and to infrastructure.

Unofficial figures put the number of dead since 1990 much higher, as high as twenty thousand. Most deaths involve innocent civilians killed in shootouts between militants and the Border Security Force (BSF), so-called custodial killings, bomb blasts and grenade attacks. Although especially severe since 1989, and, like the Punjab, in part the outcome of gratuitous interference by New Delhi over a sustained period of time, the Kashmir crisis dates back to 1947, and is tied up with the very concept of secularism itself. In 1947, along with the other hereditary rulers of over 500 Princely states, the British gave the Maharaja of Jammu and Kashmir the choice to join either India or Pakistan, but ruled out the option of becoming an independent state.

The Maharaja was a Rajput Dogra, a Hindu, the legatee of small state founded in the 1840s at the end of the Anglo-Sikh Wars by Gulam Singh. Yet a majority of its population were Sunni Muslims, concentrated in the Kashmir valley, and in the Poonch area, on the edge of the Punjabi plains. Other significant ethnic groups under the territorial control of the Maharaja included buddhists in Ladakh, (including the districts of Leh and Baltistan), Shiite Muslims in Kargil, and Hindus in Jammu and the plain districts at the foot of the Bani Lal pass.

Historically speaking, many of these groups shared a composte culture. Hinduism, Buddhism and Islamic sufism had generated a collective identity of the *Kashmiriyat*, in which issues such as language and supersitions created links between religious groups.[25] Yet this commonality can also be exaggerated. Madan, an Indian ethnographer investigating Kashmiri Pandits in the 1980s, noted that although the Hindus dealt with their Muslim neighbours on friendly, even intimate terms, they also saw them as religiously different and as potential rivals.[26] More importantly, the social and political aspirations of the Kashmiris were always regionally differentiated within the Dogra kingdom, which was a product of conquest.

Many of the Kashmiri's living in the valley districts were supportive of a secular pro-Indian political party calling itself the National Conference, led by the Sheikh Abdullah. Other Muslims, situated in the old Poonch district, west of the Jhelum, were supportive of a more Islamic party, known as the Muslim Conference. In conditions in which popular loyalty was uncertain, (for few elections had been held, and even then on a very limited franchise) it will never be known with any certainty what the Kashmiri people themselves wanted in 1947 [27] No direct reference was made to the people. In the context of the partitioning of the British Indian Empire along communal lines, the Pakistanis claimed the Dogra kingdom on the grounds of the so-called two nation theory (that the Muslims of India were culturally different from the Hindus, and must therefore inherit a separate state).

The Indians claimed Jammu and Kashmir on the basis that India was a secular republic, that one of Kashmir's prominant leaders was pro-Indian, and that the Maharaja had, albeit under rather curious circumstances, signed the so-called Instrument of Accession, under which he ceded his kingdom legally to India in the face of a Pakistani sponsored tribal invasion. The signing of the Instrument of Accession led to the first Indo-Pakistan war, and the physical partitioning of the former Dogra kingdom by a UN sponsored ceasefireline of 1948 (a divide which became known as the Line of Control by 1972). By 1948, the Indians had reiterated a commitment to 'refer to the will of the people' in settling whether Kashmir went to Pakistan, or stayed with India. The concept of a referendum (or plebescite) made no mention of what, by the mid 1970s, was to become a key demand of various Kashmiri groups, the option of independence.

India administered Jammu and Kashmir within the framework of the Indian constitution, and through the provisions of article 370, which conceeded a special status to Jammu and Kashmir. On the grounds that Kashmir was India's only Muslim majority province, and because of the senitivities of Kashmiri views on their culture, article 370 gave the state a considerable degree of autonomy. Linked to this political devolution, the state also enjoyed special priority within Indian economic planning. Yet by the mid 1970s, the principle of authonomy had been seriously eroded, in part through the centralisation of Indian politics under Indira Gandhi (as discussed above), and in part through the changes in Kashmiri aspirations and the growth of a specifically Islamic identitity.

The concept of independence then, grew in a context in which both India and Pakistan were seen to deny some, if not all, of the basic rights of the

Kashmiri people.[28] Yet the concept of Independence was not in itself clear cut. By the early 1990s it has broken down into those who seek to establish an Islamic state, and those who wish to consecrate a secular one. Even if India and Pakistan agreed to allow the option of independence, (something which in itself is extremely unlikely), the real crisis is that different regions of the former Dogra kingdom of Jammu and Kashmir want different things: the Buddhists of Ladakh want to remain with India (on slightly better terms, and with consitutional protection against threatened Hinduisation), the Hindus of Jammu wish to remain with India, as do a majority of the Kashmiri Pandits. Some Pandits however, especially those situated in the refugee camps in and around Jammu town, now wish to create their own seperate state, a Panun or free Kashmir, based on the west bank of the Jhelum river, with Srinagar as its historic capital.

The Muslims, as in 1947-8, remain divided, both in terms of doctrine (sunni versus shi'ite, and in terms of ethnicity. By the mid 1990s such was the degree of alienation from India in the valley districts that sentiments for independence were high, with apparent wide spread support for the secular Jammu and Kashmir Liberation Front. Yet other Muslims are now vocal in their support for pro-Pakistan groups such as Jamaat and Hizbul. Other Muslims, comparable with the moderate Sikhs, are willing to remain with India if they can receive the necessary assurances to retain Article 370, and to defend and indeed promote, Kashmiri culture. In the case wherein Indian national politics is itself becoming increasingly dominated by Hindu chauvanims, such assurances are hard to come by.

Across the LOC, in Pakistan administered Azad Kashmir, and further afield, in the northern territories of Gilgit and Hunza, it is not clear what popular sentiment demands. Many of the Azadi Kashmiris are Punjabi in origin, and many have moved abroad. Although notionally independent, some Azadis ae supportive of the JKLF and a united, Independent Kashmir along the lines of the former Dogra Kingdom, but others, who have come of age under Pakistani patronage, look to Islamabad, if not to a truly federal Pakistani state. Kashmiri's living in the remote Northern Territories are historically associated with the Pathanis of the old North West Frontier Province and have little, if any, romantic associations with the valley. In early 1995, New Delhi attempted to restart the political process in Jammu and Kashmir, but was overruled by the Electoral Commission. In the autumn of 1996 state elections went ahead and, with the exception of several Srinigar constituencies, candidates were duly elected. Despite reports of intimidation and a boycot by several parties associated with the Hurriyat Conference, the National Conference was returned to power. Under the control of Farooq

Abdullah, the former Chief Minister, the new state government is committed to renegotiate the Kashmir's special status within the Indian Union. Yet, like the restoration of 'politics' in Punjab, the process of normalisation remains in itself problematic.

It is impossible to separate the Kashmir crisis from the wider context of Muslim politics in India. On coming to power in the wake of his mother's death, the primacy of religious symbolism continued under Rajiv Gandhi. Between 1985-89 Rajiv Gandhi attempted to use the languages of Hindu and Muslim exclusiveness to reassure both communities that he was dealing with communal tension, while appearing to be ambivalent to communal forces generally. Such a strategy isolated Jammu and Kashmir within the Indian Union, and furthered the impression that any concession to the state were another varient of Muslim appeasement. An interesting example of the mess that Rajiv Gandhi brought about lies in the Shah Bano case, which has been described by one writer as 'a fundamental disagreement over how differing communities perceive the concept of justice and a just system of laws'. Shah Bano, a Muslim women, divorced her husband under Indian secular law and sued him for maintenance.

The husband claimed that, as a Muslim, he had divorced his wife according to the Shari'ia law and that her family were now responsible for her up keep. After a lengthy legal dispute, the Indian High Courts ruled in Shah Bano's favour on the basis of India's secular laws. Since no distinction could be made between religions, Shri Bano would pay maintenance, like any other Indian, or face further legal action. The response in the Muslim community at large was one of outrage, perceiving the move not as a principle of secularism, but as an assault upon Muslim values. Aware of such sensitivities, and aware too of their electoral importance on the approach of national elections, the Congress Party decided to legislate a special marriage code to exempt Muslims from the Indian civil code. The subsequent passing of the Congress-I sponsored Muslim Marriage Act, which exempt Muslims from Indian civil law and allowed them to follow their own religious prescriptions, enraged Muslim moderates and numerous women's groups, and further offended the Hindus who had themselves accepted a secular code on marriage and divorce in the form of the Hindu Code, discussed above.

The Shah Bano case well illustrates the difficulties of attempting to devise legal codes for differing religious 'ethnic' groups. Unlike language, which can be dealt with in a relatively egalitarian manner, differing codes of practice sanctioned by religious faith bring the principles of universal conduct into dispute. Once a community can claim to be exempt from the laws of the state on religious grounds, or claim the right to ignore a law that is inappropriate to itself, the capacity of the state to manage a pluralistic society is critically undermined. The difficulties of legislating for religious difference, without allocating primacy of one over the other, is further illustrated in 1992 with the culmination of the Babri Masjid\ Ram Janambhoomi crisis.

It was within the context of the communisation of politics that the crisis of the Babri Masjid\ Ram Janambhoomi crisis at Ayodhya became so central to the survival of the V. P. Singh government, which won election in 1989, following the defeat of the Rajiv Gandhi government. The structure at the centre of a dispute is a mosque that many Hindus believe was once a temple and the birth place of Lord Ram, an important Hindu god, central to many Hindu reformist movements. They argue that the mosque was build after the Moghul invasions and that, since the Moghuls have gone (to *their* state of Pakistan) the Temple should be restored by the Indian government to the Hindus.

Demands to demolish the mosque and reinstate the temple, or at least to reinstate the worship of Lord Ram, were made throughout the British period, and periodically since 1947. From 1987 onwards, Hindu political parties agitated for the demolition of the Mosque and the construction of a temple and organised various religious ceremonies in and near the Mosque that significantly heightened the communal temperature throughout India. In 1989 the Rajiv Gandhi government dithered between its fear of offending the Hindus and its fear of loosing the Muslim vote. The result was a political impasse into which the fundamentalist parties took the initiative.

Many religious sites in India are shared sites, many mosques are along side or close to Hindu temples, and both – despite Pakistan – are part of a sub-continental *culture*. The factual debate about the authenticity of the temple site has been rather superseded by its actual demolition in December 1992, by a mob which, incited by the BJP, clearly exceeded their intentions. Although the national leadership of the BJP resigned from parliament in an attempt to 'accept responsibility' (and indeed, the leaders were to be briefly arrested) the failure of the national Congress government – then under Narashima Rao, which had come to power in a snap general election in 1991 – to prevent the incident alarmed Muslims, throughout India, since the central government seemed paralysed by the sheer power of Hindu revivalism, and incapable of defending secularism or rallying secular forces. Muslim moderates feared that the end of a secular state would destroy their economic and political status, while more fundamentalist (and rural) Muslims feared that events at Ayodhya were the beginning of a concerted drive to 'integrate' religious minorities into Hindu culture.

CONCLUSIONS

This chapter has argued that Indian nationalism was devised in the context of a territorial state, created by the British, but actively sought by the Indian political elite. This elite came of age within the political institutions of 'representative government' and constitutionalism, and was committed both to secularism and democracy. Ethnicity was tolerated on the grounds that it would be gradually eradicated. By the late 1950s, it was clear that ethnicity was an active product of the state-nation project itself. It could not, in other words, be 'cranked out of the system', it was part of the system itself: the nature of its demands could be moderated, and it could be to some extent directed, but it could not be banished. What then mattered was to devise a concept of nationalism that accommodated specific variants of ethnicity, an accommodation that required specific institutional and constitutional devices. Language emerged as the most salient indentifer of cultural and of ethnic difference, and the Indian state proved quite capable of dealing with this. For Nehru it was a compromise, but it was one that seemed worth making, and it was to yeild significant rewards.

Yet the initial successes of the Nehruvian period were not to last. This chapter has argued that various causes lie behind the breakdown in the national consensus in India: a change in the nature of the Congress leadership, a change in the autonomy of regional institutions, and changes in the use of religious symbolism. Together, the result has been to radically alter the capabilities of the Indian state to deal with social pluralism. As long as ethnic identities defined themselves as linguistic, economic and cultural categories, the Indian state could accommodate them. However intentional or unintentional, the changes to Indian secularism generated a series of ethnic challenges to the Indian state that were much more intimately linked with religious symbolism, and therefore much harder for the state to deal with. They also generated a type of ratchet effect in which, at each subsequent turn, the state had to deal with divergent – and exclusive – religious demands simultaneously. An understanding of changes in the base of ethnicity in India cannot be arrived at in isolation from nationalism and indeed from the structure of the state. Nor can it be understood without reference to colonialism and the effects colonialism had upon Hinduism.

Given the nature of ethnicity, the current primacy of religious symbolism, and the various political proposals to deal with it, will not solve the ethnic challenge either. They may merely help to redirect it. The proposition that

Hindus are an ethnic community is full of ambiguity. Hinduism is not a unified practice or set of beliefs. As a religion, it is far more diverse than Islam, since it lacks any authoritative texts such as the Koran or the Bible. The myth of the Hindu majority is born out by an examination of caste and *jati* variations, especially between the Shudra (lower castes) and upper caste groups. Brahmanical Hinduism, which is heavily textual and drawn from the Vedic and Aryan scripts is quite alien to lower caste cults throughout southern and south-eastern India.

Many Hindu movements are in themselves anti-brahmanical, linked to the many devotional cults associated with Shiviac Hinduism and Brahmism, touched upon earlier. These devotional cults used and developed within local languages while Vedic Hinduism was linked to Sanskrit. The assertion then, that India is a hindu majority state falters on the basis that Hinduism contains a endless set of minorities.[29] No where is this more apparent than in the attempt by the V.P. Singh government to implement the recommendations of the Mandal Commission, a commission of enquiry launched in 1978 to examine the socio-economic conditions of 'other backward castes' (OBCs) and to investigate the possibility of extending job reservations along the lines of those already on offer to scheduled castes and scheduled tribes. The report, submitted to Parliament in 1982, recommended that the OBCs be given an additional reservation of 27 per cent, bringing the total number of job reservations in the public sector to over 50 per cent. Faced with sustained attempts by the BJP to create a Hindu community, the Singh government decided in September 1990 to implement Mandal's findings, and to divide the Hindu community along caste lines. While lower caste groups responded favourably, upper castes turned to violence against the government and indeed members seeking to identify themselves as OBCs.

Political support offered to the Hindu fundamentalist parties, the main one being the BJP, has on the whole been very small (less than 10 per cent) but in 1989 and in 1991 there appeared to be a visible surge in its support. In 1995 they are the second largest party in the national parliament, and there is widespread speculation that they will be in a position to take – or negotiate – national power after the 1996 elections. A large part of the explanation for this success is the attitude of the major parties – especially the Congress – towards a growing assertion of Hinduism. The apparent complicity of the Congress under Indira Gandhi in the use (and abuse) of Hinduism as a political vote-catcher allowed the fundamentalist parties, almost for the first time, to alter the agenda of the Congress. In turn, this change has been facilitated by a transformation in the basis of ethnicity from linguistic, cultural identities, to religion.

The rise of the BJP is taken by many to confirm beyond all doubt that religion has emerged as the dominant political discourse in India. In the 1996 general election the Bharatiya Janata Party continued to make impressive gains in the Lok Sabha, emerging as the single largest party in the house. The prospect of a BJP national government generated a great deal of political activity on behalf of the Congress and many of the regional parties, aimed at preventing the 'communists' coming to power. Having been invited by the President of India to form a government, Sri Vaypayee resigned after only a week, aware that he could neither muster a parliamentary majority nor convince the country that his government would not be dominated by religious bigots.

That the BJP is a force of religious chauvinism remains contested, however, and is not as clear as is sometimes suggested. The charge is denied by the party leadership, who advance the argument that the party is attempting to articulate a cultural perspective, Hindu in its ethos, but nonetheless pluralist in its ability to accommodate differing religious groups. This blurring (or, from another perspective, confusion) of religion and culture is not new to South Asia. From the 1930s onwards, the articulation of the demand for a Muslim homeland by the Muslim League was premised on the belief that Muslims and Hindus were culturally different, and as such required separate states. Once this was achieved, however, Jinnah went on to claim that Pakistan need not be confessional, theocratic state.

This distinction – between culture and religion – is a fine one, and has caused endless difficulties for the state of Pakistan since independence. Furthermore in India, the emphasis placed on culture and religion appears to be a function of factionalism within the BJP and other Hindu parties and organisations, as well as a function of the proximity of the BJP to national power. By early 1997, the BJP had entered peculiar political alliances with both the Akali Dal in Punjab and the BSP in Uttar Pradesh, a backward caste party which had resolutely opposed the BJP in the early 1990s. Such experiences, familiar to observers of Indian politics, imply that, once in power, the BJP will go the way of all political parties and that the pluralism of India will not suffer too greatly. Again lessons may be gleaned from Pakistan. There the vulnerability of culturally defined Muslim forces to manipulation by religious authorities is well documented. It would be difficult for the BJP in power to back away from a specifically Hidu agenda, even if they claimed to be able to represent Muslim and other 'non-Hindu' groups. Moreover, the BJP would face a problem encountered, though not resolved by the British: how to define a Hindu in the first place.

NOTES

1   S. Rudolph and L. Rudolph, *In Pursuit of Lakshmi: State-Society Relations in India*, Chicago, Chicago University Press, 1987.
2   Culture is used here in its widest and perhaps most useful sense as constituting a way of life in which everyday social actions and social relations are given signifying and symbolic meaning.
3   V.M. Hewitt, *Reclaiming the Past? The Search for Political and Cultural Unity in Contemporary Jammu and Kashmir*, London, Portland Books, 1995.
4   D. Quigely, *Interpreting Caste*, Cambridge, Cambridge University Press, 1994.
5   M. Srinivas, *Caste in Modern India and Other Essays,* Bombay, Media Promoters, 1962.
6   A. Jalal, *Authoritarianism and Democracy in South Asia: A Comparative History*, Cambridge, Cambridge University Press, 1995.
7   A. Smith, *National Identity*, Harmondsworth, Penguin, 1991.
8   The debates between inventors and imaginators seems to have been decisively won by the latter. The difficulties of inventing identities is that it stresses a particular degree of social, and indeed individual voluntarism which is unsustainable.
9   B. Hettne, 'Ethnicity and Development – an elusive relationship' in *Contemporary South Asia*, Vol.2, No.2, 1993, pp.123–150.
10 *Ibid.*, p.126
11 Comprehending the appropriate association between the categories of language, culture and religion are crucial in being able to locate ethnicity, especially in India. It is not, for example, my intention to imply that the shift in ethnic identities in India, away from language towards religion is a shift towards a more 'real' or 'primordial' basis. The distinctions, within Hinduism, between religion and culture are in themselves notoriously difficult to establish, and often as not have been located and policed by outsiders. See S. Madan, *Non-Renunciation:Theories and Interpretations of Hindu Culture,* New Delhi, Oxford University Press, 1987, p.144.
12 V. Oldenburg, *The Building of Colonial Lucknow.*, Princeton, Princeton University Press, 1984.
13 M. Galanter, *Law and Society in Modern India*, New Delhi, Oxford University Press, 1984.
14 *Ibid.*
15 *Ibid.*

16 V.M. Hewitt, 'The Prime Minister and Parliament' in J. Manor (ed) *Nehru to the Nineties*, London, Hurst, 1995.

17 V.M. Hewitt, *Reclaiming the Past? The Search for Political and Cultural Unity in Contemporary Jammu and Kashmir*, London, Portland Books, 1995.

18 D.L. Sheth, 'The Great Lanuage Debate: Politics of Metropolitan vs Vernacular India' in U. Baxi and P. Parekh, *Crisis and Change in Contemporary India*, New Delhi, Sage, 1995, p.187.

19 *Ibid.*

20 B. Graham, *Hindu Nationalism and Indian Politics: The Origins and Development of the Bharatiya Jana Sangh*, Cambridge, Cambridge University Press, 1992.

22 Y. Malik, and D.K. Vaypeyi, 'The Rise of Hindu Militancy' in *Asian Survey* Vol.29 (1989) pp.311–43.

22 M. Limaye, *Contemporary Indian Politics*, New Delhi, Sangam Books, 1987.

23 *Ibid.*

24 M. Tully, and S. Jacob, *Amritsar: Mrs Gandhi's Last Battle*, New Delhi, Rupa Books, 1985.

25 B. Puri, 'Kashmiriyat: the vitality of Kashmir Identity' in *Contemporary South Asia*, Vol.4 (1995).

26 S. Madan, *Non-Renuciation: Interpreting Hindu Culture*, New Delhi, Oxford University Press, 1987.

27 A. Lamb, *Kashmir 1947: The Birth of a Tragedy*, Herefordshire, Roxford Books, 1994.

28 The Indian deal was probably substantially better than the Pakistan deal, because Pakistani federalism was effectively still born after 1947, and crippled after 1973. Yet both were open to critical scrutiny, and after 1972, comparison.

29 P. Brass, *Politics of India Since Independence*, Cambridge, Cambridge University Press, 1990.

2 Russia

Accommodating Ethnic Minorities

Peter Duncan

The Russian Federation emerged as a fully independent state only in December 1991, with the formation of the Commonwealth of Independent States and the demise of the Soviet Union. Prior to that, the Russian Soviet Federative Socialist Republic (RSFSR), as it was then known, held just over half the population of the Soviet Union and three quarters of its territory. Today the Russian Federation still straddles eastern Europe and north Asia, extending from the Baltic and Black Seas in the West to the Pacific in the East, and from the Arctic Ocean to the Caucasus and the Chinese border. It covers one eighth of the world's land surface and has a population of 149 million.

Despite the name, the RSFSR and Russian Federation have never been a federation in the normal sense, where powers are divided between the centre and the component units. From the end of the Russian Civil War in 1920 until the impact of perestroika in the late 1980s, the ruling Communist Party of the Soviet Union (CPSU) sought to impose its will on the whole country, stifling unacceptable forms of dissent such as any desire to reduce the power of Moscow.

RUSSIANS AND OTHERS

Ethnic Russians (*russkie*) formed 81.5 per cent of the inhabitants of the RSFSR (*rossiiane*), according to the 1989 census. This overwhelming dominance contrasts with the situation in the USSR as a whole, in which ethnic Russians formed 50.8 per cent of the population. The Russians are closer culturally to the Ukrainians and Belorussians than to the smaller native peoples of the Russian Federation; the languages of the three East Slav nations are closely related, and most Ukrainians and Belorussians share with the Russians the traditions of Orthodox Christianity. The census identified 64 peoples who were native to the RSFSR, headed by the Tatars (3.8 per cent of the RSFSR population), the Chuvash (1.2 per cent), Bashkirs (0.9 per cent), Mordvins (0.7 per cent) and Chechens (0.6 per cent); and 64 nationalities who mostly lived outside the RSFSR, headed by the Ukrainians (3.0 per cent), Belorussians (0.8 per cent) and Germans (0.6 per cent). The smallest group defined as native to the RSFSR were the Oroks, of whom there were 179.[1] The Institute of Ethnology and Anthropology in Moscow has since declared the existence of a further 25 peoples, native to the Russian Federation, wrongly subsumed by the census-takers in other nationalities.[2]

In addition to Russian, the languages spoken by the nationalities of the Russian Federation include those of the Turkic (e.g. Tatar, Bashkir), Ibero-Caucasian (e.g. Chechen, Avar) and Finno-Ugrian (e.g. Mordvinian, Udmurt) groups. Approximately half of the members of the ethnic minorities belong to nationalities which are traditionally Muslim: the Tatars and Bashkirs from the Volga region and the Chechens and most of the other peoples of the North Caucasus. The Chuvash, Mordvins, Udmurts, Mari, Ossetians, Iakuts and Komi are predominantly Orthodox, like the Russians, and indeed traditionally belonged to the Russian Orthodox Church. Buddhism is traditional among the Buriats (among whom pagan influences are also strong) and Tuvinians near the Mongolian border, and among the Kalmyks on the shores of the Caspian Sea. Judaism has enjoyed a revival among part of the Jewish population (defined as a nationality) since the early 1970s.

The Russian Federation, as it emerged from the Soviet Union, was composed of 21 republics, the Jewish autonomous *oblast'* (province), ten autonomous *okrugi* (areas), six *krai* (territories), 49 *oblasti* and the cities of Moscow and St. Petersburg. Each of these 89 units has the status of a 'subject of the federation'. The 32 republics, autonomous *oblast* and autonomous *okrugi* were created as homes for particular ethnic groups, and with the exception of the multi-ethnic republic of Daghestan in the North Caucasus are named after them. These ethnically-based territorial units account for 18 per cent of the population of the Russian Federation. Nationalities with their own national territories within the Russian Federation account for 12 per cent of the population (around two thirds of the ethnic minorities); 7 per cent of the population are minorities actually living within their own national territories.[3]

With the dissolution of the Soviet Union, there was considerable fear that the Russian Federation might follow it to disintegration. Kiev, the historical mother of Russian cities, was now in a 'foreign' country, independent Ukraine. If republics could secede from the Soviet Union, could not the republics of the Russian Federation also leave? Regionalist pressures in Siberia and the Far East contributed to the concern. The situation did not seem propitious: from 1989 up to early 1997 output in the Russian Federation was falling, living standards showed a steady downward trend and unemployment was rising. At the same time crime and corruption were rising to unprecedented levels. The perceived loss of superpower status accompanying the demise of the Soviet Union and the apparent weakness of the Russian government of President Boris El'tsin for much of the early 1990s gave rise to doubts as to the viability of the Russian state.

RUSSIA IN THE SOVIET UNION

The RSFSR, inside the Soviet Union, was never intended to be a Russian national state. The term of 'Russian' in its title, *Rossiiskaia*, referred to territory, and not ethnicity for which the term *russkaia* would have been used. The RSFSR, and then the Russian Federation, was a residual: it was simply that part of the Soviet Union which was left over after the other Union Republics were formed. It was an artificial construct, with borders fixed by Stalin.

Before 1917, the Russian Empire had enjoyed a long period of expansion, beginning with the overthrow of the Mongol and Tatar occupiers of Russia in 1480. The capture of the Tatar khanate of Kazan by Ivan the Terrible in 1552 brought numbers of Muslims under the jurisdiction of the Muscovite Tsar. Unrelenting progress across the Urals and Siberia to the Pacific joined many small tribes to the Russian state. Proselytization by the Russian Orthodox Church often had the backing of the state. Great resistance was put up by the Muslim peoples of the North Caucasus, who fought for thirty years in the nineteenth century. The Caucasian Wars provided the backdrop to some of the classic works of Russian literature, reinforcing in the popular consciousness the idea that the region belonged to Russia.

Following the Bolshevik seizure of power in October 1917, Lenin proclaimed an end to national oppression, the equality of all nationalities and the right of all nations to self-determination, up to the point of secession. The Bolsheviks appealed for support particularly to the Muslims of Russia, seeing them as a link with the oppressed masses of India and other colonies of the imperialist powers. Originally he had rejected the idea of federalism, believing that a strong, centralized state was the most effective instrument for achieving the construction of socialism. As late as 1916 he reiterated his belief that socialism would lead to the 'fusion' of nations.[4] Even before the Civil War, however, when parts of the former Russian Empire achieved their independence, Lenin had come round to the view that a federal form of government was a necessary compromise, in order to win over the non-Russian regions. In January 1918 he called for a 'federation of the Soviet Republics of Russia'.[5] The Constitution of the RSFSR was adopted in 1918, but the state was federal in name only. During the Civil War, the Bolsheviks managed to re-conquer most of the Empire. Stalin proposed to include the regained minority territories inside the RSFSR, but Lenin feared that this would provoke minority nationalism. He proposed instead, in September 1922, the formation of a union of republics, in which the RSFSR would in form be one among equals.[6]

The result was the formation in December 1922 of the Union of Soviet Socialist Republics (USSR), with a federal constitution guaranteeing all the constituent republics, including the RSFSR, the right to secede. Within these constituent republics, known as union republics, there were units of lesser status, created to give a territorial home to nationalities which did not qualify for the status of union republic; to achieve this, the nationality had to be at least one million strong, and its territory had to have a border with the outside world. These lesser units were known, in descending order of status, as autonomous republics, autonomous *oblasti* and autonomous (formerly national) *okrugi*. Autonomous republics had their own constitution and supreme soviet, but did not have the right to secede. The other units were little more than local governments. There was in effect a hierarchy of nationalities in the USSR: those with union republics, those with territories of lesser status and those without any territorial political unit at all. The number of the union republics grew from four in 1922 to 16 in 1940, by redivision of existing republics and territorial expansion; this number was reduced to 15 in 1956, when the Karelo-Finnish Soviet Socialist Republic was downgraded to the level of an autonomous republic. By 1985 there were 16 autonomous republics, five autonomous *oblasti* and ten autonomous *okrugi* within the RSFSR. The bulk of the territory of the RSFSR, however, was composed of administrative units which were not linked to any minority ethnic group.

Federalism in the Soviet Union was, until things began to fall apart under Gorbachev, a matter of form and not substance. Most economic powers were reserved to the centre. From 1936 the USSR Supreme Soviet had two chambers, one of which, the Soviet of Nationalities, was designed to increase the representation of the non-Russians. But the Supreme Soviet was a rubber stamp, endorsing decisions taken by Party leaders. The CPSU exercised a monopoly, not merely of the exercise of power but of permitted political activity. Within the Party, the practice of 'democratic centralism' meant that all members were required to carry out the decisions of the Politburo and Secretariat of the Central Committee in Moscow. Any attempt to promote the secession of a republic was branded as counter-revolutionary and could form the basis of a criminal charge of anti-Soviet activity. This did not necessarily mean a dictatorship of ethnic Russians. Jews were very well represented and sometimes dominant in the early years of Bolshevik power, while Stalin and the secret police chief for most of his rule, Lavrentii Beria, were both Georgians. The General Secretaries of the CPSU after Stalin's death in 1953, however, were all ethnic Russians. From the later Stalin period, most ministerial posts were held by ethnic Russians, with some important posts held by Ukrainians. In the 1970s and 1980s the central Party bodies were increasingly dominated by ethnic Russians.

The RSFSR was not even federal in form: there was no division of powers between the centre and the subordinate territories. It was only in 1990 that a second chamber was introduced to give some extra representation to the non-Russians. The reality was that most powers were reserved to the all-Union level of government. Indeed many institutions which existed in the other union republics were absent in the RSFSR. Many of the all-Union ministries supervised directly the relevant enterprises and bodies in the RSFSR. There was no Academy of Sciences for the RSFSR, and until 1990 there was no Communist Party organization for the republic. Given the importance of the RSFSR within the USSR, the existence of parallel bodies would have caused a duplication of functions and a rivalry of power centres.

NATIONALISM AND LANGUAGE

The emphasis on nationality as the basis of Soviet federalism had the effect of weakening the pan-Islamic and pan-Turkic tendencies that were present among the Muslims of Russia, the Caucasus and Central Asia at the time of the Bolshevik Revolution. In 1920 Sufi Muslims in Chechnia and Daghestan in the North Caucasus had led an anti-Bolshevik revolt, which was put down the following year. The principal bearer of the ideas of pan-Islamism and pan-Turkism was, however, the Volga Tatar intelligentsia. It should be pointed out that before the revolution, the Tatars had a more highly developed trading class and a slightly higher degree of literacy than the Russians. In March 1918 the Bolsheviks proclaimed the formation of the Tatar-Bashkir Republic stretching from Kazan and the Volga region to the southern Urals, within the RSFSR, in an attempt to win the support of Muslim nationalities. Within the Communist Party, Mir Said Sultan-Galiev argued for a still greater Muslim state in Russia, including also Central Asia. This 'Turan Republic' would have removed a whole swathe of territory from Moscow's control. After winning the Civil War, the Bolsheviks backtracked on their promises to the Muslims and pursued a policy of divide-and-rule, creating separate republics for each nationality. Sultan-Galiev's ideas remained influential within the Tatar and Bashkir regional committees of the Communist Party. Sultan-Galiev himself was arrested for nationalist conspiracy in 1923 but released the following year; he was finally arrested in 1928 and executed in 1939. His followers were purged in the late 1920s and 1930s.[7]

In creating a quasi-federal system and ethnically-based local governments, the Bolsheviks were not simply seeking to deceive the non-Russian minorities. They aimed to use these territories to strike roots among the non-Russian nationalities. The principal basis of Bolshevik support was the industrial proletariat, which was mainly ethnically Russian. The Bolsheviks hoped to recruit elites from the local nationalities to join the Communist Party and administer their republics and regions, while being the loyal servants of Moscow. The intention was that these units would function in the local language rather than Russian. Many languages, particularly those in Siberia, received written alphabets for the first time. The learning of Russian was made voluntary. Much was achieved in the Soviet period in promoting the use of local languages in the schools, in the Press, radio and later television. The main advances were made in the 1920s; by the end of that decade Stalin feared that cultural pluralism was going too far and the local elites might not be loyal to the USSR. In the 1930s many leaders from the local nationalities were therefore purged and Russian was in most cases re-imposed as the language of administration, where the local language had succeeded in gaining the dominant position. From 1934 Russian nationalist images appeared increasingly frequently in official Soviet propaganda, as the leadership became concerned about the threat of war and sought to appeal to Russian traditions to mobilize support. Whereas under Lenin Tsarist Russian imperialism had been condemned, now it was seen as a 'lesser evil' that the non-Russian peoples had been joined to the Empire, since otherwise they would have been taken over by Russia's enemies, and been unable to benefit from the October Revolution. The Russian language was made compulsory in all schools in the USSR in 1938 (possibly reflecting fears that soldiers might not be able to understand commands).[8]

RELIGION

While communism gave some support to the languages of the peoples of the RSFSR, it was clearly hostile to their religions. The Bolsheviks were committed to the eradication of religion. In the early years it was not the minority religions which suffered the most, however, but the Russian Orthodox Church, which as the established region in the Tsarist Empire was identified with the old order and counter-revolution. The government tried to promote pro-Bolshevik priests within the Church while killing and holding hostage senior clerics. In 1927 Metropolitan Sergii, the acting Moscow Patriarch, was forced to give a pledge of loyalty to the Soviet regime.[9] Jewish sections (*evsektsii*) of the Communist Party were established among members of Jewish nationality in order to campaign against Judaism. The image of Russian Communists campaigning against Judaism might have stirred memories of Tsarist anti-Semitism and the pogroms. At the same time the Jews, recognized as a nationality, were given their own territory, Birobidzhan, in the Soviet Far East. Tens of thousands of Jews voluntarily migrated to the inhospitable area, which became the Jewish Autonomous *oblast'*, although Jews never formed as much as a quarter of the population.[10] Other religions suffered less, as the Bolsheviks were unwilling to lose support among the minorities.

In 1929, however, in parallel to the move towards forced collectivization of agriculture, Stalin launched a major attack on all forms of religion, leading to the closure of churches and mosques and the mass arrests of priests and mullahs. Every Buddhist monastery was closed. Religion by that time was the only tolerated form of dissent. It was feared that religious organizations, including the Orthodox Church, or even the gathering of Christian or Muslim believers to worship, might impede collectivization. The Nazi invasion in 1941 brought a relaxation, as Stalin sought to mobilize religious organizations for the war effort. Sergii had a meeting with Stalin in 1943 and was later allowed to become Patriarch, while four Spiritual Directorates were established to provide an official framework for Islamic worship on the basis of loyalty to the Soviet state.

After the war, the Moscow Patriarchate assumed a privileged position in relation to other religions. Citizens, and particularly Party members, were still discouraged from attending Church, but the Patriarchate was given a role in the consolidation of Soviet power in Western Ukraine and in the propagation of Soviet foreign policy. The official leaders of Islam were given resources, mainly to act as ambassadors in the Muslim world. After Stalin's death, CPSU First Secretary Nikita Khrushchev began a process of 'de-Stalinization', ending Stalin's use of mass terror and seeking to revive belief in the Communist future, to be achieved by 1980. Paradoxically, in relation to religion this meant an increase in repression: with communism supposedly round the corner Stalin's detente with religion had to be abandoned, for the communist society would be free of religious throwbacks. In 1959 Khrushchev launched a violent offensive against all forms of religion, Muslim, Jewish or Buddhist, forcibly closing half of the Russian Orthodox churches. Although ethnic Russians suffered along with the rest, the minority nationalities saw the anti-religious policies as directed against their own cultures, and as part of Moscow's attempt to create a uniform Soviet atheist Russian-speaking culture.

CULTURAL DOMINATION

Certainly, the non-Russians had little reason to trust Moscow. In 1941, after the Nazi attack, the Germans who had lived on the Volga since the late eighteenth century were deported and their republic was abolished. In 1944, just before the end of the Great Patriotic War, Stalin ordered the deportation of six whole nationalities living in the RSFSR: the Chechens, Ingush, Karachays and Balkars of the North Caucasus, the Crimean Tatars and the Kalmyks. Nearly one million people were forced into railway trucks and sent to Central Asia or Siberia, with a high proportion dying on the way. Their autonomous territories were abolished. They were accused of having collaborated *en masse* with the Nazis. The reality was that the ever-suspicious Stalin doubted the loyalty of these groups. The Chechens, in particular, had never been reconciled to Soviet rule, and had revolted several times before the war. The deportations would be a demonstration of Soviet firmness and a warning to other nationalities. In 1956 Khrushchev denounced the deportations and the victim-nations were 'rehabilitated'. All except the Volga Germans and Crimean Tatars were allowed to return home, and their autonomous territories were partly restored.

These deportations were the most dramatic cases of the population movements which occurred throughout the USSR from the 1930s. The most significant was the movement of ethnic Russians from the RSFSR into the other republics, and also into the autonomous territories within the RSFSR, reflecting in particular the desire to exploit the resources of Siberia. The Buriat population of their autonomous republic fell from 33.5 per cent in 1926 to 20.2 per cent in 1959, rising again to 24 per cent in 1989; the Tuvinians fell from 75.0 per cent of the population of Tuva in 1926 to 57.0 per cent in 1959, rising to 64 per cent in 1989. Most dramatically, the Yakuts in their gold-and-diamond-rich republic fell continuously from 81.6 per cent in 1926 to 35 per cent in 1989. In the Khanty-Mansi autonomous *okrug*, the share of the two titular nationalities fell from 13.8 per cent in 1959 to a mere 1.4 per cent in 1989, as Russians were drawn in for the extraction of oil and gas. In all of these cases, the minority continued to grow in absolute terms.[11]

A further threat to the cultures of the non-Russians came from Khrushchev's educational reform of 1959. This gave parents the right to choose between Russian and the local language as the medium for primary and secondary education. The result was that many non-Russian parents opted for Russian-medium education, expecting that this would be more favourable to their children's career. At the same time, within the RSFSR the provision of minority medium education was reduced. It appears that between 1958 and 1968, all native-language education ceased in Karelia, Kabardino-Balkaria and Kalmykia. In other republics of the RSFSR, native-language education was restricted to the early years.[12] Only in Tataria and Bashkiria were the full ten years available in the local language.

In the Soviet period, education and the Press in the minority languages were available only in the territory named after the particular minority. A Chuvash outside Chuvashia could be educated only in Russian or the language of the region of residence, and would be likely to adopt the Russian language. The exception was that there were Tatar-language schools in Bashkiria, where in fact the Tatar population was larger than the Bashkir. This reflected the Soviet policy of divide-and-rule: fearing the unification of the Volga Muslims, Moscow built up Bashkir education, playing on Bashkir fears of Tatar assimilation. A result of migration and the reduction of local-language education was the decline in the proportion of non-Russians in the RSFSR claiming the language of their nationality as their native language. This was true between 1959 and 1989 for all the major non-Russian indigenous groups of the RSFSR, except the Bashkirs: the Udmurts showed the most assimilation, with the proportion speaking Udmurt as a native language falling from 89.1 per cent to 69.6 per cent, while the Tatars fell from 92.0 per cent to 83.2 per cent. The Chechens lost their language hardly at all, with a decline from 98.8 per cent to 98.0 per cent over the three decades. The proportion of

Bashkirs speaking Bashkir as a native language increased from 61.9 per cent to 72.3 per cent. For all groups except the Bashkirs, rural dwellers were more likely to retain their language than those living in the more Russified cities. As might be expected, those living within their own republics were more likely to retain the nationality language as the native language, but again the Bashkirs were the only exception (although they displayed 'normal' behaviour in 1989). More research is necessary to explain the Bashkir situation, but a tentative hypothesis would be that it reflects the high degree of Tatar influence in the rural parts of Bashkiria.[13]

The Brezhnev era (1964-1982) saw a rise in national consciousness within the USSR, but this was stronger among the nationalities with their own union republics and among the Russians than in the minorities of the RSFSR. Moscow continued to promote the Russian language and (albeit with less fervour than Khrushchev) to fight religion, and to repress those who defended the interests of their language or religion too strongly. Despite seeking to overcome nationalism, the Soviet system ended up by promoting it. The structure of ethnically-based territorial units produced native elites, whose national consciousness was confirmed by the 'nationality' entry in the internal Soviet passport. Within the RSFSR, the most active area of nationality dissent was among the Jews. Following the defeat of the Soviet Union's Arab allies by Israel in the June 1967 Six-Day War, much of the Soviet media engaged in an 'anti-Zionist' campaign which in reality had the effect of promoting anti-Semitism. Much of the Soviet Jewish population suddenly discovered that despite their loyalty to the USSR, the entry 'Jewish' in the nationality section of their passport meant that they were now seen by much of officialdom as in some way alien and subject to discrimination. The result was a rise in Jewish national consciousness in the USSR, culminating in a campaign to be allowed to emigrate to Israel. Foreign pressure led to permission being granted to a quarter of a million Jews to emigrate in the 1970s.

DEMOCRATIZATION AND NATIONAL IDENTITY IN THE RSFSR

The policies of *perestroika* (restructuring), *glasnost'* (openness) and *demokratizatsiia* (democratization) inaugurated by Mikhail Gorbachev after he became General Secretary in March 1985 ultimately precipitated the collapse of the USSR. There is no space here to analyse in full the reasons for the dissolution of the Soviet Union.[14] In 1989 nationwide competitive elections were held for the first time since 1917, with the voting for the

USSR Congress of People's Deputies, and the following year competitive elections took place in the republics and localities. The forces of nationalism unleashed by the ending of political control, particularly in the Baltic Republics and Transcaucasia, showed the weakness of the central authorities. But arguably it was the pressure building up within the RSFSR itself, for the abandonment not so much of the Union as of the old Communist and centralist economic and political structures which went with it, that proved the decisive agent of change.

The independent political forces in the RSFSR, led by intelligentsia-based groups from Moscow and Leningrad, saw that the old system of central planning could not be reformed but had to be replaced, and that a precondition for both economic reform and for thorough democratization was the abolition of the leading role of the CPSU. The Russian democrats wanted to use the RSFSR as a pivot to transform the whole USSR, while conservatives sought unsuccessfully to use the RSFSR as a springboard for undermining Gorbachev's reforms. The democrats' standard-bearer was Boris El'tsin, the former First Secretary of the Moscow City CPSU organization whom Gorbachev had sacked for his radicalism. The struggle between the radical reformers and the moderate reformers manifested itself as a power struggle between El'tsin and Gorbachev. El'tsin's election as Chairperson of the RSFSR Supreme Soviet in May 1990 paved the way for the 'Declaration of State Sovereignty of the RSFSR' in the following month. This claimed the supremacy of RSFSR laws over those of the USSR, posing a mortal challenge to the Union.[15]

Gorbachev's inconsistency and his belated attempt to devolve power to the union republics provoked the attempted coup by conservative communists in August 1991. The failure of the coup showed the weakness of the centre under Gorbachev and the strength of El'tsin, who had publicly encouraged resistance to the coup. The defeat of the coup plotters led to Gorbachev as President of the USSR dissolving the leading bodies of the CPSU and El'tsin banning the Party in Russia. But it was the CPSU which had created and held together the Soviet Union, and without its control mechanisms in play it would be difficult for the Union to survive. Elites in the union republics, sensitive to growing national feeling and realizing that the centre could no longer keep them in office, declared independence. The Ukrainian vote for independence in the referendum of December 1991 led to El'tsin's decision to depose Gorbachev, terminate the existence of the USSR and form the Commonwealth of Independent States with those republics wishing to join.

Democratization also meant constitutional changes within the RSFSR and some mobilization of the minorities. The old unicameral Supreme Soviet was replaced in 1990 by a Congress of People's Deputies, which included an element of extra representation for the autonomous units, and by a smaller bi-cameral standing parliament, elected by the Congress. The smaller parliament retained the name Supreme Soviet, but was composed of two chambers of equal size, the Soviet of the Republic and the Soviet of Nationalities. (These arrangements paralleled those introduced in 1989 for the USSR legislature). Half of the seats in the Soviet of Nationalities were allocated to the autonomous units, which accounted for 17.7 per cent of the population as a whole.[16] As a result, according to Valerii Tishkov, Director of the Institute of Ethnology and Anthropology, the Russian parliament fairly reflected the ethnic composition of the RSFSR, except that the 'non-status' nationalities, those lacking their own territory, were under-represented.[17] Following El'tsin's election to the new post of President of the RSFSR, he was succeeded as Chairperson of the Supreme Soviet by Ruslan Khasbulatov, a Chechen.

In 1989 Tatar intellectuals in Kazan established the Tatar Public Centre (TOTs). Their programme demanded that autonomous republics, such as the Tatar republic, be given the same status within the USSR as union republics; democratization of the republic; a reduction in Russian immigration and in the republic's contribution to the Russian budget; cultural facilities for Tatars living outside the Tatar republic: and the Tatar language to become the state language of the republic, alongside Russian.[18] Other smaller and more extreme nationalist groups appeared, such as Ittifaq (Unity). Some of these demands were taken up by the leadership of the Tatar local committee of the CPSU. Following the Declaration of State Sovereignty of the RSFSR, the territories within the RSFSR sought to upgrade their status. After North Ossetia, Karelia, Khakassia and Komi made declarations, Tatarstan (as the Tatar republic was renamed) declared its sovereignty. By the end of 1991 all the autonomous units had declared their sovereignty. Moreover, all the autonomous *oblasti* except the Jewish had raised their status to that of a republic. Although El'tsin himself initially encouraged this process as part of democratization, it was supported by Gorbachev as a means of weakening El'tsin's control of the RSFSR. In practice the declarations were largely symbolic, but they reflected the determination of the republics to increase their autonomy. They did not represent genuine democratization: Communist leaders such as Mintimer Shaimiev in Tatarstan could try to gain legitimacy by arranging for themselves to be elected as President of their republic, but that did not stop Shaimiev from supporting the August 1991 coup.[19]

In Tuva, a nationalist Popular Front was formed which won some spectacular successes in the elections to the Tuva Supreme Soviet in March

1990. This forced the local Communist leaders to take a more nationalist line, promoting more ethnic Tuvinians. Racial clashes led to the emigration from Tuva of ethnic Russians. The Tuva Communists were discredited by their support of the August coup, and for a time a member of the Popular Front became Chairperson of the Supreme Soviet.[20] It was in the Chechen-Ingush Republic, however, that the failure of the coup had its most dramatic effects. As in Tuva and Tatarstan, the local Communist leadership had supported the coup. The opposition Congress of the Chechen People was stronger than the nationalists in Tatarstan and Tuva, however, and in September 1991 it seized the Supreme Soviet building in Groznyi and overthrew the former leaders. The leader of the Congress, General Dzhokar Dudaev, was elected President, and the new government declared independence. El'tsin attempted to declare a state of emergency and to send troops to end the rebellion, but was overruled by the RSFSR Supreme Soviet. Dudaev was appealing to the Muslim and militant anti-colonial traditions of the Chechens, and the Russian parliamentarians wished to avoid bloodshed. The Ingush declared their own independence from the Chechens, and the Ingush Republic was recognized by Moscow as a new republic within the Russian Federation, but the Chechens remained in a state of rebellion for more than three years.[21]

RUSSIANS AND MINORITIES IN THE NEW RUSSIA

A major factor in the collapse of the Soviet Union was the rise of a liberal civic nationalism, based on the RSFSR, personified by El'tsin, desiring greater powers for the republics within the USSR and opposed to the forcible maintenance of Soviet rule over the union republics. This civic nationalism was counterposed to (at least) two more well-established forms of Russian nationalism. One was the Stalinist variant of Russian nationalism, which since the late 1960s had advocated the need for a strong Soviet Russian state, devoted to keeping out Western liberal influences and maintaining authoritarian and collectivist practices. Some of these theorists glorified a 'single stream' of Russian history, in which they saw Ivan the Terrible, Peter the Great, Lenin and Stalin all strengthening Russian statehood in the form most appropriate for their time. Another was a traditional form of ethnic Russian nationalism. Some prominent writers, such as Vladimir Soloukhin, Aleksandr Solzhenitsyn, Vasilii Belov and Valentin Rasputin, from the late 1950s onwards began to portray and praise rural life before collectivization, with the Orthodox Church as the guardian of morality. This peasant nostalgia was inherently at odds with Stalinist modernization practices.

Nevertheless, under perestroika representatives of these two tendencies had increasingly found common ground. Both were hostile to Gorbachev's liberalizing efforts, and both wished to preserve the Soviet Union. With a typical colonial mentality, they saw the peoples of the Baltic States and Transcaucasia as ungrateful for the self-sacrifices made by the Russians in helping to develop their economies. The ideas of this conservative coalition of Communists and Russian nationalists helped prepare the basis of the coup of August 1991. After the collapse of the Soviet Union, they established the National Salvation Front, which formed one of the largest sources of opposition to El'tsin's rule. Paradoxically, they were helped in this unification of Communists and nationalists by El'tsin himself; by banning the Communist Party after the coup he forced the Communists to seek allies for the creation of a new organization. When in 1993 the ban on the Communists was lifted by the Constitutional Court, the new Communist Party of the Russian Federation under Gennadii Ziuganov had adopted an ideology of neo-imperial Russian nationalism, abandoning compulsory atheism and rehabilitating the Russian Orthodox Church.[22]

The independence of the Russian Federation coincided with the implementation of a programme of radical economic reforms by El'tsin's government. This involved the shift to a capitalist market economy with the privatization of most of industry and agriculture. Riding high on his popularity after the August coup, El'tsin had persuaded the Russian Congress to grant him special powers for one year to implement the transformation of the economy. This allowed him, among other things, to appoint the heads of administration in all the regions of Russia, with powers to override the Communist-dominated local authorities; and also to appoint Presidential representatives in the regions to act as his 'eyes and ears'. He did not, however, appoint the heads of administration in the republics, allowing them a free hand in the election of their presidents or chairpersons of their supreme soviets. Most republics succeeded in avoiding having presidential representatives appointed. Not surprisingly, this led to feelings of resentment in the other regions of the Russian Federation: they felt that they were being subjected to greater control from the centre because they were Russian.

Generally speaking, the elites in the republics have acted in the spirit of *nomenklatura* nationalism. Most of the leaders were high up in the local Communist nomenklatura before 1991; several had the key position of First Secretary.[23] Now that they are dependent for their posts on elections, and not the approval of Moscow, they play the ethnic card, presenting themselves as the defenders of the local culture, while at the same time seeking to avoid antagonizing the ethnic Russians who often form an important part of their electorate. More importantly, they seek to maximize the autonomy of their republic as far as possible. This may reflect a desire to hold up the reform process, but more often it reflects the local elite's desire to ensure that the process of privatization is implemented under its own control and for its own benefit, not that of interests in Moscow.

The titular nationality or nationalities accounts for the majority of the population in only seven of the 21 republics – Daghestan, Chuvashia, Tuva, Chechnia, Ingushetia, Karbardino-Balkaria and North Ossetia. Of these all except Chuvashia and Tuva are in the North Caucasus. Of the 11 other autonomous units, only the Komi-Permiak and Aga Buriat autonomous *okrugi* have a native majority. Russians are in a majority in ten of the republics and nine of the other units. Even in Tatarstan, Tatars form only 48.5 per cent and Russians 43.3 per cent.[24] Because of this demographic structure, demands from the regions for greater autonomy are more likely to reflect the shared interests of local Russians and non-Russians *vis-a-vis* the centre than ethnic demands by minorities against Russians.

Ethnic structure is a major component of the explanation for the lack of separatism in the autonomous republics of the Russian Federation, in comparison with that which appeared in the union republics of the USSR. In the union republics, the titular nationality had a majority of the population everywhere except Kazakhstan. Geographical factors are important: the union republics had a frontier with the outside world, whereas many of the republics within Russia are surrounded by it, Tatarstan, Bashkortostan and Chuvashia being examples. The North Caucasus region now borders Georgia and Azerbaijan, areas which Russia has traditionally found easier to control than the North Caucasus itself. Tuva has a border with Mongolia, but as with other autonomous units in Siberia the fear of China makes a break with Russia problematic. Historical factors are influential: the republics in Russia do not have a recent experience of independence (unlike the Baltic States and even Transcaucasia), and during the Soviet period the elites of the autonomous republics were relatively less powerful than the elites of the union republics, and included more local ethnic Russians. Financial factors are also important, with republics such as Tuva feeling themselves dependent on subsidies from the Russian budget. The economic experience of the union republics since independence, distanced from the Russian market, is also a caution against separatism. Cultural factors undoubtedly play a role, but the importance of religion should not be exaggerated. The end of the communist campaign against religion certainly led to the opening of large numbers of churches and mosques. While the Russian leadership, partly for reasons of foreign policy, sometimes draws attention to an Islamic threat, Islamism or political Islam at present seems however to have little influence outside Chechnia and perhaps some other parts of the North Caucasus.

Since January 1992, Moscow has dealt with the republics essentially by a series of elite pacts. The conditions of these pacts have varied, however. The first attempt to meet the demands of the republics within the Russian Federation by moving towards some codification of the relations between the centre and the republics was the Federation Treaty. This was signed by the Russian Federation and the republics on 31 March 1992. The treaty referred to the republics as 'sovereign republics within the Russian Federation' and as 'states'. It contained a long list of functions reserved to the Federation, another long list of areas shared by the Federation and the republics, and a provision assigning the unlisted functions to the republics. On the key question of control over resources, the treaty declared: 'The land and its resources, waters, flora and fauna are the property of the peoples living on the territories of the corresponding republics'. The use of these resources, however, would be determined by the laws of the Federation and the republics. The central government signed separate treaties with the non-ethnic regions of Russia and with the lesser ethnic autonomous units. The Federation Treaty widened the rights of the republics in relation to ownership of resources, taxation and foreign relations, putting them in a privileged position above the other regions.[25] This did not satisfy Tatarstan and Chechnia, who refused to sign. Tatarstan had voted in a referendum on 1 March that it was a 'sovereign state, a subject of international law, conducting its relations with the Russian Federation and other republics on the basis of equal treaties'.[26]

In summer 1992 the army of independent Georgia attempted to regain control over its autonomous republic of Abkhazia. The Confederation of the Peoples of the Caucasus, an informal movement of ethnic groups based mainly in the Russian North Caucasus, organized forces to help the Abkhaz. This may have suited the aims of Russian policy in Georgia; it ultimately led to Georgia being forced into the CIS and promoted the aim of imperially-minded Russians of gathering together the former Soviet republics into a new community. Nevertheless the idea of the North Caucasus peoples acting autonomously set a worrying precedent, especially since the Confederation aimed at the independence of the North Caucasus from the Russian Federation. But the divisions between the peoples seemed to rule out this possibility. In particular, divisions between the peoples who had been deported and then allowed to return and the other peoples frustrated unity. In April 1991, the RSFSR Supreme Soviet had passed a 'Law on the Rehabilitation of Repressed Peoples'. This led the deported peoples to believe that they would be given back the lands they had owned before deportation, but the law provided no mechanism for restitution.[27] In October 1992 violence erupted between Ossetians and Ingush in the Prigorodnyi *raion* (district) of North Ossetia, which had originally been part of Checheno-Ingushetia. The Ossetians feared that the Ingush returners would be given back the land which the Ossetians had occupied since the Ingush were deported. Russian troops stood by as the traditionally pro-Russian Ossetians forced up to 50,000 Ingush to flee. The revival of the Cossacks, the traditional defenders of the Empire and of Russian nationality, complicated ethnic relations in the North Caucasus still further, although Moscow increasingly saw them as a force for stability.

Through 1992 and most of 1993, the republics and other regions of Russia sought to maximize their autonomy and control over their resources by taking advantage of the power struggle between El'tsin's government and the parliament. El'tsin particularly favoured the republics, reducing their tax obligations even where they were wealthier than the non-ethnic regions. At the same time, debates took place over whether the Leninist concept of linking territory and ethnicity should be continued in the new Russia. Few if any ethnic Russians, and nobody in the government, were willing to allow any part of the Russian Federation to secede. Many Russians, from the reformist governor of Nizhnii Novgorod *oblast'* Boris Nemtsov to the imperialist Vladimir Zhirinovskii, favoured abolishing the republics and removing the ethnic principle from territorial administration. Tatarstan, for example, would then become Kazan *guberniia* (governorship), with no particular link to Tatar nationality. Others argued for putting the republics on the same level as the 'Russian regions', while allowing cultural autonomy to the minorities, wherever they were within the Russian Federation.[28] Valerii Tishkov, who was Chairperson of the State Committee for Nationality Policy for most of 1992, pointed out that any attempt to take away the forms of national statehood granted to the minorities would be likely to be met with violence.[29]

The situation was transformed after El'tsin forcibly dissolved the Supreme Soviet and Congress in September 1993. Having won in Moscow, the President sought to impose his control over the country. The new Constitution, adopted by referendum in December 1993, strengthened the powers of the executive over the legislature and the centre over the periphery. All the subjects of the Federation, republics, autonomous units and non-ethnic regions, were declared equal. All received two seats in the Council of the Federation, the upper chamber of the new Federal Assembly, which gave some degree of over-representation to the ethnically-based territories. Republics were allowed to have their own state languages. But the republics were no longer described as sovereign, and the Federation Treaty was declared valid only insofar as it did not contradict the new Constitution.[30] As Rachel Walker pointed out: 'In crucial respects, therefore, the subjects of the Federation are quite clearly subordinate to the federal authorities in ways that are not characteristic of classic federations but are rather more reminiscent of unitary states'.[31]

In practice, it was not quite so easy to bring the republics into line. The use of tanks to shoot up the parliament building in Moscow undoubtedly sent a signal that El'tsin was willing to use force to achieve his ends. In February 1994 the Russian Federation signed a bilateral treaty with Tatarstan, using a face-saving formula whereby both sides recognized each other's constitutions, despite the fact that Russia was no longer prepared to recognize Tatarstan's sovereignty. While Kazan was given the right to 'decide questions of republic citizenship' (not then allowed to other republics), it had been forced to settle for less than had been on offer at the time of the Federation Treaty. Apparently Tatarstan had been brought into line by the threat of an oil boycott.[32] In August 1994 Bashkortostan agreed a bilateral treaty with Russia on more favourable terms than those gained by Tatarstan, winning control of natural resources and the valuable oil-refining and petrochemical plants, and being allowed its own citizenship.[33]

Chechnia could not be negotiated back into the Russian Federation, and after three years of tolerating its independence El'tsin ordered the invasion of the republic in December 1994. Chechen resistance was intense, and the Russian Army responded by mass bombings of civilian areas, which upset both Russian and world opinion. After the capture of Groznyi, Russia allowed the Organization for Security and Co-operation in Europe to mediate and facilitate negotiations with Dudaev's forces. While the Chechens had the sympathy of the Ingush and among some groups in Daghestan, there was no large-scale show of solidarity in the North Caucasus. Nevertheless the leaders of other republics expressed their opposition to the use of force, and Moscow was humiliated by the episode.

Supporters of Chechen independence succeeded by the summer of 1996 in regaining control of most of Groznyi. During his short tenure as Secretary of El'tsin's Security Council, Lieutenant-General Aleksandr Lebed negotiated a ceasefire with the rebels. It was agreed that Russian forces would withdraw from Chechnia but the question of the republic's future would be shelved until 2002. All Russian troops left Chechnia by January 1997. Moscow hoped that by that time economic pressures might persuade the Chechens of the value of staying in Russia, but other observers believed that the Kremlin was being forced towards a gradual withdrawal from the Caucasus.[34]

Democracy and the rule of law in the Russian Federation is still weak. Relations between the centre and the periphery are based on pacts between leaders, reflecting the relative strength of the sides at the time, rather than an acceptance of an established set of rules. The quasi-federal structure inherited from the Soviet period, with republics linked with ethnicity, clearly benefits the titular nationalities, or at least their elites. The non-ethnic regions are jealous of the rights of the republics, and will continue to seek more autonomy. Siberia and the Far East, in particular, resent Moscow's control and look towards the Asia-Pacific region for their business partners. It will be some time before Moscow succeeds in negotiating a system which meets the demands of the regions, Russian or non-Russian, while preserving a strong and stable centre.

NOTES

1 A.S. Barsenkov, A.I. Vdovin, V.A. Koretskii, Iu.S. Kukushin, and A.I. Ostapenko, *Towards a Nationalities Policy in the Russian Federation*, Centre for Soviet and East European Studies, Aberdeen, University of Aberdeen, 1993, pp.16–17.

2 *Razdelit li Rossiia uchast' Soiuza SSR?*, leader of authors' collective E.A. Bagramov, Mezhdunarodnyi fond rossiisko-ellinskogo dukhovnogo edinstva, Moscow, 1993, p.89.

3 Aleksandr Barsenkov, Valery Koretsky and Aleksandr Ostapenko, 'Inter-Ethnic Relations in Russia in 1992', *Russia and the Successor States Briefing Service*, Vol.1, No.3, June 1993, p.3, 25.

4 V.I. Lenin, 'Sotsialisticheskaia revoliutsiia i pravo natsii na samoopredelenie', *Polnoe sobranie sochinenii*, 5th edn, 55 vols, Politizdat, Moscow, 1958–1965, Vol.27, p.256.

5 V.I. Lenin, 'Deklaratsiia prav trudiashchikhsia i ekspluatiruemogo naroda', *Polnoe sobranie sochinenii*, Vol.35, p.223.

6 V.I. Lenin *KPSS o sovetskom mnogonatsional'nom gosudarstve*, Politizdat, Moscow, 1981, pp.84–6.

7 On Muslims in the USSR, see Alexandre Bennigsen and Chantal Lemercier-Quelquejay, *Islam in the Soviet Union*, Pall Mall, London, 1967; Alexandre Bennigsen and S. Enders Wimbush, *Muslim National Communism in the Soviet Union: A Revolutionary Strategy for the Third World*, Chicago, University of Chicago Press, 1979; Marie Bennigsen Broxup, 'The last *Ghazawat*: The 1920-1921 Uprising', in Marie Bennigsen Broxup (ed.), *The North Caucasus Barrier: The Russian Advance towards the Muslim World*, London, Hurst, 1992, pp.112–45;

Marie Bennigsen Broxup, 'Volga Tatars' in Graham Smith (ed.) *The Nationalities Question in the Soviet Union*, London, Longman, 1990, pp.279–82.

8   Isabelle Kreindler, 'The Changing Status of Russian in the Soviet Union', *International Journal of the Sociology of Language*, No.33, 1982, pp.7–39.

9   Dimitry Pospielovsky, *The Russian Church under the Soviet Regime, 1917–1982*, Crestwood, N.Y., St. Vladimir's Seminary Press, 1984, esp chs.1–3.

10 On Russian Jews, see Lionel Kochan (ed.) *The Jews in Soviet Russia since 1917*, 3rd ed., Oxford, Oxford University Press, 1978.

11 Gail A. Fondahl, 'Siberia: Native Peoples and Newcomers in Collision', in Ian Bremmer and Ray Taras (eds) *Nations and Politics in the Soviet Successor States*, Cambridge, Cambridge University Press, 1993, p.498.

12 Brian D. Silver, 'The Status of National Minority Languages in Soviet Education: An Assessment of Recent Changes', *Soviet Studies*, Vol.26, No.1, January 1974, pp.28–40.

13 G. Smith (ed.), *The Nationalities Question*, pp.366-7; Ron Wixman, 'The Middle Volga: Ethnic Archipelago in a Russian Sea', in Bremmer and Taras (eds), *Nations and Politics in the Soviet Successor States*, pp.438–43.

14 Rachel Walker, *Six Years that Shook the World: Perestroika - The Impossible Project*, Manchester, Manchester University Press, 1993; John B. Dunlop, *The Rise of Russia and the Fall of the Soviet State*, Princeton, Princeton University Press, 1993; Steve Crawshaw, *Goodbye to the USSR: The Collapse of Soviet Power*, London, Bloomsbury, 1992.

15 Peter J.S. Duncan, 'The Rebirth of Politics in Russia', in Geoffrey A. Hosking, Jonathan Aves and Peter J.S. Duncan, *The Road to Post-Communism: Independent Political Movements in the Soviet Union, 1985-1991*, London, Pinter, 1992, pp.76–93.

16 *Konstitutsiia (Osnovnoi Zakon) Rossiiskoi Federatsii-Rossii*, Izvestiia, Moscow, 1992, articles 105, 107.

17 V.A. Tishkov, 'Strategiia i mekhanizmy natsional'noi politiki v Rossiiskoi Federatsii', in V.A. Tishkov *et al* (eds), *Natsional'naia politika v Rossiiskoi Federatsii. Materialy mezhdunarodnoi nauchno-prakticheskoi konferentsii (Lipki, sentiabr' 1992 g.)*, Moscow, Nauka, 1993, p.18.

18 Broxup, 'Volga Tatars', pp.283–7.

19 Richard Sakwa, *Russian Politics and Society*, London, Routledge, 1993, pp.115–16.

20 Toomas Alatulu, 'Tuva – A State Reawakens', *Soviet Studies*, Vol.44, No.5, 1992, pp.881–95.
21 An account from a pro-Dudaev standpoint is Marie Bennigsen Broxup, 'After the Putsch, 1991', in Broxup (ed.), *The North Caucasus Barrier*, pp.219–240.
22 On Russian nationalism, see Dunlop, *op. cit.*, and John B. Dunlop, *The Faces of Contemporary Russian Nationalism*, Princeton, Princeton University Press, 1983; Stephen K. Carter, *Russian Nationalism: Yesterday, Today, Tomorrow*, London, Pinter, 1990; Hosking *et al.*, *op. cit.*; Peter J.S. Duncan, 'The Party and Russian Nationalism in the USSR: From Brezhnev to Gorbachev', in Peter J. Potichnyj (ed.), *The Soviet Union: Party and Society*, Cambridge, Cambridge University Press, 1988, pp.229–44.
23 Ol'ga Senatova, Aleksandr Kasimov, 'Federatsiia ili novyi unitarizm? Povtorenie proidennogo', in Vladimir Gel'man (ed.), *Ocherki rossiiskoi politiki (issledovaniia i nabliudeniia 1993-1994 gg)*, Institut gumanitarno-politicheskikh issledovanii, Moscow, 1994, p.44.
24 Barsenkov *et al.*, *Towards a Nationalities Policy*, p.18.
25 *Konstitutsiia (Osnovnoi Zakon)*, pp.81, 84–85.
26 Barsenkov *et al.*, 'Inter-Ethnic Relations', p.15.
27 A.I. Kazannik, 'Pravovye problemy razvitiia mezhnatsional'nykh otnoshenii v Rossii', in Tishkov *et al.*, (ed.) *Natsional'naia politika v Rossiiskoi Federatsii*, p.136.
28 Barsenkov *et al.*, *Towards a Nationality Policy*, p.14.
29 Tishkov, 'Strategiia', p.16.
30 *Konstitutsiia Rossiiskoi Federatsii*, Moscow, Iuridicheskaia literatura, 1993, pp.56-57.
31 Rachel Walker, 'Democratisation and the Federal Principle: The Case of Russia', Paper prepared for the Political Studies Association Annual Conference, University of York, 18–20 April 1995, p.8.
32 Elizabeth Teague, 'Russia and Tatarstan Sign Power-Sharing Treaty', *RFE/RL Research Report*, Vol.3, No.14, 8 April 1994, pp.19-27.
33 Vladimir Todres, 'Bashkortostan Seeks Sovereignty - Step by Step', *Transition*, Vol.1, No.7, 12 May 1995, pp.56–9.
34 Paul Baev, *Russia's Policies in the Caucasus*, Royal Institute of International Affairs, London, 1997; Richard Sakwa, *Russian Politics and Society*, 2nd ed., London, Routledge, 1966.

Part Two

Bipolar Pluralism

3 Belgium

A Laboratory of Federalism

John Fitzmaurice

Belgium is, to all intents and purposes, a bi-ethnic state of Flemish and French speakers with a very small German-speaking community in the rural south-east towards the German border. Currently, about 58 percent of the population are Dutch speakers, 41 percent French speakers and 0.7 per cent speak German. Geographically, the two main communities are located to the north and south of a relatively precize language frontier that was first laid down and has varied but little since Roman times. The favourite Belgian euphemism for Flemings and Walloons are 'the north of the country' and 'the south of the country'. The fact that the administration of the post-1830 independent Belgian State was centred in Brussels led to the increasing 'Frenchization' of Brussels that had in the Middle Ages been a Flemish city. This and other centres of mixed population created a problem that could not easily be resolved by pure territorial federalism.

The ethical conflicts in Belgium are not and indeed never were simply language or even 'community' conflicts. French was the language of the dominant bourgeoisie that made the Belgian revolution of 1830 in their own image and interest and took control of the State that resulted from the success of this revolution. To them, the dominance of the French language was part of a centralising and state-building process and it was this reason as much as linguistic prejudice that explains their extreme reluctance to take on board the early demands of the Flemish movement. Thus, from the start, the conflict was a political and socio-economic one, as well as one of language.[1]

By the late 1960s, the rize of the community conflicts to become the dominant issue put the whole unitary and centralized machinery of the State and the political parties and their associated network of mass organizations under an intolerable strain. Structures organized as a function of socio-economic cleavages could not cope with new and predominant community cleavage that came to overlay the traditional cleavage. Belgium was becoming ungovernable. Even Unitarists such as Leo Tindemans were obliged to recognize that a measure of federalism was the only remedy that would save the existence of the Belgian State and head off pressures towards separatism. Indeed, part of the slowness and zig-zag nature of the process of federalization from the first revision of the Constitution recognising regions and communities in December 1970 to the enactment of the St. Michael's Agreement in the spring of 1993, is in large part due to the fact that it was promoted by an uneasy and unstable coalition of those committed federalists of the first hour and perhaps more numerous pragmatic and sceptical groups that came to accept federalism reluctantly for fear of worse or as a tactical device to 'reculer pour mieux sauter' (to step back in order to jump further). Belgian federalism and the complex processes by which it was achieved were the mirror image of Belgian society and political culture with its complex and cross-cutting, but peaceful compromizes. With the awful example of the ex-Yugoslavia before us, the peaceful evolution of Belgium from unitary to a federal state should not be underestimated or taken for granted. Naturally, the Belgian model has its downside: it is costly, complex, slow to respond to change and its consensual and consociational nature can create alienation and leave important issues unresolved. It should be seen as the very real and positive achievement that it is.

THE ORIGINS OF INDEPENDENT BELGIUM

By the late Middle Ages, the territories that today make up Belgium were a patchwork of territories with interlocking feudal allegiances, but with no common state structure. Indeed, at the time of the French Revolution, the various territories that became the Belgian state in 1830, had almost no common history, except in the most indirect manner. The Austrian Netherlands and the Principality of Liège that then covered most of Belgium south of the Meuse both had the same sovereign, the Austrian Emperor. Yet, these states were different and they belonged to different *Circles Administratives* (divisions) of the Empire.

The main building blocks of Belgium were the ecclesiastical state, the Principality of Liège, never previously united with the remainder, Brabant and Flanders. These last had, until the later Middle Ages, belonged variously to the Burgundian kingdom or owed fealty to the French king. From 1528, these territories were under the Emperor. This was confirmed by the Treaty of Cambrai in 1529. Under the Transaction of Augsburg (1548) and the Pragmatic Sanction of 1549, the Succession rules in all territories making up the Spanish Netherlands were united, making them henceforth indivisible.

During the revolt against Spain in the late 16th century that was to lead the northern Protestant provinces to independence from Spain as the United Provinces (later the Netherlands), the ten southern Catholic Provinces remained with Spain for religious reasons. After the War of the Spanish Succession, the remaining Spanish Provinces were transferred to the Austrian Habsburgs and became for almost a century, from 1713, the Austrian Netherlands.

The Emperor was represented in Brussels by a Governor board and the Minister Plenipotentiary, who was in effect the chief minister. There were three long-standing councils: the 'Conseil d'Etat' for political and military matters; the 'Conseil'for judicial and political matters and the 'Conseil des Finances' for financial matters. These councils were assisted by a series of administrative organs. There were also separate governors and councils in each of the separate principalities. There was no single representative body, as the States General did not meet any more after 1634, although various territories did still have functioning Estates based on the three estates (nobility, clergy and towns). The Principality of Liège was governed by the Prince Bishop, elected by the Chapter of the Cathedral, which was subject to joint approval by the Pope and the Emperor.

The transition period between the 'ancien regime' and Belgian independence is seen by most historians to cover the fifty-year period from 1780 to 1830. It can be broken down into three phases: (a) the late Austrian and Brabançonne period of 1780 to 1794, (b) the French period of 1794 to 1815 and (c) the United Netherlands period of 1815 to 1830.

The accession of Joseph II to the Imperial throne in 1780 inaugurated a period of accelerated reform. Joseph was a typical late 18th century enlightened absolute monarch, and he sought to impose reform from the top down, with no concern for public opinion. These reforms attacked the roots of provincial tradition and particularly in the Austrian Netherlands. The power of the church in relation to family law, education and public assistance was challenged by the first series of reforms in the 1781-84 period. These reforms opened the way to a more capitalist economy by restricting the powers of the guilds and corporations. The final straw was two clearly centralising edicts of 1st January 1787 that centralized and rationalized both civil and judicial administration, abolishing the long-standing councils and replacing them by one single council and creating nine circles and 64 districts as administrative units instead of the traditional provincial structure. There was a similar judicial rationalization.

Resistance developed in the Estates of Brabant and among the middle classes, and was influenced by the 1787 Dutch democratic revolt and the reform ideas that were to lead to the French Revolution. There were two trends in the opposition: the so-called 'statists', led by the lawyer Van der Noot, sought to defend traditional privileges. The second more modernist current led by Vonck opposed the fact that the reforms were imposed from above. Rival committees of statists (the Breda Committee) and Vonckists (the Brussels committee) were formed. Both sought external allies, but different ones. The statists sought support from the Netherlands, Britain and anti-Austrian Prussia, whereas the 'Vonckists' sought support from the democratic reformers in Liège after the democratic revolution there in August 1789 or from revolutionary France. Indeed, a committee of Belgians and Liègois was established in France. A fragile unity between the various currents – Statists, Vonckists, Liègois (more inclined to union with France) enabled an initial victory over Imperial forces at Turnhout in October 1789 and led to the proclamation of independence by the German provinces by the end of December 1789. On January 11, 1790, the Union Treaty of Twelve Articles was signed, creating a common state, but without Liège. It created a confederal state called the Republic of the United Belgian States.

The new State was strongly divided about the correct constitutional structures. In any event, Joseph II died in February, and the new Emperor was more conciliatory, enabling Austria to regain control by December 1790. In December 1792, French revolutionaries entered Belgium and after their victory at Jemappes, took Antwerp and Brussels. There were then local attempts to revive independence. These were short-lived as the Convention annexed Belgium in March 1793. The Austrians returned at the end of March and were again defeated at the Battle of Fleurus on June 25, 1794. This time the defeat of the Austrians was final and the French annexation lasted until 1814.

French rule grew increasingly unpopular due to conscription, taxation and the continental system. It did, however, have some positive and lasting effects. Inside the continental system, the nascent Belgian industrial revolution took off. A common administrative culture was imposed that was to greatly influence the new Belgian State after independence in 1830. Some Belgian leaders hoped for independence in 1814. However, in one of the few decisions of the Congress of Vienna that did not restore the status quo ante bellum, the great powers, and in particular Britain, opted for creating a larger United

Netherlands buffer state by reuniting the low countries under Dutch rule. This arrangement was never popular in the Belgian Provinces and a political opposition based on an alliance between the Catholics and the Liberals under the umbrella of unionism developed in the 1820s and organized the revolution.

THE RISE OF THE FLEMISH MOVEMENT

At the time of independence, the language issue was not understood in the manner that we now understand it. Certainly, as the 1846 census showed, there was a Flemish majority (2,471,248 to 1,827,141, that is, 57 per cent to 42 per cent and 1 per cent German speakers), which actually differs little from the present situation.[2] However, there was no standard French or Dutch usage. Flemish speakers used a variety of Flemish dialects. The 42 per cent that declared themselves to be French speakers in fact spoke Walloon dialects. French was perhaps only used by about 10-15 per cent.[3] What has happened since is that there has been clear change in consciousness and, with it, a homogenization in usage of both languages. There has also been a move towards monolithic language areas, whereas at the time of independence, Belgium was more of a linguistic patchwork. French usage has declined almost to extinction north of the linguistic border, even in such traditional Francophone centres as Ghent and Antwerp, which long retained a small but significant French-speaking minority and were manifestations of French culture. Even before independence, Brussels was the key issue. Brussels was changing. In the Middle Ages, it was a Flemish city. By 1780, there were 15 per cent French speakers in Brussels and the figure was growing rapidly.[4]

The Provincial Government adopted a Decree on language usage on November 16, 1830. This was Belgium's first language law. It granted a special privileged status to French, as it was considered that the other languages were variable from area to area. In effect it made French the only national and official language in the administration, Parliament and the Courts. Flemish and German were relegated to local languages, which were accorded a limited localized public role in exchanges with the administration. It was considered a natural step, as part of the process of nation-building. The founding fathers no doubt considered French superior to Flemish dialects, but beyond that considered that a nation needs one single language to forge its identity.[5]

Very soon, this almost self-evident dominance of French was to come under challenge as the Flemish movement entered the stage[6] and formulated its first demands. The Flemish movement was inevitably soon to become a social and political movement. French was the language of the dominant bourgeoisie which governed the new state in its own interest, though that was clearly not in the interest of the Walloon and equally French-speaking industrial proletariat any more than it was in the interest of the Flemish rural working class. But in Flanders, language demands and political and social demands more easily coincided. In a democracy, such issues ultimately turn on mobilization of political support. Belgium had, after 1831 what was for the time a very liberal constitution, but it had far from espoused universal suffrage. The franchize was very restricted and based on property qualifications. For the Lower House of Parliament, there was a mere 46,000 electors in 1830. This number grew to 79,000 after a reform in 1848 and to 136,000 in 1892.

In 1893, full manhood suffrage was at last introduced, but with a system of plural voting, based on additional votes for property and education. Hence, the 63 per cent of the voters with only one vote had only 41 per cent of the available votes in 1894. Full equal universal manhood suffrage was only introduced in 1919 after the First World War. Of course, the franchize for the Senate was even more restricted, as in 1842, for example a mere 412 persons were eligible for election to the Senate. Inevitably, almost all the pre-manhood suffrage electorate was French-speaking, as were those between 1893 and 1919 who had more than one vote. The Flemish movement could only begin to count as a potential force once universal manhood suffrage had been obtained. Indeed, the 1894 election saw election of the first large bloc (nine) of Flamingant members, committed to using Dutch in Parliament. It was however only as late as 1954 that all MPs elected in Flanders took the oath in Dutch. Formal bilingualism in both Houses was only achieved in 1898.

The Flemish movement began much earlier, developing both its political programme and working to unify the language, led by writers such as J.F. Willems and Hendrik Conscience. Support came at this stage mainly from the middle class, some clergy and ex-Orangist supporters. The first political manifestation of the movement came in 1840 with the mass petition initiated by J.F. Willems, F.A. Snellaert and Cannon J.B. David. It called for the use of Flemish in the courts in Flanders, in municipal affairs, for public officials in Flanders to be required to speak Flemish, a Flemish section at Ghent University. Moderate though it was, the petition set down issues that were to be at the centre of the demands of the Flemish movement down to the 1930s. In 1847, the Manifesto of the Flemish movement was published in Ghent. It was drafted by F.A. Snellaert and Hendrik Conscience. It developed and amplified themes from the petition of 1840. It called for full equality between the two languages, full use of Dutch in national affairs and in Flanders, support for Dutch education, full use of Dutch in the courts of Flanders. The Government established a Royal Commission to examine the Flemish demands in 1856. It reported a year later and recommended implementation, in one form or another, of virtually all the Flemish demands. It remained a dead letter at this time, though it became a permanent reference point for the Flemish movement down the years.

It developed through a series of tragic court cases, where defendants who only understood Flemish were condemned to death in French and the election to Parliament of the first Flemish activists in the 1860s, through the development of the first broader Flemish organizations such as the Willemsfonds (Liberal) in 1851 and the Davidsfonds (Catholic) in 1875; the Vlamingen Vooruit in Brussels (1858) and the Antwerp Meeting Partij (1860).

This led to the first three great packages of language legislation (1870s, 1930s and 1962–63) that was to enact the long-standing demands of the Flemish movement, by which time, despite its reversals after both World Wars as a result of its anti-Belgian attitudes and in some cases, its actual collaboration with the occupiers, it had moved on to formulate a broader political federalist programme and to mobilize a broad Flemish majority for such a programme.

Thus, laws were adopted on the use of languages in the criminal courts in 1873, in national administrations in 1878, in secondary education in 1883 and finally, providing for equal usage at the national level, including Parliament in 1898. The demand for a Flemish university became the next major goal of the movement, alongside its battle – with others – for universal equal suffrage.

In one sense, the First World War saw an apparent setback for the Flemish movement. It was divided between its activist wing that was prepared to work with the German occupier to achieve its political goals, the Frontists who were more moderate and opposed to the pan-Germanist ideas and the 'Passivists', who opposed collaboration and sought to prepare for a new step forward but only after the war. The activists tarred the whole movement with the brush of treason and collaboration, an all too convenient alibi for the Francophone establishment.

Yet, during the war, a Flemish university had been established for the first time in Ghent. More important, the first Flemish political institutions were set up, involving both administrative splitting of the administration between Flanders and Wallonia, the drawing of a language border in 1917 and above all, the Council of Flanders which, like the Czechs or South Slavs, put the issue of independence or at least autonomy on the political agenda for the first time. Clearly, these changes, all implemented by or with the active and deliberate consent of the German military authorities as part of the pro-Flemish policy, could not survive the Allied victory, but nor would it disappear without a trace.

The 1920s appeared as a quiescent decade, as the Flemish movement sought to recover its momentum. The shock was all the greater when at the 1929 victory of the activist August Borms at the by-election in December 1928. The shock waves led to a new round of language laws that legitimized much that had been temporarily imposed during the occupation. In 1930, the Ghent University was made into a Flemish institution. The 1935 law strengthened the position of Dutch in civil and judicial matters and a 1938 law provided that there should be unilingual units in the army up to regimental level. Most important for the future, was the law of 1932, building on an earlier law of 1921. This was the modern origin of the language border, leading the move towards full political and administrative unilingualism, with even fewer exceptions in each region and bilingualism in Brussels only.

As in the First World War, the Nazi occupation posed severe strains on the Flemish movement. For many, the apparent total victory of Germany by the end of 1940 was a severe temptation to take advantage of the new situation to break up the Belgian State. No doubt, many who entered on the slippery slope of collaboration were not Nazis, though some were, and did so in a naive good faith, hoping for a collaboration among equals, with reciprocation. However, the Germans were even less interested in such niceties than in 1914. Collaboration, it turned out, could only be a one-way street, on their terms and with no turning back, even or especially as the tide of the war turned after 1942. At the same time, the rank and file members of organizations such as the collaborationist inclined Vlaams Nationaal Verbond (VNV) demanded benefits from the policy of collaboration from their leaders or they would be tempted into even more unreserved collaborationist groups. Those who thought they could manipulate collaboration and limit it for their own purposes were soon caught in the net. They learned that there existed no spoon long enough for supping with the Nazi devil. Again, as after 1918, the Flemish movement was divided and discredited after 1945, but re-emerged as a political force in the 1950s. The tag of collaboration was an even more effective weapon after 1945 than after 1918.

The post-war period saw several key political events to which the north and the south reacted differently, driving a deeper wedge between them and reinforcing those in both communities who were beginning to contemplate structural reforms of the Belgian state as a serious option.[7]

The long and painful debate abut the future of King Leopold III – the so-called 'Question Royale'– was to culminate in a referendum in 1950 and his abdication in 1951 to save the monarchy and national unity exposed deep divisions between Flanders and Wallonia. The King won a majority in the country as a whole and in Flanders, but not in Wallonia. Extra-parliamentary opposition and a near civil war atmosphere in Wallonia forced the King to abdicate. The lesson and the bitterness at the fact that their democratic wishes were not respected was not lost on Flanders. The battle over subsidies for Catholic schools in 1954-58 was also a north–south conflict. The Christian Democrat – Liberal coalition sought to impose a package of austerity and anti-strike measures through the so-called 'Loi Unique'in 1960–61. The political left in Wallonia as in opposition and the Walloon wing of the FGTB Socialist trade union organized strikes, but found themselves isolated, as the Flemish wing of the FGTB did not support them.

It became clear that there were two distinct and opposed political cultures in the country. In Wallonia, the dominant culture was more left-leaning, more collectivist, more laïc (non-confessional), had opposed Leopold III and opposed any amnesty for wartime collaborators. In Flanders, the culture was more Catholic, more pragmatic, more right-leaning. The minorities in each case (Catholics and Liberals in Wallonia, Socialists in Flanders) had to accommodate themselves to the prevailing political culture.

TOWARDS FEDERALISM

As the Flemish movement increased the pressure, gaining the last part of the 'minimalist' linguistic programme from the 19th century and moving on to demands for autonomous political structures, the Walloons began to realize that they were on the defensive. Demographically, as ever, they remained a minority. They had lost their economic dynamism as the 'rust belt' industries of the first industrial revolution that dominated the Walloon economy entered a long period of decline and the new centres of economic dynamism were located in Flanders. Wallonia needed the state. It needed national solidarity. It therefore needed political clout. Its traditional ascendancy was no longer self-evident. Adjustment on both sides was difficult and painful.

At long last, a countervailing Walloon movement[8] began to develop out of defensive necessity when earlier efforts had largely failed. The Walloon movement had hitherto, despite some sporadic cultural organizations and the more spectacular Assemblée Wallonne in 1912 and the Congrès Wallon in 1945 that voted for autonomy, achieved little impact. Indeed, before then few had seen the need for such a movement. The Walloons and Francophones were a minority with a majority complex. They believed that the Belgian state was largely their state, as it had been, but that was changing fast so that they, as much as the Flemish, needed to build their own institutions and seek guarantees for their interests in the central government system.

The conflict achieved new and more political dimensions in the 1960s. The deonator was the expansion of the University of Leuven. This was seen as an attempt to expand French influence in Flanders. Demands to remove the French section of the university became insistent. The Christian Social Party then split in 1968 into two parties – the Flemish CVP and the French-speaking PSC. The other traditional parties followed suit.

By 1968, the regional parties had begun to make a serious political impact. The Volksunie nearly doubled its representation, from 12 to 20 deputies and the Rassemblement Wallon won 7 seats, compared with 2 in 1965. The new Brussels Party, the FDF, increased its representation from 3 to 5.

The 1971 election saw 21 Volksunie, 14 RW and 10 FDF returned. In all, 45 regionalists were elected. The old unitary Belgium was becoming ungovernable, reform was the only answer. The first step was taken with the revision of the Constitution in December 1970, establishing the communities and regions. It was a modest step. These new bodies seemed to have few real powers and little political or financial autonomy. In any case, the Constitution did no more than establish the principle of communities and regions, which then had to be given effect. It was, though, a key step that was to lead to the eventual federalization of Belgium in 1993.

THE BELGIAN FEDERAL MODEL[9]

Progress was slow and difficult. It required several more major constitutional amendments and a host of so-called special laws requiring approval by qualified majority.[10] As usual in Belgium, progress was complex, gradual and based on compromise. Solutions were rarely the most intellectually or theoretically elegant, but were practical, acceptable and irreversible as each stage built on the previous ones, successively tying up more loose ends as the process proceeded usually after much informal ground work had produced imaginative solutions as the raw material for the politicians to work with. This is the Belgian method. It involves lengthy gestation and dialogue, in itself a shock absorber of conflict. It involves solutions of nearly labyrinthine complexity, which also acts as a shock absorber. It is also – a basic downside – expensive as all interests have to be squared in the process of compromize, which may involve doubling institutions and expensive 'side payments'. Thus, for example, both in 1974-77, in 1988 and in 1993, the regional parties or some of them were brought into the process. It involves complex cross-cutting systems of mutual guarantees. Above all, it enables conflicts to be resolved without violence.

What are the essential characteristics of the Belgian model?[11] Belgium could not adopt a simple classical federal model based on co-equal territorial units with identical or virtually identical powers bound together under a central federal authority. There are several reasons for this. Belgium was not created a federation ex-novo, nor did independent sovereign entities come together to make a federation. Belgium was a highly centralized unitary state, bound into the obligations of the European Community and its Single Market. Furthermore, given that full control over cultural policy was a central demand of both the Flemish and Francophone movements, it was agreed from an early stage that international cooperation in these fields, including treaty-making powers (or at least, initially more correctly, the powers of ratification) would be devolved. The federal power never – from the early stages of the process of reform in 1971 – retained, as in the classic federal model, a monopoly of external policy-making or representation. This sharing of external relations functions has considerably grown and extended. The external relations competence is in essence defined as an extension of the domestic competence, under the *foro interno, foro externo* doctrine.

More importantly, the organising principle of federalism in Belgium is not wholly territorial but territorial and linguistic. The communities are linguistic, not geographic alone, because there is not complete concordance between geographic areas and people from each language community. There are both Flemish and Francophones in Brussels. Brussels could not be a language region. It must obviously be a bilingual space. Cultural and linguistic issues in Brussels could not easily be handled by any classic 'unitary' political authority. The only possible solution was to give such authority to the two linguistic communities and/or to break a Brussels authority down with component linguistic groups to handle these functions. Both approaches have been tried.

An additional problem standing in the way of the more classic of purely territorial federalism was the question of the number of sub-national units. The Flemish, with a sense of nationhood wanted to fuse socio-economic and cultural authority into one single set of symbolic and visible Flemish national political institutions, with some special arrangements to deal, as it were, extraterritorially with the Flemish minority (20 percent) in Brussels. Such a solution was unacceptable to Flemish opinion within Brussels. It was also not desired by the Walloon wing of the Parti Socialiste, as fusion of the more

Liberal Brussels with Socialist Wallonia would dilute the dominance of the PS in the area as a whole.

The small non-contiguous German-speaking community, whilst viable as a separate community, endowed with powers equal to those of the two larger communities in the cultural and linguistic fields, could not, with a mere 66,000 German speakers, constitute a separate socio-economic region.

For a long period, the Flemish side contested the right of Brussels to become a third socio-economic authority, as a full region alongside the other two. There were certain objective reasons for regarding Brussels as distinct, deriving from its enclaved status as a national and European capital city. The real basis of Flemish opposition was though political. For them, a Brussels political authority would constitute a second or even third French-speaking authority, capable of outnumbering the single Flemish authority. This resistance was eventually overcome, with a battery of complex guarantees, to which we shall return.

Another complex problem to which a difficult compromise had to be found related to the boundaries of the bilingual Brussels and the status of the

LEVEL	INSTITUTIONS		
FEDERAL LEVEL	FEDERAL GOVERNMENT **Chamber and Senate**		
COMMUNITIES	German Community	French Community French Community Commission Joint Community Commission	Flemish Community Flemish Community Commission
REGIONS	**Walloon Region**	**Brussels Region**	**Flemish Region**
LANGUAGE REGIONS	German French	Bilingual	Flemish
PROVINCES (Nine)	Naimur, Hainant Liege Luxembourg	Brabant (two provinces)	Antwerp, Limburg West Flanders East Flanders
COMMUNES 589	Unilingual	19 Brussels Communes	Unilingual

Fig. 3.1 The Belgian Federal Model

area at its immediate periphery. Over the years, French-speaking commuters, working in Brussels had moved out into the Flemish hinterland outside the boundaries of the 19 'communes' (boroughs) which make up Brussels. This process had led to French majorities and near majorities (not to mention soaring house prices) in many of the communes just outside Brussels, such as Rhode-St. Genèse or Kraainem. Six communes outside the Brussels region were permitted (or required) to retain what were initially intended to be temporary purely administrative facilities for French speakers whilst remaining in Flanders. French speakers at a minimum intended these facilities to be permanent, but also expected that in due course these communes could become part of the bilingual Brussels Capital Region. Historically, this was regarded as not entirely unrealistic. Indeed, as late as 1935, three more communes were added to the Brussels Region. This has been one of the FDF's long-standing campaign themes. It calls for a referendum in the periphery boroughs which would bring up to five more into Brussels. Clearly, by the late 1970s, the Flemish movement was strong enough to prevent any such development. A compromize consisted in retaining the facilities on a permanent basis by enshrining them in a law passed by special majority and the same for the boundaries of Brussels. This law provided that the 'Collège des Bourgmestre et Echevins' (the Mayor and Borough Executive) in the communes in Brussels and along the linguistic boundary should take decisions by consensus giving some minority guarantees. It was not accepted that the 120,000 Francophones in the periphery nor even the 40,000 in the six communes with facilities should be able to register to vote inside Brussels as some had proposed. This was a very Belgian compromize. Similar methods were applied to some other boroughs stranded on the 'wrong side' of the language border which had come to acquire some of the characteristics of an open political border.

The successive compromizes that enabled the necessary majorities to be attained have involved complex guarantees and checks and balances between the two communities. The original constitution laid down that it could be amended by a two-thirds majority of those voting in either House, provided over half the members of the House took part. In the new Belgium that recognized its communities as building blocks, this was not an adequate safeguard, especially for the Francophones as on the basis of population there are more Flemish representatives and senators. A new concept based on language groups in both Houses was introduced, the so-called double majority: two-thirds overall and a majority in each language group. Deputies and senators outside Brussels are automatically assigned to one or other language group, depending on where they are elected. Brussels members choose their language group by taking the oath of office in French or Dutch. In practice, it will depend on which unilingual party list they were elected on, as in Brussels French and Flemish lists (e.g. both PS and SP) compete.

There are also symmetrical guarantees for minorities.[12] At the national level, the Francophones are the minority and in Brussels, the Flemish are the minority. The Constitution lays down that the Federal Government (a maximum of 15 ministers in all) shall, excluding the Prime Minister, be composed of an equal number of French and Flemish speakers. This parity in the national government, which is a protection for the French speakers, is counter-balanced by the minority rights granted to Flemish speakers in the Brussels Region. There are five Brussels ministers equally divided, the Minister President (who will be a French speaker) excepted. There are complex 'double majority'requirements in the Brussels Regional Council, ensuring that the Flemish language group, though only 11 out of 75, cannot be out-voted. Under the present composition of the Council, two Flemish parties (CVP and either the SP or VLD) represent a blocking minority in the Council for certain matters. In both the National Parliament and the Brussels Council, there is also a so-called 'alarm bell' procedure, under which if, of one or other language group considers that a measure affects its vital interests, it can table a reasoned motion that suspends consideration and refers the matter back to the Cabinet for further consideration and, if necessary, a final deliberation in the Senate. The procedure can be invoked against measures in both the parliament and the community councils and can be invoked on a majority by the language groups in the parliament and by community councils.

The new Senate also provides a guarantee of minority positions. It is, however, as often in Belgium, a compromize, a hybrid body with both regional and national representation within it. It has 74 members of whom 40 members (25 Flemish and 15 French speakers) are elected at large in the two linguistic electoral colleges used for the European elections. The Flemish Council (10 members), the Council of the French Community (10 members) and the Council of the German Community (1 member) appoint another 21 members from their number. These 61 members co-opt another 10 members (6 Flemish and 4 French speakers). There is thus an element of favourable weighting for the French speakers in the Senate (29 out of the 71 members). The Senate must agree to revisions of the Constitution and by 'double majority', to all special laws, in general those relating to the structure of the state. In other federal matters, the role of the Senate will now be much more modest. In the past, the Senate was co-equal with the Chamber. Now, the Chamber has exclusive competence over the budget and other finance bills. Over other bills, the Senate can propose amendments within 30 days but the Chamber again has the last word. The Senate can initiate legislation, but the Chamber has the final word. Outside the broad area of constitutional issues, the role of Senate has been reduced to that of a revising Chamber. The Chamber alone is able to remove the Federal Government by a motion of constructive non-confidence, which requires it to elect (as in Germany) an alternative candidate as Prime Minister, who must then be appointed by the King. The Chamber, of course, is based on representation of unweighted populations, that is one vote one value.

As in must modern federations, the Belgian model involves various mechanisms for cooperation between the various authorities and devices for conflict reduction, if cooperation cannot resolve a problem by consensus. Many powers are so interrelated that they have to be exercized in cooperation over often complex arrangements for mutual information, consultation and even assent. The centrepieces of this system are the Cooperation Committee, the Conciliation Committees and the Arbitration Court. The emphasis is on prevention in advance rather than ex-post conflict resolution, in a typically Belgian pragmatic and consensual manner.[13]

The Conciliation Committee is made up of ministers from the various Federal Committees and Regional Governments. It has twelve members and an equal number of Flemish and French speakers. The Prime Minister and five Federal Ministers attend, together with the Minister Presidents of the two large communities and the three regions (five in all). For Brussels, a Flemish member of the government attends. This makes for double parity – six Federal Ministers, six regional community ministers; six Flemish and six French speakers. The Minister President of the German Community may attend when issues of concern to his community are raized. The Committee does not vote, but operates by consensus, giving each participant (perhaps regarding the federal delegation as one) an effective veto.

The texts identify conflicts of competence and conflicts of interest and open up possibilities of both compulsory and voluntary cooperation and coordination between the various levels of authorities. In the first instance, the Conseil d'Etat – an independent advisory body of lawyers – must be consulted on all draft bills (federal) and decrees (communities and regions). If the it 'finds that the proposal is ultra vires as lying outside the competent federal, regional or community powers of the body making the proposal, it shall so advize. Often, the matter can be resolved or the text is withdrawn at this early stage. If not, the Conciliation Committee, acting by consensus, examines the matter and seeks to resolve it. The Conciliation Committee cannot bind the authority concerned. If the measure is adopted anyhow, then the Arbitration Court can be seized and make a binding determination that can lead to the annulment of the act in contention.

Conflicts of interest created either by decisions of government or legislatures adversely affecting the interest of other authorities cannot be resolved judicially, but can be brought before the Conciliation Committee. A three-quarters majority in a legislature can seize the Committee where a draft measure creates such a conflict. The Senate delivers an opinion within 30 days and the Conciliation Committee issues a recommendation (that is not binding) within 60 days, but such a recommendation cannot be issued if the government or the authority where the measure is proposed objects, as there would be no consensus. The measure can therefore be suspended for conciliation for a maximum of 90 days. Governments can seize the committee of executive measures that would create conflicts of interest. These measures are useful, but inevitably can only have a limited impact.

There is provision for cooperation, sometimes compulsory between either Federal Government and regional and communities or between regions and communities. In addition, the French community and the Walloon Region may agree to delegate some functions, respectively to the Walloon Region and the Community Committee of the Brussels Region and the German Community. These provisions enable authorities to cooperate to provide efficient and rational services in areas such as transport, tourism, research and development. It is as if a degree of voluntary rationalization and even recentralization is possible, provided that the starting point is the formal devolution of competence. It is a very Belgian, very pragmatic approach.

In the first phase of the Reform of the State, the devolved authorities hardly had any real political autonomy. These political institutions were both formally and informally still closely tied into the centre. The members of community and regional councils were simply deputies and senators wearing a regional or community hat. A national political crisis destabilized the regional and community authorities for no reason. A political crisis in the community or region could not be resolved by elections. Coalitions at regional and community level were concluded only after national coalition had been formed and reflected the national arrangement. In 1988, a tentative PS/FDF/Ecolo coalition in the Walloon Region was reversed when the PS and PSC became national allies. The SP demanded inclusion in the Flemish government because it was in the national government. The Community and Regional administrations were very small and the new authorities did not have the right to expand them. The powers of the devolved authorities were often restricted by national reserve powers. The financial resources of the communities and regions were limited and dependent on grants from the central exchequer. The most radical change in 1993 – the St. Michael's Agreement – was the creation of genuine autonomous devolved authorities with their own political institutions and a critical mass of powers and resources, independent of the Federal Government.

The Federal Parliament and Government only have the enumerated competences granted by the Constitution. Residual powers are devolved. The communities are responsible for cultural matters which includes language usage, education, broadcasting; for the so-called personalized matters, which cover health, social policy (but not social security and training). The regions are responsible for a range of developed socio-economic policy areas, such as planning, environment policy, housing, water, energy policy, transport, public works, foreign trade, agriculture, employment, industrial policy. The communities and regions can also conclude international agreements within their areas of competence. The devolved authorities can of course pursue different policies, such as the majority in their institutions decide, but may not act in such a way as to undermine the single Belgian market and economic and monetary union, which clearly still limits their capacity for independent action. Exceptions such as scientific research remain divided. Nuclear power remains a national responsibility, as do pensions but not salaries in education and minimum standards for qualifications. The Federal Government is responsible for foreign policy, law and order, defence, monetary policy and powers necessary to the maintenance of economic and monetary union and solidarity (such as social security).

From modest beginning, spending by the communities and regions is now almost one-third of State spending.[14] In 1993, the Federal Government's spending was set at 1,715 billion BF. The spending of the 457 billion BF for the communities (70 per cent on education) and 309 billion BF for the regions. Under the latest devolution deriving from the St. Michael's Agreement, the share of the communities and regions will increase. Initially, the regions and communities were almost entirely financed by national block grants. Increasingly, the communities and regions are achieving financial autonomy and with it, responsibility. This was a long-standing demand by the economically stronger Flemish community which argued that federalism also meant fiscal responsibility. It opposed 'consumer federalism', whereby Wallonia could spend money regardless of its capacity raize revenue. This demand was extended to proposing federalization of social security, which involves much greater share of spending in Wallonia because of the age, health and socio-economic structure of the population. For Wallonia, social security should remain national, as a element of solidarity between the regions. The financial provisions of the reform are byzantine, as the legislator attempted to square the circle of contradictory goals: providing the communities and regions with adequate resources and financial economy, whilst ensuring that the overall tax pressure could not increase; solidarity and fiscal responsibility.

Under the excruciatingly complex compromize enshrined in the 1989 financing regime still in force, a mixture of grants, transferred taxes and autonomous taxing powers and solidarity contributions was introduced. Both the communities and regions have some basic taxing powers, but only on items not already taxed. Taxes such as gaming taxes, licensed premizes, death duties, stamp duty, vehicle excize duty have been fully transferred to the regions. A share of VAT revenue and the TV licence fee is transferred to the communities. Some specific grants from central government remain. Both communities and regions may borrow. Both receive a share of personal taxes (income tax) on the basis of the product raized in their area. The region, but not the communities, can raize additional precepts on this source of revenue. This source is unfavourable to Wallonia, with its weaker economy, higher unemployment and larger population on welfare benefits. This is partially compensated for by a national solidarity contribution both to the Walloon Region and to the French community based in the later case on an educational needs criteria. The major financing crisis in French education that arose in 1990 saw the near bankruptcy of the French community and was a major reason for the new provisions that enabled its competences to be delegated to the financially strong regions or the COCOF in Brussels.

CONCLUSION

In conclusion, the essential pragmatism of the Belgium model should be emphasized. It derived less from a clear political or ideological construct than from successive and iterative responses to immediate political necessity. It was never implemented by the most fervent partisans of the federalism in either Community though, as we have seen, they were from time to time coopted into the process, but rather by those who sought to preserve as much of the common state as possible (so-called Fédéralisme d'Union). To that end, they were prepared to make considerable tactical concessions to federalism that, cumulatively, assumed significant proportions. They, as it were, 'stole the federalists' clothes while bathing' in order to stabilize the system and pre-empt further pressures for so much devolution that the outcome would not be federalism, but confederalism or even separatism.

To the extent that such an approach has followed any clear pattern or scheme, it can best be seen as a 'Belgian method' or approach, rather than specific policy goals or theoretical constructs. This approach is based on several premizes which, while perhaps not individually unique to Belgium, might prove collectively difficult to replicate in other societies. It firstly posits a high degree of basic goodwill among all parties involved and their readiness to work within the parameters of the existing system or close to it. The Belgian method also posits that all problems are amenable to solution by dialogue and by compromizes of the 'upgrading the common interest' type or 'splitting the difference' or by side payments.

Complex and even byzantine institutional arrangements, permanent political dialogue, cross-cutting cleavages, overlapping competences, post-federalization coordination mechanisms, asymetries and minority protection measures are not considered negative, but rather useful shock absorbers. Conflict can get lost in the maze, bouncing off its walls and becoming attenuated in the process. However, these processes require constant attention and care and maintenance. They require considerable material resources in the form, for example, of infrastructure, roads, subsidies parallel school systems, especially in Brussels, in the form of side payments. They also require a considerable part of the energies of the political class, the parties and interest organizations that make up civil society.

Public opinion, as evidenced from the sharp drawing back from the polarization that took place at the time of the fall of the government in 1991 and over the St. Michael's Agreement and the rediscovery of a Belgian national sentiment on the death of King Baudouin in the summer of 1993, seemed to reject separatism in both Communities at this stage. It seems therefore to support federalism as the least worst alternative, which allows the Communities and Regions a considerable degree of autonomous development in line with their distinct political orientations, but within the common structure of Belgium.

Yet, the negative side of the Belgian consociational model is also increasingly clearly perceived by public opinion. There is widespread alienation from both the traditional political parties and the traditional politics of compromize. There is widespread awareness of the potential waste through duplication and over-politicization of policy-making. There is also denunciation of the inability of the system to respond to clear signals from the electorate in one Community or the other and its incapacity to deliver change and a clear recognition of the high costs of the model, both in terms of its absorption and scarce material and immaterial resources. At present, few would oppose federalism and most would accept that its benefits outweigh its costs. Most would recognize its value as a shock absorber, diverting conflict into institutions,though few could guarantee that this positive balance can be permanent. But most would probably raize two cheers for Belgian federalism.

NOTES

1 X. Mabille, *Histoire Politique de la Belgique: Facteurs et Acteurs de Changement*, CRISP, Brussels 1912, pp.5-138; A.Z. Zolberg, 'Les Origines du Clivage Communautaire en Belgique, esquisse d'une sociologie historique', *Recherches Sociologiques*, Vol. VII, No.2, 1976.

2 For the early history of pre-independent Belgium and independence, see Mabille, *op. cit.*; pp.16–27 for the pre-independence period, pp.101–25 on independence and J. Fitzmaurice, *The Politics of Belgium: Crisis and Compromize in a Plural Society*, London, Hurst, 1996.

3 Mabille, *op. cit.*, p.129; Zolberg, *op. cit.*, p.155.

4 H. Hasquin, 'Le Français à Bruxelles entre 1740 et 1780', in *Etudes sur le 18ième Siècle*, ULB, VI, 1979, pp.193–200.

5 Mabille, *op. cit,*, pp.125–27.

6 For a history of the Flemish movement in English, see M. Ruys, *The Flemings: a People on the Move*, Lanoo, Tielt, 1973.

7 K. MacRae, *Conflicts and Compromize in Multilingual Societies: Belgium*, Waterloo, Ontario, Wilfrid Laurier University Press, 1986, pp.32-33.

8 C. Kesterloot, 'Mouvement Wallon et Identité Nationale', *Courier Hebdomadaire* (CH) No. 1392 (1993), Brussels, CRISP, 1993.

9 See table on page 98 for the structure of the Belgian Federal State, as it was established by the 1993 reforms.

10 For a brief history of the Reform of the State and its various phases, see Fitzmaurice, *op. cit*.

11 For an up-to-date analysis of the institutional landscape, see C.E. Lagasse, *Les Nouvelles Institutions Politiques de la Belgique et de l'Europe*, Louvain-la-Neuve, *CIACO, 1990*.

12 Lagasse, *op. cit.*, pp. 279–97.

13 On conflict resolution and cooperation, see Lagasse, *op. cit.*, pp.251–78 and G. Nagel, *Communautaire Conflicten in Belgie: Systemen voor Beheersing van Conflicten Tussen de Staat, de Gemeenschappen en de Gewesten*, Het Arbitrage-Hof en de Overleg Comité Regering-Executives. Die Keure, 1984.

14 On finance, see Lagasse, *op. cit.*, pp.124–29 and pp.171–74.

4 Czechoslovakia

The Velvet Divorce

Karen Henderson

INTRODUCTION

Czechoslovakia as a multinational state represents both failure and success: although it only existed for some seventy years before dividing into separate Czech and Slovak republics, the division itself was effected quickly and smoothly, without even the threat of physical violence. It is a particularly complex and interesting case because, in the course of their coexistence, the Czechs and Slovaks were subjected to the successive sudden changes of regime which were a feature of twentieth century history for much of Europe. However, problems of ethnic diversity cannot always be addressed in ideal political circumstances, and Czechoslovakia remains an important example which should not be neglected.

Czechoslovakia was one of the successor states of the Austro-Hungarian empire, and it was the only country in central and eastern Europe to maintain democratic rule throughout the interwar period. In 1939, external German pressure divided it into a Protectorate of Bohemia-Moravia in the Czech Lands, and a quasi-independent state in Slovakia. After liberation in 1945, Czechoslovakia reformed – albeit as a smaller and less multinational state – and there was another brief interlude of democracy until the communist takeover in February 1948. There then followed more than forty years of communist rule, during which the most notable event was the 'Prague Spring' of 1968, which was terminated by the Soviet invasion in August of the same year. The only Prague Spring reform which survived the invasion was the federalisation of Czechoslovakia, and the country persisted as a federation through the 'Velvet Revolution' of 1989. Yet the federal institutions created under communist rule proved unable to mediate national disagreements in the new era of democracy, and at the end of 1992, Czechoslovakia divided into two.

It is against this background of discontinuity that national issues in Czechoslovakia must be viewed. On three occasions when the relationship between Czechs and Slovaks was clearly appearing on the political agenda – in the late 1930s, in 1945-48, and in 1968 – external events intervened and prevented the free negotiation of a solution. When the question re-emerged in 1990, the problems of rearranging the constitutional foundations of Czechoslovakia had to vie with the other pressing challenges facing the novice parliamentarians of a postcommunist democracy, such as economic reform, the maintenance of social security, and dealing with the communist legacy. The dissolution of Czechoslovakia at the end of 1992 was, however, unique in being the first major change in the system of government which had been brought about by Czechs and Slovaks themselves without massive interference from external forces.

It is for this reason that the division of Czechoslovakia will be the main focus of this chapter, yet it would be unbalanced to look merely at the country's institutions and national relations in the postcommunist period, since this lasted just three years. The events of 1989-92 are therefore initially placed in their broader historical context: they were not merely the product of postcommunist teething troubles, but also the culmination of all the failures that had gone before.

INTERWAR CZECHOSLOVAKIA

The Czechoslovak state was proclaimed on 28 October 1918, and its First Republic survived until 1938.[1] It was held to be the national state of the Czechoslovaks, a nation which comprised two branches, the Czech and the Slovak. This idea reflected both elite beliefs developed during the period of national revival in the nineteenth century, and more pragmatic considerations. In 1921, just under two-thirds of citizens were officially considered to be ethnically Czechoslovak, so that if the Czechs and Slovaks had been counted as separate nations, both the Slav identity of the country and their claim to be the 'state nation' would have been weakened. Additionally, since nearly a quarter of the population was ethnically German, the new country actually contained more Germans than Slovaks, so that any form of autonomy or special status granted to the Slovaks as a distinct nation could also reasonably have been claimed by the Germans. Ethnic Hungarians comprised a further five per cent of citizens, and there were also smaller numbers of Russians, Ukrainians, Poles and Jews. The presence of the substantial German and Hungarian minorities meant that the 'Czechoslovaks' faced a particularly complex nationality problem: not only did the country contain one of the most ethnically mixed populations in the region, but the two largest minorities were composed of people who until recently had been part of the ruling imperial nations.

In an uncertain international environment, with both the German and Hungarian minorities inhabiting borderlands next to states ruled by their own nationalities, any form of decentralisation was felt to present a threat to the country's integrity. Consequently, interwar Czechoslovak democracy was constructed on the basis of the country being a unitary whole, with the partial exception of Subcarpathian Ruthenia.[2] There was a bicameral national parliament in Prague, and elections were conducted on the basis of proportional representation and binding party lists;[3] about a third of deputies came from ethnic minorities, which was a fair reflection of the population as a whole. It must be emphasised, however, that the Slovaks were never viewed as an ethnic minority at any point in Czechoslovak history, although many of them considered themselves to be Slovak rather than Czechoslovak.

Relations between Czechs and Slovaks in the interwar period were complex. The two peoples, while speaking mutually intelligible languages, had been separated for nearly a thousand years, during which time the Slovaks

Table 4.1: National Composition of Czechoslovakia[4]

Nationality	1921 Number	per cent	1950 Number	per cent	1991 Number	per cent
Czech	8,760,937	64	8,383,923	70	9,928,005	64
Slovak			3,240,549	26	4,684,658	30
German	3,123,568	23	165,117	1	48,645	0
Hungarian	745,431	5	367,733	3	628,481	4
Ruthenian	461,849	3	67,615	1	65,768	0
Other / aliens or Unknown	521,387	4	113,513	1	220,993	1
Total	13,613,172		12,338,450		15,576,550	

Table 4.2: National Composition of the Czech Lands/Czech Republic[5]

Nationality*	1921 Number	per cent	1950 Number	per cent	1991 Number	per cent
Czech	6,727,436	67	8,343,558	94	9,871,518	96
Slovak			258,025	3	239,355	2
German	2,973,208	30	159,938	2	40,907	0
Hungarian	6,104	0	13,201	0	20,260	0
Ruthenian	3,321	0	19,384	0	7,189	0
Other / aliens or Unknown	295,693	3	102,027	1	122,986	1
Total	10,005,762		8,896,133		10,302,215	

were under Hungarian rule. In the Habsburg Empire, the Czechs had been governed from Vienna and the Slovaks from Budapest, and their experiences were vastly different. The Czechs entered the new Czechoslovak state in the fortunate position of having most of Austria-Hungary's industry on their territory, while Slovakia was comparatively underdeveloped, and what

Table 4.3: National Composition of Slovakia (inc. Ruthenia pre-1945)[6]

Nationality*	1921 Number	per cent	1950 Number	per cent	1991 Number	per cent
Czech	2,033,529	56	40,365	1	56,487	1
Slovak			2,982,524	87	4,445,303	84
German	150,360	4	5,179	0	7,738	0
Hungarian	739,327	20	354,532	10	608,221	12
Ruthenian	458,528	13	48,231	1	58,579	1
Other / aliens or Unknown	225,694	6	11,486	0	98,007	2
Total	3,607,438		3,442,317		5,274,335	

* *The 1921 and 1991 census data refer to nationality defined by native language. 'Ruthenian' includes Ukrainian and Russian speakers; Czechs and Slovaks were counted together as Czechoslovaks in the interwar period.*

industry it did possess struggled to compete in a common state with the more advanced Czech rivals. The social structure of the new state was thus markedly different in the Czech and Slovak parts: in the 1920s, the percentage of the population working in industry in the Czech Lands was more than twice as high as in Slovakia, while the percentage working on the land was only about half that in Slovakia.[7] Slovakia also lacked strong indigenous elites: Hungarian assimilationist policies had meant that there had been no advanced Slovak-language education, and Slovaks who had gained administrative experience in Hungary were suspected of having an undesirable allegiance to what was now a foreign state.[8] Consequently, in the early years of the First Republic, large numbers of Czechs moved to Slovakia to assume posts in the administrative and educational system, and while they were gradually joined by suitably qualified Slovaks, the Czechs tended to remain, thus becoming a focus for Slovak nationalist resentment.

The political cleavages in the party system of Czechoslovakia reflected both its socio-economic and multiethnic composition as well as the complexities of Czech-Slovak relationships. While the parties were largely distributed along a left-right axis, with some defined by their Catholicism, the crucial divide of interwar Czechoslovak politics was not one of left and right, but rather of government and non-government parties. For most of the First Republic, the government was formed by the *petka*, a group of five Czech or Czechoslovak parties. The consensus between them was largely facilitated by the awareness of external and internal threat. The opposition to the ruling parties came mostly from anti-system political parties which – with a few partial exceptions – did not participate in government. Apart from the communists – the only party which encompassed all the nationalities in the Czechoslovak state – the major forces involved were non-Czech ones: German, Hungarian and also Slovak. The Slovak vote, significantly, was split between the ruling Czechoslovak parties and parties advocating greater Slovak autonomy.[9]

The failure of the governing coalitions to incorporate non-Czechoslovak interests contributed to the demise of interwar Czechoslovak democracy. As the Great Depression took its toll on the Czechoslovak economy in the early 1930s, and with Hitler's rise to power across the border, the German vote consolidated behind Henlein's Sudeten German Party. When Czechoslovakia capitulated to Germany after being abandoned by its western allies at Munich in 1938, the German areas of the country were annexed by Germany, the Hungarians reclaimed the south of Slovakia, and the Slovaks finally opted for independence in March 1939. At the same time, the Czechs came under German occupation as the Protectorate of Bohemia-Moravia.

The war years represented a fundamentally different experience for Czechs and Slovaks. Among Czechs, there is consensus that the experience of occupation and the demoralisation of being forced to work for and compromise with the Germans were one of the gloomiest periods in their history. Slovak views of the war are more mixed, both because some Slovaks see positive elements in the very fact that Slovakia was nominally independent, albeit under Nazi tutelage, and also because the closing stages of the war, in autumn 1944, saw a heroic event of Slovak history in the form of the Slovak National Uprising. These two factors produced a lasting ambivalence towards the war, both in the Slovak nation as a whole and in the minds of individual citizens. Surveys conducted in the early 1990s indicated that the Slovaks were evenly divided about whether the wartime Slovak state had had more positive than negative aspects, while at the same time a majority of 80 per cent felt that the Slovak National Uprising was convincing proof of Slovak opposition to fascism.[10] Only about 10 per cent of Slovaks rejected the Uprising as having been a revolt against the Slovak state, and yet more than twice as many appeared to have positive views about the leader of the wartime Slovak state, Jozef Tiso,[11] who was executed for treason in 1947. As in the case of the interwar party system, Slovaks were more fundamentally divided than Czechs.

THE COMMUNIST EXPERIENCE

When the Czechoslovak state was reformed in 1945, its composition changed markedly. It became far less multinational: not only had much of the Jewish population been lost during the war, but Ruthenia was ceded to the Soviet Union, and the large German minority was deported in the course of 1946. The Czech or Slovak proportion of the population thereby rose from 64 per cent to over 95 per cent. Additionally, however, links between the Czechs and Slovaks themselves had been disrupted. The independent Slovak state, for all its many faults, had demonstrated the possibility that Slovakia could be run without Czech personnel, and the myth of the Czechoslovak nation was abandoned: the Kosice Government Programme of April 1945 – the first agreed between Czechs and Slovaks after the war – recognised the Slovaks as a nationally distinct people, and undertook to try to realise the principle of 'equals with equals' in Czech-Slovak relations.[12] Just as important, the previously existing Czech-Slovak links within political parties were no longer present, and in the elections of 1946, Czech and Slovak parties stood separately. There was a separate Communist Party of Slovakia, which, isolated

Table 4. 4: 1946 National Assembly Elections in the Czech Lands[13]

	per cent vote	*seats*
Communist Party of Czechoslovakia	40	93
Czechoslovak National Socialist Party	24	55
Czechoslovak Populist Party	20	46
Czechoslovak Social Democracy	16	37

from the Czechs, had participated in the Slovak resistance; and the anticommunist opposition in Slovakia largely united in the new Democratic Party.

In the period after the 1946 elections, as so often in the history of Czechoslovakia, broader developments interfered with the dynamics of Czech-Slovak relations. The predominance of the Democratic Party in Slovakia – where the communists had been less successful than in the Czech Lands – rendered Slovak autonomy undesirable in the communists' eyes, and recentralisation ensued after the communist takeover in 1948. The emergent party system of the democratic interlude of 1945-48 was replaced by Communist Party domination over several other small 'satellite' parties. Slovak national identity was acknowledged by a certain asymmetry in structural organisation, whereby, for example, a Communist Party of Slovakia continued to exist alongside the Communist Party of Czechoslovakia, but the Party had no separate Czech organisation.[14] The 1960 constitution further eroded any vestiges of Slovak autonomy.

The Slovak issue re-emerged on to the political agenda during the 1960s as free debate flourished during the 'Prague Spring' of 1968 and the federalisation of the country began to be discussed for the first time since the late 1940s, although it was an issue that appeared of greater importance to

Table 4.5: 1946 National Assembly Elections in Slovakia[15]

	per cent vote	*seats*
Democratic Party	62	43
Communist Party of Slovakia	30	21
Freedom Party	4	3
Labour Party	3	2

Slovaks than to Czechs.[16] After the Warsaw Pact invasion of August 1968, federalisation was the only of the reforms to proceed, and constitutional amendments came into force at the beginning of 1969 whereby a Czech National Council was established as well as a Slovak National Council. However, there were three aspects of the federalisation of Czechoslovakia which were particularly problematic, and these were all later to play a fateful role in the division of the country when it became a democracy.

The first is that, as pointed out by Carol Skalnik Leff, it is unusual for an established state freely to choose to convert itself into a federation:

States federalize because they must; for an existing state to federalize peacefully after a prolonged experience of centralized power, as Czechoslovakia did, is a rarity amounting almost to an impossibility. Federalization is commonly the recourse of the organizers of a new state, in the wake of revolution or war; in such cases, it is virtually a quid pro quo for statehood itself.[17]

Where a decision to federalise is essentially made by a ruling centralised power, as in the Czechoslovak case, an element of reciprocity is lacking in the relations between federal and republican governments. Since the centre has chosen to cede powers to the periphery, the danger remains that they may perceive an entitlement to take such powers back. This in fact happened in the Czechoslovak case: in 1970, as the Communist Party reasserted its control during the normalisation process, federalist structures were noticeably watered down, so that the country was left with the form but not the substance of a federation. Because Czechoslovakia was a federation but *not* a democracy and consequently both the input structures (parties, interest groups etc.) and the output structures (legislative, executive and judicial institutions) were dominated by Communist Party dictatorship, the significance of the 1970 changes became blurred against the repressive background of normalisation and authoritarian rule as a whole. However, when, after the Velvet Revolution, attempts were made to rectify the situation by creating an 'authentic federation', Slovaks were particularly anxious that the federation should be formed 'from below', by the two republics delegating power to the federation, rather than 'from above', by the federation granting greater powers to the republics. The Slovaks insisted that a State Treaty between the Czech Republic and the Slovak Republic should precede the passing of a new constitution, but many Czechs found this unacceptable since it appeared to involve the republics becoming separate states before they decided to recreate the common state.[18] The structural flaws of the late 1960s thus helped bring about the eventual demise of Czechoslovakia.

The second problem was that although both the Czech Republic and the

Slovak Republic now had their own national council, asymmetry remained where it most mattered: there was a Communist Party of Czechoslovakia and a Communist Party of Slovakia, but still no Czech Communist Party. This asymmetry was also present in a myriad of other organisations (e.g. the Academy of Sciences), with an almost universal pattern whereby the federal headquarters were in Prague, and any HQ to be found in Bratislava was sure to be that of the Slovak branch only. Communist federations functioned badly because they existed in chronically centralised states, where devolution and dispersal of power were an anathema to the rulers.

The third inherent problem in the Czechoslovak federation was that it comprised only two republics, and there was no equilibrium between them in terms of size and population. This is generally considered to be an unfavourable arrangement for the consensus-building process on which federalism is based, as it tends to polarise conflict and make all negotiations at federal level appear to be a zero sum game:[19] any gain for one republic must represent a loss for the other, and vice versa. Just as Slovak nationalists had earlier blamed their economic sufferings on the Czechs – even in periods such as the Great Depression of the 1930s and the Stalinism of the early 1950s, when the Czechs were clearly also losing[20] – so many Czechs resented federalism on the assumption that if it gave the Slovaks half of anything (e.g. investment, leadership posts) when population statistics should have entitled them only to a third, then the Czechs were losing out. The polarisation of views between Czechs and Slovaks on the issue of 'fair shares' can scarcely be overestimated: from public opinion surveys conducted after 1989, it became clear that the question 'who is paying for whom' was the single most divisive issue separating the two peoples. In the autumn of 1990, the vast majority of Slovaks (83 per cent) denied that they were being subsidised by the Czechs, while only 36 per cent of Czechs rejected the proposition; and although a vast majority of Czechs (91 per cent) denied that they were being paid for by the Slovaks, only 38 per cent of Slovaks disagreed with the statement.[21]

Amid the disillusionment of the 'normalisation' period in Czechoslovakia, however, such discontent had had few channels of expression. Communist dictatorship succeeded, for much of the time, in concealing disagreements between Czechs and Slovaks, but it did nothing to solve them.

AFTER THE 'VELVET REVOLUTION'

Postcommunist politics

Despite the lack of overt national conflict under communism, from the 'Velvet Revolution' of November 1989 to the dissolution of the Czechoslovak state took little more than three years.[22] Czech/Slovak disagreement was quick to emerge in conditions of greater freedom, with its first open manifestation being controversy over the renaming of the state in early 1990. President Havel's suggestion that the word 'socialist' should be deleted from the official name 'Czechoslovak Socialist Republic' was countered by a Slovak proposal that the word 'Czechoslovak' should be hyphenated, so that the outside world might know that the state comprised two nations. After bitter debate, the compromise title 'Czech and Slovak Federative Republic' was adopted.

Equally significant, though subject to less discussion, was the fact that the emergent party system consisted of separate Czech and Slovak parties. This pattern was established in the early days of the Velvet Revolution, when the Czechs and Slovaks set up their own citizens' movements, Civic Forum and Public Against Violence. Yet the division of the party system was not merely a decision of politicians, but also one endorsed by the electorate. The first free elections, in June 1990, were contested by 22 parties, of which five stood only in the Czech Republic and six only in Slovakia;[23] of the eleven which stood in both republics, only one – the Communist Party of Czechoslovakia – obtained seats in each.

The separate party system did not immediately appear problematic, since Civic Forum and Public Against Violence took both cooperation between the two citizens movements and the general desirability of broad coalitions, for granted. After the 1990 elections, both willingly entered coalitions with the Christian Democrats. Consensus democracy of the type familiar from the First Republic appeared still to be functioning. Problems ensued, however, when the citizens' movements split, as broad anticommunist alliances were prone to do after the first elections in postcommunist states. In the Czech Republic, the new Civic Democratic Party, led by the economic reformer and Federal Finance Minister Václav Klaus, gained the ascendancy. The division of the Public Against Violence, however, reflected the deep and traditional polarisation of Slovak society. In the spring of 1991, the Slovak Prime Minister, Vladimír Meciar was ousted from office and went on to form his own Movement for a Democratic Slovakia. In opposition, Meciar consolidated his popular support by emphasising both the economic interests of the Slovaks vis-a-vis reform impulses from Prague, and

Table 4.6: Czechoslovak Election Results 1990[24]

| | Federal Assembly | | | | National Council | |
	Chamber of People		Chamber of Nations			
Czech parties	vote %	seats (of 101)	vote %	seats (of 75)	vote %	seats (of 200)
Civic Forum	53	68	50	50	49	127
Communist Party of Czechoslovakia	13	15	14	12	13	32
Movement for Self-governing Democracy/ Association for Moravia & Silesia	8	9	9	7	10	22
Christian Democratic Union	9	9	9	6	8	19
Others	17	0	18	0	19	0
Slovak parties	vote %	seats (of 49)	vote %	seats (of 75)	vote %	seats (of 150)
Public Against Violence	33	19	37	33	29	48
Christian Dem. Movement	19	11	17	14	19	31
Communist Party of Czechoslovakia	14	8	13	12	13	22
Slovak National Party	11	6	11	9	14	22
Coexistence/Hungarian Christian Democratic Movement	9	5	8	7	9	14
Democratic Party	4	0	4	0	4	7
Green Party	3	0	3	0	3	6
Others	8	0	6	0	8	0

A 5 per cent clause operated for the Federal Assembly and Czech National Council, but only a 3 per cent clause for the Slovak National Council. The per cent vote is calculated separately for each republic. Percentages have been rounded up or down, so totals may not equal 100.

Table 4.7: Czechoslovak Elections Results 1992[25]

| | Federal Assembly | | | | National Council | |
| | Chamber of People | | Chamber of Nations | | | |
Czech parties	vote %	seats (of 99)	vote %	seats (of 75)	vote %	seats (of 200)
Civic Democratic Party / Christian Democratic Party	34	48	33	37	30	76
Left Bloc (Communist successor)	14	19	14	15	14	35
Czechoslovak Social Democracy	8	10	7	6	7	16
Republican Party	6	8	6	6	6	14
Christian Democratic Union/ Czech People's Party	6	7	6	6	6	15
Liberal Social Union	6	7	6	5	7	16
Civic Democratic Alliance	5	0	4	0	6	14
Movement for Self-governing Democracy/Association for Moravia & Silesia	4	0	5	0	6	14
Others	17	0	18	0	19	0

Slovak parties	vote %	seats (of 51)	vote %	seats (of 75)	vote %	seats (of 150)
Movement for a Democratic Slovakia	34	24	34	33	37	74
Party of the Democratic Left (Communist successor)	14	10	14	13	15	29
Slovak National Party	9	6	9	9	8	15
Christian Democratic Movement	9	6	9	8	9	18
Hungarian Christian Democratic Movement/Coexistence	7	5	7	7	7	14
Social Democratic Party of Slovakia	5	0	6	5	4	0
Others	21	0	20	0	20	0

A 5 per cent clause operated for all elections. The per cent vote is calculated separately for each republic. Percentages are rounded, so totals may not equal 100 and a party may appear to have 5 per cent of the vote yet no seats.

constitutional demands of Slovakia for greater autonomy in the guise of a confederation.

Although the first parliament, from 1990 to 1992, succeeded in passing much contentious legislation, it did not perform the major task for which its shortened, two-year term had been intended: passing new constitutions. When the second elections took place in June 1992, the results reflected a polarisation of political concerns between Czechs and Slovaks, and the hope of compromise on constitutional arrangements receded.

The victor in the Czech Republic, Klaus's Civic Democratic Party, had no obvious partner in Slovakia, and the election results made it inevitable that he had to negotiate with Meciar. When they met after the elections, Klaus, whose own political agenda was dominated by economic reform, refused even to discuss the possibility of confederation, and cornered Meciar into agreeing to the division of the state: independence was an offer it was hard for the Slovak leader to turn down, since he could scarcely retreat from his nationalist stance without losing support in Slovakia. The country was thus divided into two at the end of the year, without even the endorsement of a referendum. Neither party actually had an electoral mandate to divide the country, despite some small print in the Civic Democratic Party's manifesto.[26] The causes of the division of Czechoslovakia therefore require more detailed explanation.

Attitudes to Reform

The first explanation relates to differing Czech and Slovak attitudes to economic reform, one of the paramount concerns of a postcommunist society. Slovaks were more cautious about rapid economic change, and it is argued that divergence of opinion on the most desirable tempo for change was pre-programmed by the two peoples' differing experiences of modernisation.[27] Slovakia, like most regions which had been subjected to communist rule, had not been a modern, industrial society in earlier periods of its history; it was the Czechs Lands which were, in this respect, the exception. Consequently, although Slovak living standards had nearly caught up with those of the Czechs by the late 1980s,[28] comparisons between past and present were vastly different in the two parts of Czechoslovakia. For most Czechs, communism had been an unmitigated disaster which, in addition to political repression, had deprived them of one of the better western European standards of living which they had enjoyed in the interwar period. Hence they looked back fondly to the democratic years in the interwar First Republic.[29] For many Slovaks, however, communism had brought about progress of sorts, and, whatever its faults, they could scarcely hanker after the rural poverty into which their parents or grandparents had been born before the war. Additionally, the very nature of modernisation under communist rule itself made it inherently likely that some of the economic 'achievements' it brought about were extremely fragile.[30] Under communism Slovakia became the location of much heavy industry, notably armaments production, which declined steeply after 1989. The attendant rise in unemployment was particularly devastating in rural areas where much of the local economy had been dependent on a single state employer. At the time of the June 1992 elections, an overall Czechoslovak unemployment rate of 5.5 per cent comprised 2.7 per cent unemployment in the Czech Republic, compared to 11.3 per cent in Slovakia.[31]

Not surprisingly, the latent insecurity engendered by the historically-determined vulnerability of the Slovak economy affected public attitudes to postcommunist transition. Differences between average Czech and Slovak views first emerged about five months after the Velvet Revolution, in the spring of 1990.[32] In January of that year, 43 per cent of Czechs and 41 per cent of Slovaks favoured fast and radical reform with quick improvement over softer reform with slower improvement, but by May a gulf of ten percentage points had opened between Czechs and Slovaks, so that the figures were 61 per cent for Czechs and 51 per cent for Slovaks. In the same space of four months, fear of losing one's job had increased from 23 per cent to 36 per cent among Czechs, but from 26 per cent to 44 per cent among Slovaks.[33] These differing attitudes towards reform were reflected on a broader level in the right and left orientation of Czechs and Slovaks. Slovaks were somewhat more inclined to leftish positions on key questions such as whether incomes should be made more equal, whether individuals or the state should take responsibility for providing for every family and whether state ownership or private entrepreneurship was the better way to run an enterprise.[34]

However, although there were statistically significant differences in the attitudes to reform among Czechs and Slovaks which can be explained by differences in economic conditions with structural, historically-determined roots, this does not of itself provide an explanation for the division of the country. The divergence of views between the Czechs and the Slovaks as a whole on economic questions and regime transition was not, in fact, as great as the differences of views within each nation taken separately. It is not unusual for one region of a country to be somewhat more left or right inclined than another, and a well-functioning political system should be able to accommodate such divergent perspectives.[35]

Institutional Factors

A second explanation for the division of the country therefore lays more emphasis on the institutional structure of the emergent Czechoslovak democracy, and its inability to reconcile somewhat differing views of Czechs and Slovaks about the extent of reforms necessary. At first sight, Czechoslovakia should have benefited from the fact that federal structures had been established in the wake of the Prague Spring reforms of 1968, and Czechoslovak democracy – both in the interwar period and after 1989 – did display most characteristics of a consociational or consensus democracy.[36] However, the political structures in Czechoslovakia contained flaws which militated against the achievement of consensus.

Firstly, it could be argued that the federation's legislative arrangements gave rather too much power to the Slovaks. This was not apparent under communism, since the parliament merely rubber-stamped decisions already reached by centralised communist party structures, and was never called upon to mediate genuine conflicts of interest. The structure of the Federal Assembly was complex,[37] and for certain types of major legislation to be passed, Czech and Slovak deputies voted separately in the upper chamber (Chamber of Nations). For constitutional amendments, the majority required was 60 per cent of all deputies elected for each Republic. This provided the Slovaks with a strong safeguard against being outvoted by the Czechs, but it also hampered negotiation and consensual politics: the veto powers of both parts of the upper chamber rendered Czech/Slovak coalition-building on constitutional issues futile. However, these imperfect decision-making structures could only be changed initially by using existing institutional arrangements, and the Slovaks were unlikely to agree to anything perceived to strengthen their dependence on the Czechs. After the 1992 elections, the chances of any constitutional changes being agreed diminished, since the winners of the elections broke the mould of consensual politics which had previously been a feature of Czechoslovak parliamentary democracy.

A second problem for the Federal Assembly stemmed from the fact that the Czechoslovak federation comprised only two constituent republics, each with a democratically and directly elected National Council, a prime minister and a government. Any agreement reached by the Federal Assembly, which was unfortunately located in the largest Czech city of Prague, was likely to have questionable legitimacy in the eyes of Slovaks if it were opposed by the Slovak National Council in Bratislava.

A further disincentive to compromise was provided by the electoral system, which took for granted the fact that the country was divided into two halves. All election results, and all tables and analyses of the share of the vote obtained by individual parties, started from the assumption that one counted the Czech and Slovak vote separately. For example, while it is often stated that the Slovak National Party – the only parliamentary party which explicitly demanded Slovak independence in its election manifesto – obtained less than 10 per cent of the Slovak vote, no-one bothered to make the further computation that their supporters represented about 3 per cent of the voters in Czechoslovakia as a whole. This idiosyncratic Czechoslovak way of expressing election results was reflected in the electoral system itself. The voting system was one of proportional representation, whereby a party list had to obtain 5 per cent of the vote in order to obtain any seats in the Federal Assembly. Yet this '5 per cent clause' operated *separately* in the Czech Republic and the Slovak Republic. For a Czech or Slovak party struggling to overcome the 5 per cent hurdle, it was not, therefore, important to modify its programme in such a way that it could attract votes in the other republic. It was far more instrumental to success for party leaders to construct a political programme and electoral campaign likely to appeal in its own republic. Parties consequently did not act as an integrative force in Czechoslovakia, but rather a polarising one.

Elite politics

This leads to the third explanation of the division of Czechoslovakia, which relates to the way in which disagreements between Czechs and Slovaks were handled by the political elites in both parts of the country. Virtually all public opinion polls conducted in the period leading up to the division of the country, and some conducted afterwards, showed that a majority of ordinary citizens – both Czech and Slovak – did not want two separate states. An even larger majority felt that a decision on this issue should be made by the people in a referendum, and not by politicians, and there was a strong belief among both Czechs and Slovaks in late 1991 and early 1992 that politicians were using nationalism and national questions for their own aims.[38] A question must therefore be posed about why the Czech and Slovak elites were unable or unwilling to reach the accommodation apparently desired by the populace.

Public opinion was disregarded in part due to factors specific to the nature of postcommunist politics. Citizens had a low sense of efficacy inherited from the communist period, and had little experience in campaigning against undesired government policy. In other words, they did not believe there was anything they could do. Also, the political problems confronting a postcommunist government are both numerous and pressing, and the inevitably slow process of consensus-building amongst different parts of a federation demanded time which was simply not available in Czechoslovakia in the early 1990s.[39] Politicians were aware, for example, that although most Czechs and Slovaks opposed the division of Czechoslovakia, they shared no consensus about the basis upon which their coexistence should continue. People talked variously about federations, authentic federations, confederations etc., but there was not even agreement about what such terms actually meant.[40] Therefore a referendum, requiring a yes/no answer to a straight question, was unlikely to produce a concrete solution to the country's problems – even in the unlikely event that the wording of such a referendum could ever have been agreed by the labyrinthine parliamentary decision-making procedures. A final specifically postcommunist factor is that the atomisation of political life under communism had meant that no formal structures were permitted to exist independently of the communist power monopoly. The only noncommunist political contacts which did exist were, therefore, informal ones, and such links are greatly impeded by lack of geographical proximity. One result of this was that the Prague elite and the Bratislava elite had rarely come into contact with each other.

These factors form part of another explanation for the failure of the political elites to save the common state, which is that conditions in postcommunist Czechoslovakia were almost diametrically opposed to those normally considered conducive for the smooth functioning of a consociation.[41] A consensus democracy relies on a high level of cooperation between the elites in the different parts of a divided society, but such an arrangement is usually the response to a common external threat – a situation which applied to interwar Czechoslovakia, but not to postwar Czechoslovakia. Other factors conducive to consociational democracy are the presence of more than two political communities, and a low burden on the decision-making apparatus to prevent the threat of immobilism.[42] Czechoslovakia did not fulfil either of these conditions. The confrontational style of politics which followed Klaus and Meciar's election victories may therefore be viewed less as a personal failing of the Czech and Slovak political elites, and more as a result of objective circumstances.

Separate nations

Finally, however, in order to understand the failure of Czechoslovakia as a common state one must question why no overarching political elite could be formed in the country. One answer lies in the suggestion of the Czech sociologist Jiri Musil that no 'Czechoslovak society' had ever been established.[43] There were *separate* Czech and Slovak societies. Czechs and Slovaks differed not only in their historically-determined economic and material situation, but they also had fundamentally separate identities.

On a symbolic level, this point can be most graphically illustrated by listening to the Czechoslovak national anthem, which comprises a Czech folk song followed by a totally unconnected, shorter Slovak folk song, with an often audible gap in the middle (which, it was sometimes jokingly suggested, represented Moravia). Neither part of the national anthem makes any reference either to Czechoslovakia, or to any common myths, symbols, achievements or aspirations of the Czech and Slovak peoples. This led to the ultimate absurdity whereby, at the end of 1992, the Czechoslovak national anthem was, like most other possessions of the common state, neatly divided up in the ratio of two to one. Both nations then carried on using their respective folk songs as the national anthems of the Czech Republic and the Slovak Republic.

What can be suggested from this is that Czechoslovakia came apart because, at an emotional level, it had never been joined together properly. The lack of genuine Czechoslovak symbols was in part historically determined, as the two peoples had almost never stood together at the turning points in their history: they had, for example, few common dead, having largely fought separately in both the first and second world wars. The invasion of 1968 was the only heroic moment which they had shared, yet even this had been overshadowed by the demoralising and divisive normalisation experience which followed. In surveys conducted in both 1968 and 1990, Czech and Slovak respondents proved to have vastly different images of their own history, too. When asked to name the historical personalities of whom they were most proud, Czechs rarely mentioned Slovaks, with only one appearing in the ten most cited names in 1968, and two in 1990; the Slovaks, on the other hand, mentioned Slovaks more often, but the number of Czechs who managed (and often only just) to reach the Slovak 'top ten' declined from five in 1968 to two in 1990. Only three people appeared on both the Czech and Slovak lists both times: the interwar president, T.G. Masaryk, the Prague Spring leader Alexander Dubcek, and Ludvík Svoboda, president from 1968 to 1975. And even in the case of these three, there were enormous differences in their ranking by Czechs and Slovaks, with the Slovak Dubcek, in 1968, being mentioned by 56 per cent of Slovaks but only 20 per cent of Czechs, and the Czech Masaryk in 1990, being mentioned by 46 per cent of Czechs and only 4 per cent of Slovaks.[44] Similar discrepancies emerged when Czechs and Slovaks were asked about the most glorious periods in their history. In 1990, a slight majority of the 'golden eras' mentioned by Czechs were periods up to the end of the First Republic, whereas more than three-quarters of the periods mentioned by Slovaks had occurred after that date. It should also be noted that half the Slovak respondents but only a third of the Czechs could not think of any time in their history at all of which they were proud.[45] Czechs would appear, therefore, to have had a stronger sense of being rooted in a glorious past than the Slovaks, and, quite clearly, both peoples were looking back at very different pasts.

Czechs and Slovaks not only had different histories, but their contemporary identities were also structured differently. In early summer 1991, Czechs and Slovaks were asked if they also thought of themselves as being Czechoslovak, as well as being Czech or Slovak: 71 per cent of Czechs did, compared to only 26 per cent of Slovaks; of these, 55 per cent of Czechs but only 39 per cent of the smaller Slovak group regarded Czechoslovak as their first identity.[46] This may not necessarily mean that the Slovaks had a lesser degree of attachment to the common state as such; an alternative conclusion that can be drawn is that – as in the common English language usage – Czechs perceived the terms 'Czech' and 'Czechoslovak' to overlap to a substantial degree, whereas Slovaks did not.

However, it is not only the lack of a common Czechoslovak past and Czechoslovak identity that is important, but also the fact that from the 1960s onwards, practical steps towards creating such an identity virtually ceased – for example, school classes no longer went on officially organised excursions to the other republic.[47] Federalisation reinforced this tendency for the two societies to be allowed to develop separately, and the intermingling of the two nations actually decreased over time. Whereas, in the early 1950s, about 9 per cent of citizens who changed address had moved from one republic to the other, this proportion gradually decreased to around 4 per cent in the early 1980s.[48] Education patterns changed, too: an analysis of the education of Czechoslovak elite, derived from a Czechoslovak 'Who's Who' from 1969, showed that during the First Republic half the future Slovak elite had been educated in the Czech Lands, but that this declined to one third in the period up to 1968.[49]

A first consequence of this was that the Slovak elite which was maturing at the time of the 1989 revolution was far more strongly oriented towards its own republic than at any previous time during the existence of the Czechoslovak state. This was reflected, for example, in the tendency of Slovak party leaders, from 1990 onwards, to stand for seats in the Bratislava-based Slovak National Council rather than the Prague-based Federal Assembly.

The second consequence was, as Skalnik Leff wrote in the late 1980s, that 'the existence of Slovakia is largely extraneous to the life choices of Czechs'.[50] Czechs had little reason to go to Slovakia, other than for a holiday in the mountains, whereas Slovaks had tended to be more exposed to the Czechs than vice versa for economic reasons as well as the fact that the latter were the majority in the country. In a survey conducted in the autumn of 1990, it was found that 60 per cent of Slovaks but only 47 per cent of Czechs had spent several weeks in the other republic, and that 51 per cent of Czechs, but only 28 per cent of Slovaks, had neither relatives nor friends in the other republic.[51]

There is also some evidence that Czechs felt somewhat more uncomfortable about the idea that the country comprised two nations than the Slovaks did, and that this tendency may have been particularly strong among the Czech elites. Unpublished public opinion surveys conducted in the communist period – however questionable their reliability may be – indicated that more Slovaks (73 per cent) than Czechs (60 per cent) thought that the relations between Czechs and Slovaks had improved since the interwar period[52], and, interestingly, the lowest proportion (47 per cent) was found in Prague.[53] Likewise, more Slovaks (28 per cent) than Czechs (13 per cent) thought relations had got better, rather than remaining the same, since the federalisation of the country, and more Slovaks were optimistic about further improvements in the future.[54] There were also some signs that there were more negative feelings among Czechs with university education.[55] These findings were to an extent confirmed by surveys carried out in more objective circumstances after 1989. In October 1990 – at a time when considerable national emotions were being manifested in Slovakia about new laws concerning the position of Slovak as the sole official language – it was found that 60 per cent of Slovaks but only 38 per cent of Czechs evaluated relations between Czechs and Slovaks as good. It is likely that manifestations of Slovak nationalism looked far more serious and threatening to the Czechs, watching from afar, than they did to the Slovaks. Slovaks were more aware both that manifestations of extreme Slovak nationalism represented the views of a small minority, and that more reasoned Slovak criticisms were directed at 'pragocentrism' – i.e. the system by which the country was governed – rather than at the Czechs as individuals.[56] It was also found that when Czechs and Slovaks were asked to evaluate the national characters of themselves and the other nationality, 41 per cent of Czechs saw Slovaks solely in a negative light, and that the most commonly found profile of such respondents contained such features as more 'men, people with higher education (particularly in comparison to citizens with only basic education), people in early middle age (35-40), those holding higher managerial position, inhabitants of larger settlements, especially Prague, people who have neither relatives or friends among the Slovaks...'[57] The above categories virtually correspond to a description of the Czech elite.

What emerges in total is a picture of Czech and Slovak society in the early 1990s containing a Slovak elite which, for the first time, had been able to fulfil itself by remaining in Slovakia, pitted against a Czech elite which may have held more pessimistic views about coexistence with the Slovaks than the population as a whole. These rather different and separate elites were competing in a political system structured in such a way that there was no apparent advantage to them in burying their differences, and for many of them, the separation of the state may have brought no personal disadvantage.

AFTER CZECHOSLOVAKIA

It is an irony that, throughout Czechoslovak history, it was the Slovaks who took the lead in demanding greater autonomy, yet in the first two years after independence, it was the Czechs who came to terms with it most easily. In a survey conducted at the end of 1994 where Czechs and Slovaks were asked what their preferred future arrangement of the relations between Czechs and Slovaks would be, 57 per cent of Czechs, compared to only 38 per cent of Slovaks opted for two independent states. 30 per cent of Czechs but only 11 per cent of Slovaks, stated that they had originally opposed the division of the country, but now thought it was right; and 8 per cent of Slovaks, but only 2 per cent of Czechs, stated that they had originally supported division, but now thought it had been a mistake.[58]

There were a number of reasons why the Czechs were more easily able to adapt to independence than the Slovaks. One was that the Czechs sensed they had much to gain from uncoupling themselves from the weaker Slovak economy, although the opposite did not necessarily apply to the Slovaks, since most Slovaks had never acknowledged that they were in any sense subsidised economically by the Czechs. Another factor is that – precisely because the Czech and Czechoslovak identities had always been less distinct than the Slovak and Czechoslovak identities – the termination of the latter was more noticeable in Slovakia. Czech allegiance to Czechoslovakia had been, at best, somewhat superficial.

A final reason, however, why more Slovaks than Czechs mourned the passing of the common state is that Slovakia continued, after 1992 as in the entire Czechoslovak period, to be a profoundly divided society. While the

Czech party system was clearly characterised by a left-right divide largely based on socio-economic issues, political cleavages were more complex in Slovakia. Parties were divided not only on a left-right axis, but also on questions of national identity. After the elections of September/October 1994, both the government and the opposition contained a full left-right spectrum of parties.[59] Additionally, Hungarian parties were separate from both. Slovakia generally had far more problems with its own sense of identity than the Czech Republic. With the exception of Dubcek, who had been killed in a car accident in autumn 1992, there was virtually no figure in Slovak politics who was overwhelmingly regarded as positive by all citizens, and controversy remained about the evaluation of the Slovak past.[60] It was from the consequences of such internal Slovak polarisation that the Czechs had freed themselves by dividing the state.

Czechoslovakia, however, had always been more than the sum total Czechs and Slovaks. The separation of the two peoples did not release them from the dilemma of coming to terms with other national groups. Once the 'Slovak problem' was solved, Czech relations with Germany were an increasing focus of national grievance, and racism against the Roma minority was a running sore. The Slovaks, too, were left to cope with the demands and anxieties of a Hungarian minority that comprised more than 10 per cent of its citizens, as well as a minority of Roma larger than that in the Czech Republic. Questions of national tolerance had been simplified by the division of the state, but the state nations of the new democracies were still faced with the need to define their relations with other communities.

CONCLUSION

History has demonstrated that Czechoslovakia, as a multinational state, was not a long-term success. Yet it remains an interesting case because – within a relatively short period of 74 years – it tried out a diverse range of constitutional arrangements, both as a democracy and otherwise. None succeeded. The new democracy after 1989 was left to confront the legacy of earlier history with a benevolent bafflement and the simple inability to cope with so many problems at once.

One reason for the repeated failures was that, despite experiments with federalisation, the country was never really organised as a multinational state. It was not only uninformed foreigners who regarded Czechoslovakia as the nation state of the Czechs; the Czechs, too, tended to react to inputs and demands from other national groups as *problems* which intruded into the smooth running of the state, rather than as a normal part of day-to-day politics. Periods of stability ensued when the government of the country was successfully dominated by the Czech political agenda, but this arrangement was not sustainable in the long term. Established democracies are not normally affected by secession. Czechoslovakia, however, never became a stabilised democracy. Historical circumstances never granted Czechs and Slovaks a long enough breathing space to come to grips with the intricacies of their mutual relationship.

NOTES

1   The period from the Munich Agreement of September 1938 until the complete dismemberment of Czechoslovakia in March 1939 is designated as the 'Second Republic'.

2   See Chapter 1, Paragraph 3 of the 1920 constitution, *Ústava republiky Československé z roku 1920*, Prague, Auctoritas, 1992, p.11; Joseph Rothschild, *East Central Europe between the Two World Wars*, Seattle & London, University of Washington Press, 1974, pp.73–135.

3   For further details of the election system, see: Eva Broklová, *Československá demokracie: Politický systém ČSR 1918–1938*, Prague, Sociologické nakladatelství, 1982, pp.79-85; Oskar Krejčí, *Kniha o volbách*, Prague, Victoria Publishing, 1994, pp.134–41.

4   Compiled from census data in: Václav L. Beneš, 'Czechoslovak Democracy and its Problems 1918–1920', Victor S. Mamatey & Radomír Luža (eds), *A History of the Czechoslovak Republic 1918–1948*, Princeton, Princeton University Press, 1973, p.40.

5   Compiled from census data in: Federální statistický úřad, *Historická statistická ročenka ČSSR*, Prague, SNTL/ALFA, 1985, p.62, 429, 630.

6   Compiled from census data in: Český statistický úřad, *Statistická ročenka České republiky '93*, Prague, Český statistický úřad/Český spisovatel, 1993, p.413.

7   For statistics of distribution of population by profession, see: Beneš, 'Czechoslovak Democracy', pp.42–3.

8   See: Stanislav J. Kirschbaum, 'Czechoslovakia: The Creation, Federalization and Dissolution of a Nation-State', *Regional Politics and Policy*, Vol.3, No.1, 1993, p.85.

9   The best account of Slovak politics in this period is contained in James Ramon Felak, *'At the Price of the Republic': Hlinka's Slovak People's Party, 1929–1938*, Pittsburgh, University of Pittsburgh Press, 1994.

10 Pavol Frič, Zora Bútorová, Tatiana Rosová, 'Česko-slovenské vzťahy v zrkadle empirického výskumu', _Sociológia_, Vol.24, No.1–2, 1992, pp.43–74.

11 FOCUS, _Aktuálne problémy Slovenska po rozpade ČSFR, Október 1993_, Bratislava, 1993, pp.6–8.

12 Jan Měchýř, _Slovensko v Československu: Slovensko-české vztahy 1918–1991_, Prague, Práce, 1991, pp.50–65.

13 Krejčí, _Kniha o volbách_, p.158.

14 See: Carol Skalnik Leff, _National Conflict in Czechoslovakia: The Making and Remaking of a State, 1918–1987_, Princeton, Princeton University Press, 1988, pp.98–102.

15 _Ibid._

16 See: Jaroslaw A. Piekalkiewicz, _Public Opinion Polling in Czechoslovakia, 1968–69_, New York & London, Praeger, 1972, pp.110–12.

17 Leff, _National Conflict in Czechoslovakia_, pp.249–50. Leff states that she can find no other case such as Czechoslovakia among contemporary federal governments, but was writing before the federalisation of Belgium.

18 For more detailed discussion of this issue, see: Mathernova, 'Czecho?Slovakia: Constitutional Disappointments', A.E. Dick Howard (ed.), _Constitution Making in Eastern Europe_, Washington, Woodrow Wilson Center Press, 1993, pp.68–75; Jiri Pehe, 'The State Treaty between the Czech and Slovak Republics', _Radio Free Europe Report on Eastern Europe_, 7 June 1991, pp.11–15; Jan Obrman, 'Further Discussions on the Future of the Federation', _ibid._, 20 September 1991, pp.6–10; Jiri Pehe, 'Czech and Slovak Leaders Deadlocked over Country's Future', _ibid._, 28 November 1991, pp.7–13.

19 See: Arend Lijphart, _Democracy in Plural Societies: A Comparative Exploration_, New Haven, Yale University Press, 1977, pp.56–7.

20 Leff, _National Conflict in Czechoslovakia_, pp.278–82.

21 Frič, Bútorová, Rosová, 'Česko-slovenské vzťahy v zrkadle empirického výskumu', pp.66–8.

22 The best English language account of this period is contained in Carol Skalnik Leff, _The Czech and Slovak Republics: Nation versus State_, Boulder, Colorado, Westview Press, 1997.

23 Peter Bugge, 'The Czech Republic', Bogdan Szajkowski (ed.), _Political Parties of Eastern Europe, Russia and the Successor_

States, Harlow, Longman, 1994, p.150.

24   Federální statistický úřad, Český statistický úřad, Slovenský statistický úrad, *Statistická ročenka '91 České a Slovenské Federatívní Republiky*, Prague, SEVT, 1991, pp.629–30.

25   *Statistická ročenka České republiky '93*, pp.433–41.

26   The bottom paragraph of one page of a 77-page manifesto contains the sentence: 'Dividing the state is not our programme; but if it proves to be necessary, we will be able to come to terms with it.' *Svoboda a prosperita: volební program ODS volby 1992*, Prague, 1992, p.17.

27   For further discussion of this point, see: Jiři Musil, 'Czech and Slovak Society', *Government and Opposition*, Vol.28, No.4, 1993, pp.479–95. This issue, as well as many others surrounding the division of Czechoslovakia, are dealt with in Jiři Musil (ed.), *The End of Czechoslovakia*, Budapest, Central European University Press, 1995.

28   See: Pavel Machonin, 'Česko-slovenské vztahy ve světle dat sociologického výzkumu', Fedor Gál a kol., *Dnečni krize česko-slovenských vztahů*, Prague, Sociologické nakladatelství, 1992, pp.97–101. More detailed figures, such as historical comparisons for food consumption and consumer goods, can be found in official statitistical yearbooks, such as Federální statistický úřad, *Historická statistická ročenka ČSSR*, pp.580–83 and 779–82.

29   Questioned in late 1990/early 1991, Czechs provided very much more positive responses to questions about the First Republic. See: Frič, Bútorová, Rosová, 'Česko-slovenské vzťahy', pp.44–74.

30   For an account of the situation of the Slovak economy after 1989, see: *Slovensko a jeho premeny na začiatku 90. rokov*, Bratislava, Sociologický ústav SAV, 1994, esp pp.144–55. For detailed comparative Czech and Slovak data on economy and society in the entire Czechoslovak period, see Jaroslav Krejčí and Pavel Machonin, *Czechoslovakia, 1918–92: A Laboratory for Social Change*, London, Macmillan, 1996.

31   *Budování státu*, Vol.3, No.7, 1992, p.13.

32   See for example Jan Hartl, 'Jací jsme a kam směřujeme', *Respekt*, 6–12 September 1993, p.6; Marián Timoracký, 'Verejná mienka o česko-slovenských vzťahoch', Gál, *Dnešní krize*, pp.97–101.

33   AISA, *Czechoslovakia – May 1990: Survey Report*, Prague, 1990, appendix, p.1.

34   AISA, *Czechs and Slovaks Compared: A Survey of Economic and*

Political Behaviour, Studies in Public Policy No.198, Glasgow, University of Strathclyde, 1992, pp.6–7.

35   For more detailed discussion of this point, see: Karen Henderson, 'Divisive Political Agendas: the Case of Czechoslovakia', Patrick Dunleavy and Jeffrey Stanyer (eds), *Contemporary Political Studies 1994: Proceedings of the Political Studies Association's 1994 Annual Conference*, Belfast, Political Studies Association of the United Kingdom, 1994, pp.408–12.

36   For further explanation of the terms, see: Arend Lijphart, *Democracies: Patterns of Majoritarian and Consensus Government in Twenty-One Countries*, New Haven and London, Yale University Press, 1984.

37   For further discussion of this point, see: Karen Henderson, 'Czechoslovakia: Cutting the Gordian Knot', *Coexistence*, Vol.31, No.4, December 1994, pp.314–17; Mathernova, 'Czecho?Slovakia', pp.64–5; David Olson, 'The Sundered State: Federalism and Parliament in Czechoslovakia', Thomas F. Remington (ed.), *Parliaments in Transition: The New Legislative Politics in the Former USSR and Eastern Europe*, Boulder, Colorado, Westview Press, 1994, pp.100–3.

38   For a useful summary of public opinion surveys, see: Sharon Wolchik, 'The Politics of Ethnicity in Post-Communist Czechoslovakia', *East European Politics and Society*, Vol.8, No.1, 1994, pp.176–81.

39   For further explanation of this argument, see: Henderson, 'Czechoslovakia: Cutting the Gordian knot', pp.312–17.

40   For an interesting analysis of the confusion surrounding the use of terms such as 'confederation' in Czechoslovak political discourse, see Ján Bunčák, Valentína Harmadyová, Zuzana Kusá, *Politická zmena v spoločenksej rozprave*, Bratislava, VEDA, 1996, pp.34–54.

41   See: Karen Henderson, 'Czechoslovakia: The Failure of Consensus Politics and the Breakup of the Federation', *Journal of Regional and Federal Politics*, Vol.5, No.2, 1995.

42   For a more detailed account of factors crucial to successful consociationalism, see: Lijphart, *Democracy in Plural Societies*, pp.53–103.

43   Musil, 'Czech and Slovak Society', p.479.

44   For figures, see: Archie Brown and Gordon Wightman, 'Czechoslovakia: Revival and Retreat', Archie Brown and Jack Gray (eds), *Political Culture and Political Change in Communist States*,

London, Macmillan, 2nd edn, 1979, pp.159–196; Frič, Bútorová, Rosová, 'Česko-slovenské vzťahy', pp.44–52.

45   *Ibid.*

46   AISA, *Czechs and Slovaks Compared*, p.30.

47   See: Ján Bunčák, 'Slovensko – spoločnosť v rekonštrukcii', *Sociológia*, Vol.25, No.1–2, 1993, pp.6–7.

48   Federální statistický úřad, *Historická statistická ročenka ČSFR*, p.83.

49   See Leff: *National Conflict in Czechoslovakia*, pp.288–93.

50   *Ibid.*, p.292.

51   AISA, *Czechoslovakia – November 1990: Survey Report*, Prague, 1990, Table 2. For further statistics on the same subject, see: Frič, Bútorová, Rosová, 'Česko-slovenské vzťahy', p.56.

52   'Ústav pro výzkum veřejného mínění při FSÚ', *Názory na socialistické vlastenectvo: Záverečná správa 78–3*, Prague, 1979, pp.7–8.

53   The pattern whereby people in Prague gave the least positive responses was repeated again in a 1983 survey asking about friendly relations towards other nationalities. 'Ústav pro výzkum veřejného mínění při FSÚ', *Názory na vzťahy národov a národností ČSSR: Záverečná správa z výskumu 83–3*, Prague, 1983, p.19, p.26.

54   'Ústav pro výzkum veřejného mínění při FSÚ', *Názory na socialistické vlastenectvo*, pp.13–14.

55   'Ústav pro výzkum veřejného mínění při FSÚ', *Názory na socialistické vlastenectvo*, p.30; *Názory na vzťahy národov a národností ČSSR*, pp.27, 35.

56   Timoracký, 'Verejná mienka o česko-slovenských vzťahoch', pp.83–4.

57   Frič, Bútorová, Rosová, 'Česko-slovenské vzťahy', p.54.

58   FOCUS, *Aktuálne problémy Slovenska December 1994*, Bratislava, 1995, pp.37–9.

59   For 1994 Slovak election results, see: Karen Henderson, 'The Slovak Republic', Szajkowski (ed), *Political Parties of Eastern Europe, Russia and the Successor States*, p.534.

60   FOCUS, *Aktuálne problémy Slovenska po rozpade ČSFR, Október 1993*, pp.6–8.

Part Three

Complex Pluralism

5 Lebanon

The Two Republics

Fida Nasrallah

INTRODUCTION

Lebanon is an Arab Republic situated on the Eastern shore of the Mediterranean. Its population numbers around 3.5 million excluding the approximately 350,000 Palestinian refugees residing on its territory. Its official language is Arabic although French and English are widely spoken.

The ethnic composition of Lebanon is 90 per cent Arab in addition to a sizeable Armenian population, some Kurds and some Jews. The main religions are subdivided into 17 different sects which include: Maronite, Greek Orthodox, Greek Catholic (Melchites), Armenian Orthodox, Armenian Catholic, Protestants (Evangelists), Syrian Orthodox, Syrian Catholic, Latins, Assyrians, Chaldaens, Nestorians, Jews, Sunnis, Shi'as, Alawis and Druzes. For political reasons, Lebanon has not had a census since 1932 so no accurate information on the numbers of the various confessions is available.

Lebanon became a Republic in 1926. In its relatively short existence, the first Republic of Lebanon (1926-1990) suffered a series of crises. These crises were the result of internal demands – either for domestic reform and greater participation in the political system, or over matters of foreign policy and greater involvement in regional issues – that clashed with external pressures. The creation of the State of Israel in 1948 had serious repercussions on Lebanon. The first wave of refugees that fled their original homes in Palestine seeking refuge in Lebanon would, in time, have important consequences on the country both by altering the country's confessional balance (most of the refugees were Sunni Muslim) and by involving Lebanon in the Palestinian question.

1958 was also a dramatic year in the history of the modern Lebanese state, when domestic politics fused with regional inter-Arab rivalries and caused a civil war in the country. In 1969, with the signing of the Cairo Agreement which gave Palestinian guerillas freedom to launch a war of liberation against the State of Israel from Lebanese lands, Lebanon's problems became very closely linked with the Palestinian question. The situation became more acute in 1971 when the Palestine Liberation Organisation (PLO) was expelled from Jordan and relocated its headquarters in Beirut. In 1975, domestic calls for greater political participation from one segment of the Lebanese population, coupled with alliances between internal groups and external foreign powers, had a heavy toll on the Lebanese system and caused its collapse. April 1975 marked the beginning of what came to be known as the 'Lebanese civil war', a war which lasted 15 years until the second Republic of Lebanon was officially proclaimed in September 1990. This was the date when the Lebanese Parliament amended the Constitution and incorporated reforms to the political system. Lebanon's new Constitution was based on the controversial Charter of National Reconciliation, a document drafted by foreign powers but signed by Lebanese Members of Parliament in the Saudi city of Ta'if in September 1989. This Charter is more popularly known as the Ta'if Accord.

HISTORICAL BACKGROUND

The year 1514 marked the transition from Persian to Ottoman rule and the fall of the Arab world under the Ottoman Empire for approximately 400 years. At that time the principality (*Imarah*) of Mount Lebanon was under the rule of its local chief, Emir Fakhreddine I, a member of the Ma'ni dynasty. His supremacy was recognised by the victorious Ottoman Sultan Salim who conferred upon him the title 'lord of the land'.[1] In 1696 the leadership of the principality of Mount Lebanon fell into the hands of the Shihabi dynasty until the collapse of the principality in 1841.

Under Ma'ni rule, the Maronites (a monotheistic Christian sect) and the Druzes (initially an offshoot sect of Ismaili Shi'i Islam who have come to be considered as a separate religion), the principal inhabitants of the Mountain, co-existed and co-operated. Although co-existence was mainly confined to the leaders of the two sects, and co-operation restricted to military and political matters[2] there nevertheless prevailed a desire to live together – 'the nearest known approximation of a social contract'.[3] And it was this type of co-operation and collaboration that was the prime factor that ensured the viability of the principality.

In 1788 Bashir al-Shihabi II acceded to power. Under his rule, co-operation and collaboration between the two major sects foundered. Bashir's policies exacerbated Maronite-Druze relations and civil war erupted in 1841. The principality was abolished and, under the weight of European intervention and internal resistance, Mount Lebanon was partitioned into two administrative districts and the Dual Governorate of Mount Lebanon *(Nizam al-Qa'immaqamiyyatayn)* was created.

Under this system, the northern district was placed under the rule of a Maronite Governor and the southern district under a Druze Governor. But since neither district was homogeneous, this settled little. In 1845, following more civil unrest, a new settlement was negotiated by the Ottoman authorities. This settlement stipulated that the Governor would be advised by a 5-member Council comprising a Sunni, a Maronite, a Druze, a Greek Catholic, and a Greek Orthodox. Since the Ottomans did not recognise the Shi'as as a separate sect, the latter were represented by the Sunnis. The implications of the new settlement for Lebanon were far-reaching. It created, for the first time in the history of Mount Lebanon, an institution that was based on the formal representation of the religious communities.

The partition of the Mountain lasted 15 years when, in 1860, another, fiercer civil war broke out.[4] This war ended in 1861 when the five Great European powers proclaimed a new statute for the Mountain (the Reglement Organique) which turned Mount Lebanon into an autonomous Province *(Sanjak)* of the Ottoman Empire whose status the Powers guaranteed. The Governorate of Mount Lebanon, known as the *Mutasarrifiyya* was thus created. The new statute stipulated that Lebanon would be governed by a non-Lebanese Christian Governor and established an Administrative Council that would represent all the religious communities. Initially, all communities were to be represented equally regardless of their numerical importance. But in 1864 the Reglement Organique was amended and a system of quasi-proportional representation was introduced. The additional factor of demographic strength was to operate alongside communal representation. The Reglement Organique became the Constitution of Mount Lebanon remaining in effect until the Great War.[5]

The *Mutasarrifiyya* was a considerably reduced version of the old principality – the justification given was to render its population more homogeneous.[6] This territorial reduction of Mount Lebanon became a source of discontent although the new system had many benefits. Under it Lebanon acquired the basis for its modern administration. Political experience bred political ambitions and, for the Christians in general and the Maronites in particular, minimal autonomy under an Ottoman Governor was no longer sufficient. They wanted self government and sought independence.[7]

LEBANESE IDENTITY AND THE MODERN STATE

Perhaps the most important development that occurred under the *Mutasarrifiyya* was the cultural awakening that took place in the Mountain. The mostly Christian inhabitants of Mount Lebanon, educated by Western missionaries and in Western schools, developed a different approach to the West from that of the mostly Muslim inhabitants living outside the *Mutasarrifiyya*. They also developed a feeling of distinctiveness and a distinct Lebanese identity.[8] 'The establishment of the Mutasarrifiyya of Mount Lebanon gave the Lebanese identity ... a legal definition. To be Lebanese was to enjoy citizenship in the Mutasarrifiyya and the various privileges that went with it'.[9]

But the cultural awakening that was taking place in the Mountain did not assume identical forms inside and outside the *Mutasarrifiyya*. The Christians and Muslims residing outside the *Mutasarrifiyya* had a different education and different traditions. They were sent to schools which taught in the Arabic language, with an emphasis on Arabic culture and heritage and a strong penchant towards Islam. They too developed a cultural awakening but of a different kind – an Arab awakening.

This Arab awakening was Christian inspired. The Christian inhabitants of the territories lying outside the *Mutasarrifiyya* sought to create, with their Muslim colleagues, an independent, secular Arab state separate from the Ottoman Empire. But the Muslims did not share the same goal and considered the creation of an independent secular state as both impossible and undesirable.[10] What they wanted, in contrast, was to reform the existing administration and demand more political and civil rights so as to strengthen the Empire and return to pure Islam and Muslim institutions.[11]

In the crucial years that followed, there developed a schism between Arab nationalists and Lebanese nationalists. The former wanted the formation of an Arab Empire with Muslim overlordship which, to the Christians, constituted no great change from Ottoman Muslim rule; the latter called for a separate Lebanese state where Christian rights would be guaranteed and where compromises would not have to be made.[12] This schism proved to be the most pervasive source of tension in Lebanese society surviving well into the creation of the modern Lebanese state.

The Republic of Lebanon, the present Lebanese state, came into being at the end of the first World War with the collapse of the Ottoman Empire. As a result of the Paris Peace Conference of 1919, the state of Greater Lebanon was proclaimed in 1920. Greater Lebanon became the first Republic of Lebanon after obtaining its own Constitution in 1926.

The state of Greater Lebanon was formed by adding to the territory of Mount Lebanon a number of districts that had been under direct Ottoman rule. The autonomous Governorate was enlarged so as to render the newly created independent state economically more viable. The districts that were annexed to the new state included Tripoli, Sidon, Tyre, Beirut and Baalbeck, as well as the fertile Bekaa valley. Greater Lebanon was mandated to France under the League of Nations.

But with the enlargement of the province of Mount Lebanon into the state of Greater Lebanon came a loss in social cohesion.[13] Even though the addition of the new territories almost doubled the size of the former Province, it also increased its Muslim population. Consequently, the clear majority which the Christians had enjoyed in Mount Lebanon was almost wiped out by the extension of its frontiers into Greater Lebanon.

THE FIRST REPUBLIC

A Lack of Consensus

Despite the loss of their overall majority, the creation of Greater Lebanon was a political victory for the Maronites. They regarded the new entity as primarily a Christian country in the Arab world, pro-Western and Christian in orientation. Situated as it was, it would naturally cultivate friendly ties with its Arab neighbours. However, it would remain independent and would not be incorporated into any other Arab country.

The creation of the modern Lebanese state was not welcomed by the populations of the newly annexed territories. In fact it aroused much hostility and opposition from various sects – from the Sunnis in Beirut, the Shi'as in Tyre and the Bekaa, the Druzes in the Chouf, and some of the Greek Orthodox and Protestant communities of Beirut.

For the Sunnis, the creation of Greater Lebanon dealt a fatal blow to the dream of unification into an Arab Nation (*Ummah*). They resented being merely a community amongst many others in an independent Lebanese state rather than being part of the dominant community in a single Arab state. Not sharing the feelings of distinctiveness, of Lebanese identity, that flourished in the Mountain they saw no reason for the creation of a separate and independent Lebanese state. They did not feel that Lebanon possessed social or cultural traits of its own that differentiated it from the rest of the Arab countries. Consequently, they felt that the country had no reason to exist on its own and that it ought to have been incorporated into a larger Arab or Syrian state. They considered Lebanon's existence as temporary, until the final goal of unification could be achieved.[14]

The Druzes (although they had been one of the two dominant communities in Mount Lebanon) were equally unhappy with an independent Lebanon. They feared that the state of Greater Lebanon meant a Maronite country under Maronite hegemony. Under such circumstances they preferred that Lebanon be incorporated into a larger Arab state even if that meant Sunni rule. Sunni Muslim overlordship was considered the lesser of two evils.

The Shi'as were also opposed to the creation of the modern state. A heterodox Muslim sect, they had always viewed the Sunnis with suspicion and had always wanted for themselves the official status of a separate community, independent of the Sunnis. Even though separate status had been denied them by the Ottoman authorities, they had nevertheless enjoyed some measure of autonomy in Jabal 'Amil. They figured that this autonomy would be safeguarded by an Arab government, whereas it was not certain that it would survive under Christian rule. Thus they too were opposed to becoming part of a Christian-led Lebanon under French protection.

Some Christians, too, were opposed to the creation of an independent Lebanese state. The Greek Orthodox community itself was split. Those who had been living in the Kourah district of Mount Lebanon and had been part of the autonomous Province sympathised with the Maronites and their allegiance went to an independent Lebanon. But the majority of the rich and important members of that community living in Beirut, although they too feared Muslim rule, were equally suspicious of Maronite Catholic supremacy, so they supported union with Syria. So did the Protestants of Beirut who had always had pro-Arab leanings, and unification with Syria was deemed preferable to Maronite hegemony.[15]

Muslim unhappiness with the creation of an independent Lebanese state initially led to resistance against it, a refusal to accept it, and demands that it be incorporated into Syria. In the first decade and a half after the creation of the state when the country was still under the French Mandate, the Muslims boycotted state institutions refusing to participate in Lebanese political life.

But with the consolidation of political and administrative institutions came a grudging Muslim acceptance of the state. They realised the importance of participating in the public service, since their boycott had resulted in a mostly Christian civil service. They realised the advantages available to them through active co-operation in the affairs of the Lebanese state. Their desire for incorporation into a greater Arab state had still not withered away. However they were equally aware that unification could only come about with the consent of their Christian compatriots.

The Search for a Common Identity

By successfully enlarging the autonomous Province into Greater Lebanon, the Maronites succeeded in creating a state. The challenge was to create a nation, to devise a mythology for the young emerging country. To create a nation, it was essential to create a common Lebanese identity. It was also essential to create a viable political association from the array of heterogeneous communities divided in terms of religion, culture, wealth, traditions and customs.

A national image therefore had to be cultivated – if not invented. One attempt was made by Michel Chiha, a Greek Catholic banker from Beirut who was the main architect of the Lebanese Constitution. Chiha sought a Lebanese common denominator to unify this heterogeneous society and returned Lebanon to its ancient past. In his attempt to dissociate Lebanon from any Islamic or Arab links, he cultivated the myth that Lebanon was the modern version of ancient Phoenicia and that the Lebanese, therefore, were not Arabs but Phoenicians.[16] Chiha emphasised the uniqueness of Lebanon in the Arab East. To him Lebanon was a pluralist multi-confessional society; a society where Christianity and Islam were in a state of equilibrium, a unitary society which could accommodate different religious communities. For Chiha, Lebanon was the only Christian country in Asia.[17]

Chiha's vision and image of Lebanon was unacceptable to the Muslims who rejected the whole concept of Phoenicianism and considered themselves Arabs first. The Muslims also rejected the idea of Lebanon as a unitary society where different religious communities were integrated. They viewed Lebanon as a society where various religious communities, holding different ideologies and political traditions, and hence working at cross purposes, might be able to coexist. They therefore put forward an Arabist ideology. To them, if Lebanon should exist at all, it should not be Christian, but secular. Moreover, Lebanon's connections with Arabism and Islam should not be forgotten or disregarded. Being Arab in speech and tradition, Lebanon should consider itself part of the Arab world 'suffused with a memory of the Arab and therefore Muslim past'. Its identity was Arab, its descent Arab, not Phoenician.[18]

The Islamic overtones associated with Arabism meant that such a conception of Lebanon could not be acceptable to the Christians. Moreover, the idea of Arabism granted supremacy to the unity of the Nation over any state's territorial integrity. Thus if Phoenicianism was rejected by the Muslims because it disregarded Lebanon's Arab heritage, the Arabist formula was deemed equally unacceptable by the Christians because it jeopardised Lebanon's sovereignty.[19]

Liban asile, Liban refuge was another device to forge a common identity. This new ideology portrayed Lebanon as a haven – a protectorate for persecuted minorities. Ideas such as these were cultivated and made the basis for a Lebanese national identity. Circulated by Pere Lammens, they had potential amongst Christians, Druzes, and Shi'as alike but not amongst the Sunnis: this ideology 'was considered hardly complimentary ... to the Sunni Muslims ... who were presumed to have been, historically, the persecutors and oppressors'.[20]

In 1943 an attempt was made to overcome the lack of consensus about Lebanon's identity through a 'gentlemen's agreement' known as the National Pact. The National Pact was a political compromise between the Maronites and the Sunnis in which the Muslims finally accepted the separate independence of Lebanon and in which the Christians conceded that Lebanon had 'an Arab face (*un Liban a visage arabe*). The Christians agreed to renounce Western protection in return for Muslim renunciation of union with Syria or any other Arab entity. Lebanon would retain its cultural links with the West although it would collaborate closely with the Arab states. In inter-Arab conflicts Lebanon would remain neutral.

This compromise over identity was also a compromise over power-sharing. All the communities would participate in the exercise of power although the highest echelons of the state would go to the two major communities – the Maronites would get the office of the Presidency of the Republic and the Sunnis would get the Premiership. Cabinet posts and positions in the civil service would be distributed on a confessional basis. Parliamentary seats would be divided on a 5:6 ratio in favour of the Christians. This ratio was calculated on the basis of the 1932 census which had then given the Christians a slight majority.[21]

It was hoped that this compromise over identity and agreement on power-sharing would herald the creation of a true multi-confessional pluralistic nation. But this compromise did not satisfy everyone in Lebanon and Arab nationalists remained singularly unconvinced since the Pact did not envisage outright involvement with an Arab national destiny. They did not feel that the National Pact constituted a long-term solution to the problem of identity because its outlines were too broad and unspecific. The compromise boiled the issue down to the main common denominator leaving all other questions unanswered[22].

Many decades were to pass before the issue of Lebanon's identity would finally be settled and it was not resolved through the creation of a common vision or an established interpretation. That Lebanon was *Arab* was first conceded in 1983, 8 years after the beginning of the Lebanese 'civil war' at a meeting in Geneva amongst the contending factions. That Lebanon's identity was Arab *and* that it was the *definitive* state of all the Lebanese was conceded in the Charter of National Reconciliation signed in September 1989. This document was the compromise that finally put an end to the fighting in Lebanon. Amongst other things, it reformed the 1943 confessional system and formed the basis of the second Lebanese Republic.

In the final analysis, Lebanon as an independent state acquired its legitimacy amongst the entire population simply by its very existence over seventy years. That alone is its justification. Thus 'the Lebanese have become Lebanese simply by the process of living together and sharing in a common national life ... [for over half a century]. While the search for a historical and philosophical basis for Lebanon's nationality continues, it is in the main, by the day-to-day process of being Lebanese that the people of Lebanon [have] becom[e] more and more ... a nation'.[23]

The Creation of a 'Lebanese' System

Chiha's political philosophy, in contrast to his vision of a Lebanese identity, made a lasting contribution to Lebanon's political institutions. Chiha sought to devise a stable system based on constants such as history, geography, the environment and the legacy of the past rather than on ideology. His aim was to devise a system that would ensure the survival of the precarious state in a hostile environment, surrounded as Lebanon was by two belligerent neighbours, Israel and Syria – the latter believing in the geographic indivisibility of Lebanon and Syria. It was essential to formulate a stable yet adaptable system – a system capable of accommodating external demands without losing its character.

Internally, what was needed was a political system which could accommodate the realities of religious and sectarian differences. This is why it was decided to adopt a plural, liberal and open system – a system designed to promote individuality yet able to accommodate contending ideologies; a system designed to encourage the society's heterogeneity, originality and cultural variety. It was hoped that under such a system these different communities, free from the pressure for forceful assimilation by the state, would work together to strengthen that very state which safeguarded their rights and guaranteed their individualism.

Lebanon's external policy was designed primarily to protect its independence. This required a policy which kept up the country's reliance on the West while remaining on friendly terms with the Arab states. An open economic system with minimum taxation was adopted to enable Lebanon's citizens to be materially better off than their neighbours. The rationale for such a system was that it would discourage them from calling for the adoption of modes of political rule similar to those in other Arab states. No attempt at cultural or social integration was even contemplated since it was perceived that such a policy might breed rebellion and work against a feeling of solidarity and national unity.[24] In foreign affairs, neutrality was seen to be the best role that Lebanon could play. Lebanon could best serve the Arab world in general and the Palestinian question in particular by remaining above inter-Arab rivalries.

Being an 'association of confessional minorities', Lebanon had therefore to maintain itself in a constant state of equilibrium. This equilibrium could only be reached through national representation.[25] The objective of Lebanon's political institutions, therefore, was to forge a feeling of solidarity amongst its communities. By working together, it was hoped that the country's opposing factions could develop a feeling of 'a national public spirit which, in the absence of homogeneity, would at least permit agreement on essentials'.[26]

Parliamentary representation was the answer. It was the only system able to accommodate heterogeneity yet guarantee the various communities a voice and participation in power. Parliament's role was to be 'the meeting place of confessional minorities which form the state'.[27] It would function as the country's political integrator – the place where communal differences were overcome and a denominator common to all was found. Parliament was to achieve its integrative objective primarily through its legislative power.[28] It provided a means by which the new emerging middle class could seek power without having to replace the traditional feudal families. Geographically, it became a forum where different parts of the country, having different allegiances and loyalties, could meet and map out a common programme.

DEMOCRACY 'LEBANESE STYLE'

Institutions

A multi-confessional and heterogeneous state lacking a shared political culture and living in a hostile environment could preserve its delicate existence only through stability and the maintenance of the *status quo*. Lebanon's fragmented body politic could solely be maintained through a complex balance-of-power among the various communities and this balance could only be exercised through representative institutions that would act as the guarantor of its stability.

Democracy in Lebanon was not a typical Western-style popular democracy but a confessional one: the proportional distribution of parliamentary seats amongst its multiple *confessions* – the official groups which the country recognises – as a guarantee that their minimum interests could be defended.[29] Confessionalism was adopted as a temporary institution and 'with great reluctance'; yet it was felt that the country could not reject confessional representation as it was still suffused with a confessional spirit and it was easier to accommodate confessional allegiance than forcefully to reject it. Solidarity between the different communities was not yet sufficiently strong to enable political confessionalism to be eliminated.[30]

Under the first Republic, Lebanon's was neither a strictly parliamentary system nor a purely presidential one. It was a presidential Republic where Parliament was elected directly by the people every four years and the President elected by Parliament for a period of six years. The President could not seek immediate re-election without a constitutional amendment. The Prime Minister and the ministers were designated by the President after consultation with Parliament. They constituted a Cabinet responsible to Parliament.

The Lebanese system under the first Republic was designed to render the executive branch much stronger than the legislative. In fact the President was vested with exceptionally great powers and prerogatives. Nevertheless, the system remained strongly parliamentary in the sense that its major concern lay in ensuring that all the communities were represented in proportion to their demographic importance. Moreover, confessionalism imposed the adoption of certain procedures which were strictly parliamentarian and hence conferred upon the system its special parliamentary character.[31]

The Electoral System

Lebanon's complex electoral system was also designed to ensure proportional representation of the various regions as well as of the multiple religious communities residing in these regions. Thus each district was assigned a fixed number of seats which were then distributed among the various sects to which the electors of that particular district belonged.

Since Article 7 of the Constitution of 1926 stipulated that each deputy was 'supposed to represent the entire nation', the system, which was a list system, obliged the voter to vote for the entire list of candidates for his or her district. The candidates themselves belonged to various sects. In this manner, any one representative was not answerable solely to the voter of his or her own faith but to all the electors of his or her district. This meant that one of several minority sects may hold veto power over the candidates of the majority sect.[32] However, it was possible to replace the name of one candidate on the list by the name of another candidate from another list provided they both belonged to the same sect. This method, known as *tashteeb*, was designed to replace inter-sectarian competition with intra-sectarian competition.

The process of districting was another important legal loophole. Conflicts arose over the advantages of large districts with their long ballots and small districts with their short ballots. The procedures for districting and re-districting were guided, in principle, by the desire to ensure better representation and create homogeneity.

The Power of the Executive

'We emerged from the first World War miraculously unscathed albeit bruised, with no homogeneous public opinion, without any organised political parties, divided amongst communities, ... weakened by clan rivalries, subjugated by the influence of the notables, and above all, needing to confront, with considerable urgency, the difficulties of independence. With whom could we entrust power? With a juvenile Parliament? We opted instead for the President of the Republic'.[33]

The weakness inherent in Parliament led to the creation of an alternative organ known as the Council of Ministers (the Cabinet) that would guarantee greater representation and efficiency. Executive power was placed in the hands of the President who shared his powers with this Cabinet.

The confessional and geographic constraints which applied to the choice of the members of Parliament also applied to the choice of the members of the Cabinet, even though the Cabinet itself was divided equally between Christians and Muslims. The Cabinet therefore represented the various communities on the executive level. One advantage which the Cabinet enjoyed over Parliament, however, was the fact that its deliberations were secret, so issues considered taboo in Parliament (communitarian questions, contending Christian and Muslim viewpoints, Arabism, Lebanese nationalism, etc.) were debated in the Cabinet.[34] But such debates usually ended up in a stalemate and decisions were rarely made. And since Ministers were unlikely to be sacked (because of the geographic, sectarian, economic, ideological and personal interests involved), they became disloyal and indiscreet.

The structural weakness inherent in Parliament and the government meant that ultimate power rested in the hands of the President who was not responsible to the Chamber. Presidential powers included the right to participate in the formulation of laws; to amend the Constitution; to veto bills; to dissolve the Chamber; to appoint and dismiss the Prime Minister and his Ministers; to negotiate and ratify treaties; etc. But the President also acted as a balancer of power and his role consisted mainly in playing the judicious and active arbiter, in conciliating the multiple and often contradictory interests of such a divided country, and in guaranteeing the stability of its institutions. However, the President had always to take into consideration the attitudes and interests of extra-parliamentary influential leaders such as the Maronite Patriarch; the President also had to cater to the needs of important business groups and of paramilitary forces. He always had to engage in balance-of-power politics in order to obtain consensus. Neglect of any segment might lead to open rebellion and the subsequent breakdown of the system.[35]

THE SYSTEM AND ITS SUCCESS

It is difficult to argue that the Lebanese system was successful in the light of the conflict that erupted in 1975 and was to last 15 years. Yet it is equally difficult to pin-point one single reason which led to the breakdown of the system and therefore to conclude that the demise of the system was due solely to inherent structural problems. Indeed, whether the blame lies on the political institutions or on foreign involvement remains open to debate. There is a strong case for arguing that the young Lebanese political system could have succeeded in accommodating domestic pressures and demands for reform without the need to resort to violence in the absence of the involvement of external forces.

Inherent Difficulties

Whichever factor one wishes to emphasise as constituting the root cause for the break-up of the Lebanese state, one thing is clear: the system itself did have some structural flaws that made it amenable to outside pressures.

One flaw resided in the dualistic nature of the executive branch in Lebanon – the power-sharing formula between a Maronite President and a Sunni Prime Minister. The fact that the executive branch was a duumvirate made the system open to exploitation. In times of crisis, this dualism turned the executive into a bicephalous body and the consequences of this bicephalism affected Lebanon's national unity, its Arab foreign policy and its relations with the various Arab states. However, the nature of the executive branch notwithstanding, it is important to keep in mind that the existence of a dualistic parliamentary regime in Lebanon in the midst of a region where strong presidential authoritarian systems were (and still are) the norm put Lebanon *a priori* at a disadvantage and made it vulnerable to the external environment.[36]

The electoral law and the problems associated with districting and electoral lists was another inherent structural difficulty. The argument in favour of a large district was that it would always contain a variety of important sects making it impossible for one sect to predominate over another in a long ballot. But large districts had two disadvantages: they alienated the voters from the candidate and made it easier for the regional feudal chief or a rich rural proprietor to gain an edge over the other candidates. Even though this risk was decreased in a small district with a correspondingly short list, a short list accentuated sectarian sentiments due to homogeneity of a small district. In such cases, the candidate counted on the votes of his or her co-religionists so inter-community co-operation was neither needed nor encouraged.[37]

The list system also made the choice of candidates very difficult. Only a moderate and compromising candidate was appropriate, and very frequently his or her views were so middle-of-the-road that they no longer spoke for their community. The result was that members of Parliament ended up representing neither their community nor the nation. Under such conditions, Parliament ceased to be a representative institution thereby defeating the original purpose for which it was created.[38]

Lebanon's confessional system made it particularly difficult for political parties, particularly ideological ones, to function (even though the role of political parties in Lebanese political life has always been marginal). Political parties could not guarantee that the integrity of the list would be respected – given the freedom enjoyed by the voters with their right to *tashteeb*; and those with an ideology had to alter their programme considerably if they were to be able to join a list. They therefore had to choose between alienating their followers or undermining their chances of being elected.[39]

Moreover, the emphasis on stability and moderation also meant that membership in Parliament remained restricted to those who wished to maintain the *status quo*. In addition, districting was seldom motivated by the desire for more homogeneity and greater representation and often enabled the leading *za'ims* (patrons) to recruit the largest number of their supporters to Parliament.[40] The nature of its composition made it such that Parliament effectively avoided discussing matters of a confessional nature. As a political institution, therefore, it was unable to resolve the communities' fundamental problems. Ideological conflicts were kept at bay lest they destroy the country's political institutions.

It can also be argued that the bases on which the Lebanese economy rested contributed to the country's instability. Being neither an agricultural nor an industrial country, Lebanon's economy was one which was based on the services sector, on tourism and trade, particularly with its Arab partners. This policy became a source of the country's weakness because it became susceptible to the vicissitudes of all the other states. The country's dependence on Arab markets, on Arab tourists, and on the Arab countries in general to host its emigrant population, made Lebanon susceptible to Arab and international economic and political pressure.[41]

Lebanon's foreign policy orientation also became a source of instability, particularly since it was so closely tied to its crisis of identity. The Lebanese ideology of neutrality in foreign affairs made no provisions for 'participation', that is, for active involvement in the Arab-Israeli question out of a sense of Arab solidarity. Neutrality bred instability as Lebanon's Muslim population could not tolerate being dissociated from the problems of the Arab world. This part wanted participation, and with that, the country's independence was jeopardised.

The absence of a firmly established national identity made it possible for Arab states and Western powers to play upon inherent contradictions to further their interests. This process was facilitated by the fact that different sects, at different times, sought help from foreign countries to improve their internal situation. For example, the cultural and political identification of Lebanon's Sunni Muslim population with the Arab countries – an identification which also sought to promote their power in Lebanon – paved the way for greater Arab intervention. Arab identification meant that Lebanon had to adopt policies in line with the policies of the Arab states. This clashed with the political identification of the Maronite Christians who preferred to look to

the West in general and to France in particular. Thus sectarian cleavages '...
transformed Lebanon into a battlefield where Lebanese factions, often
unknowingly, ... fought the undeclared wars of other nations by proxy'.[42]

The communal nature of Lebanese society was also a factor that weakened
the state, particularly since community and family loyalties transcended state
loyalty. Communal loyalties cast doubt on the state's legitimacy and
contributed to the fragility of the state's institutions.

Demands for Reform

Demands for reform under the first republic addressed many issues. One
issue was the inequality in power between the Maronite President and the
Sunni Prime Minister prompting Sunni demands for a more influential role.
Another was the confessional nature of the system itself. Indeed, in matters
of power-sharing, the confessional political formula made no provisions for
demographic change. Thus other communities in Lebanon became
increasingly disillusioned with the Maronite-Sunni duumvirate because this
formula barred them from attaining the most powerful offices of the state.
The Druzes and the Shi'as were a case in point, the latter believing themselves
to be the largest Muslim community. As a result they called for a review of
the division of offices and the confessional system became the target,
particularly since some positions (such as the Chief-of-Staff of the Army,
the Governor of the Central Bank, the Director of Military Intelligence and
State Security) were considered to be the 'preserve' of the Maronite
community.

This call for reform resulted in claims by some for the complete
secularisation of state and society. What this meant in practice was the
abolition of the jurisdiction of the religious communities, the extension of
civil law to cover personal matters, issues of family and inheritance, and the
suppression of the proportional representation of confessions in political office
as well as the scrapping of the quota system in the civil service. These claims
were put forward by some Christian and leftist political parties. Total
secularisation, however, was unacceptable to the Muslims, both Sunni and
Shi'a alike, because it threatened their status as a pure Muslim community.
Instead, the Shi'as called for the 'abolition of political sectarianism' which
meant simply the suppression of the Lebanese system of proportional
representation and the removal of the quota system in the civil service whilst
retaining the jurisdiction of the religious communities. This demand was
rejected by the Christians because it implied a diminution of their status to

that of a tolerated minority in an Islamic state.

Other demands for reform concerned the confessional distribution of seats in Parliament; the holding of a new census and the conditions under which it would be conducted; and the allocation of seats in the civil service with the Muslims demanding the imposition of a quota system based on the principle of collective justice and the Christians stressing the advantages of a system of merit and competence based on the principle of individual justice.[43] However, this problem was resolved in 1958 by the introduction of a system of strict parity.

THE SECOND REPUBLIC

In September, 1990 the 'civil war' that erupted in Lebanon in 1975 officially came to an end. This date coincides with the ratification, by the Lebanese Parliament, of the Charter of National Reconciliation which forms the basis of the Second Republic.

The causes of the 1975 war were many. They were an amalgamation of domestic difficulties exacerbated by regional and international interventions. The war passed through many phases, and involved a large array of protagonists that changed over time. The development of the war in Lebanon was very closely linked to developments in the Arab-Israeli question; it was also tied to superpower politics and the Cold War.

The war in Lebanon ended for a variety of reasons. By 1990 the Cold War was at an end. Syria was eager to improve its relations with the one remaining superpower, the United States, which involved a change in orientation. The United States itself was eager to reap the benefits of a rapprochement with Syria in order to broker an Arab-Israeli peace of its own making. The timing of the Gulf crisis, and the subsequent Gulf war, was equally opportune. As a *quid pro quo* for Damascus' joining the alliance against Iraq, the US had to make concessions to Syria over Lebanon. The Charter for National Reconciliation was therefore internationally and regionally endorsed and the fighting in Lebanon came to an end. Having achieved its hegemonic aims through the imposition of a political accord of its own making, Syria no longer saw it in its interests to perpetuate the war in Lebanon.

The war ended when all domestic opposition to the Charter of National Reconciliation was eliminated. It ended because the warring factions had exhausted their supply of external allies. Equally, the population was physically and morally exhausted after one and a half decades of war. The war in Lebanon ended with Lebanon remaining united. The country's sovereignty, on the other hand, remained fractured; its territorial integrity, compromised.

THE 'NEW' SYSTEM

It is ironic that what became known as the phenomenon of 'lebanonisation' – the break-up of states – did not, in the final analysis, apply to Lebanon. Whether by common consent or bowing to external pressures, Lebanon was put back together again and opted for unification.

The Charter for National Reconciliation, which was a practical translation of this unification option, was divided into four sections: the first dealt with domestic reforms; the second with the restoration of Lebanese sovereignty over all of Lebanon's territory; the third with the liberation of southern Lebanon from the Israeli occupation; and the fourth with creating 'privileged relations' with Syria.[44]

The section dealing with the domestic reforms is what concerns us here. Despite some alterations to the 1943 system, the Ta'if document retained the traditional division of power: the President would remain a Maronite, the Prime Minister a Sunni, and the Speaker of Parliament a Shi'i. However, the powers of the President were reduced to virtually a ceremonial role. Although he remains Supreme Commander of the Armed Forces and Chairman of the Defence Council, he is bound by Cabinet decisions. Chairing Cabinet sessions is no longer his prerogative by right, although he could still do so if he so chose, without, however, having the power to vote.[45] Although he can still appoint the Prime Minister, after obligatory consultations with Parliament, he cannot dismiss him. The President no longer heads the executive; executive powers now reside in the Council of Ministers. Moreover, Presidential decisions now require the co-signature of the Prime Minister except when appointing the Premier and upon accepting the government's resignation. In contrast, the powers of the President of the Council – the Sunni Prime Minister – are greatly increased. The Premier, by right, chairs the cabinet sessions and he alone is responsible for implementing the decisions of the Council of Ministers. The President of the Council can only be dismissed by Parliament.

Supreme executive power thus rests in the hands of the government as a collective body. The introduction of bills is exclusively its prerogative. It oversees the implementation of laws, controls the administration, and appoints civil servants. A separate seat of government for the Council of Ministers was created – distinct from those of the President and the Prime Minister.

Cabinet decisions are to be taken by consensus (in Arabic the term used is *tawafuqiyyan*; the French equivalent is *par concordance*). When consensus is impossible, decisions on 'issues of vital concern' require a two-thirds majority. These 'vital concerns' include general mobilisation, declaration of war and conclusion of peace, international treaties, the budget, long-term development plans, the appointment of senior civil servants, administrative reform, the dissolution of Parliament, the electoral law, the law on nationality, laws on personal status and the dismissal of ministers.

The role of the Speaker of Parliament is also enhanced. His term is extended from two to four years and any premature dismissal (effective after two years) requires a two-thirds majority. His duties as President of the Chamber of Deputies give him very strong powers: he is consulted by the President before the latter nominates a Prime Minister and by the Deputies before they elect a President. Parliament itself is increased from 99 deputies to 108 (subsequently expanded to 128) on the basis of parity between the Christians and Muslims. The Ta'if reforms also mention the creation of a Senate, after the election of the first non-confessional Parliament. However, it remained clear that as long as deconfessionalisation did not take place, Parliament would be elected on a confessional basis.

A NEW CONSENSUS?

The Ta'if reforms retained the 1943 confessional formula and basically redistributed power. The implication of retaining the old system meant that the new Lebanese consensus rested in the retention of Lebanon's confessional formula. The Ta'if reforms failed to introduce a totally new system of government.

Whilst some erstwhile problems such as those relating to the question of identity and the acceptance of the state are no longer an issue, other, more fundamental problems remain. Indeed what is still to be determined is the type of state that the Lebanese of all denominations actually want. Even though Lebanese leaders have once again settled for some form of consociationalism, some movements and political parties are sceptical of the ability of the new system to survive, and may still harbour alternative visions for the future of Lebanon.

One such vision propagated by the more hard-line Christians, is for a federal Lebanon. They believe that such a solution would allow all the Lebanese communities to retain their individualism. But questions remain as to the viability of this option knowing that foreign policy would rest in the hands of the federal government and that many of the problems of the first Republic had actually revolved around questions of foreign policy. Even though some issues deemed contentious in the past have either disappeared or have changed, it is doubtful that a federal government would be able to resolve them if disagreements over foreign policy were to reappear in another form. One answer, of course, would be neutralisation. But for neutralisation to happen its status would have to be guaranteed by the powers concerned and it is doubtful whether the two belligerent powers surrounding Lebanon would find it in their interest to give such a guarantee. And judging by their actions and their attitudes in the recent past, it is equally unlikely that either the United States or France would be prepared to offer such a guarantee.

But more importantly, federalism, dubbed as partition by its opponents, was never and can never be a realistic option. Attempts to homogenise certain areas in Lebanon, initiated by the Christian militias but subsequently adopted by all the rest, were perceived by Syria as part of a grander strategy for partition and elicited unambiguous statements from the then Syrian Foreign Minister Mr Abdel Halim Khaddam: 'We shall not allow Lebanon to be divided. Any such step would necessitate our immediate intervention. Lebanon was part of Syria [sic!] and we shall reclaim it as soon as it actually attempts to split up ... Lebanon should either be a single state or else it should return to Syria'.[46]

The federal option was therefore dismissed and the consociational model was reaffirmed. The Ta'if reforms altered the powers of the most important organs of the State and the division of power amongst the various communities. The Accord renewed the contract amongst the communities – although it still aspired towards the ultimate abolition of the confessional system even though no timetable was put in place.

Despite the changes that were introduced by the Ta'if Accord it nevertheless did not satisfy everyone. The 'new' domestic formula was criticised by the Druzes because it merely revived the confessional system; it was also criticised by some Shi'as for failing to introduce a democracy based on numbers; it was denounced by the more hard-line Shi'i groups for failing to establish an Islamic state in Lebanon; it was criticised by the Maronites because it stripped them of their privileges. The Ta'if Accord was also rejected by those who opposed conceding to Syria any undue influence in Lebanon.[47]

Whatever the Ta'if reforms proposed in theory, in practice they resulted in the creation of a *de facto* tricephalous body. The jockeying for power by each of the three 'presidents' (the president of the Republic, the president of the Chamber and the president of the Council of Ministers) has led to a confusion between the legislative and executive powers. It has also led to immobility. Whilst these frustrations are not liable to re-ignite the war, they do not perpetuate an image of a working or workable system and it is difficult to predict how long the system will be able to survive without a radical overhaul.

Whatever the Ta'if reforms proposed in theory, the manner in which these reforms have been implemented has led to a high degree of resentment by the population. The conduct of the 1992 parliamentary elections, which were boycotted by most Christians and many Muslims, was at best flawed and did not provide a solid basis for national reconciliation. The whole electoral exercise produced a feeling of disillusion, particularly on the part of the Christian community. Indeed the boyvott resulted in the marginalisation of most of the Christian leadership. It was thus believed that such disillusion could be redressed by participating in the parliamentary elections of 1996. But the 1996 elections were as flawed as those of 1992 and the Christian opposition found itself divided, adding to the community's disenchantment, even though morale was temporarily lifted following the visit of Pope John Paul II in May 1997.

Christian disillusion can also be attributed to the selective and partial implementation of the Ta'if Agreement. Whereas the Christian militias have been disarmed, other militias (namely the Shi'i militia Hizballah) are allowed to operate under the guise of a 'movement of national liberation' aimed at liberating southern Lebanon from the Israeli occupation. Whereas one of the Christian militia leaders has been tried and sentenced to life imprisonment, other militia leaders have been rewarded with the highest political offices. Thus actions and gestures that could have formed the basis for proper national reconciliation were mishandled, and the opportunity for comprehensive accountability that could have led to a genuine catharsis of Lebanese society was lost.

Christian disenchantment with the new political system is matched by Muslim unhappiness at still being denied the highest office in the land. Equally the Druzes are disillusioned at not having been given a position of power commensurate with their historical role. What they were offered was the leadership of a non-confessional Senate, an offer that is not likely to materialise in the foreseeable future.

The economic policy being vigorously pursued by the post-Ta'if government, and the role it seeks to forge for the Lebanon of the future, is almost identical to the role of the past. The decision that Lebanon should regain the role it once had is open to criticism since it ignores the regional developments of the past fifteen years and the fact that the country no longer possesses the monopoly of financial services that it enjoyed in the past, even though Lebanese entrepreneurs still enjoy considerable business expertise. Moreover, the absence of a social policy and the government's emphasis on large-scale reconstruction projects targeted to the wealthy has created great social unrest in the country. Riots brought the government down in May 1992 but were suppressed by force in July 1995. Economic recovery was further shaken following Israel's 'Grapes of Wrath' operation against Lebanonin April 1996. But the xountry proved very resilient and quickly succeeded in bouncing back.

Thus disillusion with the new system mirrors the old. Even though the first system broke down, arguably under the weight of foreign intervention, the second system was established with the blessing of the main intervening power. The new system has granted Syria uncontested hegemony in Lebanon and the final say in the latter's domestic and foreign policies. Short of a radical change in the nature of the Syrian regime, it is difficult to imagine a change in the conduct of policy under Lebanon's second Republic. As long as policy is conducted in tandem with the interests of Damascus, it is reasonable to conclude that the system in Lebanon will be preserved. By force, if necessary.

NOTES

1 Philip Hitti, *Lebanon in History,* New York, St. Martin's Press, 1967, p. 357; A.J. Abraham, *Lebanon at Mid-Century: Maronite-Druze relation in Lebanon 1840–1860: A Prelude to Arab Nationalism,* New York, University Press of America, 1981, p.28.

2 Kamal S. Salibi, *The Modern History of Lebanon,* New York, Caravan Books, 1977, p.xiv.

3 *Ibid.,* p.xxvii.

4 See Leila Fawaz, *An Occasion for War: Civil Conflict in Lebanon and Damascus in 1860,* Oxford and London, Centre for Lebanese Studies and I.B. Tauris and Co. Ltd., 1994.

5 For an excellent account of the history of Lebanon under the *Mutasarrifiyya* see Engin Akarli, *The Long Peace, Ottoman Lebanon 1861-1920,* Oxford and London, Centre for Lebanese Studies and I.B. Tauris and Co. Ltd., 1993.

6 Henri Lammens, '40 ans d'autonomie au Liban', in *Etudes* 92, 1902, p.36.

7 Kamal Salibi, *Op Cit.*, pp.117–18.
8 John Spagnolo, *France and Ottoman Lebanon 1861–1914*, London, Ithaca Press, 1977, p. 54.
9 Salibi, *op. cit*, p.78.
10 Zeine Zeine, *The Emergence of Arab Nationalism*, Beirut, Khayats, 1966, p.69.
11 *Ibid.*
12 Albert Hourani, 'Middle Eastern Nationalism Yesterday and Today', in Albert Hourani, *The Emergence of the Modern Middle East*, London, Macmillan, 1983, p.186.
13 Philip Hitti, *Lebanon in History*, 3rd edn, London, Macmillan, 1967, pp.490–1.
14 Albert Hourani, *Minorities in the Arab World*, Oxford, Oxford University Press, 1947, p.69.
15 Meir Zamir, *The Formation of Modern Lebanon*, London and Ithaca, Cornell University Press, 1988, pp.120–36.
16 Kamal Salibi, 'The Lebanese Identity' in *Journal of Contemporary History*, Vol.6, No.1, 1971, pp.83–4; Albert Hourani, 'Ideologies of the Mountain and of the City' in Roger Owen (ed.), *Essays on the Crisis in Lebanon*, London, Ithaca Press, 1976, p.38.
17 Hourani, 'Ideologies', p.38.
18 *Ibid.*
19 Kamal Salibi, 'The Lebanese Identity' in *Journal of Contemporary History*, Vol.6, No.1, 1971, p.85.
20 *Ibid.*, pp.85–6.
21 For an analysis of the 1943 National Pact see Farid el-Khazen, *The Communal Pact of National Identities: The Making and Politics of the 1943 National Pact*, Papers on Lebanon No.12, Centre for Lebanese Studies, Oxford, 1991.
21 'Neither Westernization nor Arabization': It is upon this double negative that Christianity and Islam have based their alliance. What kind of unity can one derive from such a formula? It is easy to see what half of the Lebanese do not want. And it is easy to see what the other half do not want. But what the two haves actually both want – that one cannot see' Georges Naccache, 'Deux Negations ne font pas une nation', quoted in David Gilmour, *Lebanon: The Fractured Country*, Oxford, Martin Robertson & Co., 1983, p.53.
22 Salibi, 'The Lebanese Identity', *op.cit.*, p.86.
23 Abdo Baaklini, *Legislative and Political Development in Lebanon, 1842–1972*, Durham, Duke University Press, 1976, pp.107–8.

24 Michel Chiha, _Politique Interieure,_ Beyrouth, 1964, p.81.
25 Jean Salem, _Introduction a la pensee politique de Michel Chiha_ Beyrouth, Librairie Samir, 1970, p.94.
26 Chiha, _op.cit._, p. 202.
27 Baaklini, _op.cit._, p.274; Salem, _op.cit._, p.99.
28 Malcolm Kerr, 'Political Decision-Making in a Confessional Democracy' in Leonard Binder (ed.), _Politics in Lebanon,_ New York, John Wiley & Sons Inc., 1966, p.188.
29 See Pierre Rondot, _Les institutions politiques du Liban,_ Paris, Institut de l'Orient Contemporain, 1947, p.80.
30 Charles Rizk, _Le regime politique libanais,_ Paris, Librairie General de Droit et de Jurisprudence, 1966, p.81.
31 Pierre Rondot, 'Les structures socio-politiques de la nation libanaise' in _Revue Francaise des Sciences Politiques,_ Vol.IV, No.1, January-March 1954, p.94.
32 Antoine Azar, _Le Liban face a demain,_ Beyrouth, Librairie Orientale, 1978, pp.38–9.
33 Rondot, 'The Political Institutions' in Binder, _op. cit._, p.192.
34 See Rizk, op.cit., p. 32; Ralph Crowe, 'Parliament in the Lebanese Political System' in A. Kornberg and L. Musolf (eds), _Legislatures in Developmental Perspectives,_ Durham, Duke University Press, 1970, p.300; Salem, _op.cit._, p.104; Michael Hudson, 'Democracy and Social Mobilization in Lebanese Politics' in _Comparative Politics,_ Vol.1, No.2, January 1969, p.250.
35 Antoine Messarra, _Le modele politique libanais et sa survie,_ Beyrouth, Librairie Orientale, 1983, pp.435-6.
36 See Rizk, _op. cit._; Rondot, 'Les structures' _op. cit._; Baaklini _op. cit._; Fu'ad Chahin, _Al-Ta'ifiyya fi Lubnan: Hadiruha wa Judhuriha al-Tarikhiyya wal-ijtima'iyya,_ Beirut: Dar al-Hawadith, 1980.
37 See Chahin, _op. cit._, p.109; Ralph Crowe, _op. cit._, pp.297–9; Rondot, 'Les structures', _op. cit._, p.96.
38 Baaklini, _op. cit._, p.148.
39 For elaboration on this point, see for example Chahin, _op.cit._, p.109.
40 M.C. Hudson, _The Precarious Republic,_ New York, Random House Inc., 1968, p.95.
41 Maroun Kisrwani, 'Foreign Interference and Religious Animosity in Lebanon' in the _Journal of Contemporary History,_ Vol.15, No.4, October 1980, p.685.
42 Theodor Hanf, _Co-existence in Wartime Lebanon: Decline of a State and Rise of a Nation,_ Oxford and London, Centre for Lebanese Studies

and I.B. Tauris & Co. Ltd, 1993, pp.86–97.

43 For an analysis of the Ta'if agreement see Joseph Maila,*The Document of National Understanding: An Analysis*, Prospects for Lebanon No.4, *The Document of National Understanding, An Analysis*, Oxford and London, Centre for Lebanese Studies, May 1992.

44 Albert Mansour, *Al-inqilab 'ala al-Ta'if*, Beirut, Dar al-Jadid, 1993 p. 48.

45 *Al-Ra'i al-Aam* January 1976.

46 See Fida Nasrallah, 'The Treaty of Brotherhood, Cooperation and Co ordination: An Assessment' in Youssef M. Choueiri (ed.), *State and Society in Syria and Lebanon*, Exeter, University of Exeter Press, 1993, pp.105–11

6 Switzerland*

An Alternative Model

Jonathan Steinberg

Is Switzerland a multinational state? At first glance the answer must seem obvious. If language defines nationality, then a federation of twenty- six little, sovereign republics, where the inhabitants speak four 'national languages' (only three are used officially by the federal government), could hardly be anything else. Against that evidence I am going to argue that Switzerland is not a multinational state in the usual sense of the word but an exceptional historic entity which defies easy categories. Switzerland represents an alternative model of European development in which the national state evolved only very recently.

SWISS IDENTITY IN EUROPE

Let me begin with a few necessary facts. Switzerland is a small country with a population in 1990 of 6, 873, 000 of whom 1, 245,000 are foreigners. From west to east it covers only 350 kilometres and from north to south 250 kilometres. Mountains, lakes, rivers and steep valleys dominate its geography and divide its people into specific, often very different, communities. Of the 4,128,458 hectars of surface area, 2,693,898 are classified as 'Alps, Pre-Alps and Southern Alpine Slopes' or 65.2 per cent of the total surface area. Thirteen important Alpine passes, including the Gotthard, make Switzerland one of the most important way-stations in the European transport system and a land of trade and tourism. Switzerland is among the richest countries in the world by almost every statistical indicator. The Swiss live under a federal system but of an unusual kind. In addition to the federal government with its capital in Bern, there are 26 semi-independent states called 'Cantons' with capitals such as Zurich, Luzern or Geneva and, in addition, 3015 communes or *Gemeinden* which, as we shall see, have their own semi-autonomous status, elected governments and powers to levy taxation. In addition to the usual forms of representative democracy, the Swiss deploy an array of referendums and popular initiatives, which add a plebiscitary element to the institutional mix. Of the resident population, including foreigners, 63.6 per cent speak German, 19.2 per cent speak French, 7.6 per cent speak Italian, 0.6 per cent speak Romansch, and 8.9 per cent are officially classified as speaking 'other' languages (Spanish, Serbo-Croat and Portuguese are the most numerous).[1]

The simple facts as set out show how complex and unusual Swiss reality is. The sense that they are not like other people makes the Swiss feel both superior and uneasily inferior to other states. On the one hand, by comparison with their more homogeneous neighbours like the French, Germans or Italians, they feel somehow abnormal. As a result they describe themselves as a *Sonderfall*, a special case, as if the laws of history and the evolution of national identity had made a detour around the Alps. On the other hand, they do not see themselves as 'multinational'. They use words like 'Mehrsprachigkeit', 'diversité', 'molteplicitá culturale' to describe their peculiar sense of identity. All of them feel 'Swiss' outside Switzerland. As one Swiss put it to me, 'Swissness, which is strong in New York, evaporates in the train from Zurich to Solothurn'.[2] Inside the country they disintegrate into all sorts of micro-identities – cantonal such as Basler, Zürcher, Vaudois, Jurassien or regional like the Italian Swiss who divide into' Sottocenerini' and 'Sopracenerini' [those who live above and those who live below Monte Ceneri] or ultimately into identities as citizens of one of the over 3000 communes.

Outsiders find this hard to understand. There is something unnatural about a country without a proper national identity. Ever since the French Revolution, nationalists of every colour have attempted to seduce or browbeat the three main Swiss linguistic communities to surrender their apparently unnatural allegiance to Switzerland. Nowhere is that more true than the Italian-speaking Canton of Ticino. The Swiss Italian historian, Raffaele Ceschi, cites an anonymous proclamation issued in Milan in 1859 which urged the residents of Ticino to detach themselves from what it called the 'bizarra ed informe federazione elvetica' [the bizarre and shapeless Helvetic Confederation].[3] The fact that Italian Swiss have consistently said no to siren voices from across the border has historical explanations, but such explanations are complicated, not easily expressed in a few words. What remains is the idea that Switzerland is both 'bizarre' and 'shapeless', not natural or organic. The Swiss react to this by citing their determination to remain Swiss, a determination which finds its verbal representation in the phrase 'Willensnation', a 'nation by will'. In this sense the Swiss see themselves not as a multinational entity but as a fragile set of communities held together by a sort of 'volonté générale'. After all, the phrase was invented by Rousseau, who signed his famous work 'Du Contrat Social' simply as 'J.J. Rousseau, citoyen de Genève'.

In recent years, under the mounting pressure of European integration, this sense of specialness has begun to swing from positive to negative. The Swiss passport has become a liability not an asset. As 'non-Europeans' the Swiss have to wait in long queues at airports with the 'others', while the fortunate travellers from the European Union sweep by without further formalities. In European Union countries, young Swiss cannot get work permits or scholarships; they pay foreign not 'home' fees, and Swiss businesses have had to move production beyond their borders to enjoy the full benefits of the common market.

Yet paradoxically, it is 'Europe' which has forced the Swiss to confront their identity problems all over again. Whereas the threats of nationalism, fascism, nazism or communism from outside Switzerland strengthened the determination of the Swiss to remain apart, the threat of Europe is exactly the opposite. The Helvetic Confederation developed its institutions to confront external enemies. Now it is surrounded by friends. Germany, France, Italy and Austria are peaceful, capitalist, bourgeois republics, and all are members of the European Union. The European Union, because it is multi-national and confederal, calls into question, at least as the Swiss now feel it, the need for their special case to survive.

On 17 January 1989, Jacques Delors offered an apparent solution to the Swiss identity crisis. He proposed in a speech to the European parliament in Strasbourg a 'structured partnership with common decision-making and administrative institutions' for the members of the European Free Trade Area (EFTA).[4] The Swiss as members of EFTA began to negotiate a new status of partial membership. As State Secretary Franz Blankart, the Swiss negotiator, put it to me, they were hoping for European Union membership 'extra muros'.[5] The EFTA members found it more difficult than they had anticipated. Brussels demanded that EFTA negotiate as a bloc and accept as a pre-condition the so-called *acquis communautaire*, around 11,000 pages of legislation derived from over 1400 directives and regulations.[6] The promise of common decision-making and administrative institutions disappeared during the course of the negotiations and the EFTA partners began to divide. The European Union offered EFTA the so-called four freedoms – free movement of goods, services, persons, and capital – but at a high price. Sweden, Austria and ultimately Finland decided to join the European Union and Switzerland was left isolated and weakend. On 20 May 1992, Switzerland applied formally for membership of the European Union [7]

The referendum set for 6 December 1992, on Switzerland's membership of the European Economic Area had been planned long before the Swiss application for full membership. The referendum on the issue took place under inauspicious circumstances. Many Swiss voters could not – quite understandably – separate the EEA from the EU and voted against the latter rather than the former. There was an exceptionally vigorous No campaign and in the event the voters did, narrowly, say No by a margin of 23, 195 out over three and a half million voters. Turnout at 78.3 per cent was unusually high for Swiss referendums, but even more striking was the distribution of Yes and No votes. In French-speaking Switzerland more than 70 per cent of the population voted Yes, while in the German part of the country 56 per cent voted against.[8]

This division of sentiment frightened many Swiss. It called to mind those perilous moments in the Swiss past when German and French Swiss had divided on 'national' issues, taking the sides of Germany and France in the Franco-Prussian or the First World War. For a moment it looked as if the so-called 'Graben' [trench] had once again divided the two groups. Switzerland seemed to be a multinational state after all. Subsequent and calmer analysis showed a more differentiated picture. In March 1993, the Federal Statistical Office published a study of voting in the 1992 referendum, carried out by the Forschungszentrum für Politik of the University of Bern, which showed that the divisions ran just as sharply between city and country voters or between higher and lower income groups as between language communities. The urban, middle classes voted for Europe while German- or Italian-speaking workers in the towns and peasants and lower middle classes in the Alpine areas tended to vote No. Certainly French Switzerland was more solidly pro-European than German but language was only part of the story. After all, the half-cantons of Basel, both German-speaking, had also voted Yes.[9]

Two years later the picture had changed very little. In April 1995, the *Neue Zürcher Zeitung* published a survey of attitudes to eventual membership of the Europe Union by party, by degree of activism and by linguistic areas. In French Switzerland, members of all political parties from right to left were still more inclined to join the European Union than German Swiss, but only the Socialist Party of Switzerland had majorities for membership in all three language regions. Members of other parties and those without affiliation in German and Italian Switzerland rejected membership altogether.[10]

If Switzerland is not exactly a multinational state, what is it? Firstly, it is a state profoundly divided by religion. From the Reformation to the present the line between Protestant and Catholic has been, perhaps, the deepest of all the 'trenches' separating Swiss from Swiss. Northern Ireland and Bosnia remind us painfully that religion divides communities at a level nationality itself rarely reaches. After all Bosnian Orthodox, Catholics and Muslims all spoke the same Serbo-Croat with Sarajevo's characteristic local accent until civil war tore them apart. The Swiss had a series of religious wars between Protestant and Catholic. The last of these, *Sonderbundkrieg* of 1848, in which Catholic Switzerland took up arms against Protestant Switzerland, may have been bloodless by Bosnian standards (Bismarck called it a 'hare shoot')[11] but it left scars not yet entirely healed. Until the 1990s Switzerland did not have normal diplomatic relations with the Vatican and had, among its other claims to uniqueness, the curious diplomatic anomaly that, whereas from 1920 there had been a nuntius in Bern, there was no Swiss ambassador at the Holy See. As a senior Swiss diplomat explained it to me, there were still political obstacles, not least the existence of a specifically Protestant People's Party, to the establishment of a permanent embassy to the Pope, obstacles which no longer apply. [12]

It is not the problem of religious hostility but its solution that marks the Swiss case as special. The existence of the sovereign cantons, which even the radical, anti-clerical, liberals of 1848 never questioned, made it possible for Catholics to withdraw into their enclaves and yet retain some political authority. The most eloquent spokesman of nineteenth-century Catholicism was a Luzern patrician called Philipp Anton von Segesser (1817–1888). Segesser belonged to one of the old '*regimentsfähigen*' families of Luzern, that is, the ruling patrician caste. His ancestors served in Imperial and French armies, as office-holders in the cantonal government, and as comfortable incumbents of baroque church livings. Philipp Anton entered politics as naturally as certain old Etonians become Tory MPs and, like some of the 'wetter' among them, he incorporated the paradox of the aristocrat as democrat. Late in life he described his long career as representative of his class, church and canton in these words:

I spoke and voted in this chamber, as everywhere in my public life, as a democrat, as a federalist, as a catholic. These three concepts determined my actions. [13]

The existence of representative institutions on local and cantonal level gave the minority Catholic community a weapon to use against the Protestant, anti-clerical majority. The Catholic conservatives had discovered a deep truth about democracy, known to the Greeks but obscured in the English-speaking world by the fusion of the terms 'liberal- democratic', that democracy can be turned to entirely reactionary ends if the sovereign people wills them. As Segesser wrote in 1866,

> My firm conviction is that we of the conservative camp must put our-selves entirely onto a democratic basis. After the collapse of the old conditions nothing else can provide us with a future and a justification except pure democracy. Even if democracy has its dark side it is preferable to the quasi-bureaucratic aristocracy of the representative system. [14]

The gradual transformation of violent confrontation into political obstruction changed the terms of Catholic-Protestant hostility. They loved each other no better but found ways to get along. Segesser's tactics allowed Swiss Catholics to survive the ferocity of the *Kulturkampf* of the 1870s better than their German cousins. Bismarck's liberal, half- constitutionalism gave the embattled Catholics of the Rhine, Ruhr and Danube the options of surrender or siege. The German church chose siege and drew the faithful into a closed Catholic 'milieu', a kind of sectarian ghetto, from which the state could be excluded. This left the German Catholic community, as Thomas Gauly has written, with a '*Bildungsrückstand*' – an educational and cultural deficit – even as late as the 1960s. [15] Swiss Catholics also retreated into what the Swiss historian Urs Altermatt has called their 'ghetto' but they counterattacked with referenda, intitiatives and constitutional reforms. As Altermatt argues, the loose network of Catholic societies, singing, yodelling and hiking clubs, the charitable, devotional and educational societies gave conservatives like Segesser the perfect weapon against the liberal, bourgeois, Protestant and capitalist majority:

> In numerous referenda they organized oppositional voting alliances, which slowed or halted the radical law-making machinery. In this way the Catholic-conservative opposition, excluded from executive authority in the government, found a compensation for its powerless-ness in parliament. [16]

Two consequences flowed from this democratic activity. By the end of the 1880s radical majorities began to seek compromises with conservative minorities. It is not a coincidence that 1891 saw simultaneously the establishment of the 1st of August as the Swiss national holiday; the celebration of 600 years of Swiss history held in the Catholic canton of Schwyz; the election of the first Catholic member of the national executive, federal councillor Joseph Zemp; the great papal encyclical on the 'social' question, Pope Leo XIII's *Rerum novarum*; and the adoption by the German social democrats of the complete Marxist programme of revolution in their so-called 'Erfurt programme'. The depression of the early 1890s frightened liberals and Catholics out of their sectarian trenches. The rise of an industrial proletariat and the spread of slums threatened them both.

FEDERALISM: SWISS STYLE

Swiss national identity developed slowly and painfully as a process of conflict resolution. In the nineteenth century the very idea of a 'Swiss' identity was controversial. The radicals, who made the Swiss constitutions of 1848 and 1874, who fought the fight for 'progress' against what they saw as Catholic superstition and reaction, saw a world in which secularism, moderate Protestantism, liberalism and capitalism would reinforce and invigorate each other. Their vision of Switzerland included a strong and increasingly centralised government, the *Bund*, embodied in Victorian statues of Helvetia, armed and watchful, standing guard before the banks and bourses of the new age. The reaction to that came from people like von Segesser:

> For me Switzerland is only of interest as long as the canton of Luzern – this is my fatherland – is in it. If canton Luzern no longer exists as a free, sovereign member of the Helvetic Confederation, then Switzerland is as irrelevant to me as the lesser or greater Tartary... I shall be either a free man or a subject. If as a Luzerner I cannot be a free man, I should rather be a subject of the king of France or the emperor of Austria or even the sultan himself than of some Swiss republican diet. [17]

Federalism is more than simply a form of government which the Swiss happen to have chosen; it embodies the painful experience of conflict and its resolution. By allowing very different ethnic or religious groups to govern themselves, in effect, by compartmentalising political identity into small units, the system reduces the amount of political friction among hostile groups. The combination of direct democracy and federalism allowed the two sides of the religious *Graben* to lay down their arms, because religion remained a matter for the cantons, not the federal government. The constitution of 29

May 1874 states the premise in Article 3:

> The cantons are sovereign, in so far as their sovereignty is not limited by
> the federal constitution, and exercise all those rights, which have not been
> transferred to federal power.' [18]

In this respect the Swiss federal system seems to be very much like the
American. The Tenth Amendment of the U.S. Constitution makes the same
claims as Article 3 of the Swiss. Here is the American version:

> The powers not delegated to the United States by the Constitution, nor
> prohibited by it to the States, are reserved to the states respectively or
> to the people.

The difference is not in theory but in historical custom. Since cantons are
the result of complex historical aggregation, with bits and pieces added and
taken away over time, they can, if necessary, be divided or adjusted, as long
as the Sovereign People gives its consent to such changes. Division of political
units often eases a conflict. During the 1830 revolution the aristocrats in
Basel city, threatened by rebellious peasants demanding greater rights in
government, preserved their regime by allowing the peasants to secede. They
accepted a division into two half-cantons, a city-state called 'Basel-Stadt'
and a country canton called 'Basel-Land', which in spite of reunification
efforts remain half-cantons to this day. When in the 1960s, the Catholic,
French-speaking communities of Canton Bern began to agitate for
'independence', often using violence and chanting very un-Swiss slogans
such as 'Jura libre', the system slowly and painfully accommodated them.
Like a kind of political jigsaw puzzle, bits of Bern were detached and
transferred to a new canton called Canton Jura. The remaining French-
speaking, largely Protestant, communities either opted to stay with Bern or,
as in the case of the Catholic but German-speaking Laufenthal voted to join
Basel-Land. Finally in 1995 more than thirty years after the agitation began,
the tiny French-speaking commune of Vellerat, composed of 70 voters,
decided to transfer its allegiance to Canton Jura. At each stage, the communes
voted, the cantons voted and the whole Swiss population voted on these
territorial swaps.[19]

The jigsaw of communal sovereignty produces jagged and irregular
cantonal boundaries and in some cases results in bits of territory not
contiguous with the cantonal borders. Such bits and pieces are called
'enclaves' or 'exclaves'. Splitting political units in this way acts to reduce

friction or, at least, to contain it in the smallest element of tolerable dissatisfaction. Swiss federalism is both absolute and relative at the same time. The system works because the parts are moveable.

In addition, cantons retain a variety of crucial rights which allow them to preserve threatened religious, cultural, linguistic or other identities. They determine the educational system and maintain universities. They provide the legislation under which the semi-autonomous communes operate and raise substantial revenues from their own tax bases. They constitute an essential element in Swiss national identity, an element which at first glance seems to make Switzerland look multinational: linguistic variety. Of the twenty-six cantons and half cantons 17 use German as their official language, four use French, three (Bern, Fribourg and Valais) use German and French, one (Ticino) uses Italian and one (Graubünden) uses German, Italian and Romansch.[20] Yet even that conceals further complexities, for among the German cantons *Schwyzertütsch*, an Alemannic dialect, is the spoken language of the people, while High German, or what the Swiss call 'Schriftdeutsch', is the written variant. The differences between High German and Swiss German are at least as great as between German and Dutch. A German-speaker cannot normally understand Swiss German, any more than he or she would expect to understand Dutch.[21]

The peculiar status of language in German Switzerland creates a variety of problems of self-definition. The fact that the 'national language' is imperfect in the sense that, unlike Dutch, it cannot be used in all situations and is almost never written, turns German Switzerland into an incomplete national community. The boundaries of dialect usage remain fluid. Of late more 'dialect' will be heard in public and on the mass media than would have been true twenty years ago, but Swiss German can never replace written German. Hence German Swiss use a foreign language even when they speak German and tend to be uneasily aware that they speak it clumsily in comparison to 'real' German speakers.

For the other linguistic groups Swiss German poses a peculiar problem. It is not taught in schools, varies from place to place, has only limited use outside Switzerland and almost no literature. The obvious thing to do is to learn 'proper' German, an international language with some hundred million speakers, a vast literature, and great prestige. Yet Schwyzertütsch is what their fellow Swiss actually speak among themselves and they constitute the overwhelming majority of the Swiss population. According to the official statistics of the government's working party on the linguistic situation 73.5 per cent of Swiss citizens speak German, 20.1 per cent French, 4.5 per cent Italian and 0.9 per cent Romansch.[22] Hence non-German speakers face a thicket of dialect which they cannot easily penetrate and on the whole refuse to try.

Language like religion divides the Swiss profoundly but like religion has become the subject of complex political and practical compromises. The formation of the modern federal state led to the first linguistic provisions. As with religion, so with language, federalism acts to compartmentalise differences and reduce friction. Article 109 of the constitution of 1848 stated:

> The three main languages of Switzerland, the German, the French and the Italian, are national languages of the Federation

When the constitution of 1848 was revised in 1874, that paragraph became 116 of the new constitution but an additional article 107 provided that all three national languages may be used in the Federal Court. In 1938, as the Swiss began to defend themselves against the surrounding totalitarian states, they added Rhaetoromantsch to the group of 'national' languages but left the three previous languages as 'official'.[23]

In the 1980s, agitation from Romansch representatives prompted the Department of the Interior to set up a working party to revise the linguistic provisions of the constitution. This turned out to be much harder than the Department had anticipated. The rights of language groups, as so often in Swiss politics, rested on the 'unwritten' constititution, that set of behaviour patterns that Swiss observe in public life almost without thinking about them. The working party found that there were in fact two antithetical principles in operation in Swiss daily life: the 'territorial principle' and the principle of 'freedom to use one's own language'. Under the former the cantonal authorities determine which language will be permissible and where; under the latter, every Swiss should have the right to speak his or her language before any public body. In ordinary life the latter principle generally holds. Whenever a body of Swiss from different language areas meets, each member speaks in whatever language he or she chooses. In parliament the same freedom to use one's own language is self-evident, although Italian and Rhaetoromantsch speakers recognise the need to reach their audience and normally use either French or German.

The attempt to legislate for these usages failed. In 1993 and 1994 parliament rejected the suggested clarifications and reaffirmed the present, undefined situation. Representatives of French, Italian and Rhaetoromantsch areas prefer the territorial principle because it protects their linguistic integrity against the German Swiss, who dominate industry, commerce, banking and tourism.[24] In a recent case, the Federal Court has ruled that a German-speaking motorist who ran into the car of the French- speaking public prosecutor in Fribourg had no right to demand that the investigation be carried out in German, although in principle Fribourg is bilingual and the public prosecutor ought to be competent in both languages. The court's decision in favour of the territorial principle meant that for the time being the language question has been settled. [25]

Linguistic division certainly matters in Switzerland but the lines of that division do not run along those of religion. French-speaking cantons are both Protestant and Catholic, as are German-speaking cantons. Hence the linguistic trench cuts across the religious one. Both fault lines reinforce the importance of the micro-authority of canton and commune. The existence of Romantsch-speaking communes and the sovereignty of Canton Graubünden which has the power to grant it status as one of the Canton's three official languages allows the tiny, embattled Rhaetoromantsch community a chance to survive.

Cantons and federalism make up essential pieces of the Swiss political machine. As we have seen, they act as receptacles for dissatisfaction and reservoirs of threatened, minority identities. They vary hugely in size and significance. Canton Zurich has well over a million inhabitants and as a political unit is both richer and more populous than independent states like Estonia or Slovenia. The tiny Appenzell half-cantons with 50,000 and 13,000 would not merit more than district councils in English local government. Yet the Appenzells and Zurich share the same attributes of sovereignty and form part of the same federal state. Their politics reflect certain general features of Swiss political reality and need to be understood. Although every imaginable activity is, as the Swiss ruefully admit, 'different from canton to canton', they are more alike than different and a look at one will serve to illuminate how they all work.

Canton Zug with its 239 square kilometres and population of about 85,000 people is very small. Even among Swiss cantons it ranks near the bottom in area and population; yet it is number one in national income per head. Its sovereign status allows it to enact a very relaxed taxation system which has encouraged companies to register their head offices in its capital town.[26] Canton Zug has its own constitution, dated 31 January 1894. Like all Swiss constititutions it was ratified by popular referendum and has been amended more than thirty times over the past century. Swiss constitutions are not sacrosanct pieces of ancient parchment but a form of running record of the decisions of the 'Sovereign', as the Swiss call the people.

The first article proclaims that Canton Zug is 'a democratic free state'.[27] Like the twenty-five other Swiss cantons and half cantons Zug has all the attributes of sovereignty – constitution, executive, legislative and judiciary, its own system of laws and practices, a flag and coat of arms. It has a proper parliament with eighty members elected by proportional representation for four year terms.[28]

Like Switzerland itself, even a small canton like Zug breaks down into semi-autonomous communes. The communes enjoy the same sort of semi-sovereignty within the canton that the canton enjoys within the federation. Article 2 of the 'Gemeindegesetz' (communal law) of 4. September 1980 recognizes and regulates the status of communes in phrases very like those of the federal consititution's Article 3:

Tasks of the communes can be all affairs which affect the well-being of the commune, which are not exclusively tasks of the Federation or the Canton.'[29]

Within that framework the *Gemeindegesetz* regulates the election, powers and rights of communes. The *Einwohnergemeinde* or residential commune is the primary political unit of cantonal politics. Article 59 lists the powers of the residential communes: conduct of elections and other referenda or initiatives; security of essential needs; law and order; primary schooling; social and welfare services; promotion of culture and health; civil defence; local planning; public transport; police and fire services; civil registration office and maintenance of cemetaries.[30] Article 64 states that

the highest organ of the commune are those persons entitled to vote, who exercise their rights at the ballot box or in the general communal assembly.'[31]

Communes are substantial enterprises and raise taxes to defray their costs. In 1989 the communal taxation level per head of all communes in Canton Zug at Sfr 2,363, was much larger than the cantonal tax yield per head at Sfr 1463 and raised for the eleven communes of the canton the stately sum of Sfr 250,561,000, compared to the cantonal total of Sfr 244,094,000. Total cantonal receipts were, of course, higher because federal transfer payments to the canton amounted to more than Sfr 110,000,000.[32] Communes vary in size, wealth, political representation, percentage of foreigners and taxation per head. The largest, the city of Zug, has over 21,000 inhabitants and the smallest Neuheim only 1500.[33] Yet even little Neuheim has its rights and powers.

The executive of a commune is the elected *Gemeinderat* (communal council) which according to Article 83 of the *Gemeindegesetz* in Canton Zug must be composed of five members plus the elected *Gemeindeschreiber* (communal clerk). This form of executive repeats itself at every level of Swiss politics from Neuheim to the Federal Council in Bern. The number of members in the council may vary but the formula is constant, a number of elected councillors plus an elected chief civil servant. At federal level the chief civil servant is the Federal Chancellor elected by the Federal Assembly; at cantonal level in Zug, there is the *Landschreiber* elected by the cantonal parliament and at local level, as we have seen, the *Gemeindeschreiber* elected by the people of the commune.

POLITICS

All of these offices are highly politicised. Party affiliation is deep and absolutely natural to the Swiss and constitutes an aspect of self- identity. In a Catholic canton like Zug the largest party historically has been the old Catholic-Conservative Party, renamed and redirected as the *Christlichdemokratische Volkspartei* (Christian Democratic People's Party) or CVP. In Zug the main opposition to Catholicism comes from the *Freisinnige Demokratische Partei* (the Radical Democratic Party) or FDP. In neighbouring Luzern with its different history, an urban, patrician Liberal Party plays the role of the Zug FDP. In Protestant cantons, other variants exist. Two other main parties mark the Swiss landscape: the *Sozialdemokratische Partei der Schweiz* or SPS (Social Democratic Party of Switzerland) and the *Schweizerische Volkspartei* or SVP (the Swiss People's Party). The SPS and SVP differ from the CVP and FDP in that their origins and identity have at least as much to do with class as with ideology. The SPS represents industrial workers, the unionised white collar workers and a part of the intelligentsia, where the SVP looks after the independent small business sector, the lower middle classes and increasingly a segment of disgruntled right-wing voters.

In traditional Swiss politics families would pass on a liberal or conservative affiliation from generation to generation. These identities, although diluted by the mobility of modern life and the gradual erosion of ideology everywhere, nevertheless, continue to operate in Swiss life at every level. The sheer number of elected bodies on communal and cantonal level ensures that party affiliation retains its importance. Party organisations at every level of Swiss politics select personnel and give ideological direction to daily affairs. In a typical commune in Canton Zug, not only will the *Gemeinderat* be elected on party lines but the other elected organs of the community, such as the building committee, the welfare boards, school boards. and so on.

As in the case of the religious and linguistic compromises, the Swiss have solved their ideological and class conflicts by inclusion rather than exclusion. The multi-member executives allow the operation of a 'magic formula' by which each of the four great national parties has a share of executive seats in some rough proportion to its share of the vote. In Zug, where the lower middle class and shopkeeper classes have historically been included in the CVP, the SVP is weakly represented. The cantonal executive in Zug, the *Regierungsrat*, has seven members and at present there are 3 CVP members, 2 FDP, 1 SPS and 1 Socialist-Green.[34] Canton Zug and Ticino are the only two cantons to use a party-based proportional system for the elections of the *Regierungsrat*. Other cantons prefer a majority system because it increases the personal and reduces the purely party element in elections for the executive.

A striking example of how sophisticated voters are in these matters was provided by the 'Sovereign' in Luzern. The SVP, which had hitherto had no presence in a traditional, central Swiss Catholic canton, broke into parliament in April, 1995 on a noisy anti-Europe, anti-Bern and anti- Everything campaign. Suddenly 15 SVP deputies joined the 170 members of the Luzern cantonal parliament at the expense of the traditional governing Liberals and CVP.[35] The elections for the executive produced a very different result. On the first ballot six of the seven candidates, all incumbents, got more than the 50,000 plus votes necessary to be re-elected, but one seat, formerly held by the SPS candidate, Paul Huber, remained open. On 7 May, Huber was overwhelmingly re-elected against a shirt-sleeve populist Hans Ulrich Buhler for the SVP. The correspondent of the *Neue Zürcher Zeitung* assesed the result in these words:

> In the conviction that the left-green spectrum should be represented in the government the voters expressed themselves once more for the traditional composition of the government as it has existed since 1959: four Christian Democrats, two Liberals and a Socialist...a cold shower for the SVP. [36]

It is worth pausing for a moment to reflect on this phenomenon. Swiss voters in Luzern have not changed the colour of their governing coalition since 1959. In spite of what by Swiss terms was a landslide alteration of cantonal politics, many CVP voters went out to vote for a Socialist because they want the present arrangement to continue. In addition Huber was a 'bisheriger', a member of the executive already, having served for eight years and Swiss voters almost never at any level vote out a 'bisherigen'. Arthur Gilgen continued as education minister of Canton Zurich for twenty- four years even though he had long severed conections with the party that put him there.[37] The late Emil Landholt served on the city council of Zurich equally as long and was mayor for seventeen years. He chose to step down at the age of 71; nobody would have forced him to go. In a long obituary, Alfred Cattani summed up Emil Landholt's virtues, those essential qualities that made him the perfect 'Stapi', a dialect and rather affectionate abbreviation for 'Stadtpräsident':

> Emil Landholt gave to Zurich during his term of office the charm and familiarity of a village. He knew, or so it seemed, each and everybody, and used the familar 'Du' with many of them. If one invited him to something, he would come, and if you met him on the way to one of his countless receptions, he would spontaneously invite you, whether it was a grand official occasion or a private party...His 'be nice to each other' [in dialect, of course, 'sind lieb miteinand' – JS] was directed at those whom he wished to tie into the personal and political consensus. [38]

Landholt embodied every virtue the Swiss value in politics. He was not grand, nor abrasive. He put consensus and community above ideology, even though he became the first 'bourgeois' mayor after a long period of 'Red' dominance. He said 'Du' to people, spoke dialect and made Zurich seem like a village not a megalopolis.

These virtues are precisely those to be found among long-serving politicians in Neuheim or in Bern. In 1991 I interviewed three members of the Federal Council. They received me with an unstuffy and relaxed manner, as if they had all the time in the world to sit in a cafe and chat. René Felber, then foreign minister, comes from Le Locle in Canton Neuchâtel. He trained as a teacher, joined the Socialist Party in 1958, and was elected a member of the legislative body of the commune. He rose to be successively mayor from 1964 to 1980, member of the cantonal parliament from 1965 to 1976 and member of the national parliament from 1967 to 1981. From 1981 to 1987 he served in the government of the Republic and Canton of Neuchâtel as finance minister until he was elected Federal Councillor on 9 December, 1987.[39] He has served at every level and in both executive and legislative capacities. At one and the same time M. Felber was mayor of Le Locle, deputy in the cantonal and in the national parliaments, uniting in his person the three levels of Swiss federalism.

All the other six members of the Federal Council have exactly the same experiences and curricula. Like the members of the *Regierungsrat* of Canton Luzern, Federal Councillors operate within the constraints of a 'magic formula', which since 1959 has produced at national level a 2-2-2-1 division among FDP, CVP, SPS and SVP. Federal councillors are elected every four years by the newly elected parliament, with both houses sitting together. The operations of the 'magic formula' become particularly complex in Bern because the cantons, language groups and latterly sexes have to be adequately represented.

The members of the two chambers behave like all other Swiss. They rarely vote a Federal Councillor off the Council, but may register disapproval by re-electing him or her with a reduced majority. This process which operates at every level of Swiss politics is called giving the incumbent a 'Denkzettel', [sending somebody a warning note]. It means – do a better job or we shall humiliate you again. Vacancies in the Federal Council are trickier. The party which claims the vacancy nominates a candidate, but all members of the two houses vote on them by secret ballot. In 1973, the Socialist, Christian Democrat and Radical parties nominated official candidates, and all three lost to unofficial candidates. The Socialists have seen this happen to them four times, 1959, 1973, 1983 and 1993; on each occasion the National Assembly chose a less extreme Socialist.[40]

There is a variety of consequences which arise from the way the Swiss executive is chosen. The first is that nobody controls a Swiss cabinet. Federal Councillor Otto Stich explained that, as finance minister in a magic formula cabinet, he has no prime minister to lean on, no parliamentary majority behind him, indeed, no political leverage of any kind. He cannot impose a tight budget on recalcitrant colleagues. Everything must be negotiated within a collective body, which in turn accepts collective, executive responsibility towards parliament. Of course, the other councillors are in the same position with regard to him. Each must read the other's position papers and all must arrive at a consensus before each can act. The executive is a collective of persons of different parties, but united in responsibility.[41]

Federal Councillors have an ambivalent relationship to their parties. A member of the Federal Council is not the leader of his party in either house nor, as Federal Councillor Flavio Cotti pointed out, can he be said to represent his canton or linguistic community. He retains his party membership, linguistic and cantonal identity, the right, indeed duty, to attend parliamentary party meetings and conventions, but he is not party spokesperson. A Federal Councillor may often end up having to represent policies which his party opposes. As Signor Cotti said to me, when he was president of the CVP, he used to think 'how unfortunate that the party president is not the Federal Councillor. Now I think how fortunate that he is not.'[42]

THE SWISS MODEL OF DEMOCRACY

This thicket of executive and legislative practice makes Swiss politics anonymous and to the outsider impenetrable. Yet its principles resemble that of a complicated machine whose wheels and gears always return to the point of rest. It aims to reduce friction and to channel external pressures into smaller and containable units. The Swiss speak of their system as a 'Konkordanz-Demokratie', a democracy based on concordance rather than conflict. In this it represents the opposite of the American system. As James Madison put it in *Federalist Paper* No. 51:

> Ambition must be made to counteract ambition. The interest of the man must be connected with the constitutional rights of the place. It may be a reflection on human nature that such devices should be necessary to control the abuses of government. But what is government itself but the greatest of all reflections on human nature? If men were angels, no government would be necessary. If angels were to govern men, neither external nor internal controls on government would be necessary. In framing a government which is to be administered by men over men, the great difficulty lies in this: you must first enable the government to control the governed; and in the next place oblige it to control itself. Dependence on the people is, no doubt, the primary control on government; but experience has taught mankind the necessity of auxiliary precautions. [43]

Experience seems to have taught the Swiss a very different lesson. The elegance and disdain for the masses which can be heard in Madison's tone makes a sharp contrast with the homely virtues of Swiss politics. Madison's view of government as a system of control is not Swiss. The highest organ of a polis, says the Zug *Gemeindegesetz*, are persons entitled to vote. Certainly the Swiss observe quite strictly constitutional separation of powers but there is in Swiss constitutional practice very little that limits or controls the sovereign people. Each canton and commune has elaborate provisions for direct intervention by the citizenry in politics. There are referenda, some of which are mandatory, some optional. There are various provisions for initiating legislation on all three levels of politics, so that people have the machinery to exercise Madison's 'primary control on government'. Many cantons have obligatory fiscal referenda on expenditure above a certain level and all have them for changes in constitutional practice. What applies to lower levels applies at the top. The Federal Council as supreme executive and the two legislative organs, the National Council and the Council of States, may pass legislation which can then be repealed by the Sovereign. The most famous case of that was the rejection in December, 1992, of Swiss membership in the European Economic Area.

Swiss citizens vote on their own taxes. On 28 November, 1993, they adopted by an overwhelming majority of 66.7 per cent 'Yes' to 33.3 per cent 'No' a Value Added Tax of 6.5 per cent, which in 1977, 1979 and 1991 they had turned down. On the same day the citizens of the *Gemeinde* of Wallisellen in Kanton Zurich voted by 2987 Yes to 684 No to spend Sfr 38 million on the reconstruction of the community's old peoples home, while in ten other cantons the citizens decided issues as varied as the purchase of snow cannons in Bern (No), voting rights for foreigners in Canton Geneva (No) and an end to sexual distinctions in the Solothurn fire department (Yes).[44]

None of this is unusual to the Swiss. In 1993, for example, six initiatives came to national vote, compared to four in 1992. Seven new initiative campaigns to collect the necessary signatures were begun. Six optional referenda were held, the same number as in 1992, making a total of 120 such popular referenda on pieces of legislation since the adoption of the constitution of 1874.[45] The voters go to the polls four times a year on federal matters. Normally on the same day cantonal and local referenda are also on the ballot.

This network of popular, direct democracy provides an outer framework around the entire Swiss political machine, limits its flexibility, slows its decision-making but greatly increases its legitimacy. The sovereign people rule and not just reign. Since they may act in the tiniest communes as well as in the greatest conurbations, they provide a counter-force to government but also a justification for the micro-mesh of authorities and overlapping identities. If you don't like what is taught in school, you know how to get it changed. If you don't want that superstore in your community, you need not wait on the pleasure of some distant and alien ministry. Organise the petition, collect the votes and win the initiative. Nothing more unpalatable to the Sir Humphreys of Europe can be imagined. Brussels is 'top down'. It issues 'directives' and they bind the directed. Swiss identity collides with European reality most painfully on this issue.

The final piece in the puzzle is neutrality. Unlike neutrality for Swedes or Austrians, neutrality for the Swiss is as much a domestic as a foreign political reality. Neutrality began in humiliation. After the defeat at Marignano in 1515, the hitherto unbeatable Swiss realised that their own disunity, organised in a loose confederation, could not compete with the new kingdoms of Henry VIII or Francis I. Within a few years religious civil wars set Swiss against Swiss, so that by the time of the Thirty Years War the whole Swiss confederation looked likely to be tugged to pieces, pulled by religious ties to Protestant or Catholic Europe. The Peace of Westphalia of 1648, which ratified the religious armistice in Europe, also confirmed that the Swiss Confederation no longer owed allegiance to the Holy Roman Empire and nor were its courts subject to Imperial oversight. For the next 150 years a very loose and irregular Helvetic Confederation, made up of leagues of cantons with overlapping borders and authorities, survived on both slopes of the Alps.

When the French overran Switzerland during the revolutionary wars in the 1790s, they put an end to all the messy decentralisation of Swiss practice and introduced a shining, modern, centralised, rational and uniform state which they proudly called the Helvetic Republic. The unpopularity of the new state led to revolt and revolt threatened French military lines across the Alps. Napoleon, ever the realist, 'mediated' a new Swiss Confederation on more democratic lines in 1803 and thus bequeathed to Switzerland its present shape. In 1815 the victorious allies recognised Switzerland's permanent and unconditional neutrality.[46]

Swiss neutrality is 'armed'. Switzerland maintains a very large land army but it is, like the Israeli, an army of citizens. 'Every Swiss is obliged to do military service', Article 18 of the Federal Constitution states. In peacetime the Swiss army at any one moment comprises a cadre of some 1500 regular officers. There are two annual intakes of twenty year-olds who undergo fifteen weeks of basic training and about 400,000 officers and men who return regularly for the so-called 'Wiederholungskurse' (refresher courses).[47] Those who go on to be officers spend, in the end, years of their lives in the services. One major in his forties reckoned that over the years since his twentieth birthday he had amassed 1200 days of duty.[48] The 'militia' system of military service casts its shadow over many aspects of Swiss life. Parliament on national and cantonal level is said to be a 'militia', as is practically all communal service. Even executive members in cantons have only recently become full- time, paid public servants. As the Swiss theologian Hans Küng puts it, 'Switzerland does not have an army; it is an army.'[49]

Neutrality and the militia army reinforce Swiss national identity. If Switzerland can be seen as an equilibrium system, 'armed' neutrality is its outer casing. Universal suffrage and universal service in a militia army reinforce each other and erect the protective shell against external threats. That is why mythology focuses on images like William Tell or more recently the heroic resistance to Nazism during the second world war. According to popular mythology, the 'reduit national', fortress Switzerland, convinced Adolf Hitler not to invade the country. However questionable the claim may be as history it is deeply and widely believed.

To change the army is to change the very essence of Swissness. That was why the initiative of 26 November, 1989, to abolish the army so startled public opinion. Left-wing initiatives are always being launched but nobody expects them to get the necessary 100,000 signatures. This one, promoted by the Socialist Youth, did so quite easily. Nobody expected, least of all the young socialists, that 68.6 per cent of those eligible to vote would turn out and that 35.6 per cent of those would vote Yes.[50] The shock waves went through the Swiss political system and still generates the occasional tremor. One third of the Swiss, and much more among the age groups likely to have to serve, voted, it appeared, to dismantle an essential feature of Swiss national life.

The army and citizenship consititute an essential binding force in Swiss national identity and the domestic mythology is no less important than the foreign political. If 'armed' neutrality preserved Swiss liberty from Hitler and his Reich, the army shows Swiss democracy at work. In service to the Fatherland all Swiss, so it is said, are equal. The company director and the worker mess together and the civilian boss may find his employee as his military superior. In reality no institution more subtly reflects the reality of class behind the facade of classlessness in Switzerland than does the Swiss army. In the past officers were generally men who had 'studied' [have degrees]; the men in the ranks had not. Until recently anybody who wanted to rise to the top in Swiss industry would rise to officer rank, the higher the better. Here too changes in Switzerland's international position and the pressures of modern business have eroded certain automatic career assumptions. Modern businesses, under constant pressure to 'downsize', are less prepared to allow important executives to disappear for weeks on end to serve the extra tours of duty required by senior officers.

CONCLUSION

Switzerland is not a multinational state but is not a conventional national state either. Its institutions have evolved in a matrix of conflict – religious, ideological, linguistic, economic, social and military – and have turned into systems of concordance and conflict- resolution. The preservation of the autonomy of even the tiniest of authorities gives the system a uniquely 'bottom up' character, quite unlike the 'top down' authorities of traditional states like France or Britain. Its complex representative machinery, its magic formulae and multi-member executives, its referendums and initiatives, its jigsaw puzzle of territories, turn the political machinery into an acute and sensitive device for registering, channelling and resolving the movements caused by twitches of the body politic. Identity crises and conflicts, however sharp in one micro-unit of politics, may not be so fierce in the unit next door. Around and through the entire set of structures the values – longevity in service, anonymity, a certain populist coziness, a general awareness of how things are done according to the 'unwritten rules' – unify behaviour across all the differences. Switzerland is Swiss from Chiasso in the south to Basel in the north, and every visitor feels it the moment he or she crosses the border.

Swiss national identity arises from these shared values and attitudes. A strong rootedness in place marks every Swiss. The former deputy chairman of Ciba-Geigy explained to me that thirty-five years in Basel had not made him less a Zurich man, and a world-travelling management consultant told me that he is still a Thurgauer although born and raised in Zurich. Switzerland's long historic evolution has marked its citizens more deeply than they imagine. The idea that Switzerland will simply crumble, if the citizens stop willing it to continue, is not plausible.

The structures to control and compartmentalise conflict grew out of the resolution of conflicts within society. Catholic and Protestant faced each other across the religious trenches. Urban and rural communities fought for control of politics, as did liberals and conservatives. There was a near revolution in 1918 when Swiss socialists tried to mount a general strike and imitate the successful Bolsheviks. Switzerland escaped none of the disturbing currents which troubled other European societies. Its 'bottom up' system of representation, the confines of tiny, homogeneous units, the cats-cradle of over-lapping identities, ensured that lines of ideology or interest rarely coincided. Not all German Swiss were Catholic, conservative, rural, democrats; only some were. Not all French Swiss were Protestant, liberal, urban, patricians, though some were. Not all Italian Swiss were clerical or rural and so on.

Switzerland today faces a double identity crisis. Internally, the ebbing of commitment to the great ideologies of the twentieth century, instant communication with the outside world, physical mobility and the disintegration of the historic 'milieus', have hollowed out the compartments of Swiss domestic politics. None of the old structures stands as firmly as in the past because the old conflicts which those structures redirected have lost power. Catholic cantons are less Catholic, rural life less rural, trade unions less solid and so on. The Swiss behave more like their neighbours because they have become less idiosyncratically Swiss.

On the other hand, Switzerland faces an external identity crisis. The

European Union, which now surrounds it, has begun to develop into a loose, multinational confederation not unlike what Switzerland was at an earlier stage. State Secretary Franz Blankart, who negotiated with the European Union, sees in these negotiations an irony of history: the long struggle from 1291 to free the Swiss Confederation from the Holy Roman Empire may end with Switzerland joining that Empire's unlikely successor, the European Union.[51]

My guess is that Switzerland will join the European Union. The Sovereign may vote No a few more times but will vote Yes in the end. Then Switzerland will gradually loose its distinctive features as its citizens make their way into European Union politics. Nothing lasts forever, and the Helvetic Confederation has no inherent right to permanence. A Confederation which has resisted its enemies for seven hundred years may well surrender to its friends.

NOTES

* What I know about Switzerland I owe to all those Swiss who over thirty years have explained their country to me. The list has grown too long to be included, but there are some special cases. I must begin by thanking Federal Councillor, Signor Flavio Cotti, and former Federal Councillors M. René Felber and Herr Otto Stich. All three gave me lengthy interviews and allowed me to record what they said. It was a rare privilege to hear how the Swiss executive works from those who work it. State Secretary Franz Blankart gave me his exceptionally frank view on the negotiation with the European Union. I am grateful for very helpful interviews to State Secretary Jakob Kellenberger, Ambassador Jenö Staehelin, Ständerätin Rosemarie Simmen, Divisionär (a.D.) Gustav Däniker, Signor Marco Cameroni, Herr Egon Zehnder, Herr Dr Albert Bodmer, Professor Dr Urs Altermatt, Dr Raffaele Ceschi, Herr Max Frenkel, M. Pierre Baudère, and, in particular to Dr Hans Windlin, *Landschreiber* of Kanton Zug, who supplied me both with an exceptionally helpful interview and a useful selection of written matter. My work has been made much easier by the fact that Europe's best newspaper, *Die Neue Zürcher Zeitung,* is Swiss. It is a newspaper which takes its function as newspaper of record seriously and provides statistics and information in great richness and variety.

1   *Statistisches Jahrbuch der Schweiz 1995* Bundesamt für Statistik/ Verlag
     Neue Zürcher Zeitung, 1994, Tables T 1.3, p.26, Section 2, p.57, Table

T. 2.6, p.66, and on wealth in comparison to other states, see World Bank *Atlas* 1994, as reported in *Neue Zürcher Zeitung*, 31 December 1994, Switzerland's gross domestic product divided by population amounted to $36 410 which made it the 'richest' country in the world. These figures are misleading to the extent that they rest on nominal exchange rates, rather than real purchasing power. Switzerland will be in the top five by any measure.

2   Interview with Professor Urs Altermatt, University of Fribourg, 6 April, 1991.

3   Raffaele Ceschi, 'Buoni ticinesi e buoni svizzeri. Aspetti storici di una duplice identità' in *Identità in Cammino* a cura di Remigio Ratti e Marco Badan, Locarno: Armando Dadò Editore; Bellinzona: Coscienza Svizzera, 1986, p.23.

4   Sophie de Skowronski, *Switzerland and the European Community; the EEA Referendum of 1992,* Cambridge University M. Phil. Dissertation, 1994, p. 20.

5   Interview with State Secretary Franz Blankart, Bundesamt für Aussenwirtschaft, Bern, 11 April, 1991.

6   Sophie de Skowronski, *Switzerland,* p.21.

7   'Die Schweiz stellt EG Beitrittsgesuch' and 'Kein Schicksal sondern Chance. Der Bundesrat zur europäischen Zukunft der Schweiz' in *Neue Zürcher Zeitung* (abbrev. NZZ) 20 May 1992, p. 27 and 22 May 1992, p. 29.

8. VOX *Analyse de la votation fédérale du 6 décembre 1992* GfS, Publication No.47, Février 1993.

9   *Ibid.* 4. 'Le profil du vote', pp.31–41; 'Mehrere Gräben in der Europapolitik', NZZ, 28 February 1993, p.26.

10 'Die Parteien auf dem Weg zu Europa' NZZ, 20 April 1995, p.25.

11 Jonathan Steinberg, *Why Switzerland?* 2nd edn, Cambridge, Cambridge University Press, 1996, p. 46.

12 Luigi Maglione was accredited as the first papal nuncio to the Helvetic Confederation on 8 November 1920. For an analysis of the complex negotiations leading to that point, Fabrizio Panzera, 'Benedetto XV e la Svizzera negli anni della Grande Guerra', *Schweizerische Zeitschrift für Geschichte*, Vol.43, No.3 (1993) pp.321 ff. Interview with Ambassador Jenö Staehelin, Bern, 12 April 1991.

13 *Briefwechsel Philipp Anton von Segesser (1817–1888).* General editor: Victor Conzemius, Zurich, Benziger Verlag, 1983–1989. Vol.1 p.xiii.

14 *Ibid.* Vol.4, pp.215–16

15 Thomas Gauly, *Katholiken: Machtanspruch und Machtverlust*. Bonn, Bouvier Verlag, 1991. P. 181

16 Urs Altermatt, *Katholizismus und Moderne. Zur Sozial- und Mentalitätsgeschichte der Schweizer Katholiken im 19. und 20. Jahrhundert*. Zürich: Benziger Verlag, 1989. P. 146. See also Urs Altermatt, *Der Weg der Schweizer Katholiken ins Ghetto. Die Enstehungsgeschichte der nationalen Volksorganisationen im Schweizer Katholizismus 1848-1919* (Zurich: Benziger Verlag, 1972).

17 *Briefwechsel von Segesser,* Vol. 1, p. 494

18 Bundesverfassung der Schweizerischen Eidgenössenschaft (vom 29 Mai 1874), Erster Abschnitt, Art. 3

19 For the background to the Jura crisis,Jonathan Steinberg,*Why Switzerland?*, pp 89-97. See also 'Berns schwieriger Umgang mit dem Nachbarn Jura, NZZ, 17.11. 1990, p. 32. The Laufenthal voted to join Basel-Land on 12 November, 1989, which was confirmed by the Bernese parliament on 25 June, 1991. The negotiations were complicated by claims and counter-claims, law suits and referenda. The final stage was reached on 25 June, 1995, when the Swiss voters nationally approved Vellerat's decision to switch cantonal allegiance.

20 Paul Stadlin, *Die Parlamente der schweizerischen Kantone* (Zug,1990) Synoptische Tabellen über Organisation und Verfahren, No. I

21 For a discussion of language usage and its problems, Jonathan Steinberg,*Why Switzerland?* Ch. 4 'Language', pp. 129ff

22 *Zustand und Zukunft der viersprachigen Schweiz.* Abklärungen, Vorschläge und Empfehlungen einer Arbeitsgruppe des Eidgenösssischen Departementes des Innern, August 1989 (Bern: Schweizerische Bundeskanzlei, 1989) p. 30

23 Ibid. p. 160

24 The lower house approved a version of the new article 116 on 22 September, 1993, which omitted both the territorial and the freedom of language principles. For the debate, see 'Eidgenössische Räte', NZZ, 24 September, 1993, p. 31. In June, 1994, the upper house restored the territorial principle to the text of the constitutional amendment but not the freedom of speech. They also elevated Rhaetoromantsch to the dignity of 'official' language. For the text, cf NZZ, 17 June, 1994, p. 32. In March, 1995, the upper house referred the matter back to committee, where at this moment the matter rests. 'Letzte Chance für den Sprachenartikel', NZZ, 15 March, 1995, p. 25

25 'Aus dem Bundesgericht: 'Sprachenfreiheit gegen Territorialitätsprinzip', NZZ, 4 May, 1995, p. 27

26 *Statistical Data on Switzerland*, Swiss Federal Statistical Office, Bern, 1991, Table 1,p.2 and Table 4, p.7. Also interview with Dr Hans Windlin, Zug, Landschreiber des Kantons Zug, 5 April 1991.

27 *Verfassung. Gemeinde- und Wahlgesetz*, Herausgegeben von der Staatskanzlei des Kantons Zug, 1985.

28 After the elections of 1994 the eighty were divided among the parties as follows (1990 results in brackets): CVP – 33 (36), FDP – 28 (25), Social Democrats – 11 (–), Socialist-Green Alternative – 3 (4), SVP – 3 (0), Gleis 3 – 1 (1), Forum Oberägeri/Forum Cham – 1, Staatskanzlei des Kantons Zug cf.'Linksrutsch bei der Zuger Wahlen', NZZ, 13 November 1990, p.21

29 'Gesetz über die Organisation und die Verwaltung der Gemeinden (Gemeindegesetz)' (vom 4 September 1980) in *Verfassung. Gemeinde- und Wahlgesetz*, Zug, Herausgegeben von der Staatskanzlei des Kantons Zug, 1985 p.95.

30 *Ibid.*, p.110

31 *Ibid.*, p.111

32 'Kantonaler Finanzhaushalt' *Zug in Zahlen 1990*, Zuger Kantonal Bank, 1990.

33 *Ibid.*, 'Gemeinde Neuheim'.

34 'Wahlen im Kt Zug 1994: Regierungsrat', Sitzzuteilung, Staatskanzlei des Kantons Zug.

35 SVP als Gewinnerin der Luzerner Wahlen', NZZ, 3 April 1995 p.19.

36 Paul Huber bleibt in der Luzerner Regierung', *ibid.*, 8 May 1995, p.11

37 'Arthur Gilgen - Politiker mit unverwechselbaren Profil' NZZ 6 May, 1995, p.31

38 Alfred Cattani, 'Erinnerung an Emil Landholt', NZZ, 21 April 1995, p. 32.

39 Interview with Conseiller Fédéral M. René Felber, Bern, 11 April 1991.

40 For an account of the 1973 debacle, Jonathan Steinberg,*Why Switzerland?* pp.120-21 and for an account of more recent unsuccessful elections, 'Regeln und Ueberraschungen bei Bundesratswahlen', NZZ, 25 February 1993, p.27.

41 Interview with Bundesrat Otto Stich, Bern, 12 April 1991

42 Interview with consigliere federale Flavio Cotti, 12 April 1991.

43 No.51: Madison in Clinton Rossiter (ed.),*The Federalist Papers: Hamilton-Madison-Jay*, New York, 1961, p.322.

44 'Finanzpolitischer Durchbruch. Die Mehrwertsteuer im vierten Anlauf erfolgreich', NZZ, 30 November 1993, p.15 and 'Kanton Zürich' *ibid.* p.32.

45 'Starker Gebrauch der Volksrechte' *ibid.* 6 January, 1994, p.22.
46 For an account of this, Jonathan Steinberg, *Why Switzerland?*, pp.11–12, 42.
47 Marko Milivojevic, 'The Swiss Armed Forces' in M. Milivojevic and Pierre Maurer (eds), *Swiss Neutrality and Security: Armed Forces National Defence and Foreign Policy*, Leamington Spa, Berg, 1990, p.25.
48 Interview with M. Pierre Baudère, Zurich, 5 April 1991.
49 Hans Küng, *Die Schweiz ohne Orientierung? Europäische Perspektiven* Zurich, 1992, p. 68.
50 Marko Milivojevic, 'The Swiss Armed Forces', p.3.
51 Interview with State Secretary Franz Blankart, Bern, 11 April 1991.

7 Yugoslavia
Rise and Fall of Communist Pluralism

Christopher Bennett

INTRODUCTION

Visitors to Yugoslavia in the 1970s and 1980s often had the country's complexity explained to them as follows: Yugoslavia was one country with two alphabets (latin and cyrillic), three religions (Catholicism, Orthodoxy, Islam), four languages (Slovene, Macedonian, Croat, Serb), five nations (Serb, Croat, Slovene, Macedonian, Montenegrin), and six republics (Slovenia, Croatia, Bosnia-Hercegovina, Serbia, Montenegro, Macedonia). While contrived, this description formed an integral part of every Yugoslav's education as, for over 40 years from the end of the Second World War, Yugoslavs of all nationalities were taught, by their schooling and media, to love one another and to celebrate the diversity which made their country unique.

By virtually every criterion Yugoslavia defied simplification. Its national composition was the result of centuries of rule by two great, adversarial empires – the Habsburg and the Ottoman. Several cultures and peoples lived side by side; East met West; Islam confronted Christianity and Catholicism came up against Orthodoxy. In some regions, notably Slovenia, a single nation formed an overwhelming majority of the population. In others, notably Bosnia-Hercegovina[1] and Vojvodina,[2] the population was mixed to a bewildering extent.

Yugoslavia was born on 1 December 1918 at the end of the First World War. The first incarnation, a constitutional monarchy, survived just over 22 years before being defeated and dismembered by Nazi Germany in 1941.

Between 1941 and 1945 the territory of Yugoslavia was engulfed by war, pitting Yugoslavs of all nationalities against one another. At the end of the Second World War Yugoslavia reemerged as an independent state within expanded borders. The second incarnation, a communist dictatorship, survived just over 46 years before it, too, erupted in war. Yugoslavia formally died on 15 January 1992 when, after six months of fighting, all 12 members of the European Union recognised Slovenia and Croatia as independent states.

Yugoslavia means the land of the south Slavs. Strictly speaking, this was a misnomer. Of the country's 1918 population 16.5 per cent were not Slavs,[3] while most Bulgarians who most definitely were south Slavs, lived outside the country. For the first decade of Yugoslavia's existence the country was known not as Yugoslavia but as the Kingdom of Serbs, Croats and Slovenes. In many ways this was a more appropriate name, since, though only 71.13 per cent of the population in 1918,[4] the relationship between Serbs, Croats and Slovenes was key. While the country's other peoples – most obviously the Muslim Slavs, but also Macedonians, Hungarians and Albanians – have borne the brunt of the fall-out from Yugoslavia's disintegration, they were little more than bystanders for most of the country's history and played a minimal role in the events leading to the outbreak of war in 1991.

In the course of the 20th century Yugoslavia changed almost beyond recognition. In 1918 the country was essentially agrarian and even in 1945 only three cities, Belgrade, Zagreb and Ljubljana, had more than 100,000 inhabitants. Yugoslavia's 73-year history and especially the period after the Second World War were years of accelerating development and rapid change throughout the world, and of urbanisation, industrialisation and modernisation at home. Until the recession of the 1980s, Yugoslavs were beneficiaries of rising living standards, greater access to education and improved health care. The growth of industries and the move to the city radically altered both the landscape of Yugoslav society and the ethnic composition of the country (see tables below).

While some form of national awareness existed among Serbs, Croats and Slovenes in 1918, it was by no means a fully-formed identity. Moreover, national consciousness among Yugoslavia's less-developed peoples was very much in its infancy. Indeed, despite an apparent obsession with the distant past among contemporary Serb and Croat propagandists, the modern national identity of all Yugoslavia's peoples is largely a product of the 20th century. Most citizens of the Kingdom of Serbs, Croats and Slovenes, irrespective of nationality, were peasants. Burdened by the daily struggle for survival, few devoted much thought to national questions.

Table 7.1: Ethnic composition of the Kingdom of
Serbs, Croats and Slovenes in 1918

Ethnic Group	Number	Per cent
Serbs and Montenegrins	8,140,452	36.30
Croats	579,023	2.58
Slovenes	4,428,005	19.75
Muslim Slavs	1,753,554	7.82
Macedonians and Bulgarians	1,999,957	8.92
Other Slavs*	1,339,729	1.45
Germans	513,472	4.27
Hungarians	427,409	3.93
Albanians	441,740	3.68
Romanians and Vlachs	229,398	1.91
Turks	168,404	1.40
Jews	64,159	0.53
Italians	12,825	0.11
Others	80,079	0.67
Total	12,017,323	100.00

*Czechs, Ruthenes, Slovaks, Russians, Ukrainians, Poles
Source: Ivo Banac, *The National Question in Yugoslavia*,
p. 58, extrapolated from the 1921 census.

Serbs were always the most numerous nation in Yugoslavia but never constituted an absolute majority of the population.[5] Together with Montenegrins[6] they formed 38.83 per cent of Yugoslavia's 1918 population, spread throughout the country in both former Ottoman and former Habsburg lands, except Slovenia. By 1981, though the proportion of Serbs and Montenegrins remained almost identical, their geographical concentration had shifted somewhat.[7] However, the historical experience of the many Serb communities across Yugoslavia was very different and they were by no means a homogeneous nation. In many respects, Serbs from Vojvodina had more in common with their German, Hungarian and Croat neighbours than with Serbs from the Kingdom of Serbia, as did Serbs and Croats from Croatia and Serbs, Croats and Muslim Slavs from Bosnia-Hercegovina.

Croats were the second most numerous nation making up 23.77 per cent of the population in 1918 (19.75 per cent by 1981) and living almost entirely in the former Habsburg lands.[8] Slovenes were the third most numerous nation in 1918 forming 8.53 per cent of the population (7.83 per cent in 1981) and living exclusively in the former Habsburg lands. By 1991 the proportion of Slovenes had declined to the extent that there were actually more Muslim Slavs, Albanians and even Macedonians in Yugoslavia. Nevertheless, as Yugoslavia's wealthiest republic, Slovenia played a role in Yugoslav affairs which belied its size and the number of Slovenes in the country.[9] By the 1981 census people considering themselves primarily Yugoslav and not Serb, Croat or any other nationality made up 5.44 per cent of the population. These 'Yugoslavs' were generally the offspring of mixed marriages and were especially numerous in regions such as Bosnia-Hercegovina and Vojvodina.

Today, images of Yugoslavia are those of ethnic hatred and war. The overriding question is how the country broke down. Prophets of doom began to speculate about Yugoslavia's future as soon as Josip Broz Tito died in 1980. They argued that deep, historical fault-lines divided the country. The north and west were comparatively wealthy, the south and east poor, and the gulf between rich and poor unbridgeable. Serbs, Montenegrins and Macedonians were Orthodox and had lived under Ottoman rule, while Croats and Slovenes were Catholic and had lived within the Habsburg Empire. Moreover, during the Second World War, fanatical Croat and Serb nationalists had done their best to wipe each other out. Yugoslavia, they claimed, was an artificial creation, plagued by atavistic and irrational hatred, and, in the absence of Tito's charismatic leadership, the country would surely not survive. Yet there were excellent reasons both for the creation of a Yugoslav state and for its continued existence.

Firstly, after the disintegration of the Habsburg and Ottoman empires, Yugoslavia was the best framework within which to reconcile the national aspirations of all south Slav peoples and ensure that they did not fall out over rival claims to ethnically-mixed territories. Secondly, the south Slavs faced a common external threat. In school Yugoslavs were taught that their neighbours were a constant menace and the message was reinforced with the word *brigama*, meaning worries, which was derived from the first letter or each of the neighbouring states.[10] Thirdly, Yugoslavia held a certain geopolitical significance in the eyes of much of the international community. In 1919 the country satisfied the principles contained in Wilson's 14 points and in the interwar period it formed part of France's system of alliances designed to contain German ambitions. Moreover, following the break with Stalin, Yugoslavia assumed an importance way beyond its size as a buffer between East and West.

Table 7.2: Ethnic composition of Yugoslavia in 1981

Ethnic Group	Number	Per cent
Serbs	8,140,452	36.30
Montenegrins	579,023	2.58
Croats	4,428,005	19.75
Slovenes	1,753,554	7.82
Muslim Slavs	1,999,957	8.92
Macedonians	1,339,729	5.97
Other Slavs*	143,563	0.64
Germans and Austrians	10,114	0.05
Hungarians	426,866	1.90
Albanians	1,730,364	7.72
Romanians and Vlachs	87,017	0.39
Turks	101,191	0.45
Jews	1,383	0.01
Italians	15,132	0.06
Bulgarians	36,185	0.16
Gypsies	168,099	0.75
Yugoslavs	1,219,045	5.44
No response / regional affiliation	72,415	5.44
Others	172,617	0.32
Total	22,424,711	100

*Czechs, Ruthenes, Slovaks, Russians, Ukrainians, Poles

Source: The 1981 census.[11]

HISTORICAL EVOLUTION OF YUGOSLAVIA

1 Evolution of Yugoslavist philosophy: 1830-1914

2 First World War: 1914-1918
    Greater Serbia: 1918-1929
    Royal Dictatorship: 1929-1939
    Sporazum: 1939-1941

3   Second World War: 1941-1945
    Stalinist Titoism: 1945-1951
    Evolutionary Titoism: 1951-1974
    Post-Titoism: 1974-1986

4   Disintegration: 1986-1991
    Yugoslav Wars: 1991-

FROM YUGOSLAVISM TO THE SECOND WORLD WAR

Frustrated south Slav nationalists in the Habsburg Empire may have dreamed of a Yugoslav state, but they had no clear vision of the form that state might take. Most Slavs in Austria-Hungary were loyal to the Habsburgs and the most that Yugoslav nationalists could aspire to was a third, south-Slav tier to the Empire. Unification with Serbia and Montenegro came suddenly in the wake of the disintegration of Austria-Hungary. Habsburg authority was being replaced by anarchy across parts of Croatia and Bosnia-Hercegovina, while Italian armies were threatening to hive off Dalmatia and the new states of Austria and Hungary also claimed lands with a south Slav population. Predominantly Serb regions of Austria-Hungary spontaneously declared themselves for Serbia and the Serbian Army reconquered all of Serbia and Montenegro. To south Slav politicians from the Habsburg lands, union with Serbia appeared to offer salvation, but no groundwork had been prepared for a common state.

During the war attempts were made by *émigré* Habsburg south Slavs to forge a common policy with Serbia, but they foundered on diverging visions of the post-war settlement. While the *émigrés* had vague hopes for a common south Slav state, Serbian war aims were specific and achievable without recourse to an alliance with the Habsburg south Slavs. Serbia was fighting to liberate all Serb lands and had no intention of annexing any purely Croat or Slovene territories. At the end of the war, when Serbian politicians met with their Habsburg counterparts in Geneva, they failed to find common ground.

The Geneva impasse reflected the diverging traditions and historical experience of the Serbs of Serbia and of the Habsburg south Slavs. The pattern of national awakening and the nature of modern nationalisms in the Balkans were clear by the beginning of the 19th century. For Serbs from the Ottoman Empire, the path to national emancipation was straightforward; for the Habsburg south Slavs, the Croats in particular, it was more complicated. Serbs lived in a decaying empire with a clear enemy, the Ottoman, and knew that they could win their freedom by armed struggle. By contrast, the Habsburg south Slavs belonged to an empire which, despite many faults, appeared to be in no real danger of collapse. Moreover, the Habsburgs had been their benefactors against the Turks and more recently against the Hungarians.

Yugoslavism, that is the vision of a single south Slav entity, can be traced back to the 1830s and the Illyrian movement in Croatia. The Illyrianists were essentially Croat intellectuals who believed fervently in the ethnic, linguistic and cultural unity of all south Slavs.[12] They also provided an intellectual explanation for the very real physical need among Croats for unity with Serbs and even Slovenes in the face of aggressive, non-Slav nationalisms. While Serb nationalism developed within the context of armed struggle against Ottoman rule, Croat nationalism evolved as a reaction against predatory German, Italian and, in particular, Hungarian nationalisms.

In the 19th century Serbia developed a centralised state administration and standing army enabling the Kingdom to achieve most Serb national aims by war. Serbian victories did not pass unnoticed in Croatia. Far from being perennial enemies, there were times when Croat admiration for Serb achievements knew no bounds. To Croat nationalists, Serbia's dynamic expansion was both a cause of envy and a source of inspiration. However, whereas Croats looked to Serbs to help achieve their national goals, Serbs were doing very well on their own and had no comparable psychological or political need for Croat support. And while Serb achievements spawned a following in Croatia, there was no reciprocal movement of comparable size and influence in Serbia.

Unification would have been difficult under any circumstances, but after four years of war the task proved beyond the new country's political leaders. Though the first Yugoslav incarnation failed to win over its many peoples or to develop any framework for national coexistence, three separate approaches to governing the country were tried between the two world wars. The first was the Greater Serbian option; the second was an attempt by the monarch to impose an artificial 'Yugoslav' identity on all Yugoslavia's peoples; and the last approach entailed an accommodation with the state's most vociferous opponents, the Croats. In the event, the Greater Serbian option poisoned relations between Serbs and Yugoslavia's other peoples and soured the prospects of any future south Slav state. The second managed to alienate all peoples, including Serbs, and the third approach was overtaken by the onset of the Second World War and never had the time to succeed.

The Greater Serbian option appeared natural to Serbian leaders and Habsburg south Slavs were hardly in a position to make demands. In addition, the most senior Habsburg politician, Svetozar Pribicevic, was himself a Serb convinced that the best solution was integration with Serbia. And the Croat position was further undermined by the Croat leader, Stjepan Radic, who chose to boycott parliament in the country's formative years.

In the absence of Croat political parties, a highly-centralised constitution was pushed through in 1921. However, since no nationality formed an absolute majority and no political party could ever win a parliamentary majority on its own, government was of necessity by coalition. Despite his mishandling of the early parliaments, Radic's popularity soared on the back of Croat disillusionment with the new state. When he finally entered parliament, just as before the First World War in Austria-Hungary, the Croat bloc used its parliamentary muscle to filibuster and make government farcical.

Though the Serbian parties came to accept the need to accommodate Croatia, the gulf between fundamental positions proved too great. The Serbian parties considered the 1921 constitution as the basis of the state, while Radic insisted on renegotiating the terms of unification. By 1927 Pribicevic, recognising the shortcomings of centralism, began to espouse federalism and formed a parliamentary alliance with Radic. It was an alliance of the Serbs and Croats of the former Habsburg Empire against the Serbs of the former Kingdom of Serbia. Relations between Serbia and the former Habsburg lands deteriorated until on 20 June 1928 a Montenegrin deputy shot Radic and four other members of the Croat Peasant Party in parliament. When Radic died of his wounds on 8 August Pribicevic withdrew the opposition from parliament and five months later, King Alexander dissolved parliament and took the reins himself.

Alexander hoped to reconcile both Serbs and Croats within his own vision of Yugoslavism. He renamed the country Yugoslavia, broke it up into administrative units bearing minimal resemblance to historic or ethnic entities, and, in 1931, introduced a new constitution designed to ensure that real power remained with the monarch. But Alexander succeeded only in alienating all groups: Croats feared he was trying to create a Greater Serbia by the back door, while Serbs objected to the loss of their political liberties.

Soon after Alexander imposed the dictatorship Pribic evic went into political exile and Vlatko Macek, who had already succeeded Radic as head of the Croat Peasant Party, became the leading opposition figure. Meanwhile, Ante Pavelic, then a minor figure, founded the Ustasha, a Croat Revolutionary Organisation committed to the creation of an independent Croatia by any means. The Ustashas fled to Italy where Mussolini took them in as part of his wider scheme to undermine Yugoslav security. Pavelic's most famous victim was King Alexander who was gunned down on a state visit to France in 1934.

Ironically, relations between Serbs and Croats were never better than in the late 1930s as their political leaders cooperated against the dictatorship, which Alexander's successor, Paul, the Prince Regent, maintained after his cousin's death. The electoral system was designed to ensure victory for the monarch's supporters, but the vote of the United Opposition, a Serb-Croat coalition headed by Macek, increased with every election. At the same time, Prince Paul attempted to integrate Croatia into Yugoslavia.

Negotiations between Prince Paul's representative, Prime Minister Dragic a Cvetkovic, and Macek, but behind the back of the Serbian parties, bore fruit in 1939. The outcome was the so-called *sporazum* which set up an autonomous province of Croatia within Yugoslavia. However, it was not necessarily a solution to Yugoslavia's national question. Serbian and Slovene political parties resented the settlement because Croatia appeared to have won a privileged position. Macek remained Yugoslavia's Vice Premier and Croatia's politicians retained a say in Yugoslav affairs, even though Serbian and Slovene politicians had no reciprocal say in Croatian matters. Moreover, of a population of 4.4 million, the autonomous province included about 866,000 Serbs and 164,000 Muslim Slavs. In the event, the deal lasted less than two years and was never fully implemented.

The *sporazum* only provided for Yugoslavia's two largest ethnic groups. It did nothing for the many national minorities, including the German, Hungarian, Albanian, Macedonian and Muslim Slav communities. Officious and corrupt Serb police dominated many regions and often made life miserable for non-Serb populations. In Kosovo, Albanians waged a guerila war against the Yugoslav state during much of the 1920s and, though the majority, were encouraged to leave for Turkey, as were Muslims from Bosnia-Hercegovina and the Sandcjak.

Nevertheless, Royal Yugoslavia was not an unmitigated disaster doomed to end in the slaughter of the Second World War. That it did has more to do with foreign intervention and the exceptional circumstances of 1941, than any innate desire of Serbs and Croats to wipe each other out. Since Yugoslavia had not been on Hitler's immediate agenda, he had made no preparations for the country's occupation. In the event, he parcelled out whatever he could to neighbouring countries with territorial claims against Yugoslavia.[13] And in the regions which could not be hived off – inner Serbia, a truncated Croatia, a piece of Vojvodina and Bosnia-Hercegovina – Hitler looked for Quisling leaders. In Serbia he found General Milan Nedic . But in Croatia Macek, the undisputed Croat leader, refused to cooperate so that, by default, Hitler turned to Pavelic .

There was no precedent for the Ustashas. When they came to power,

Macek broadcast a statement advising Croats to obey the new authorities, before withdrawing from political life. Macek had not anticipated, and could not anticipate, what the Ustashas were about to do. Croatia's Serb population would probably have been willing to respect Ustasha rule, had they been the opportunity. Indeed, even when Ustashas began wiping out Serb villages, survivors went to Zagreb to protest, convinced that the government could not be involved.

To understand the Ustashas, it is important to bear in mind that, above all, they were terrorists who had overnight been handed total power. Moreover, they had been handed total power over lands in which only a little more than half the population were actually Croats. The Independent State of Croatia contained all of what became the republic of Bosnia-Hercegovina and included about 750,000 Muslim Slavs as well as 1.9 million Serbs. When they came to power, the Ustashas lacked popular support, since even according to their own estimates they only had about 40,000 supporters. Yet they viewed being a Serb as an act of political aggression against their Croatian state and hence their plan to kill a third. expel a third to Serbia and convert the remainder to Catholicism.

The simplified picture of the Second World War in Yugoslavia is of Serbs – whether under Mihailovic or Tito – on the allied side and Croats on the German side. However, the actual picture was far more complex. To a large extent the Second World War in Yugoslavia was several civil wars which had little to do with the wider war raging outside the country. All groups, with the exception of the Slovenes, fought against Serbs, though not in unison, while extreme nationalists on all sides were able to indulge their wildest fantasies.

THE TITOIST EXPERIMENT: 1945-86

An open discussion of the Second World War in its immediate aftermath might have helped restore trust between Yugoslavia's peoples and given the country's second incarnation a more secure foundation. However, the victorious communists ruled out such a dialogue. According to Marxism-Leninism, nationalism was a feature of bourgeois society which would disappear as soon as the proletariat won power and the inequalities which had bred nationalism were eradicated. As far as Yugoslavia's communists were concerned, their triumph was part of the march of history and the nationalisms which had torn Yugoslavia apart between 1941 and 1945 were sure to fade away.

In partisan folklore, all anti-communists were demonised and labelled collaborators. The Second World War was interpreted as an epic anti-fascist struggle and proletarian revolution, but not a civil war. This simplistic version of the events of 1941-45, which conflicted with personal recollections, became the official communist history of the war. However, an alternative history was passed on by word of mouth to succeeding generations, ensuring that open wounds continued to fester long after the war was over.

Tito's national policy was a key element in the partisans' military victory. The Communist Party was a club anyone could join. By trading national loyalties for allegiances based on a universalist ideology, the communists drew recruits from Yugoslavia's Slav peoples, though they attracted few non-Slavs. In Bosnia-Hercegovina, the main theatre of war, partisan units contained all three major national groups, Serbs, Croats and Muslim Slavs, fighting together under the slogan 'brotherhood and unity' .

The foundations of the post-war state were laid at the second meeting of the Anti-Fascist Council at Jajce in Bosnia on 29 November 1943. In the event of a communist victory, Yugoslavia would become a federation consisting of Serbia, Croatia, Macedonia, Slovenia, Montenegro and Bosnia-Hercegovina. Exactly two years after the Jajce meeting a communist-dominated constituent assembly abolished the monarchy and proclaimed the Federal People's Republic of Yugoslavia. And just over two months later on 31 January 1946 the country's first communist constitution was unanimously approved. It was Yugoslavia's third constitution in 25 years establishing the federation of six republics agreed at Jajce. In addition, Kosovo became an autonomous region and Vojvodina an autonomous province within Serbia because of the large Albanian and Hungarian communities living there.

The federal system was not meant to divide the country but to create as equitable a balance as possible between Yugoslavia's peoples and to prevent conflict over disputed territories. Republican borders were drawn up on a mixture of ethnic and historic principles. In this way, Macedonians won recognition of their separate national identity and their own republic. Montenegro became a republic in its own right in respect of its independent history, while Bosnia-Hercegovina maintained its former Ottoman contours, including an outlet on the Adriatic coast. The border between Croatia and Vojvodina meandered between villages depending on whether they had a Croat or a Serb majority. Autonomy for predominantly Serb regions of Croatia was considered but deemed unnecessary. Presumably, had autonomy been granted to these regions, then the same status would have had to be accorded to the predominantly Muslim Sandcjak in Serbia and, in time, to predominantly Albanian regions of Macedonia.[14]

The 1946 constitution was modelled on the Soviet 1936 constitution drawn up by Stalin. According to article 12, inter-republican borders could only be altered after negotiations between the republics themselves with the agreement of all sides. Each republic, but not Vojvodina and Kosovo, had the right of secession and self-determination, although clearly these were rights which they were not meant to exercise. The communist revolution was supposed to be the culmination of a historical process and there was certainly no provision for a possible break-up of Yugoslavia. Officially, Yugoslavia's peoples had exercised their right to self-determination 'once and for all' during the national liberation struggle, when they chose to live together in a multinational federation. In reality, though not mentioned in the constitution, all power lay with the Communist Party just as in the Soviet Union. The highest authority in the land was Tito and his trusted lieutenants, Alexander Rankovic , Milovan Djilas and Edvard Kardelj. Despite its federal structure, Yugoslavia was if anything more unitary and centralist than under King Alexander.

Communist Yugoslavism attempted to cultivate a multinational and thoroughly Yugoslav patriotism out of the wartime struggle for national liberation. It was revolutionary, idealistic and aspired to universal, socialist goals. National equality was fundamental and extended as far as participation in the national liberation struggle. According to the official interpretation of the Second World War, all Yugoslavia's peoples had contributed equally to the defeat of fascism. It was an attempt to wipe the national slate clean and allow all peoples to join the new state free of historical mortgage.

Though Slav peoples were all well represented in Tito's army by 1945, few non-Slavs joined the partisans. Yugoslavia's German, Albanian and Hungarian populations remained for the most part allied to the Axis powers until the end of the war and, consequently, the commitment to national equality did not include them. The fate of the German minority in Yugoslavia was the same as that of German minorities throughout eastern Europe. It disappeared. Yugoslavia's Hungarians and Albanians were more fortunate but remained suspicious of the new state's intentions towards them. The Yugoslav communists hoped to deal with the non-Slav minorities within the wider context of a union of communist states of eastern Europe or at least a Balkan federation and did not address the question immediately. The break with Stalin in 1948, however, forced them to evolve a more comprehensive national policy.

The eventual solution was supposed to be scientific but was in reality complex and arbitrary. Yugoslavia's peoples were split into nations and national minorities. Initially, nations corresponded to those peoples who had a home republic, that is Slovenes, Croats, Serbs, Macedonians and Montenegrins. But in 1971 the status of Muslim Slavs was elevated to that of a constituent nation. Meanwhile, the Hungarians and Albanians, as well as all other peoples living in Yugoslavia, were classified as national minorities. Each republican and provincial constitution listed the nations and national minorities living there and officially both nations and national minorities had identical rights and duties. For example, in Bosnia-Hercegovina Serbs, Croats and Muslims were listed as the republic's constituent nations. In Croatia and Vojvodina Croats and Serbs were listed as the constituent nations. Hungarians who lived in both Croatia and Vojvodina were listed as national minorities in both even though they outnumbered Croats in Vojvodina. Albanians were classified as a national minority in Kosovo, even though they formed the majority there and despite the fact that by the 1980s there were more Albanians in Yugoslavia than Montenegrins, Muslim Slavs, Macedonians and Slovenes.

As in all communist countries, propaganda played a central role in Yugoslav society. From an early age Yugoslavs were indoctrinated, via their schooling and the media, with love for Tito, Yugoslavia, Titoism and each other. In school, children studied the histories and cultures of all Yugoslavia's peoples as well as their own. Education was multicultural and aimed at bringing Yugoslavia's peoples together. All citizens of Yugoslavia, including the non-Slav Albanians and Hungarians, were taught that they could be their own nationality and Yugoslav at the same time and that they should be proud of both.

Great winners in Tito's Yugoslavia were the country's smaller and less-developed peoples, the Macedonians, Muslim Slavs, and to a lesser extent Hungarians and Albanians, who were shielded from the aggressive potential of Croat and, in particular, Serb nationalisms. The security provided by the Titoist system allowed Macedonians and Muslim Slavs to thrive culturally as never before and to evolve a modern and confident national identity. As a result, affection for Tito and Titoism survived longest in Macedonia and Bosnia-Hercegovina. The Titoist state also bent over backwards to make sure the Serb minority in Croatia as well as the Croat minority in Vojvodina felt secure.

The break with Stalin was critical to Yugoslavia's development since it forced Tito to change course and led, in time, to the evolution of the Yugoslav way. Without Western economic support the country would probably have crumbled in the face of a concerted economic blockade by the Soviet bloc. But in September 1949 the Truman administration granted Yugoslavia a $20 million aid package and by 1960 Yugoslavia had consumed more than $2 billion of non-repayable Western aid. As far as the Western powers were concerned, aid was an insurance policy against Yugoslavia slipping back into the Soviet camp. For Tito, who made sure that the aid came without any strings, it enabled him to remain a communist, albeit independent of Moscow. Aid became fundamental to Yugoslavia's development and allowed Yugoslavs to live way beyond their means, while Tito and his successors became expert at raising the spectre of the Soviet bogey to procure yet more economic assistance. The result was communist extravagance paid for by a seemingly endless supply of Western credit.

As the immediate Soviet threat receded, but while Stalin was still alive, Yugoslavia's communists set out to develop their own Marxist-Leninist ideology. They decided that Stalinism had gone astray in its concentration of power within the state and the expansion of the bureaucracy. In Yugoslavia, by contrast, they determined that the state should wither away and that power should be devolved to the workers. Herein lay the foundations of Worker Self-Management.

The Stalinist blueprint for economic development was shelved and in 1953 Yugoslavia began to decollectivise agriculture. The CPY changed its mane to the League of Communists of Yugoslavia (LCY) and in the 1953 constitution Workers' Councils were set up to devolve power to the lowest level. Worker Self-Management, however, was a sham and the celebrated Workers' Councils were but an additional tier of bureaucracy. Despite its new title, the LCY remained a Marxist-Leninist party unwilling to renounce its historical mission in society. On this, all attempts of the 1950s and 1960s to liberalise the economy were bound to founder.

Whatever the precise constitutional arrangement, relations between Yugoslavia's peoples were certain to remain stable in Tito's lifetime. He was Yugoslavia's ultimate arbiter and his unassailable power base enabled him to step in and resolve any conflict which he feared might be getting out of hand. During 35 years at Yugoslavia's helm, Tito moulded the country in his own image, so that when he died he was genuinely mourned in every republic.

Tito's fourth constitution, which was Yugoslavia's sixth and last, was drawn up when he was 82 to cater for conditions after his death. Though the constitution finally made him President for life, he had lost interest in the day-to-day affairs of state, which he was happy to delegate to his juniors, while still strutting the world stage he had grown to love. The 1974 constitution was an intricate series of checks and balances designed to prevent any individual from acquiring as much power as Tito himself, and to prevent any of Yugoslavia's peoples from dominating the federation. It codified the arrangement which had evolved after the liberal experiment of the 1960s and, in particular, the aftermath of the Croatian Spring of 1971 and attempts to emancipate the Albanians of Kosovo.

During the first 20 years of communist rule Tito made little attempt to integrate Albanians into Yugoslav society.[13] Order in Kosovo was left to the security apparatus and the secret police, which were dominated by Serbs. However, with the fall of Alexander Rankovic , Tito's hardline police chief, in 1966, policy towards Kosovo and Yugoslavia's Albanians changed as part of a series of measures to liberalise the regime. As repression eased, Albanians were finally able to manifest their discontent which exploded in 1968 into street demonstrations demanding republican status for Kosovo. Instead of a return to repression, Tito decided to emancipate the Albanians and to try to win them over to Yugoslavia and Titoism.

Reversing more than half a century of discrimination was an exceptionally ambitions undertaking which only someone of Tito's stature could consider. In his advancing years Tito may have fallen victim to his own propaganda for one factor motivating him was undoubtedly his desire to keep all Yugoslavia's peoples happy. Police rule in Kosovo was a stain on Yugoslavia's record and ran counter to the benevolent image Tito liked to project. Whatever his motives, Tito attempted to win over Kosovo's Albanians through a combination of increased autonomy, cultural gains and economic aid. Kosovo's status was raised to that of autonomous province alongside Vojvodina, and both provinces acquired most of the attributes, including the autonomy, of a republic, though not the name. To make Kosovo a republic was not an option because it was unacceptable to both Serb and Macedonian opinion. Albanian became an official language of Kosovo in addition to Serbo-Croat, and Pric tina, the provincial capital, acquired its own university and Albanalogical Institute.

In Croatia, Tito intervened to preempt what he considered a potentially dangerous upsurge in nationalism and purge that republic's League of Communists in 1971. The upsurge of Croat nationalist in the late 1960s began as a cultural movement. But, instead of stamping out the early and seemingly innocuous manifestations as Tito would have expected, Croatia's leadership attempted to harness it to their own cause. At the federal level Yugoslavia was divided between economic reformers in the wealthier republics and economic conservatives in the less-developed regions and the result was deadlock. Croatia's leaders were prepared to use nationalism to back up the demands of their economic programme. However, their gamble failed as the national movement gained a momentum of its own, feeding off the rise in unemployment which accompanied and resulted from earlier economic reforms. As the movement became more militant, it also assumed an anti-Serb character. When student leaders called a strike, Tito intervened and the Croatian Spring petered out in a purge of Croatian society.

The purge finally ended Yugoslavia's experiment with economic liberalism as Tito took the opportunity to move against the meritocrats who had risen to power during the 1960s throughout the federation. Leading Communists in Slovenia and Serbia were also purged and replaced by a generation of mediocrities whose credentials for government were fidelity to Tito and Titoism. At the same time, Tito decided to give way to many of the devolutionary demands of the Croatian communists whom he had just purged.

The devolution process which began in the early 1950s following the break with Stalin had by the 1970s turned Yugoslavia into a federation with some of the characteristics of a confederation. According to the constitution, all Yugoslavia's republics were sovereign and independent. Foreign affairs, defence and essential economic matters remained the prerogative of the federal centre, but required a consensus among federal units. Otherwise, the republics and provinces were able to pursue their own, often conflicting, policies. The bonds which tied the country together were Tito himself, the armed forces, which Tito had created and still dominated, and the LCY, which Tito had just purged. At a time when he was already in his eighties and could not expect to live much longer, Tito had made himself more indispensable to Yugoslavia than ever.

Federal institutions, from the Presidency and National Bank to cultural and sporting bodies, contained representatives from all federal units. Offices were rotational so that every republic and autonomous province had equal access to positions of power. While the system was designed to be manifestly fair, it exacerbated the post-Tito malaise. Federal Presidents and office-holders in general had neither the time nor the authority to iron out the failings of the Titoist system. At the same time, republican leaderships were wary of moves to expand the powers of the federal centre at their expense and prepared to use their representatives in the federal institutions to maintain the status quo.

Devolution turned the LCY from a highly centralised body into little more than a talking shop for the eight republican and provincial Leagues of Communists. While all eight Leagues were committed to Tito, they were short of talent in the aftermath of his purge of meritocrats and reformers. Loyalty to Tito and ideological orthodoxy replaced ability as the key to advancement within communist ranks. In the absence of liberal thinkers each republic pursued its own development strategy with predictable results. At a time when European economies were integrating and converging, Yugoslavia's mini-economies were actually fragmenting.

BREAKDOWN

The Achilles heel of all Europe's communist states was the economy. For an ideology which promised a better future, Marxism-Leninism was an economic catastrophe. Declining living standards, a lack of consumer goods and shortages of even the basic essentials had become the harsh reality of life in the 1980s throughout eastern Europe. Despite its detachment, Yugoslavia was not immune to the malaise afflicting the entire Eastern bloc. Attempts at reform during the 1950s and 1960s foundered as soon as the side-effects, such as unemployment, began to appear. In the 1960s and early 1970s more than a million Yugoslavs moved abroad to live and work, principally in West Germany. Money they sent home to their families boosted the country's balance of payments, but began to decline in the wake of the First Oil Shock of 1973. As work in western Europe dried up, many were forced to return home and by the mid-1980s the number of Yugoslavs working temporarily abroad had halved. The quintupling in oil prices between June and December 1973 devastated Yugoslavia's balance of trade and exacerbated the inherent deficiencies in the economy. In response, Yugoslavia borrowed from private Western banks, extending its foreign debt from under $3.5 billion in 1973 to more than $20.5 billion in 1981.

When the loans dried up, Yugoslavia had to begin repaying its debt. The crunch came about the time of Tito's death. and coincided with recession in western Europe stemming from the Second Oil Shock of 1979. The debt burden was aggravated by high interest rates and an exceptionally strong dollar and the government moved to cut imports. Between 1982 and 1989 the standard of living fell nearly 40 percent and in December 1989 inflation peaked at more than 2,000 percent. The extravagance of Tito's Yugoslavia ended with the 1980s' austerity package. Yet the fundamental causes of Yugoslavia's malaise were not addressed. In Tito's absence, Yugoslavia's federal centre lacked sufficient authority to assert control over the economy of the whole country. The system could not reform itself, yet it was so bankrupt both structurally and politically that it would not even permit the media to discuss the debt question. The nail in the coffin of communist credibility came in 1987 when Agrokomerc, a Bosnian food processing company, disintegrated. It was the 29th largest company in Yugoslavia and, though bankrupt for years, had survived on 'political' loans. It went under with debts of almost $900 million in a scandal implicating the Central Committee of Bosnia's League of Communists.

Against this background of economic crisis, Slobodan Milosevic launched his assault on the federal system. The decisive battle in Yugoslavia's disintegration was fought not in 1991 but in 1987. The struggle was not between Serbs and non-Serbs but between two wings of the League of Communists of Serbia (LCS); between advocates of a Serb nationalist ideology which was incompatible with a multinational society and those who defended the concept of a multinational state. This power struggle came to a head in September 1987 at the eighth plenum of the LCS when Milosevic had his principal rival, Dragic a Pavlovic , expelled from the Party. Triumphant in Serbia, he set his sights on Vojvodina, Kosovo and Montenegro.

Milosevic's role in Yugoslavia's disintegration cannot be over-estimated. Indeed, his career is testimony to the impact that an individual can have on the world around him, given exceptional circumstances and ruthless ambition, and comparisons with both Stalin and Hitler are not far-fetched. For, like the 20th century's tow most notorious dictators, Milosevic is essentially an aberration. Though he has played the Serb national card, he is not, and never has been, a Serb nationalist. Moreover, Milosevic is no more typical of Serbian statesmen than Hitler was of German leaders, and there is no precedent in Serbia's past either for the man or for the destruction he has sown.

That Milosevic had such a huge impact on events in Yugoslavia is not simply a result of the economic malaise afflicting Yugoslavia in the mid-1980s. It is also, in part, due to the nature of communist societies in general. The Party apparatus in any communist country was an astonishingly powerful mechanism for control, and, from the moment that he became President of the LCS in 1986, in exactly the same manner as Stalin in the Soviet Union, Milosevic put it to work shaping Serbian society in his own image. At the same time, Milosevic capitalised on the desperate economic climate prevailing in Serbia in the mid-1980s. But instead of attempting to correct the deficiencies of the existing economic system, he offered only simplistic solutions and scapegoats.

The Serb case against Tito's Yugoslavia was not Milosevic's creation but grew out of the thinking and writing of Dobrica Cosic, one of Serbia's most distinguished writers. Though a former partisan and personal friend of Tito, Cosic could not come to terms with Albanian emancipation and was purged from the LCY for nationalism in 1968. After his fall, Cosic developed a complex and paradoxical theory of Serb national persecution under communism which over two decades evolved into the Greater Serbian programme, set out in the now notorious 1986 Memorandum of the Serbian Academy of Arts and Sciences.

The Memorandum stated what was essentially an elaborate, but crude conspiracy theory. It alleged that Tito's communists had imposed an alien, that is federal, model of Yugoslavia onto a reluctant Serb nation. According to its authors, Croats, in the person of Josip Broz Tito, and Slovenes, in the person of Edvard Kardelj, had deliberately pursued a policy of 'strong Yugoslavia, weak Serbia'. Moreover, Tito had ensured Serbs would remain weak by dividing them between several federal units and carving the autonomous provinces of Vojvodina and Kosovo out of Serbia in the 1974 constitution. Serbs faced discrimination throughout Yugoslavia, the Memorandum alleged, while in Kosovo they were being subjected to 'genocide' at the hands of irredentist and separatist Albanians!

Had the opinions in the Memorandum remained those of a tiny faction of frustrated intellectuals, they could have done nobody any harm. But in the hands of an unscrupulous politician these views posed a serious threat to the Yugoslav federation, since the Memorandum's xenophobia and simplistic analysis struck a chord among many Serbs at a time of declining living standards. Though liberal reformers had, hitherto, been more influential in Serbian society than the nationalists, once Milosevic added the weight of the LCS to the nationalist cause, the liberals were rapidly silenced.

The key to Milocevic's rule and an understanding of modern Serb nationalism is the Serbian media and their sustained campaign to generate national hysteria. At least three years before the shooting war formally began in Yugoslavia, a war psychosis had already set in in Serbia – though not in the Serb communities of Croatia and Bosnia-Hercegovina, since, at that time, they had not yet been exposed to the media offensive. Irrespective of whether or not Serbs were facing genocide in much of Yugoslavia, as the Serbian media alleged, Serbian society was gripped by fear and ordinary people genuinely came to believe that they were under siege and, critically, began behaving as if they were surrounded by enemies determined to wipe them out.

Milocevic's ability to wreak havoc in the Yugoslav federation was largely the fault of the Titoist system itself, since the centre lacked sufficient power to bring Serbia back into line, but it is a also the result of the malaise in the rest of the country. Montenegro, Macedonia and Kosovo had gone bankrupt, the leadership of Bosnia-Hercegovina was compromised by the Agrokomerc scandal and Croatia was still governed by the generation of mediocrities installed after the Croatian Spring. Moreover, the Macedonian leadership generally sympathised with Serbia in its conflict with Kosovo's Albanians, since its relations with Macedonia's own Albanian minority were increasingly strained.

When finally some form of credible opposition materialised it came from outside the official channels, from Slovenia where a rainbow alliance of opposition groups pressurised a reluctant Slovene leadership to challenge Milosevic. And it was this rift which developed between Slovene and Serbian Communists which went on to destroy Yugoslavia in form. By April 1989, after Milosevic used the Yugoslav military to crush Kosovo, the country was already dead in spirit.

Slovenia was a very different proposition from the rest of Yugoslavia. In the absence of a significant non-Slovene minority, Slovenes were in a position to detach themselves from the rest of the country. The Yugoslav state had generally been good to Slovenes and had certainly fostered the evolution of a modern Slovene national identity. Since the emergence of the new Serb nationalism in Milosevic's Serbia, however, the Yugoslav connection had become a liability. By the late 1980s, a continued Slovene presence in Yugoslavia was, in many ways, more important to Yugoslavia than to Slovenia, as Slovenia had become an essential counter-weight to Serbia. But, as war appeared imminent in the rest of the country and Serbia refused to moderate its hardline position – which included an economic boycott of Slovene products – Slovene leaders decided to distance themselves from the rest of the country.

By the beginning of 1989 Yugoslavia was already in an advanced state of decay, but developments abroad exacerbated the country's crisis and hastened its demise. As communism collapsed in the rest of eastern Europe and the threat of Warsaw Pact invasion disappeared, the unique geopolitical position Yugoslavia had occupied in world politics for more than four decades disappeared. Diplomatic activity and foreign investment shifted towards eastern Europe's emerging democracies, and, without the Soviet bogey to hold the country together and Western money to bail out the economy, Yugoslavs found themselves for the first time entirely on their own. As long as their internal quarrels did not spill over into neighbouring countries, the international community no longer cared what happened.

Though Yugoslavia remained a single entity in the eyes of the world, communism had held it together for almost 45 years, and its demise made a major reorganisation of the state unavoidable. In effect, the debate which had preoccupied Yugoslav politicians during the 1920s as to the best form of government for their common state had been reopened. Future inter-republican relations were ostensibly negotiable, and in a climate of goodwill it would certainly have been possible to erect a third Yugoslavia out of the ruins of the communist state. However, in the 17 months between the break-up of the League of Communists and the outbreak of war talks never even got off the ground. On 27 June 1991 the Yugoslav People's Army moved against Slovenia and Yugoslavia was no more.

CONCLUSION

The shift from a centralised state to a federation failed to prevent Yugoslavia's disintegration. That said, the failings of Yugoslav federalism were very peculiar to Yugoslavia and do not necessarily bode ill for federal experiments elsewhere in the world. Indeed, the critical flaws were principally those of communism, not of federalism. Yugoslavia's communists never managed to place the economy on a sound footing and never properly addressed the issue of the atrocities which took place during the Second World War. Moreover, they failed to construct a civil society based on the rule of law which could guarantee that human rights would be respected. Impeded by ideology, crippled by debt and excessively reliant on one man's charisma, Tito's Yugoslavia lacked the flexibility to cope with the crisis it faced in the late 1980s in his absence.

Federalism appealed to Yugoslavia's smaller ethnic groups and remained their preferred form of government until the very end. But the settlement could never satisfy the maximalist goals of either Serb or Croat nationalists. While alive, Tito managed to keep these tensions in check, but by the late 1980s nationalists had a free rein in Serbia. Ironically, their ideal arrangement was essentially that which had already been tried and found wanting in the early years of Royal Yugoslavia, namely a centralised, Serb-dominated state. The attempt to recentralise the country under Serb domination, however, was almost certain to end in failure simply on account of demographics. While there were sufficient Serbs in Yugoslavia to destabilise the country, there were too few to rule it.

NOTES

1   According to the 1981 census, Muslim Slavs accounted for 39.5 per cent, Serbs 32 per cent and Croats 18.4 per cent of Bosnia-Hercegovina´s population.
2   According to the 1981 census, 56.6 per cent of Vojvodina's population were Serbs or Montenegrins, and the remaining 43.4 per cent were a

mixture of peoples, including Hungarians (19 per cent), Croats (5.4 per cent), Czechs, Slovaks, Ruthenes and Romanians.

3	The non-Slav population had declined to 11.3 percent by 1981.

4	By 1981 the proportion of Serbs, Croats and Slovenes in the population had declined to 66.45 per cent.

5	According to the 1981 census, Serbs formed an absolute majority of the population in both inner Serbia and Vojvodina of 85.4 per cent and 56.8 per cent respectively. They formed 32 per cent of the population in Bosnia-Hercegovina, 13.2 per cent in Kosovo, 11.6 per cent in Croatia, and 2.2 per cent in Macedonia.

6	Banac estimates that there were 168 392 Montenegrins in Yugoslavia in 1918 but points out that only a fraction considered themselves distinctively Montenegrin, rather than Serb.

7	The relationship between Serbs and Montenegrins is in many ways akin to that between Austrians and Germans. They speak the same language and belong to the same church, but have different historical experiences and have thus evolved two separate identities over the centuries.

8	According to the 1981 census, Croats made up 75.1 per cent of Croatia's population, 18.4 per cent of Bosnia-Hercegovina's, and 5.4 percent of Vojvodina's.

9	*Per capita* income in Slovenia was about three times greater than in Kosovo in 1945 and six times greater by the late 1980s.

10	Bulgarija, Rumonija, Italija, Greka, Albanija, Madgarska (Hungary), Austrija.

11	A census was also carried out in 1991 in the months immediately preceding the outbreak of war. While the results of this census are generally accurate, they are incomplete since Yugoslavia's Albanians boycotted it.

12	The most prominent Illyrian was Ljudevit Gaj, the language reformer who standardised literary Croat. That literary Serb and Croat are so similar reflects Gaj's desire for south Slav unity. The dialect Gaj chose as the basis for literary Croat was that which his Serbian counterpart, Vuk Karadjic, had chosen for literary Serb and was actually closer to that spoken by a majority of Serbs than that which most Croats spoke.

13	Slovenia was divided between Germany, Italy and Hungary. Italy, which already possessed Istria, also grabbed much of Dalmatia and constructed a Montenegrin protectorate. Parts of Croatia, including Baranja, Medjimurje and a strip of Slavonia went to Hungary, as did much of Vojvodina. German parts of Vojvodina, the Banat, became self-governing under German administration. Bulgaria acquired Macedonia as well as a corner of Serbia, and Albania, itself an Italian protectorate, swallowed Kosovo.

14 Albanians live in both Kosovo and western Macedonia. Because of a high birthrate their proportion of the population has grown throughout the 20th century. Today they form more than 90 per cent of the population in Kosovo and 20 per cent in Macedonia.

Part Four

Ethno-regionalism

8 Britain

The United Kingdom?

Michael Keating

THE UNION STATE

The United Kingdom comprises a single state containing several nations. The constitutional means for achieving this has been defined as a 'union state'[1]. This is a state which is neither federal nor strictly unitary but which, under a common system of authority, accommodates elements of diversity within state and civil society. This formula has permitted the development of an informal and flexible system of government, generally able to incorporate the multinational reality of the kingdom. Yet it has periodically come under challenge. It failed in Ireland and at the close of the twentieth century, is under increasing strain in Scotland, Wales and England itself.

The building of the United Kingdom can be understood by reference to the familiar core-periphery model. Starting from the core in south-eastern England, the state expanded by accretion until 1800, when it encompassed the entire British Isles. The Anglo-French dynasties of the Middle Ages (Norman and Plantagenet) consolidated the English kingdom and extended their feudal influence into Ireland, Wales and Scotland. Yet, despite the efforts of Edward I, Ireland remained largely unsubdued, Wales was only partly assimilated and in Scotland a separate kingdom survived. Wars over the French possessions and internal dynastic struggles preoccupied the English monarchy in the late fourteenth and fifteen centuries and it was only the kingdom of England which Henry VII secured in 1485. The Tudor monarchs consolidated the English state and turned their attention again to securing the whole archipelago. Under Poyning's Law, Ireland was subordinated to

215

the English Parliament and Henry VIII proclaimed himself king of Ireland. In 1536, Wales was legally incorporated into England. In Scotland, the Reformation reignited the struggle for influence between England and France, culminating in the triumph of the pro-English party and the succession of James VI of Scotland to the English throne in 1603. In 1707 Scotland and England were united in a parliamentary union. The motives were related to security, to prevent Scotland falling back under French influence, and dynastic, to secure the Protestant succession against Jacobite claims. Similar security concerns underlay the union with Ireland in 1800, amid the Napoleonic wars. This created the United Kingdom of Great Britain and Ireland.

Despite this underlying historic theme of English expansionism, the creation of the United Kingdom should not be seen merely as the establishment of Greater England, or as a colonial venture. As always in the study of nation-building, historiography is strongly coloured by the biases of the historians. So one school of thought sees the creation of the United Kingdom as a natural progression towards unity and enlightenment. This is, broadly, the view of the Whig historians. Nationalist historiography in the peripheral nations, by contrast, stresses the elements of coercion and the dominance of English power, English values and English institutions in the UK state. Even more misleading are the efforts of well-meaning outsiders[2] to convince the peripheral parts of the UK that they are the victims of colonial exploitation analogous to that practised by western powers against the peoples of the Third World. There is a strong teleological element in these accounts and a tendency to anachronism in projecting national identities back into the pre-national era.

Reality is more complex. The various parts of the United Kingdom acceded to the union in different ways and on different terms, and this legacy continues to affect contemporary politics. Ireland was conquered and governed, at least until the late nineteenth century, in a largely colonial mode. English descriptions of the Irish consistently portray them as alien, not easily assimilable. They were dispossessed of their lands by English and Scottish landowners and settlers and excluded from political participation by virtue of their religion. Wales, by contrast, was incorporated legally into England from 1536 and policy was largely characterized by assimilation. Scotland followed a third mode of incorporation, by negotiated union allowing its own indigenous elites a place in the British political order.

There was an effort at British nation-building in the late eighteenth and nineteenth centuries,[3] but it proved less thoroughgoing and successful than that of other European states (notably France). The main bases for this were Protestantism, monarchy and imperialism. As Colley[4] has shown,

Protestantism united majorities in England, Scotland and Wales against the French enemy and provided internal cohesion. Defence of the Protestant succession against Jacobite intrigues after 1688 served the same purpose. The Empire furnished an external support system for the union. It provided common symbols, and opportunities for trade and careers for upwardly mobile individuals in the peripheral nations. Excluded from the nation-building project were Catholics, which meant the majority of the Irish and parts of Scotland. The Scottish Highlands were incorporated only after the defeat of their traditional culture at the battle of Culloden (1746); their symbols were then pressed into the service of the British state. Rural Wales preserved its own strong culture, rooted in language.

On the institutional level, too nation-building was rather sporadic and incomplete. The UK state is the lineal descendant of the English state and has inherited its constitutional traditions and practices. Under the Tudor settlement, confirmed after 1688, England was a parliamentary monarchy, in which sovereignty was shared between the crown and the territorial oligarchy, represented in parliament. There was no separation between state, personified by the monarch, and society, represented by the dominant social and economic elites in the country. The territorial oligarchy remained the leaders of the local society, providing collaborators for the central regime except in Ireland.[5] Experiencing neither monarchical absolutism nor revolutionary jacobinism, the UK did not, before the twentieth century, establish a centralized bureaucracy, a standing army or a uniform set of administrative institutions. It thus partially escaped the 'national revolution' undertaken in other parts of Europe by nation-building states.[6]

Distinctive features of the pre-union societies remained and, in some cases, were strengthened in the course of modernization. In Scotland, the Union of 1707 (described in England as an Act and in Scotland as a Treaty) preserved elements of Scottish civil society while abolishing its parliament. The most important were the Church (Kirk) of Scotland which, under the doctrine of the 'twa kingdomes' had extensive powers of moral regulation as well as control over most of the education system; Scots law; the education system; and the self-governing burghs. These served to sustain Scottish identity and provided a measure of informal self-government within the Union.[7] This was not without tensions. Although the Union also abolished the English parliament, replacing it with a brand new parliament of Great Britain, the latter came to regard itself as the continuation of the English institution. It assumed sovereignty, though the principle has no basis in Scottish constitutional law and within five years of the Union had restored lay patronage in the Kirk, in defiance of its terms. Generally, however, London had to deal with Scottish society rather than merely imposing its will and was content to leave much day-to-day policy to its local representatives. Mediation between Scottish interests and British politics was undertaken until the 1830s by clientelistic system known as 'management'.[8] Whoever was recognized as the Scottish manager had the task of delivering Scottish MPs to the government in power in return for a free hand in patronage.

In Ireland, the carriers of identity were religion and social class. The mass of the population remained Catholic, with little in common with their largely Protestant landlords and social superiors. In the north-east of the island, a Protestant minority descended from Scottish and English settlers, did not integrate into the Irish population, in marked contrast to earlier generations of immigrants (including Danes, Normans and even Cromwellian settlers). Ireland was governed in a quasi-colonial mode even after the union of 1800. Power land in the hands of the Lord Lieutenant and the Secretary for Ireland, both responsible to the government in London; there was no need for either to be Irish. Dublin Castle, the seat of the administration, was thus removed from the local society.

In Wales, the principal marker of identity was language, sustained by the availability of a Welsh bible and the Protestant practice of bible-reading. From the eighteenth century, the spread of non-conformist religion served to distinguish the mass of Welsh both from the English and from their own anglicized gentry. Thereafter, the existence of an established Anglican Church was regarded as an affront, as it was in Ireland. Unlike Scotland and Ireland, Wales was legally and administratively assimilated to England, with no laws of its own before the late nineteenth century, and very few administrative institutions.

THE FIRST TERRITORIAL CRISIS

In the course of the nineteenth century, there were two competing sets of forces in the UK periphery, towards assimilation and consolidation of the state on the one hand and towards differentiation on the other. The union with Ireland in 1800 abolished the Irish parliament and provided for Irish representation at Westminster. Catholic emancipation in 1829 and the progressive reforms of the franchise after 1832 allowed the people of Ireland the right to be represented for the first time. Expansion of education eroded the Celtic languages, especially in Ireland and Wales. The Scots language had gone into decline, at least in official use and among the upper and middle classes, after 1707. The growth of the interventionist state consequent on franchise reform was another integrating force.

There was always resistance to assimilation. In Ireland, O'Connell's Repeal movement shook the country and only died out with the Famine of the late 1840s. In Scotland, there were occasional protests against tendencies to anglicization or the destruction of traditions. By the third quarter of the century, more serious challenges to the order emerged. One was a series of agrarian revolts which from the mid-nineteenth century, shook the UK periphery as they did other parts of Europe. The most significant were in Ireland, where the land reform movement became a potent political force, and in the Highlands of Scotland, where the crofters secured the election of their own Members of Parliament.[9] Religion proved another disruptive element, as the Anglican Church was rejected by the great mass of the people in Ireland and Wales. Religious revivals in both nations showed up the alienation of the people from the established religion. The growth of the interventionist state itself also provoked a series of reactions in the periphery. The informal union had accommodated a range of local customs and traditions. The modern bureaucratic state tended to be uniform and impersonal. Education was a central issue in the process of modernization and cultural formation. In 1870 a single Education Act and Department was proposed for the whole of mainland Britain. This was seen as a challenge to the Scottish tradition of independent provision and, after some argument, a separate Act was passed for Scotland, administered by a separate Scotch Education Department. Thus was begun a tradition of differential administration of Scottish matters which has been progressively extended up to the 1990s. In Wales, the need to pay tithes for the support of Anglican schools sparked a series of revolts in the late nineteenth and twentieth centuries. The 1870 Education Act ignored the Welsh language; already in the 1840s, the hostile attitude of the Commissioners of Education to the Welsh language had provided fuel for opposition. In Ireland, the campaign for a national university challenged the monopoly in higher education of Trinity College, a bastion of Protestantism and Unionism.

The emerging labour movement also took distinct forms in the UK periphery. In Scotland, a native movement was steeped in local traditions and inclined to independent action and nationalist themes.[10] In Wales, the labour movement was influenced by anarcho-syndicalism and stressed communitarian themes, especially in the mining areas.[11] At the turn of the century, the industrial areas of Scotland and Wales were among the economic power-houses of the Empire, giving a confidence to labour that it could advance on its own. The Irish labour movement had to accommodate a strong nationalist dimension in the south. In the north, it increasingly divided on sectarian lines as Catholics were excluded from high status and skilled occupations. Capital on the periphery, by contrast, was more closely tied to the imperial order and its markets and little tempted to nationalist ideas.

The result was a crisis of territorial representation across the UK periphery, as across other European peripheries in the late nineteenth century.[12] These were not, as social scientists have often assumed, backward-looking protests against modernity[13] but were rather attempts to control the process of modernization and give it a native form. This was the age of nationalism in Europe and was an important moment in the formation of national identity as we know it in the British Isles. Of course, Ireland, Scotland and Wales had distinct identities before this - but it is in the late nineteenth century that we can first speak of nationalism as a mass political movement aimed at the construction of a different type of political system. The UK state was faced with competing nation-building projects and competing foci of national identity. It is important to emphasize that I am not arguing merely that the United Kingdom is a multi-ethnic society. That claim could be made for its constituent parts individually. Ethnic complexity can be managed by a variety of policy instruments, including language rights, educational provision and civil institutions. The claim that the UK is multinational implies much more than this, that territorially based movements claim the right of self-determination and regard themselves as part of the family of European nations. In the modern era, where the claim is made that each nation should have its own state, this poses serious problems.

This is not to say that the nationalisms of the British periphery are of the same type. On the contrary, they exhibit very different characteristics. Scottish nationalism is territorially-focused and largely civic in nature. It does not emphasize ethnic purity, language or ascriptive identity but rather the characteristics of Scottish society. Its carriers are Scottish institutions and the historical memory of independent statehood. Its demands tend to be economic and institutional. Welsh nationalism, by contrast, has traditionally emphasized culture and language. Its constitutional agenda has often been vague and Welsh nationalists have often placed more emphasis on the values of community than the forms of government. Irish nationalism has taken two distinct forms, though they overlap and both may be found within the same individuals. One tradition dates traces its lineage to the United Irishmen of 1798, admirers of the French Revolution, and is civic, republican, democratic and non-sectarian. The other strand is ethnically-based, rooted in the Catholic community and opposed to accommodation with the Protestant minority. This strand has in the past also emphasized Ireland's Gaelic heritage and resisted 'foreign' influences. There is a violent tradition in Irish nationalism, which is largely absent in the other two cases, and which competes with a constitutional and non-violent tradition.

In the late nineteenth century, nationalist movements around the British periphery generally espoused Home Rule. This is a peculiarly British term, without a translation into other languages. It implies the devolution of power the constituent parts of the kingdom, but not necessarily in a consistent or symmetrical manner. Home Rule movements are more than merely regionalist, since they base their claims on national identity; yet their demands fall short of separatism. A section of British political opinion, generally found on the centre-left, is prepared to make concessions to the periphery in the form of Home Rule. In 1886, 1892 and 1910 Liberal governments brought forward legislation on Home Rule for Ireland. In 1975 and 1977 a Labour government did the same for Scotland and Wales. In between, a series of measures was proposed by backbench members of parliament. None of these succeeded. The first and last measures split the governing parties. All were bogged down in interminable discussions as to the role of members of the British parliament from the peripheral nations in the event of Home Rule. In principle, the union state formula, which permits diversity in unity, should be able to accommodate this type of moderate nationalist demand. In practice, it has proved impossible. In the twentieth century, separatist movements emerged in all three peripheral nations, partly as a result of the failure of the state to accommodate the multinational reality.

The dominant response to nationalist demands on the UK periphery has been an adamant refusal to compromise. This is the unionist position. While the (highly qualified) success of British governments in refusing to compromise with peripheral nationalism is often taken as a sign of the weakness of the nationalist appeal[14] exactly the opposite is true. The unionist recognizes that, in the absence of a deep-seated and unitary sense of national identity or a system of constitutional law, the only firm principle of the union is that of parliamentary sovereignty. Setting up national parliaments for the constituent parts of the UK would run the risk that these, drawing upon a sense of national identity, would constitute themselves as the primary reference point for their societies and so enjoy legitimacy greater than any mere regional or provincial unit. This argument is made in the classic unionist polemic of Dicey.[15] It is repeated by Wilson's[16] dissent to the Conservative's Scottish Constitutional Committee.[17] A visceral Unionism even led the Conservative Party to countenance armed resistance to Irish Home Rule in the years before the First World War.

A third response is exceptionalism in policy, either in the form of concessions to the peripheral nations, to assuage the discontent behind nationalist agitation, or in the form of peculiar measures of coercion. Coercion has most often been used in the case of Ireland, concessions in the cases of Scotland and Wales. Governments have also responded with institutional reform stopping short of political autonomy. This has permitted some differentiation in policy, enabled central government to present a local face, and provided opportunities to co-opt local leaders. These devices of territorial management proved a failure in the case of Ireland but for most of the twentieth century allowed the union state to govern largely unchallenged in Scotland and Wales. In the late twentieth century, their viability is again in question.

In Ireland, British territorial management was a failure. Politics was forged in a nationalist mode from the 1870s as the British parties failed to establish roots in the newly enfranchised Irish electorate. Irish nationalism was rejected vehemently by Protestants in the north of the island, and their connections with the British Conservative Party gave them a veto on constitutional change. An alternative strategy, of 'killing Home Rule by kindness' was pursued in the late nineteenth and early twentieth centuries. This included extensive land reform, creating a landowning peasant class; and the establishment of county councils in 1898, providing opportunities for patronage for the Catholic middle classes. Yet the counterpart to this was coercion and exceptional measures to deal with civil unrest. The constitutional nationalist Irish parliamentary party was undermined by splits in their own ranks, and by the failure to deliver on their Home Rule platform, given Conservative intransigence. This encouraged more extreme nationalist elements who, in the aftermath of the 1916 Easter Rising, were able to set the movement on the road to independence. In 1918 Sinn Fein won a sweeping victory in the general election in Ireland and unilaterally declared independence. After a violent conflict, a Treaty was signed in 1922 establishing two regimes, the Irish Free State in the south and the province of Northern Ireland in the north. Both were to be self-governing within the British Empire. In practice, the Free State became independent and in 1949 declared itself a republic and left the British Commonwealth. In Northern Ireland, the Protestant majority set up a regime to guarantee their ascendancy at the expense of the Catholic minority.

This removed the Irish question from British politics for nearly fifty years. Irish representation in the Westminster parliament was reduced to twelve members from Northern Ireland, so allowing a two-party alternating system of government to develop, with governments normally securing majorities. Speakers' rulings prevented matters within the purview of the Northern

Ireland government being raised at Westminster, further ensuring the insulation of mainstream British politics from Irish issues, despite the Stormont regime's violation of democratic norms and civil rights.

Discontent in Wales was less deep-rooted and amenable to policy concessions. After a long campaign, the Church in Wales was disestablished in 1921. The main leaders of the Welsh revival entered the leadership of the British Liberal Party by the end of the nineteenth century,[18] and one of them, David Lloyd George, was to become prime minister.

In Scotland, nationalist agitation peaked in the late nineteenth century and then again after the First World War. As in Wales, it declined as the issues which had fueled it, including land reform, church disestablishment, temperance, moved off the political agenda. Economic crisis forced Scotland into closer dependency on the British state. Leading figures in Scottish politics threw in their lot with the British Liberal Party and, after the first world war, Labour.

THE TERRITORIAL REGIME, 1922-72

With the Irish treaty and the subsiding of nationalist agitation in Scotland and Wales, British territorial politics went through a period of some fifty years of quiescence. It was during this time that commentators developed the 'homogeneity thesis', arguing, in the words of Finer that:

> Britain too has had its 'nationalities' problem, its 'language' problem, its 'religious' problem, not to speak of its 'constitutional' problem. These are problems no more.[19]

Blondel[20] described Britain as probably the most homogeneous of industrial nations. By the 1980s, few informed observers still inclined to this view.[21] The period c.1922-1972[22] should rather be seen as an exceptional time, in which territorial politics was not so much eliminated as successfully managed. The bases of the mid-century regime can be analyzed under the headings of values; economic dependence; institutional differentiation; the party system; social class; and the external support system. By the late 1960s the first signs of strain were seen in this system of territorial management.

Support for the United Kingdom has been underpinned by a set of values, shared to a greater or lesser extent by its component parts. Religion has already been mentioned as a factor uniting most Britons but excluding the majority of the Irish. In the post-1922 regime, Protestantism was the principal basis

for the union of Northern Ireland with the United Kingdom, legitimizing the
Stormont government in the eyes of the local majority but systematically
excluding the Catholics. In Scotland, by contrast, the substantial Catholic
minority was brought into the political mainstream by the 1918 Education
Act, which provided for separate Catholic schools supported by general
taxation. In Wales, education was taken out of the hands of the Anglican
Church and administered by local authorities responsive to the majority
electorate.

Shared national identity was an important factor in Scotland and Wales,
where it was possible to retain a Scottish/Welsh identity while being British
at the same time. This dual national identity is a source of mystery to
foreigners, brought up on the belief that national identity is singular and that
it can be accumulated, at the most, with a strictly subordinate local or regional
one. In Northern Ireland, by contrast, identity was mainly a matter of religion.
Catholics regarded themselves as Irish while Protestants tended to describe
themselves as British, though this did not necessarily imply adherence to the
political values of the British mainland.

The welfare state provided a set of common values after the Second World
War. It was essentially a British institution, in advance of most other countries
and built on the sense of national solidarity forged during the war. Even the
Stormont government, despite its conservative instincts, shadowed British
welfare legislation and the welfare state was often pointed out as an advantage
which Northern Ireland possessed over the Republic. Hopes that this would
lead Catholics to identify with the United Kingdom, however, collided with
sectarian divisions pointing in the other direction.

Scotland, Wales and Northern Ireland all suffered severely in the slumps
of the 1920s and 1930s, their traditional heavy industries being particularly
badly affected. The local bourgeoisies went into decline, as their industries
collapsed, moved or came under external ownership. From the 1930s and
particularly after the Second World War, the peripheral economies became
dependent on public ownership, state aid and regional incentives. This
provided a powerful argument, frequently repeated, for retaining strong links
with the UK. Fiscal transfers also became important. Stormont was originally
supposed to pay its own way and also make an imperial contribution to general
UK expenses, but its financial difficulties meant that this disappeared in the
1930s and by the 1940s, the principle had been established that the UK
government would pay to bring Northern Ireland's services up to British
standards.[23] Expenditure for Scotland had in the nineteenth century been set
according to population relativities under the Goschen formula. By mid
twentieth century, the fall in its relative population meant that its expenditure

share was proportionately higher. After the Second World War, the Goschen formula fell into disuse but the inherited relativities were maintained and even increased, as the Scottish Office bargained with the Treasury function by function.[24] Relative expenditure levels in Wales were also higher than in England, though lower than in Scotland. In the 1960s, elaborate regional development policies were developed to appeal to the peripheral nations and regions.

During this period, the party system in Scotland and Wales was the same as that in England. While the balance between the main parties was rarely identical, both Conservatives and Labour had a political base in Scotland and Wales and the alternation of parties in power ensured that the peripheral nations would at least periodically be on the winning side and provide members in the government. Scotland, until the mid-1950s, was rather evenly balanced between Conservative and Labour and represented in governments of both parties, but especially the Conservatives. Wales leaned more strongly to Labour, as did Scotland from the 1960s. In Northern Ireland, a separate party system existed. The Ulster Unionists were affiliated with the British Conservative Party and occasionally provided a government minister at the centre. It was not, however, possible to vote for the British Labour Party since it did not present candidates there.

Underlying the party system was social class, which provided the most important, although by no means the sole basis for political alignments. The Conservative Party was dominated until the 1960s or 1970s by representatives of the traditional aristocracy and gentry, a class which was truly UK in scope. The great landed families often held lands in all parts of the kingdom, they attended the same schools, and they possessed an instinctive feel for the Union. Among the working class and the labour movement, class loyalty tended in this period to attenuate territorial politics. Labour politicians in Scotland and Wales, previously sympathetic to Home Rule politics, now attacked it and all manifestations of minority nationalism as a diversion from real politics and a means of dividing the working class. This corresponded to electoral realities, as class voting reached a peak in the 1950s and 1960s.

Institutional differentiation served to isolate territorial politics from Westminster, so permitting the development of a two-party, class-based politics. Yet at the same time access was provided to decision-making at the centre. These two principles were constantly in conflict. Isolation was taken furthest in the case of Northern Ireland. Speakers' rulings had established that matters under the purview of Stormont could not be discussed at Westminster. As long as civil peace prevailed, British governments took little interest in Northern Ireland matters. While Stormont mirrored much of British social and economic policy, it was allowed to install a system of pervasive sectarian discrimination in administration and civil rights.

Scotland was much more integrated into the UK, though with a measure of differentiation. A Secretary of State for Scotland, by convention an MP from the ruling party elected in Scotland, presided over the Scottish Office. Gradually, this assumed responsibility for most domestic administration in Scotland, with the major exception of the social security system. The Secretary of State and the Scottish Office perform three main roles:

- They administer those functions which, for reasons of administrative convenience, are best handled on a Scottish level. This has long included the distinctive education and local government systems and matters of Scots law. Now it includes most domestic policy, except taxation and Social Security.
- They modify UK policy to fit into the Scottish legal and administrative system. This puts a Scottish face on UK policies, making them more acceptable to Scottish opinion. There is a minor degree of discretion on policy content, but usually only on matters of low political salience or low partisan importance.
- They lobby for Scottish interests in the Cabinet, with the Treasury and in the Whitehall policy networks. This is arguably the most important role. Much policy is made jointly by the Scottish Office and UK departments, with the UK department taking the lead role and the Scottish Office seeking to influence the policy as it develops.[25]

The role of the Secretary of State is buttressed by that of the Scottish Office bureaucracy, which also feels a loyalty to Scotland and an obligation to defend Scottish interests.[26] Scottish members of parliament also play a role of territorial representation, with a sharp distinction between a minority of UK-oriented MPs, who play on the UK political stage and avoid Scottish matters, and the majority, who are immersed in Scottish committees and the work of the Scottish Office and only venture into the UK arena where Scottish interests, normally economic, are directly affected.[27] These arrangements allow for a degree of insulation of Scottish issues from mainstream UK politics, while ensuring that the main policy lines are followed. Another device to include Scottish interests was the convention of appointing Scottish MPs to specific UK departments. Until 1979, there was always a Scottish MP in the Ministry of Agriculture, after 1974, a Scottish MP was appointed Energy Minister with responsibility for North Sea oil, and under Labour governments, there was always a Scottish miner in the government.

From 1964 a similar system was extended to Wales. A Secretary of State was appointed and gradually the Welsh Office took over responsibility for large areas of Welsh administration. There are fewer Welsh laws because of the absence of a Welsh legal system so that Welsh affairs are less self-contained than their Scottish counterparts.

Policy concessions could be made in Scotland and Wales on matters where high politics or party principles were not at stake. The language issue in Wales was handled by concessions to bilingualism, including Welsh language education, bilingual road signs and broadcasting in Welsh. In both nations, regulations on liquor licensing were different from those in England. Scotland for some time had a more restrictive divorce law than England and Wales.

This system of administrative devolution was intended to assuage nationalist pressures and contain Scottish and Welsh politics within a UK mould. It succeeded to a considerable degree, in that the UK parties in Scotland and Wales argued that any move to Home Rule would put at risk the role of the Offices and thus their privileged access to power at the centre. Given the economic and fiscal dependence of Scotland and Wales, this was a powerful argument. Yet at the same time, administrative devolution served to sustain and strengthen territorial identity by framing issues in a Scottish or Welsh context and raising expectations as to what government could do for these nations.

The external support system was provided by the British Empire and Britain's world role. The UK had been formed contemporaneously with the Empire and until the First World War was often identified with it. Home Rule proposals until that time usually distinguished between local and 'imperial' affairs (hence the imperial contribution from Stormont). The gradual transformation of Empire into Commonwealth did not at first alter this perception, though the Statute of Westminster of 1934 presaged important changes. Usually remembered for its concession of independence to the dominions, the statute also implied by subtraction that the UK was henceforth an independent state, but the implications of this were not fully felt until the aftermath of the Second World War and decolonization.

THE RETURN OF TERRITORIAL POLITICS

This territorial regime started to break down in the late 1960s and by the mid-1970s was in another crisis. While that crisis appeared to have been transcended by the end of the decade, longer term trends continued to undermine the territorial regime during the 1980s and 1990s.

The first breach of the regime was in Northern Ireland, where a civil rights movement emerged among the Catholic population, encouraged by a reforming Stormont administration under Terence O'Neill. Initially this challenged the union state on its own terms, by demanding the civil rights to which Catholics should have been entitled as *British* citizens. When a Protestant backlash threatened bloodshed on a wide scale, the British government was forced to intervene, sending in the army, initially to protect the Catholic population. It was not long before the conflict assumed more familiar contours, as the civil rights movement gave way to traditional nationalist themes, notably the demand for unification of Northern Ireland with the Republic. As before, two strands of nationalism were present, a constitutional and non-violent one associated with the Social Democratic and Labour Party, and a violent one associated with the Irish Republican Army (IRA) and its associated party, Sinn Fein. The breakdown of the regime and British intervention led, on the Protestant side, to the demise of the old monolithic Unionist Party and the emergence of militant competitors such as the Democratic Unionists of Ian Paisley, as well as Protestant paramilitary groups.

British responses to the Northern Ireland problem have been consistent with its historic treatment of Irish matters. It has attempted to contain the problem within the confines of Ireland, to externalize it from mainstream British politics, and has resorted to exceptional measures not used on the mainland. After the fall of the Stormont regime in 1972, direct rule was imposed under a Secretary of State with no political base in the province. After 1974, Ulster Unionist MPs at Westminster no longer took the Conservative Whip, so breaking the only partisan linkage between British and Northern Irish politics. Consistent attempts have been made to re-establish a devolved government in the province, this time with built-in provisions for power-sharing between Catholics and Protestants. Proportional representation has been introduced for elections in Northern Ireland. In the 1980s, Conservative governments, traditional upholders of the Union, went even further. They effectively abandoned a central tenet of their philosophy, the maintenance at all costs of the Union. Under the Anglo-Irish Agreement of 1985, Britain accepted a role for the Republic of Ireland in the government of Northern Ireland, while in the Downing Street Declaration of 1994 it went so far as to insist that it had 'no selfish strategic or economic interest in Northern Ireland'. For its part, the Labour Party officially committed itself to Irish unity, albeit only with the consent of the population of Northern Ireland.

In Scotland, the underpinnings of the union have eroded more slowly.

There was a dramatic breakthrough by the Scottish National Party in the 1974, when they won 30 per cent of the Scottish vote and 11 of Scotland's 71 parliamentary seats. This was enough to force the Labour Party to revert to its historic policy of Home Rule and try, unsuccessfully, to establish a devolved Scottish assembly. In the 1979 General Election, the SNP lost all but two of their seats. Yet in the longer run, the factors sustaining the union have been diminishing. Shared welfare values are largely intact but have come under increasing strain since the 1980s. In Scotland, the collectivist consensus remains stronger, at both mass and elite level.[28] Time-series data on identity are not available, but by the late 1980s most Scots identified themselves as exclusively Scottish or more Scottish than British.[29] Class identity no longer cross-cuts and weakens national identity. Rather, Scottish and working class identity tend to reinforce each other.[30] The pattern of economic dependency began to change in the 1970s with the discovery of North Sea oil. In the 1980s the rundown of diversionary regional policies in the UK (as in other European countries) as well as privatization, has lessened the need for access to central decision-making. so Scotland has become less of a dependency of the UK state and more a dependent of multinational capital.[31] The party system no longer serves to integrate as it did in the past. From the 1970s, the presence of the SNP has provided a competitor to the major parties in the nationalist quarter. In the 1980s, a large gap opened up between the UK parties, with the Conservative vote collapsing in Scotland and the Labour vote in England. On the previous occasion when such a gap had existed, in the early 1920s, it gave rise to a surge in support for Home Rule. This time, the gap was of longer duration and, until the early 1990s, there seemed little prospect of Scotland being on the winning side in UK politics.

In these circumstances, the system of administrative devolution came under increasing strain. It had sufficed to bridge minor differences in Scottish and English political preferences, especially when Scottish politics was conducted largely away from parliamentary scrutiny. Secretaries of State could plausibly claim to speak for a Scottish interest when they had substantial support in Scotland, and were listened to when Scotland was politically important to the government of the day. All this changed in the new political circumstances of the 1980s. The devolution debates of the 1970s concentrated attention on Scotland's public spending advantages and the Secretary of State had to fight harder, with a weaker political base to retain it. In the late 1970s, a new spending formula was introduced, the 'Barnett formula', consolidating most Scottish expenditure into a block, with increases or decreases each year calculated according to a population-based proportion of the changes in corresponding English programmes.[32] This focused attention on the Secretary of State as manager of Scottish priorities. Yet the Secretary of State, with minority support in Scotland, faced problems of political legitimacy. At a purely practical level, the Conservatives faced difficulties in staffing the ministerial ranks of the Scottish Office, given their reduced numbers of Scottish MPs.

The self-governing institutions in civil society and the quasi-governmental sector also came under attack from the Thatcher government, especially from its second mandate. Local government's powers were drastically curtailed, trade unions' privileges were cut back, and universities were subject to more detailed political intervention. Quasi-governmental agencies were brought under closer political control. Although the Thatcher government had been pledged to cut down on 'quangos', it proceeded to establish new ones, often staffed with political placemen. The Scottish Development Agency was replaced by Scottish Enterprise, with a stronger private sector presence and a much less interventionist remit, while Local Enterprise Companies were filled with business appointees who handled large amounts of public money. This was seen in Scotland as an attack on the remnants of informal self-government, the installation of placemen as a return to patronage in the eighteenth-century mode. Again, there is nothing unconstitutional in abolishing local governments, curtailing their powers, restricting trade unions or interfering in university matters; but it does represent an attack on the unwritten conventions underpinning the union state. Parliamentary sovereignty is tolerated only so long as it is not pushed too far. Many of the self-governing groups within Scotland had been lukewarm or hostile to home rule in the 1970s, fearing that a Scottish government would be more interventionist and threaten the niches which they had carved out for themselves within the state, civil society and the system of administrative devolution. The result of Conservative policies in the 1980s and early 1990s was to convert many of these to home rule. Local government, which had been wary of the devolution proposals in the 1970s, swung heavily in favour. Trade unions, brought into the UK state during the first world war, were increasingly alienated and looked to Scottish self-government and to Europe for escape. Opposition to home rule in the universities diminished. The Education Institute of Scotland, the main teaching union, which has long supported home rule, complained volubly about the 'Englishing of Scottish Education' (its enemies complained about the decline of vocabulary standards in the teaching profession).

A critical factor in undermining the old regime has been the European issue. British governments in the post-war era sought to replace the Empire successively with the Commonwealth, the 'special relationship' with the

United States and then the European Community (EC). EC entry in the 1960s and 1970s was pressed as a means of modernizing the British economy through external competition. Yet the political implications were down-played and Europe was clearly seen by most of the political elite as a new external support system for the existing state. The 1975 referendum pitched the forces of the old consensus, favourable to EC membership, against radicals of left and right. Opposition to entry was higher in Scotland and driven by a combination of party/class and territorial/nationalist objections. The argument that the Community was a capitalist organization which would prevent socialist measures in Britain was felt most strongly within the Labour Party in Scotland; and Labour itself was stronger in Scotland than in England. Nationalists opposed membership as a threat to future Scottish sovereignty and took as their model the Scandinavian democracies. More generally, Scottish interests saw EC membership as increasing Scotland's peripherality to the benefit of southern England, which was more favourably placed to take advantage of it. In the 1975 referendum, Scots voted to stay in the EC but by 58 per cent, against 69 per cent in England.

In the 1980s, these attitudes shifted radically. This is part of a general shift in the European periphery from contesting European integration to engagement in it with a view to obtaining more favourable treatment.[33] Margaret Thatcher played a role as Labour, trade unions and Nationalists in Scotland figured that anything which she opposed as strongly as European political integration must have some merit. At the British level, both Labour and the trade unions were also brought round to acceptance of Europe. The shift in the SNP came in the late 1980s. Former Labour MP Jim Sillars, who had been thinking about the link between Europe and Scottish home rule since EC entry in 1973, joined the SNP and converted them to a policy of independence-in-Europe. So now nationalists see Europe less as a support system for the old British state than as a support system for an independent Scotland. Labour does not support Scottish independence but does link home rule with Europe, proposing ways in which a future Scottish parliament could have an influence in EU policy. More generally, the whole debate on home rule and independence is now conducted in the context of European integration.

To a lesser degree, these factors can be seen in Wales. Support for the nationalist party, Plaid Cymru has not increased at general elections in the last twenty five years, but it has concentrated in the Welsh speaking areas, allowing the party to benefit from the plurality electoral system.[34] This association of nationalism with the Welsh heartland and the language was the principal reason for the heavy defeat of the devolution proposals in the

1979 referendum. Since the 1980s, a new type of Welsh consciousness has developed and diffused. The management of the language issue has defused tensions between English and Welsh speakers to that nationalism is not seen as exclusively tied to Welsh speaking. Modernization of the economy has entailed the end of mining and heavy industrial culture of the south. This has permitted the development of a modernized Welsh identity, focused on economic development and growth. An extension of administrative devolution has provided a Welsh focus for political issues but at the same time raised the question of democratic accountability. Unlike Scotland, it is politically possible to appoint a non-Welsh MP as Secretary of State; but whereas much Welsh opinion was flattered by the appointment of the heavyweight and decidedly non-Thatcherite Peter Walker in 1983, the appointment of hard-liner John Redmond after the 1992 election was not seen as a conciliatory gesture. Staffing of agencies by Conservative placemen has also been an issue. As in Scotland, Europe is an important influence.[35] In both nations, a modernized, civic nationalism has emerged, geared to contemporary issues. Cultural representations of the nation confirm this, now less concerned with nostalgia than with a mature consideration of contemporary society. In the new Europe, where nation, identity and political authority no longer always coincide, their traditions of shared sovereignty, pactism and dual identity may prove assets.

THE PROSPECTS FOR THE UNION STATE

Since the emergence of the modern state in the nineteenth century, the United Kingdom has experienced competing forms of national identity and projects for state building. The territorial regime of 1922-1972 succeeded in accommodating a complex set of territorial politics within the Westminster regime. This has come under increasing strain as a result of developments in the peripheral nations, failures of the UK state and changes in the external environment, notably membership of the European Union. In Northern Ireland the legitimacy of the state is challenged not only by Irish nationalists but also by Protestants who consider that Britain has sold them short. In Scotland and Wales, there is a search for a new political dispensation, which would provide a greater degree of self-government within a European context. Between the general elections of 1987 and 1992, a Scottish Constitutional Convention brought together representatives of the Labour and Liberal Democrat Parties, together with those of civil society, including churches, trade unions, local government and the voluntary sector. Agreement was reached on a programme of constitutional reform, with a Home Rule parliament. The parties supporting the Convention gained an absolute majority of votes and 58 of Scotland's 72 seats at the 1992 General Election. The response of the state has been confused and inconsistent. Northern Ireland has been externalized and the UK has virtually abandoned its claim to sovereignty there, agreeing to share power with the Republic of Ireland. Home Rule is pressed upon the province, irrespective of the wishes of its inhabitants. In Scotland and Wales, the response has been very different. Conservatives have adopted the traditional Unionist position of a refusal to consider even modest measures of Home Rule on the grounds that sovereignty cannot be divided. This echoes their attitudes to the European Union which most of them refuse to see as anything more than a free trade area. Instead, they have stretched administrative devolution even further, extending the functions of the Scottish and Welsh Offices. This has increased the burden on the Secretaries of State as territorial managers while further focusing political debate on Scottish and Welsh themes. The Labour Opposition, for its part, advocates a Home Rule solution, with elected Scottish and Welsh assemblies responsible for domestic affairs, while retaining representation in the Westminster parliament. This runs into the familiar question of equal representation, raised in the Irish Home Rule debates of the nineteenth century and, in the form of the 'West Lothian Question', the devolution debates of the 1970s.

Perhaps the biggest issue in the future of the union state is not the question of Scotland and Wales, where there is a growing consensus on Home Rule and on Europe, but that of England. As the dominant partner in the Union, the English have rarely had to question their national identity, which they have tended to equate with the UK itself, except when it has been challenged, from within the UK by peripheral nationalists, and from without in the form of European integration. Unless the question of England is answered, finding a stable place for Scotland and Wales within the UK may be impossible. The writhings of the contemporary Conservative Party over Europe are symptoms of a deep identity crisis. Conservative Europhobes attack integration in the name of national sovereignty, yet they are unsure just what the nation is whose sovereignty they are defending. The attack nationalism on the periphery yet defend it at the centre. They demand subsidiarity in Europe and deny it at home. Their are several nationalist traditions in England, on both right and left, yet in the contemporary era it has failed to develop a mature collective identity, one distinct from the UK, and which could recognized the limits of sovereignty in the modern era. Such an English identity could permit the recognition of Scottish and Welsh identity. It might eventually allow the reformulation of British identity as explicitly multinational. It might even permit the English to decide their place in Europe.

NOTES

1   S. Rokkan, and D. Urwin, *Economy, Territory, Identity, Politics of West European Peripheries*, London, Sage, 1983; M. Keating, *Nations against the State. The New Politics of Nationalism in Quebec, Catalonia and Scotland*, London, Macmillan, 1996; J. Mitchell, *Strategies for Self-government: The Campaigns for a Scottish Parliament*, Edinburgh, Polygon, 1996.

2   M. Hechter, *Internal Colonialism. The Celtic Fringe in British National Development, 1536-1966*, London, Routledge and Kegan Paul, 1975.

3   L. Colley, *Britons. Forging the Nation 1707-1837*, London, Pimlico, 1992; K. Robbins, 'The United Kingdom as a Multi-national State', in J. Beramendi, R. Maiz and X. Nunez (eds) *Nationalism in Europe. Past and Present*, Vol.11, Santiago de Compostela, University of Santiago de Compostela, 1994.

4   L. Colley, *op cit*, 1992

5   J. Bulpitt, *Territory and Power in the United Kingdom. An Interpretation*, Manchester, Manchester University Press, 1983.

6   M. Keating, *State and Regional Nationalism. Territorial Politics and the European State*, London, Harvester-Wheatsheaf, 1988.

7   G. Morton, 'A Tale of Two States: Scotland in the Eighteenth and Nineteenth Centuries', in J.G. Beramendi, R. Main and X.M. Nunez (eds), *Nationalism in Europe: Past and Present*, Santiago de Campostello, University de Santiago de Campostello, 1994; C. Harvie, *Scotland and Nationalism. Scottish Society and Politics, 1707-1977*, London, Allen and Unwin, 1977; Paterson, L., *The Autonomy of Modern Scotland*, Edinburgh, Edinburgh University Press, 1994.

8   M. Fry, *Patronage and Principle. A Political History of Modern Scotland*, Aberdeen, Aberdeen University Press, 1987.

9   In both cases, middle class and even landlord leadership was involved.

10 M. Keating and D. Bleiman, *Labour and Scottish Nationalism*, London, Macmillan, 1979.

11 B. Jones and M. Keating, *Labour and the British State*, Oxford, Oxford University Press, 1985.

12 M. Keating, *op. cit.*, 1988.

13   S.M. Lipset, 'The Revolt against Modernity', in *Consensus and Conflict: Essays in Political Sociology*, Ithaca, Cornell University Press, 1985.

14   A more sinister claim is sometimes made that the absence of violence of unconstitutional action in Scotland and Wales means that government does not need to take the constitutional aspirations in these nations seriously.

15   A.V. Dicey, *England's Case against Irish Home Rule*, Richmond, Richmond Publishing Company, 1886, 1973 edition.

16   C. Wilson, 'Note of Dissent', in *Scotland's Government. The Report of the Scottish Constitutional Committee*, Edinburgh, The Scottish Constitutional Committee, 1970.

17   Conversely, the failure to see the difference between a region and a nation is at the basis of the naïve proposals of Peacock and Crowther-Hunt's dissent to the report of the Royal Commission on the Constitution, in which they propose a uniform system for Scotland, Wales and the English regions. Lord Crowther-Hunt and A. Peacock, Volume 11 Memorandum of Dissent, Royal Commission on the Constitution, 1969-73, London, HMSO, 1973.

18   K. Morgan, *Rebirth of a Nation. Wales 1880-1980*, Oxford, Oxford University Press, 1982.

19   S. Finer, *Comparative Government*, Harmondsworth, Penguin, 1970.

20   J. Blondel, *Voters, Parties and Leaders*, Harmondsworth, Penguin, 1974.

21   This is not a mere matter of hindsight. In the mid-1970s a number of us were arguing for the multinational interpretation of British politics. As late as 1987, Finer could still write a student text on British politics with no reference to Scotland or Wales, but referring to 'England's status and role in the world' S. Finer, 'Politics of Great Britain', in R. Macridis (ed.), *Modern Political Systems: Europe*, 6th edn, Englewood Cliffs, Prentice Hall, 1987.

22   Periodization is necessarily a rather arbitrary matter. The date of the Anglo-Irish treaty is 1922 and the effective abandonment of Home Rule by Scottish Labour politicians as they entered the UK parliament *en masse*. The date of the suspension of the Stormont parliament is 1972. In 1973 the Royal Commission on the Constitution recommended devolution and in 1974 the SNP made their major parliamentary breakthrough and the Labour Party reverted to Home Rule for Scotland and Wales.

23   D. Birrell and A. Murie, *Policy and Government in Northern Ireland:*

Lessons of Devolution, Dublin, Gill and Macmillan, 1980.

24   D. Heald, *Public Expenditure*, Oxford, Martin Robertson, 1983; A. Midwinter, M. Keating and J. Mitchell, *Politics and Public Policy in Scotland*, London, Macmillan, 1991.

25   A. Midwinter et. al., *op cit.*, 1991.

26   M. Keating, *The Role of the Scottish MP*, PhD thesis, CNAA, 1975.

27   M. Keating, *op cit.*, 1975.

28   M. Keating, *op cit.*, 1996.

29   J. Brand, J. Mitchell and P. Sturridge, 'Identity and the vote. Class and nationality in Scotland' in D. Denver (ed.), *British Elections and Parties Yearbook*, New York, Harvester-Wheatsheaf, 1993.

30   J. Brand et. al., *op cit.*, 1993.

31   M. Keating, *op cit.*, 1996.

32   D. Heald, *op cit.*, 1983.

33   M. Keating and L. Hooghe, 'By-Passing the Nation-State? Regions and the EU Policy Process', in J.J. Richardson (ed.), *European Union: Power and Policy Making*, London, Routledge, 1996.

34   In 1992, Plaid Cymru won one seat for every 38 598 votes, against 209 852 for each SNP seat. The Conservatives, the next most favoured party, gained one seat for every 41 811 votes.

35   M. Keating and B. Jones, 'Scotland and Wales. European Integration and Peripheral Assertion', *Parliamentary Affairs*, 43.3, pp.311-24, 1991.

9 Canada

The Politics of Deep Diversity

Don MacIver

Canada is one of the most peaceful, prosperous and well-ordered states in the modern world. As a multinational state, however, it is one of the most complex and in recent years its diversity and internal divisions have from time to time placed its survival in question. This chapter addresses the nature of ethnic diversity in Canada, discusses the fragmented political identity it has produced and examines the strains it has placed on Canadian national unity. It then assesses the attempts to accommodate these divisions and considers why they have so far not been entirely successful.

Canada is the second largest country in the world but much of its territory is located in northern latitudes with a generally extreme climate, which offers an inhospitable environment for human settlement. Most of the population of 29 millions[1] is concentrated along a narrow east-west corridor within about 200 miles of the United States border. This corridor is segmented by mountains and rivers which divide the country into a number of distinct regions and create natural lines of communication north-south towards the United States. Distances between major centres are immense and the country is held together by the railway, the 5,000 mile Trans-Canada highway, the trans-continental air-routes, and a network of telecommunication, radio and satellite links. The significance of this is that Canadian national unity is a continuous act of imagination and political will in defiance of the logic of both geography and economics[2].

A LAND OF MINORITIES

The problem of unity is intensified by the diversity of Canadian society. In addition to the socio-economic and ideological divisions characteristic of modern industrial societies, there are significant territorial and ethno-cultural cleavages. There are ten provinces and two federal territories which range widely in income, wealth and resources, although efforts are made to minimise the effects of such inequalities. There are five time zones, several distinct regions and over 100 ethno-cultural communities.[3] English is the principal and most widely used language in most regions but French, spoken by about a quarter of the population, is the principal language in the Province of Quebec. English and French are both official languages and many other languages are in daily domestic use.[4]

Canada today is a land of minorities (Figure 9.1) and its population has been changing in recent years faster and more visibly than ever before.[5] The population now includes four broad ethnic categories: British, French, people of other origins and the aboriginals. Canadians of purely British origin are still the largest group but have declined from nearly 60per cent to just under 30per cent of the total population in the last one hundred years (Figure 9.2).

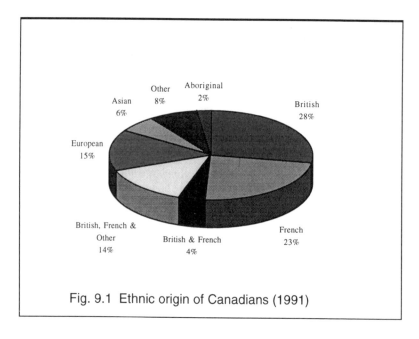

Fig. 9.1 Ethnic origin of Canadians (1991)

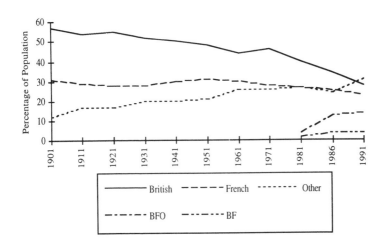

Fig. 9.2 Population by ethnic origin

The French proportion of the total population has been declining steadily for even longer and now stands at about 23%. Both the British and French populations have experienced low birth rates since the 1960s but, whereas a significant proportion of the British population is of recent immigrant stock, the French are almost entirely (99%) Canadian born, descendants of the original seventeenth and eighteenth century colonial settlers. The British have intermarried with other groups more than the French, thus creating a relatively large British and other category which is concealed in the rather inexplicit census category of British, French and Others and helps to explain the apparently steep decline of the British group since 1971.[6] Although nearly one third of the population is neither French nor British in origin, the politics of ethnicity continues to be dominated by the French-English cleavage, partly perhaps because of its long and unique history, although other issues have intruded significantly since the 1980s.[7]

While the proportion of British and French in the population has declined, that of other ethnic origins has expanded steadily throughout the twentieth century and these now constitute a very diverse group which makes up about one third of the population. It includes people of German, Italian, Ukrainian and Scandinavian origin, with growing numbers of Asians, Afro-Caribbeans and Latin Americans.[8] This reflects a shift in the source of immigrants from the British Isles and northern Europe to eastern and southern Europe and then to the third world, especially southern and south-east Asia. Most of these have settled in the anglophone cities of Ontario and the West, deepening the contrast between urban and small town populations.[9]

The smallest group is the aboriginals, whose ancestors were living in Canada before the European colonists. The total aboriginal population is just under one million and includes the Indians, who now style themselves the First Nations, the Metis or people of mixed blood and the Inuit, who inhabit the far North. Altogether they make up less than three per cent of the total population, the Indians being by far the most numerous group. Traditionally the Indians have adapted very closely to their environment and there are consequently very considerable cultural differences between the tribes of the high tundras, the temperate forests, the plains and the west coast. According to the Assembly of First Nations the Indians comprise about 600 bands or autonomous groups, ten different language groups and 53 nations, each one claiming to be a distinct society with its own culture.[10] The Inuit also believe that their language (Inuktatut, with twenty dialects and two alphabets) and culture also entitles them to be regarded as a distinct society.[11]

Canada is thus a very diverse and pluralistic society. This pluralism has its roots in the country's colonial heritage and the unique course of its political development.

THE ROOTS OF DIVERSITY

Colonial Heritage

Canadian society originated in the colonies established by European explorers, traders and settlers in the sixteenth century and after. The early history of the country was shaped by the rivalry between Britain and France for control of North America which ended with the British capture of Quebec, the principal French settlement and military capital. This, and the subsequent separation of the United States from British North America, created the essential framework and conditions in which Canadian society and political institutions developed over the next two centuries. For well over half a century after the conquest the French continued to be a majority of the population in Canada, a fact acknowledged in the institutions of the colonial government. A sequence of legislation including the Quebec Act of 1774 recognised the distinctive features of Quebec society, guaranteed its language, religion, legal system, social customs and provided its elite with a share in the exercise of political power.[12]

As Canada developed and expanded the proportion of the population of British origin increased to become a majority in the country as a whole, but the French were always to remain a majority in Quebec. This shift in the balance of the population and the territorial concentration of the English and French communities produced tensions which led to a brief rebellion in 1837. Lord Durham found 'two nations warring in the bosom of a single state' and believed the main cause of the trouble to be 'the vain endeavour' of the colonial power to preserve a distinct French Canadian society.[13] He recommended a union of Upper Canada (now Ontario) with Lower Canada (now Quebec) and the establishment of responsible government. As Upper Canada was predominantly anglophone and francophone Lower Canada was dominated by an anglophone elite, he thought Union would lead to the assimilation of the French. Durham's plan was implemented immediately, but responsible government was delayed until 1847–48, when it was introduced as a result of pressure from the colonies themselves. Contrary to what Durham expected, however, the Union produced a bicultural, consociational polity governed by a moderate, progressive coalition of Anglo-French parties. Unfortunately the system did not work entirely satisfactorarily. Whereas cooperation and understanding between leaders enabled it to work, mistrust and suspicion between the communities at large often caused deadlock and paralysis. Observing the rules of the system made it difficult to reach decisions, but disregarding them simply increased social tensions.[14]

The major weakness of the Union was that, while it was based on democratic principles, albeit rather Whiggish ones, it gave equal representation to the two provinces. This did not much please the French at first, as they still had the greater population, but it pleased the English even less as their population increased and they demanded a reform of the Union in order to give Upper Canada a greater share of representation. This antagonised the French, who feared that such a reform would lead to English domination and the loss of their privileges. The English, on the other hand, felt that if representation by population was not forthcoming, they would have to endure a French minority influence on their public affairs.[15] By the 1860s it became clear to the leaders of both communities that the solution was to create two self-governing provinces with a central government to look after their common interests, including the development of British North America. This idea was also attractive to some in the Maritime colonies and it was not long before representatives of all the colonies met and eventually agreed a continental union or confederation. Thus modern Canada began in 1867 as a union of four self-governing colonies, to which other colonies and territories later acceded between 1870 and 1949.[16] Underlying the agreement on confederation was a shared commitment to a vague, but tacitly understood conception of Canadian identity. This identity was based on a belief in parliamentary institutions and the British connection and mistrust of the United States, fuelled partly by the memory of the invasion of 1812 and partly by suspicion of American intentions in the aftermath of the Civil War.[17]

Ethnicity and Nation Building

The four provinces which formed the original Confederation were motivated more by pragmatic and careful calculation of common interests than by fine ideals, but this is not to say that the enterprise was lacking in idealism and vision. Confederation was intended to be the start of a great experiment in nation-building, inspired by the vision of a Canadian nation 'from sea to sea'. To implement this vision three principal strategies were deployed which came to be known collectively as the National Policy. These were a high tarriff against foreign (mainly American) manufactures, a transcontinental railway linking the country from Atlantic to Pacific and a government sponsored programme of immigration to colonise and develop the West.

The greatest enthusiasm for this project was amongst the British of Upper Canada, while the Maritime colonies gave their support with reservations. The most serious misgivings were expressed by the French in Lower Canada, for whom the proposed union presented a genuine dilemma. They were suspicious of the Upper Canada British, still fearful of Anglophone domination, and doubtful that they would ever be allowed an equitable share in the development of Canada. On the other hand, they welcomed the prospect of a self-governing province in which they could arrange their domestic affairs without interference; moreover, they had nowhere else to go and shared with other Canadians a desire to unite under British protection in face of the American threat. These factors, reinforced by the promise that their special status and privileges would be protected and that French and English would be treated equally, finally persuaded them to accede to the Union.

The leaders of both the English and French communities thought that ethnic conflict could be controlled in Confederation, but they were soon disappointed as difficulties arose in the West. At Fort Garry in the Red River colony near present day Winnipeg, there was a brief rebellion by the Metis people who feared that the expected growth of anglophone settlement in the West would threaten the rights and status of francophones. On the creation of the province of Manitoba in 1870 most of these rights were guaranteed, but the Metis leader, Louis Riel led another rebellion in 1885 to extend these rights to the Metis of the western territories.. This second rebellion was put down by the army, the Metis were repressed and Louis Riel was hanged. Such a severe response was greeted with dismay and anger in Quebec, where many regarded Riel as a patriot defending French rights. Across central Canada positions were taken on ethno-cultural lines which soon affected other issues and contaminated the whole political system. Ethnically charged rhetoric from some quarters in Ontario and Quebec brought anglophones and francophones closer to confrontation and intensified the difficulties facing the leaders of both communities.

This smouldering situation was inflamed in 1890 when the government of Manitoba, now an increasingly Protestant province, decided to establish a secular education system in which there would be no public support for Catholic schools. Although the issue was ultimately resolved, the anger it caused had scarcely died down when it was revived by a decision of the government of Ontario in 1913 to restrict the use of French in Ontario schools. The distress of French communities in Manitoba and Ontario over the schools question resonated in Quebec, where it was taken as further proof that confidence in the Confederation bargain had been misplaced. It united clerics, intellectuals and bourgeoisie, patriots and people, indeed almost every section of society in opposition to English Canada. It emphasised the extent to which Quebec was different, not simply because it was French, but because it was Catholic. It permitted a resurgence of the influence of the deeply traditional Roman Catholic hierarchy at a time when the economy was beginning to modernise and Quebec had the opportunity to develop a more secular, open and mobile society. Instead Quebec increasingly withdrew behind its own cultural, political and provincial boundaries which reinforced rather than weakened its isolation from the rest of Canada.

Thus for two hundred years Quebec remained a traditional, defensive and inward looking society. Cut off from France by the conquest of 1759 and further alienated from it by the anti-clerical republicanism of the 1789 Revolution, it developed separately from both France and British North America. By the twentieth century it was a distinct and self-contained, francophone society, remote from its European origins and suspicious of its English Canadian neighbours. Thus early twentieth century Quebec did not identify with France and felt little or no commitment to British or imperial interests and its alienation from the rest of Canada was only further intensified when the federal government introduced military conscription during the First World War. While conscription was accepted in English Canada as a necessary contribution to the imperial war effort, it was met with widespread and outraged resistance in Quebec. Nothing had ever so completely divided

Quebec from English Canada; nothing so fully demonstrated the detachment of Quebec from the Canadian nation building project; and nothing so clearly indicated that two distinct societies, cultures and identities had evolved within Canada. The conscription issue mobilised the conservative, catholic and nationalist forces in Quebec society which eventually came together as the Union Nationale in the 1930s and, thereafter dominated Quebec politics until the late 1950s.

Constitutional Development

While the colonial heritage and the vicissitudes of nation building were important, another important factor in shaping the diversity of Canada was the development of the constitution. Canada was formed and its constitution established by the British North America Act (now known as the Constitution Act) 1867.[18] The Act reflected the concern of the founding fathers to unite the colonies and territories, to provide for their common defence and create an integrated economy bound together by a trans-continental railway and a strong central government. It ennumerated 49 powers, of which it assigned 29 to the federal government, 17 to the provincial governments and left 3 to be concurrent. It also gave a number of general intervention powers to the federal government, which have since been repealed or otherwise fallen into abeyance. The Fathers of Confederation thus sought to strike the balance of powers in favour of the federal government and for some time it seemed that they had succeeded. From an early stage in the development of the new constitution, however, judicial review upheld the autonomy of the provinces and continued to do so for several decades. The court (the Judicial Committee of the Privy Council) insisted that the federal government could not use either its general powers or any specific power, such as the trade and commerce power, in such a way as to undermine the independent jurisdiction of the provincial governments.

The Judicial Committee has been heavily criticised by constitutional lawyers and academics in Canada for this reversal of the presumed intentions of the founding fathers.[19] One of the major issues at confederation, however, was the stubborn independence, indeed parochialism of the colonies (especially Nova Scotia) and their reluctance to yield any of their political autonomy or fiscal independence to the proposed federal government. Thus, while the Fathers of Confederation pressed for as powerful a central authority as they could get, an essential part of the Confederation bargain was that substantial autonomy was left to the provinces, who never relinquished their claim to exercise it. It was repeatedly confirmed by judicial interpretation, augmented by the growth of state activity in areas of provincial jurisdiction and sustained by the political determination of the provincial governments to protect it. Contrary to what has been argued from time to time by the exponents of centralised federalism, provincial autonomy is not a novel concept, nor one invented by the Judicial Committee, but one that was established by the Constitution Act itself. Moreover, provincial autonomy was not an artefact of confederation but a condition of it, which is perhaps why it has been so durable and tangible in its effects.[20] In recent decades in particular it has enabled Quebec to develop and maintain a distinct legislative and administrative system and has been the occasion of long standing disputes over the status of the provinces between the West and the federal government.[9]

In the years since confederation the idea of provincial autonomy has been one of the most important factors shaping the structure and culture of politics in Canada. The diversity of Canada together with the complex history of its people are reflected in the fissures in its political culture, the most notable of which are Quebec nationalism and regional alienation, particularly in the West. Both these movements articulated demands for recognition of the distinctive experience of particular regions within the Canadian political system.

THE FRACTURED POLITY

Quebec nationalism

Quebec has always consciously differentiated itself from the rest of Canada. Over the last three or four decades, however, the basis and quality of this differentiation has changed. In the past emphasis was placed on language, culture and religion as the principal indicators of difference. This cultural nationalism, which characterised French Canadian society in the nineteenth and early twentieth centuries, was replaced by a more radical and more secular political nationalism which focussed on the status of Quebec as a separate society and the unique nature of the Quebec provincial state as the guardian of that society. The new nationalism, which has dominated Quebec politics throughout the second half of the twentieth century, emerged in the 1950s and fuelled the Quiet Revolution of the 1960s. The shift of emphasis which it introduced was associated with underlying changes in Quebec society and politics.[21]

Until the twentieth century, despite increasing industrialisation, the French population of Quebec was predominantly rural. Most people lived in small agrarian, forest and village communities usually centred around the church, which fostered traditional and conservative attitudes. The economy and society of Quebec was dominated by an anglophone elite, while francophones were mostly in low paid and low status occupations. After the Second World War, a rapid expansion of higher education, based on a secular curriculum and taught by an increasingly lay staff in universities and colleges, produced a new secular intelligensia which challenged both the social leadership of the traditional clerisy and the domination of the economy and business by anglophones. Education at all levels, previously controlled by the church, was taken over by the provincial government, whose Ministry of Education looked to France as the model of a modern francophone education system. A number of Quebec industries and public utilities were nationalised or brought under closer government regulation and the scope and activity of public administration in Quebec was expanded. There was an expansion of popular interest and government support for Quebec culture, including publishing, film and television, as well as the traditional and popular arts.

This rapid transformation of Quebec society promoted both the self-confidence and the self-interest of francophones in Quebec. These changes increased the share of economic activity controlled by francophones and created employment opportunities for the enlarged pool of graduates and professionals produced by the new education policy. This new intelligentsia transformed itself into an urban middle class of salaried professionals and officials; they demanded that the provincial state manage the modernisation of Quebec society while protecting its distinctiveness; the slogan *maitre chez nous* (masters in our own house) expressed their determination to see the process through to a conclusion and eliminate anglophone domination from all areas of Quebec society. Their own professional and career interests were linked to the success of this project which became the engine of the new nationalism. Their demands also led to the establishment of French as the official language of everyday life in Quebec, to restrictions on English schools and the proscription of English language signs.[22]

Within the new nationalism in Quebec there were two divergent approaches to the expression of identity and the promotion of the French language. The first, whose most notable protagonist was the federal Liberal leader and Prime Minister, Pierre Elliot Trudeau, sought to give French equal status as an official language across Canada, thus improving the employment opportunities, access to public services and the general esteem of all French Canadians.[23] The exponents of this approach devoted immense energy to the promotion of biculturalism and their monument is the Report of the Royal

Commission on Bilingualism and Biculturalism. Their greatest success was the 1969 Official Languages Act which established bilingualism in all federal institutions with considerable advantage to Francophones at a time of federal government expansion. The policy encountered initial resistance and even hostility, especially in the West, but bilingualism has now been accepted as the norm in the federal public service and the leading sectors of business and a significant proportion of the anglophone middle class across Canada has acquired French language skills.[24]

The second approach, embraced by many Quebec privincial politicians but associated more with the Party Quebecois (PQ) and its founder, Rene Levesque, was based on the assumption that French language and culture could only survive in Canada if it was secured in Quebec by the powers and resources of the provincial state.[25] Hence the Office de la Langue Francaise was created in 1961, followed by a sequence of legislation intended to enhance the status and role of the French language in Quebec. In 1977 the nationalist PQ government introduced the Charter of the French Language, making French the sole official language in Quebec, prescribing French as the language of public services, commerce and the workplace and the principal language of education for all except Canadian born English speakers. These laws were generally accepted, even by Anglophones, but serious controversy was created by the Sign Law, which required that all advertising and commercial signs, even in small shops, must be in French. Its opponents challenged it as an infringement of individual rights while its supporters saw it as a device to ensure the collective rights of Francophones to protect their language and culture. Although this law was invalidated by the Supreme Court the provincial government insisted on keeping it in place, invoking the 'notwithstanding' clause, which allows a provincial government to take measures, otherwise unconstitutional, which it regards as vital to the interests of the province. Even on the evidence of the Conseil de la Langue Francaise, however, these language laws have been less than wholly effective. They were mainly inspired by the PQ and were generally more rigorous and draconian than was necessary to satisfy public opinion in Quebec. After many years of controversy, their scope and severity were reduced by the Bourrassa Liberal government in 1993.[26]

In general the new nationalism was a dynamic, modernising and creative force in Quebec society, but in its early stages it remained culturally defensive, inward looking and largely anglophobe. It had an extremist fringe including a short lived terrorist group, the FLQ (*Front pour Liberation de Quebec*) and non-violent groups like the St. Jean Baptiste Society, although such groups were always peripheral and never had any decisive influence on the course of Quebec politics. A more durable characteristic is a certain ethnocentrism, expressed in a pride in *pûr laine Quebecois*, signifying descent from the original French colonial settler stock. The greatest significance of the new nationalist ideology, however, is that it challenged earlier views of Quebec's relationship with the rest of Canada and radically politicised traditional conceptions of that relationship. Where the people of Quebec once described themselves as *Canadiens Francais*, a minority in Canada, they now describe themselves as *Quebecois*, a dominant majority in their own land. To the Quebecois the view that Quebec is part of French Canada seriously understates its significance and role. Over 90% of Canadian francophones live in Quebec, whose population was 82% francophone in 1991. In the nationalist view Francophone communities outside Quebec are minorities which are ultimately unviable as separate cultures and must face the realities of life in an overwhelmingly anglophone society. Quebec, however, is a vigorous, self-contained and autonomous community, the bastion of French culture in the whole American continent. Thus Quebec is not just a province like the others. Indeed Quebec is not a province, but a nation. As such it needs political self-expression to promote the economic development and cultural well-being of its members, which ultimately implies the appropriation of the resources of the state and their internalisation within Quebec. This simply means that Quebec needs greater autonomy and political powers than the other provinces.[27]

This view, widely accepted in Quebec, has brought the Province into confrontation with the other provinces and the federal government. The only question is whether the autonomy demanded can be accomplished within the existing Canadian constitutional framework with Quebec having greater autonomy and powers than the other provinces (assymetric federalism) or whether it is only possible through independence for Quebec. The former is the position of the Quebec Liberal Party which advocates asymmetric federalism, that is greater powers for Quebec within the federal system; the latter is the view of the Parti Quebecois and the Bloc Quebecois, which advocate sovereignty-association, that is political independence for Quebec and economic association with Canada on the EU model. Public opinion in Quebec is fairly evenly divided most of the time, but possibly inclines more against independence than for it. Public opinion polls generally register a majority against independence and two referendums in 1980 and 1995 have rejected it with increasingly narrow majorities. In some respects the PQ's separatist strategy may have been effective in putting pressure on the rest of Canada to acknowledge Quebec's demands. On the other hand, it may have actually stiffened resistance to these demands and polarised opinion in

Quebec.

Regionalism

As might be expected in such a vast country as Canada, regionalism is an important factor in the culture and popular heritage. A perception of difference from the rest of the country, intensified by a sense of remoteness, economic grievance and political exclusion are the common factors contributing to regional identity.[28] Canada may be considered to consist of five regions, the Atlantic or Maritime region, Quebec, Ontario, the West and the North.[29] Each of the regions has a coherent historical identity and there are notable differences between regions in economic development, lifestyle, political culture and the structure of politics. Most Canadians identify with their region and perceive their country in regional terms, with the result that competing regional identities and demands also increase the strain on Canadian unity.

While the regions each have a strong sense of identity, they are also internally diverse and polycentric and the identification of regional interests is not always unanimous. Moreover, while the central regions of Ontario and Quebec have provincial governments which give some coherence to the articulation of their interests, other regions lack this institutional and political cohesion. The North, which has a relatively small population, consists of the Yukon and the North West Territories and contains a significant proportion of Canadian natural resources. The region has always been the administrative responsibility of the federal government which has given it some coherence. The people of the North, however, have come to resent this distant, paternalistic rule and to demand provincial status with representative and responsible government like the rest of Canada. In pursuit of this, the North has recently experienced far reaching economic and political change and has now become the newest region to articulate its own separate interests and to project a distinct political identity.[30]

In the Maritimes and the West there are strong regional identities and efforts have been made to promote closer regional cooperation and integration; but none of the existing regional bodies has any corporate decision making powers, although the Maritime Economic Initiative has created a framework which could encourage further integration.[31] The Maritime region includes some of the oldest societies in Canada whose origins reach back to the earliest colonial times, but after several decades of economic decline it is now one of the poorest. Although the Maritimes played a crucial part in confederation and the making of Canada, today the region feels peripheral and dependent, with a deep suspicion of central (or 'upper') Canada and the federal government, which are usually blamed for the economic plight of the region.[32]

Regional discontent is not necessarily a function of economic deprivation or development. Even in Ontario, the richest region of Canada and generally regarded as its centre, there have been some expressions of regional discontent. The former NDP provincial government conducted an inquiry into Ontario's relative position in the federation and Premier Rae demanded that 'Ontario must be treated fairly'.[33]

Regional protest is probably strongest in the West where per capita income levels are well above the Canadian national average. Possibly the most significant recent expression of Western regional sentiment, however, is the emergence of the Reform Party, launched in Winnipeg in 1987 with the slogan 'the West wants in', a vivid and poignant evocation of the Western sense of alienation and exclusion. Historically Western alienation is rooted in a strong sense of economic injustice and political frustration and what Westerners want most of all is to be treated as equal partners. They have long believed that the West has been treated like an internal colony, its economy dominated by Central Canadian commercial elites who exploited the West for their own gain. From the western point of view, therefore, the nation building strategy and its economic components, particularly the industrial tariff, the railway freight rates and the development of natural resources, were all directed and administered for the benefit of central Canada at the expense of the West. In more recent years Westerners have felt that, despite its growing wealth and the importance of its resources to the Canadian economy, the interests of their region have again been neglected by federal governments more concerned about Quebec.[34]

These perceptions have created a deep sense of grievance that underlies the Western suspicion of central Canada and the federal government. It partly explains the resentment of Westerners at the special treatment which they believe is given to Quebec's demands compared to their own. It underlies the belief that Western interests have been persistently betrayed through most of the twentieth century by Liberal governments which were able to ignore the West because they drew the bulk of their support from Central Canada. This point was made repeatedly for Westerners at general elections, such as 1980, when the Liberal Party was able to declare a majority before a single seat had been counted in the West.

A feeling of political exclusion and disempowerment is part of the western outlook and has long been reflected in the structure of politics in the West. Since 1980 the Western Premier's Conference has sought to facilitate economic cooperation amongst the western provinces and to coordinate their approach to the federal government on political issues, but progress has been inhibited by their own disparate interests and political cultures.[35] From the

1940s Westerners put their faith in the Conservative Party to safeguard Western interests at the federal level, but were disappointed again in the late 1980s, when a Conservative government with strong support in Eastern Canada as well as the West was seen several times to act against Western interests. The Reform Party won support by promising to defend the interest of the West against Central Canada and the federal government. It articulates a conservative political philosophy with a strongly fundamentalist moral position on political issues. It now claims to speak not only for the West but for all of English Canada. It is critical of Quebec's demands and the apparent acceptance of its claims by the federal government. It has proposed a tighter immigration policy, a reversal of bilingualism and a reform of the constitution which would strengthen the position of the provinces and regions.

THE QUESTION OF CANADIAN IDENTITY

Models of Diversity

While the diversity of Canadian society causes political tensions, the way in which that diversity is perceived and understood is also problematic. There are at least two competing views or models of Canadian diversity, the two nations model and the national unity model, each of which is rooted in a particular set of interests, ideas and interpretations of history and each with its own prospectus for managing diversity. The active coexistence of these models and the conflicting perceptions and demands articulated through them by their protagonists creates the unique discourse of identity in Canadian politics.

The two nations view, sometimes known as dualism, is that Canada is composed of two distinct ethno-cultural communities which have developed from the two founding peoples, the French and the British.[36] In Quebec the idea that Canada is a partnership between two nations is not merely a political theory but a deeply rooted article of faith and the basis of Quebec's claim to be a distinct society and a province unlike the others. In Canadian political discourse, however, there are two versions of dualism. Cultural dualism, describing the relationship between French and English communities throughout Canada, was recognised in the early days of confederation and underlies the contemporary federal policy of bilingualism. Political dualism, on the other hand, generally rejected in English Canada, but supported by a large majority in Quebec, refers to the relationship between Quebec and the rest of Canada and claims a special political status for Quebec. While English Canadians outside Quebec generally acknowledge the existence of two nations and two cultures, most find it difficult to recognise Quebec's claim to special status within the federation . The two nations model is thus problematic and politically ambivalent. It is more than a description of division within Canadian society and is in itself a divisive idea.

One of the problems with the two nations view is that it fails to recognise the diverse and pluralistic character of English Canada whose complex territorial and ethnic cleavages English Canadians describe as a mosaic. In the metaphor of the mosaic Canadians come from many different regions, social backgrounds and ethnic origins, but they are one nation. The mosaic describes a multi-ethnic society in which every group can proclaim its own culture and individual identities can be celebrated in a partnership which is capable of promoting development and integration. The origins of the much celebrated Canadian mosaic are almost as old as the two nations theory dating back to the loyalists, whose numbers included many of non-British origin who chose the empire in preference to the republic after the American revolution.[37] The mosaic has probably contributed to the civil order and stabilty of Canadian life by enabling Canadians (or English Canadians at least) to create a polyethnic society which has apparently excluded no-one and given a place to everyone. It may also have assisted them to accommodate to the changing ethnic composition and increasing diversity of their country during the twentieth century. The difficulty is that it finds little or no support amongst French Canadians who, although part of the mosaic as conceived by English Canadians, have always regarded such a view as a denial of their conception of themselves as one of the founding nations.

The idea of the mosaic underlies the national unity model which is that, whatever its social diversity, Canada is one country with one national government for all its citizens. There is thus a national interest which is greater than the interest of any particular group or region and it is the responsibility of the national government to ensure that this interest is protected by maintaining the framework of a national society with a community of rights for all Canadians. The federal government, therefore, must maintain a clear presence across Canada, claiming sole responsibility for national policy matters, especially the management of the economy.[38] This view flourished most strongly under Trudeau's leadership but it may now be losing support in Canada, its main protagonists being the Liberal Party and the agencies of the federal government itself. The problem with the national unity view is that, although there is a widespread desire for national unity, the strength of ethnic and regional identities undermines it, while the efforts of the federal government are frequently regarded as intrusion and resisted by the provinces. The role of the federal government has become less dominant as it is persistently challenged over jurisdictions and tax revenues by the provinces, especially Quebec. While the national unity view thus remains an important factor in Canadian politics, it is increasingly on the defensive,

English, French and Others

The increasing diversity of Canadian society has complicated the management of ethnic relations which have traditionally been dominated by the English-French cleavage. While this cleavage has apparently become deeper and wider, there is no universally accepted political view of Canadian diversity that provides a framework for common citizenship and government.[39] The national unity model is treated with suspicion especially in Quebec, where many regard it as an ideology of anglophone federalst hegemony and assimilation. Like the mosaic it has always been embraced primarily by Anglophone Canadians, and more fully by British than others, and rejected by French Canadians, especially the Quebecois. The two nations model, on the other hand is not widely accepted outside Quebec. The rise of Quebec separatism, by transforming the ethno-linguistic dichotomy of French and English into an ethno-territorial polarisation of Quebec and the rest of Canada, has made this divergence of approach more rather than less intractable. One effect has been to broaden the resistance to Quebec's claim to be treated as a distinct society and intensify the challenge to the two nations model and its assumptions.

Resistance to the two nations model and to Quebec's demands has come from a number of sources including the federalist supporters of national unity, the other provinces, the ethnic minorities and the aboriginals. In the first place, the federalists and supporters of national unity have an, emotional and material interest in maintaining a united federal Canada and fear that this may not be possible if Quebec gains special status or secedes. They include both the anglophone minority in Quebec and the francophone minorities outside Quebec. The former, after several generations of privilege and hegemony, are now experiencing falling numbers and a struggle to maintain their committment to Quebec. The latter, having been accustomed to a difficult existence, only marginally ameliorated by whatever comfort they may have derived from the influence of Quebec, now face abandonment to the rigours of life in an anglophone culture.[40]

Secondly, the other provincial governments particularly in the West, having reluctantly accepted bilingalism and biculturalism, are even more reluctant to recognise Quebec's claim to special status. Some provincial leaders fear that such recognition would give Quebec additional powers and an unfair advantage in the federal system. They have declared that each and every province is a distinct society with its own particular history, culture and ethnic composition and that it would not be desirable to acknowledge special status for any single one. Ontario has been virtually alone amongst the provinces in being prepared to recognise and endorse Quebec's claims. Thirdly, the other ethnic minorities of neither British nor French origin reject the two nations model because it excludes them. They resent the privileged constitutional status of the French language, having themselves assimilated to English and in many cases lost the use of their original languages. They feel that Quebec's claim to special treatment diminishes the validity of their own identities and feel that a multicultural concept of Canada would give them more recognition.

Finally, the aboriginals, having been in Canada before the French or the British, find the concept of two founding peoples simply unacceptable. Statements by the First Nations have been consistently unsympathetic to all expressions of the two nations idea. The Assembly of First Nations has declared Quebec's claims to distinctiveness to be less valid than those of the aboriginal peoples. They stress that the distnctions between French language or culture and those of other European peoples is much less than the distinctions between these and the language and culture of the aboriginal peoples.[41]

Multiculturalism

The failure of any of these models to gain general acceptance highlights the lack of consensus on the perception of diversity which has been the outstanding feature of ethnic politics in Canada. It has led the federal government, several provincial governments, political parties, think tanks and a host of academics to undertake enquiries into the causes and possible solutions to the problem of Canadian identity. It brought one such enquiry to the conclusion that national unity could only be achieved if Canada resolved its deep differences on dualism and regionalism.[42] It underlies the proposition that Canadians will only be able to persist as a single sovereign people, if they can accept their diversity and agree to disagree on certain fundamental issues.[43] It drives the search for a more versatile model which might be universally acceptable and provide a secure basis for a Canadian national identity, common citizenship and statehood into the foreseeable future. Some believe that the idea of multiculturalism provided them with such a model. It may be reasonably argued that Canada actually is a multicultural society. Despite the experience of assimilation, there are many examples of strong surviving cultures, such as the Gaels of Cape Breton, the Acadians of New Brunswick, the Italians of Toronto and Montreal, the Ukranians of the West, the Chinese of British Columbia and some of the more recent immigrant groups such as the Sikhs and the West Indians. The resistance to the two nations model and its possible implications for the structure of power in Canada has not been merely a rejection of French claims, but also an affirmation of the claims of others. Moreover, it provided evidence of the breadth as well as the depth of Canadian diversity and drew attention to its multicultural quality. Recognition of this inspired an authentically Canadian concept of multiculturalism and its development into a new model of Canadian diversity which could contribute to national unity and the reconciliation of differences. Multiculturalism was promulgated as a federal policy in 1971 and consolidated by the Charter of Rights and Freedoms (1982) and the Canadian Multiculturalism Act (1988). It has been used to promote the virtues of ethnic pluralism, good race relations and respect for different cultures and social values and to facilitate the integration of new and visibly different immigrants.[44] However, it is not clear that it has been wholly successful.

First, few are prepared to accept the consequences of a policy of true multiculturalism in economic and social opportunities. More than two fifths of Canadians in a 1993 survey declared their loss of confidence in multiculturalism and *ipso facto*, in the ideal of the mosaic. Moreover, nearly half of all Canadians called for a reduction of immigration, with a substantial proportion demanding a return to a mainly European sourcing of immigrants.[45] Second, multiculturalism has not been entirely welcome in Quebec, which has chosen to regard it as merely a revised version of the mosaic. Yet Quebec is itself becoming a rather more multicultural society as a result of increased immigration from francophone South East Asia, The Middle East, Africa and the Carribean. This together with the new school and language laws and the newly reduced birth rate of the established francophone population will gradually transform Quebec society. The question is whether an anglophone and a francophone multiculturalism can coexist and converge within the federal framework of a diverse pluralist culture or whether the 'two solitudes' will persist and develop exponentially.

Multiculturalism does provide an alternative model of Canadian society, which, if applied flexibly, has the potential to account for the depth and the breadth of its diversity and the different perceptions of that diversity. Thus it could also function effectively as a basis of citizenship policy and national unity. Multiculturalism, however, is also a style and a mode of accommodating differences and resolving conflict. As such it requires not only a political discourse to give it expression but also an agreed constitutional framework within which it can operate. So far this has not been forthcoming.

THE CONSTITUTION, NATIONHOOD AND NATIONAL UNITY

Structures of Accommodation

At both elite and mass levels in Canada there is a relatively sophisticated awareness of the country's diversity and the range of its ethnic, cultural linguistic, and religious cleavages This awareness has ensured that the differences have been noticed and to some extent understood, but not that they have been satisfactorily accommodated. In the past differences have been accommodated within hegemonic, consociational and federal structures. For well over a century an Anglo-Scottish elite maintained a largely hegemonic relationship with francophones, with various immigrant groups and with the aboriginal peoples in all parts of Canada. These hegemonies were mainly economic, but they did have social and political consequences to the disadvantage of the subordinate groups.

Consociational modes of accommodation occur more frequently in the Canadian experience. Consociational practices were part of the political process in Quebec almost from the beginning, although they have become less significant as the power of the English community in Quebec has declined. Elsewhere a form of consociationalism developed in the Red River colony in the early nineteenth century andalso featured in the government of the United Province of central Canada in the mid nineteenth century. In this case there were bi-ethnic coalitions, shared ministries, equal representation in decision making, rotation of offices and meeting places, including the provincial capital. Some of these practices continued into Confederation notably the proportional composition of the federal cabinet and the joint chairing of Royal Commissions and certain parliamentary committees.[46]

The practice of bi-ethnic governing coalitions was perpetuated in the bi-ethnic political parties which dominated Canadian politics for the first fifty years after Confederation and which the Liberal Party still exemplifies. The political parties, however, both inside and outside parliament, have generally failed as instruments for the accommodation of ethnic and regional interests, especially at the centre of decision making. The possibility of the parties performing this role is now even less, because the parties themselves have become so much more dependent on regional support. Of the three major national parties, the Liberal party has for long had little support west of Ontario while the New Democratic Party has had scarcely any east of Ontario; the Conservative Party after a surge of support in Quebec during the 1980s was electorally annihilated across Canada in 1993. The strength of ethno-regionalism appeared to be demonstrated in 1993 and confirmed in 1997 by the rise of the Reform party and the Bloc Quebecois, both relying on exclusively regional support and expressing largely ethnic interests.

It could be argued that the Canadian federal system was designed more to reassure the original colonies and clinch the union than to resolve conflicts within the union once it was established. None of the federal institutions is well-adapted to the purpose of resolving the complex multilateral conflicts that occur in the Canadian federal system.[47] The Senate, which indirectly represents the provinces and regions, has too little power to be effective and repeated efforts to reform it have come to nought. In the House of Commons strict party discipline has usually made regional interaction and cooperation across party lines all but impossible. The federal cabinet tends to be a microcosm of the party in power and reflects the rigidities of partisanship as much as the pluralities of the polity. The federal bureaucracy, with limited power and little responsibility for the delivery of services, rarely has either the capability or the opportunity to influence political outcomes. The judiciary has always had a major influence on the federal system, but many feel that its impact is too narrow to shape the political development of the system.

Because of the shortcomings of other federal institutions conflict resolution has been conducted mostly through the machinery of federal provincial inter-governmental relations. This process, aptly described as federal provincial diplomacy, has more in common with the politics of international organisation than with most other federations.[48] Nevertheless, federal-provincial collaboration is essential not only to the smooth working of the Canadian federation, but to its actual survival and the federal-provincial conference is the only possible forum for such collaboration. The clearest example of this is the process of constitutional reform, for many years the focus of debate on ethnic diversity in Canadian politics.

Nationhood and Constitutional Reform

Constitutional reform became an issue because the Canadian constitution, defining the form of government, the distribution of powers and certain aspects of the relations between ethnic groups in Canada was an Act of the British Parliament which could only be amended by the British Parliament. In 1980 Prime Minister Pierre Trudeau and his cabinet decided to patriate (ie., bring home) the constitution as a symbol of Canadian nationhood and national unity.[49] The provinces insisted on being included in the process on the grounds that the federal government could not act unilaterally in constitutional matters. Thus, the federal-provincial conference, with its convention of unanimity, became the forum for negotiation on the constitution.

The issue became inextricably involved in the complexities of Canadian domestic politics, complexities which were woven around the familiar fault lines of provincial autonomy, regionalism and Quebec nationalism. The presence of an avowedly separatist government in Quebec (in the early 1980s, as in the mid 1990s) demanding sovereignty-association and promising a provincial referendum on the question, helped to crystallise the issues and concentrate minds. It forced the other provinces to demonstrate that a rejection of sovereignty-association was not simply a vote against Quebec, but a vote for an alternative view of the constitution. Nevertheless they simply rejected the Quebec government's proposals on Sovereignty-Association on the grounds that Quebec was trying to enhance its status and maximise its own interests at the expense of others. They argued that granting association to a sovereign Quebec would not be in their economic interest, would threaten the integrity of Canada and was not an acceptable political framework within which to continue Quebec's participation in the Canadian common market, with its complex sharing of costs and benefits amongst equals.[50]

The other provinces, particularly the Western provinces, were concerned to deal with the federal government as well as Quebec and to present their own grievances, interests and demands in constitutional terms. The federal position stressed the need for a strong central government with sufficient fiscal and institutional resources to maintain federal programmes and protect its view of the national interest. The major difference between federal and provincial proposals was that where the former emphasised bi-lingualism, civil rights, the amending process and the strengthening of federal institutions, the latter emphasised provincial autonomy, the division of powers and greater influence for the provinces.

In the years after the federal government's initiative on patriation, the search for a constitutional settlement developed in three stages.[51] First was the 1982 Constitution Act which entrenched the Charter of Rights and Freedoms, made some concessions to the demands of the Western and Maritime Provinces and defined the role of the provinces in the amendment process. It was ratified by the Parliament of Canada and nine of the provinces and thus became, technically at least, the new constitutional order of Canada. It was rejected by the Quebec National Assembly, however, and an overwhelming majority of opinion including all political parties in the province. People in Quebec felt betrayed. Many believed that Trudeau had promised to deliver a 'renewed federalism' which would be better than the old and preferable to 'sovereignty-association'. Since the new constitution failed to meet several of Quebec's key demands, it could not be a practicable or permanent settlement.

Trudeau and the Liberal Party produced an essentially federalist solution to the constitutional question. In many ways their national unity rhetoric highlighted rather than concealed their failure to satisfy both Quebec's dualist and the West's regional conception of the political system. At the 1984 general election Trudeau and his party paid a high price for Trudeau's constitutional vision. Faced with increased disaffection in the West, they were left with scarcely a seat west of the Great Lakes, while the Conservatives drove them out of their traditional stronghold of Quebec. The Conservatives owed this success very largely to the Quebec origins and connections of their leader Robert Mulroney, who was now expected to deliver a Quebec solution, where Trudeau had failed. The question was whether he could do so without alienating traditional Conservative support in the West.

The second stage, initiated by Mulroney and generally referred to as the 'Quebec' round was primarily an attempt to meet the demands of Quebec.[52] A formula was arrived at in April 1987 known as the Meech Lake Accord which had to be ratified by all the provinces and the federal government. The Accord recognised Quebec's demand to be treated as a distinct society and its need for special constitutional powers to protect this status. Although all provincial governments subscribed to the Accord, the results of provincial elections altered the political balance in three provincial legislatures which then refused to ratify, the Meech Lake formula. Defeat for the Accord came in the Manitoba legislature as Elija Harper, the sole Indian member, cast his vote against it, thus denying the required unanimity. As the ratification deadline of June 1990 passed, the Meech Lake Accord itself faded into history, another witness to the complexity of Canadian politics.

Almost immediately the third stage got under way. The ruling Quebec Liberal Party and then the Quebec National Assembly reported on Quebec's conditions and timetable for a settlement.[53] The federal government established a series of consultations which attracted groups previously not included in the process, notably the aboriginal peoples.[54] A new series of First Ministers Conferences got under way, but on this occasion Quebec stood aside on the grounds that it knew what it wanted and it was up to the rest of Canada to decide. The process was concluded in the Charlottetown Agreement of August 1992[55]which, for the first time, satisfied all parties and was endorsed by all eleven governments of Canada, the two territorial governments and the four recognised aboriginal organisations.[56] A nationwide referendum in October 1993, however, resulted in the Agreement being rejected by a clear majority of the people across the country, including Quebec. Undoubtedly the referendum question became entangled in other political issues such as dissatisfaction with the Mulroney government and growing impatience with the constitutional process itself, especially in the West and Quebec, However, the failure of the political leaders to campaign effectively for acceptance of the Agreement must be considered at least partly responsible for its rejection.[57]

The fate of the Charlottetown Agreement was especially disappointing because all the participants gained something from it. This applied particularly to the newer participants such as the aboriginals, who have since insisted on the implementation of the agreements affecting them. The debate about the nature of the Canadian polity and society gave the aboriginals an opportunity to renew their own historic claims to recognition and protection of their traditional way of life. They gained considerable recognition for their demands, including their insistence on the right of self-government.

It is now increasingly accepted that the aboriginals do have an inherent right of self-government and that it only remains to settle its legal status.[58] Such a right has never been recognised by parliament or the courts, but it was included in the Charlottetown Agreement of 1992. It is also accepted that implementation of such a provision implies the establishment of a third order of government, which would share jurisdictions, powers and responsibilities with the federal and the provincial governments. The aboriginals want some powers in respect of land, resources and development and the capability to provide at least some of their own police, education, health and social services, most of which are in the jurisdiction of the provinces, The aboriginals prefer to negotiate with the federal government, who are mostly responsible for aboriginal affairs and who would probably be required to provide the finance for any scheme of aboriginal self-government. A satisfactory arrangement, therefore, would require the active participation and support of the provinces, the federal government and the aboriginals. In any case it is now clear that any comprehensive and secure political settlement of ethnic and regional issues in Canada will have to include a solution to the aboriginal rights issue.

NATIONAL UNITY AFTER CHARLOTTETOWN

At Charlottetown, Canada for the first time arrived at an apparently secure and comprehensive constitutional settlement. The Charlottetown Accord was the culmination of a series of negotiations of unprecedented range and intensity. After the referendum, however, a settlement was as far away as it had ever been and the coalition of political leaders, parties and groups involved in the process was dissolved and could probably never be recreated. Moreover, a number of other developments further complicated the situation. The Free Trade Agreement with the United States created considerable dissension in English Canada, especially Ontario, where it was blamed for subsequent economic setbacks and recession. The relationship between Quebec, which welcomed the Free Trade Agreement, and the rest of Canada hardened and became more polarised as they made divergent assessments of the outcome. Simmering discontent in the West and continuing hostility towards 'eastern' interests, including the federal government, consolidated opinion in that region as well.

These new realities were soon reflected in the stucture of politics. Even before Charlottetown, the Quebec caucus of Conservative MPs had already split away from the party to form the Bloc Quebecois, dedicated to independence for the province. As western alienation deepened again in the late 1980s, the Reform Party, presenting itself as the guardian of Western interests, attracted growing popular support which overwhelmed the Conservatives. The general election of October 1993 clearly exposed all the fault lines of Canadian politics.[59] The Bloc Quebecois took most of the seats in Quebec and the Reform Party swept the West, thus lining up the two most demanding and intractable regions and their rival conceptions of the political system, not simply against the centre, but against each other. With the Liberal Party, the political home of multiculturalism and traditionally the strongest exponent of the national unity view, now forming the national government, each of the principal models of Canadian politics now had an influential political voice at the centre. This made the prospects for a resolution of the Canadian political conundrum more uncertain than ever.

These prospects seemed even more remote after the Quebec provincial election in September 1994, which brought the Parti Quebecois back to power, clearly committed to a referendum on sovereignty. At the outset it seemed that the result of a referendum would be similar to that of 1980. The new Premier, Jacques Parizeau, however, was determined that there should be a positive result and the provincial government took great care in preparing its approach. It undertook a substantial campaign, including extensive popular consultations, to raise support for the sovereignty option. The referendum was postponed from June to October so as to allow opinion time to move, while advance polling sought to discern the most favourable wording of the question. As it was ultimately formulated, the referendum question was relatively vague in its commitment to sovereignty and critics of the process argued that it was too imprecise to be capable of deciding anything.[60] In the campaign the sovereigntists engaged the issue energetically with an emotional appeal to Quebec nationalism, while the federalists appeared to take a relaxed view of the outcome up until the last few days. In the end the result was very much closer than generally expected with the question being lost by a margin of only 1.2 per cent. The federalists declared the result to be a decisive 'vote for Canada', taking comfort in the reflection that the margin was three times greater than that gained by the PQ in the provincial election on which result they had based the legitimacy of the exercise in the first place.[61]

The referendum result resolved little or nothing and simply highlighted the urgency of dealing with the unresolved problems which alienate Quebec and threaten Canadian unity. Perhaps, as some believe, these questions can be settled by realistic negotiation in the traditional style of Canadian politics.[62] Federalists within and outside Quebec believe that support for Quebec independence would crumble if people feared that it could jeopardise their economic future.[63] Some could be influenced by the clear threat by the anglophone Cree Indians of northern Quebec that they would themselves secede from an independent Quebec, taking a large part of its territory and natural resources with them.[64] There might also be rather less or less strong support for independence amongst the young and the professional classes than there was in the 1970's, despite the evidence of the 1995 referendum.[65] Even in Quebec, it is recognised that a substantial portion of separatist support is driven less by demand for independence than by the feeling that Quebec's reasonable claims have been repeatedly rejected by the rest of Canada over more than a quarter century of constitutional negotiations. It is thus possible that an imaginative and well crafted offer of 'renewed federalism' could still avert separation and swing opinion behind the federalist option and thus secure the future of Canada.[66]

Renewed federalism is substantially what was included in the Charlottetown Agreement. Largely because of its rejection, Canada may now be facing one of the most critical situations in its political history. The long and sometimes bitter dispute about the constitution between Quebec and the rest of Canada, especially the federal government, appears to have reached a decisive and possibly fateful point. Whether or not the outstanding issues are resolved by negotiation, there is likely to be another referendum on the Canadian question in Quebec. Some doubt the legality of a unilateral decision by Quebec on separation from Canada, but it is generally accepted that an informed and democratic decision by Quebec would be politically irrestible.[67] If secession is the outcome of this process, it is likely that Canada as we have known it will come to an end. This would also bring to a close one of the most ambitious, creative and in many ways successful political constructions of modern times.[68]

This chapter has attempted to trace the origins of this predicament and concludes that they can only be understood by appreciating the diversity of Canada today and the complexity of its history. It is clear that the legacies and experience of 'deep diversity' have provided Canadians with different visions of Canada, but it is not yet clear that these are all compatible with the persistence and survival of Canada itself. On the other hand, the paradox of the Canadian experience may be that the concern with the apparent disfunctions of the Canadian system has actually provided continuity and a kind of stability. The continued debate on the constitution and national identity, always conducted within the parameters of democratic values and practice, may be the hallmark of Canadian identity. It may be an unexciting, even a tiresome way to manage the politics of diversity, but it has advantages over some of the alternatives. It could also provide a model for other multinational states seeking to resolve conflicting interests and cultures within conditions of expanding democratisation and increasingly demanding pluralism.

NOTES

1   Statistics Canada, 1991 Census, update 1994.

2   See C.F.J. Whebell, 'Geography and Politics in Canada: Selected Aspects', in John H. Redekop, *Approaches to Canadian Politics*, Scarborough, Prentice Hall, 1978.

3   *Ethnic Diversity in Canada*, Ministry of Supply and Services, Ottawa, 1990.

4   B. Harrison and L. Marmen, *Languages in Canada*, Ottawa, Statistics Canada and Prentice Hall, 1994.

5   Jane Badets and T.W.L. Chui, *Canada's Changing Immigrant Population* Ottawa, Statistics Canada and Prentice Hall, 1994.

6   John Porter, *The Vertical Mosaic*, Toronto, University of Toronto Press, 1965 p. 61.

7   *Ethnic Diversity in Canada*, Ministry of Supply and Services, Ottawa, 1990.

8   Jane Badets and T.W.L. Chui, *op. cit.*, pp.17–18.
9   *Ibid.*, pp.10–11; Daniel Hiebert, 'Focus: Immigration to Canada', *Canadian Geographer*, Vol.38, No.3, 1994, pp.255–7.
10 *Ethnic Diversity in Canada*, Ministry of Supply and Services, Ottawa, 1990; *The Canadian Indian*, Ministry of Supply and Services, Ottawa, 1990.
11 *The Inuit*, Ministry of Supply and Services, Ottawa, 1990.
12 B. Young and John A. Dickinson, *A Short History of Quebec*, Toronto, Copp Clark Pitman, 1988, pp.59–64; Mason Wade, *The French Canadians*, Toronto, Macmillan, 1968, pp.47–92.
13 Gerald M. Craig, (ed.), *Lord Durham's Report*, Toronto, McClelland & Stewart, 1963, pp.28 and 150.
14 S. Noel, *Patrons, Clients and Brokers 1791–1896*, Toronto, University of Toronto Press, 1990; Denis Moniere, *Ideologies in Quebec: The Historical Development*, Toronto, University of Toronto Press, 1981, pp.124–9; Gordon T. Stewart, *The Origins of Canadian Politics*, Vancouver, University of British Columbia Press, 1986, pp.32–58.
15 J.M.S. Careless, *The Union of the Canadas: the Growth of Canadian Institutions*, Toronto, McClelland & Stewart, 1967.
16 The original provinces were Nova Scotia, New Brunswick, Quebec and Ontario; Nova Scotia tried to secede almost immediately, but was prevented from doing so. The first of the other provinces to accede was Manitoba in 1870, followed by Prince Edward Island in 1871, British Columbia in 1873, Alberta and Saskatewan in 1905 and Newfoundland in 1949.
17 Gordon T. Stewart, *op. cit.*, Ch.3; Kenneth McNaught, *History of Canada*, Harmondsworth, Penguin, 1969; G. Stevenson, *Unfulfilled Union*, Toronto, Gage, 1979, Ch.2; Young and Dickinson, *op. cit.* pp. 164–7.
18 Department of Justice, *The Constitition Acts 1867 to 1982*, Ministry of Supply and Services, Ottawa, 1993.
19 For a comprehensive and concise review of the legal and academic debate on the judicial review of the constitution, see Alan Cairns, 'The Judicial Committee and its Critics', *Canadian Journal of Political Science*, Vol. 4 (1971), pp.301–345.
20 This is the writer's view, but there is a long-standing and continuing debate on the question of provincial autonomy. See, for example, F.R. Scott, *Essays on the Constitution*, Toronto, University of Toronto Press, 1977, and particularly 'Centralisation and Decentralisation in Canadian Federalism', p.252. More recent contributions include David E. Smith,

'Empire, Crown and Canadian Federalism', *Canadian Journal of Political Science*, Vol. 24 (1991), pp. 452–473 and Paul Romney, 'The Nature and Scope of Provoncial Autonomy: Oliver Mowat, the Quebec Resolutions and the Construction of the BNA Act', *Canadian Journal of Political Science*, Vol. 25 (1992), pp. 3–28.

21 Kenneth McRoberts, *Quebec: Social Change and Political Crisis*, Toronto, McClelland & Stewart, 1988, Ch.4; W.D. Coleman, *The Independence Movement in Quebec 1945–1980*, Toronto, University of Toronto Press, 1984; Denis Moniere, *Ideologies in Quebec: The Historical Development*, Toronto, University of Toronto Press, 1981, pp.228–301; Susan Mann Trofimenkoff, *The Dream of Nation*, Toronto, Gage, 1983, pp. 266–315.

22 Rejean Lachapelle, 'Evolution of Language Groups and the Official Languages Situation in Canada', in *Demilinguistic Trends and the Evolution of Canadian Instititions*, Ottawa, Association for Canadian Studies and the Office of the Commissioner for Official Languages, 1990, p.7–33; J. Laponce, 'The French Language in Canada: Tensions Between Geography and Politics', *Political Geography Quarterly*, Vol. 3 (1984), pp. 91–104; J. Laponce, 'On Three Nationalist Options', *Political Geography Quarterly*, Vol.13 (1994), pp.192–4.

23 Pierre Elliott Trudeau, *Federalism and the French Canadians*, Toronto, Macmillan, 1968.

24 Andre Raynauld, 'The Advancement of the French Language in Canada', in *Demilinguistic Trends and the Evolution of Canadian Instititions*, Ottawa, Association for Canadian Studies and the Office of the Commissioner for Official Languages, 1990, p.93–104; Gilles Grenier, Bilingualism Amongst Anglophones and Francophones in Canada', *ibid*, p.35–45.; B. Harley, 'After Immersion: Maintaining the Momentum', *Journal of Multilingual and Multicultural Development*, Vol.15 (1994), pp.229–44.

25 René Levesque, 'National State of the French Canadians', in F. Scott and M. Oliver, *Quebec States her Case*, Toronto, Macmillan, 1964; René Levesque, *My Quebec*, Toronto, Totem Books, 1979.

26 Legislation of 1969 left the language of education largely to parental choice. Under nationalist pressure this was changed by legislation of 1974 (Bill 22) which made French the sole official language of Quebec and the normal language of education. Further legislation of 1977 (Bill 101, the Sign Law) made French the only legal language of public communication (public administration, business, work and education,

with the sole exception of Quebec born anglophones) and established the Office de la Langue Francaise to enforce it.

27 J. Yvon Theriault, 'The Future of the French Speaking Community Outside Quebec' in *Demilinguistic Trends*, *op. cit.*, p.131–40.

28 Robert J. Brym (ed.), *Regionalism in Canada*, Toronto, Irwin Publishing, 1986.

29 The Atlantic Region includes Newfoundland and the three Maritime Provinces (Prince Edward Island, Nova Scotia and New Brunswick); the West includes British Columbia and the three Prairie Provinces, (Manitoba, Saskatewan and Alberta), but British Columbia is sometimes regarded as a separate region; The North includes Yukon and the Northwest Territories, although the northern parts of Manitoba, Ontario and Quebec share some of its environmental and cultural characteristics.

30 Mark O. Dickerson, *Whose North?*, Vancouver, University of British Columbia Press, 1992; Graham White, 'Westminster in the Arctic: The Adaptation of British Parliamentarism in the Northwest Territories', *Canadian Journal of Political Science*, Vol. 24 (1991), pp.499–523.

31 Charles J. McMillan, *Standing Up to the Future: the Maritimes in the 1990s*, Report to the Council of Maritime Premiers, 1989; *Challenge and Opportunity*, Discussion Paper on Maritime Economic Integration, Council of Maritime Premiers, 1991; *In the Spirit of Cooperation: Laying the Foundation*; Council of Maritime Prremiers, 1993; Carman Miller, the Restoration of Greater Nova Scotia', in David J. Bercuson, *Canada and the Burden of Unity*, Toronto, Macmillan, 1977.

32 D. Bell and L. Tepperman, *The Roots of Disunity*, Toronto, McClelland & Stewart, 1979, pp.188 and 195–7; Ernest R. Forbes, *Maritime Rights: A Study in Canadian Regionalism*, Kingston and Montreal, McGill-Queens University Press, 1979.

33 Since 1985, there has been growing concern that federal government actions have adversely affected the Ontario government and the residents of Ontario'. Paper prepared for the Ontario Ministry of Intergovernmental Affairs, Informetrica, Toronto, 1993.

34 T.D. Regehr, 'Western Canada and the Burden of National Transportation Policies', in David J. Bercuson, *op. cit*, pp.115–41; David E. Smith, Western Politics and National Unity', in *ibid*, pp.142–68; David Kilgour, *Uneasy Patriots: Western Canadians in Confederation*, Edmonton, Lone Pine Publishing, 1988, pp.34–42 and 55–77.

35 *Working Together: An Inventory of Intergovernmental Cooperation in Western Canada, 1980–1993*, Edmonton, Western Premiers' Conference, 1994; Western Premiers' Task Force on Constitutional Trends, *Third*

Report, Victoria, Western Premiers' Conference, 1979; Glen Toner and François Bregha, 'The Political Economy of Energy', in Michael S. Whittington and Glen Williams, *Canadian Politics in the 1980s*, Toronto, Methuen, 1984.

36　David R. Cameron, 'Dualism and the Concept of National Unity', in John H. Redekop, *op. cit.*, pp.228–46; Edwin R. Black, *Divided Loyalties*, Montreal and London, McGill-Queens University Press, 1975, Ch.5–8; Donald V. Smiley, *Canada in Question*, Toronto, McGraw-Hill Ryerson, 1976, Ch.6 and 9; Patricia Smart, 'Our Two Cultures', in Eli Mandel and David Taras (eds), *A Passion for Identity*, Toronto, Methuen, 1987, pp196–205; Robin Mathews, *Canadian Identity*, Ottawa, Steel Rail Publishing, 1988, Ch.7 and *passim*.

37　D. Bell and L. Tepperman, *op. cit.*, pp.85–7.

38　See, for example, D. Johnson (ed.), *Pierre Trudeau Speaks out on Meech Lake*, Toronto, Knopf, 1990, p.43; Government of Canada, *Shaping Canada's Future Together*, Ottawa, Ministry of Supply and Services, 1991, p.27.

39　Attempts to reconcile the divergent views of Canadian identity have met with little success. See W.L. Morton, *The Canadian Identity*, Toronto, University of Toronto Press, 1972, pp. 83–9 and 147–50; Charles Taylor, *Reconciling the Solitudes*, Montreal and Kingston, McGill-Queens University Press, 1993, pp.155–86; Charles Taylor, 'Shared and Divergent Values' in Ronald L. Watts and Douglas M. Brown, *Options for a New Canada*, Toronto, University of Toronto Press, 1991, pp.53–76; *Shared Values*, Ottawa, Ministry of Supply and Services, 1991.

40　Richard Fidler, *Canada Adieu? Quebec Debates its Future*, Lanzville and Halifax, Oolichan Books and The Institute for Research on Public Policy, 1991, Ch.6 and 10; Reed Scowan, *A Different Vision*, Toronto, Maxwell Macmillan, 1991.

41　First Nations Circle on the Constitution, *To the Source*, Ottawa, Assembly of First Nations, 1992, pp.37–41; The Native Council of Canada, Constitutional Review Commission, 'Aboriginal Directions for Coexistence in Canada' (summary), in *Public Policy and Aboriginal Peoples,* Vol.2, Ottawa, Royal Commission on Aboriginal Peoples, 1994, pp.343–5.

42　Task Force on Canadian Unity, *A Future Together*, (The Pepin–Robarts Report), Ottawa, Ministry of Supply and Services, 1979, pp.21–32.

43　Peter Russell, *Constitutional Odyssey*, 2nd edn, Toronto, University of Toronto Press, 1993, pp.3–11.

44　A. Fleras and J.L. Elliott, *Multiculturalism in Canada*, Scarborough,

Nelson, 1992, pp.2, 98–9 and 143–5; V. Seymour Wilson, 'The Tapestry Vision of Canadian Multiculturalism', in *Canadian Journal of Political Science*, Vol. 26 (1993), pp.646–69.

45   *The Reid Report*, Vol.8, April 1993; Y. Abu Laban and D. Stasiulis, Ethnic Pluralism Under Seige', in *Canadian Public Policy*, Vol.8 (1992), No.4.

46   S. Noel, *op. cit.* ; Herman Bakvis, *Federalism and the Organisation of Political Life: Canada in Comparative Perspective*, Kingston, Queen's University Institute of Intergovernmental Relations, 1981, pp.71–89.

47   Garth Stevenson, *op. cit.*, Ch.8.

48   R. Simeon, *Federal-Provincial Diplomacy: The Making of Recent Policy in Canada*, Toronto, University of Toronto Press, 1972; Alan C. Cairns, The Governments and Societies of Canadian Federalism', *Canadian Journal of Political Science*, Vol.10 (1977), pp.695–734;

49   Kenneth McNaught, 'History and the Perception of Politics', in John H. Redekop, *op. cit.*, pp.103–112.

50   *The Response to Quebec: Other Provinces and the Constitutional Debate*, Kingston, Queen's University Institute of Intergovernmental Relations, 1980.

51   A full account of the process is provided in David Milne, *The Canadian Constitution*, Toronto, James Lorimer and Co., 1994 and Peter Russell, *op. cit.*

52   Patrick J. Monahan, *Meech Lake: the Inside Story*, Toronto, University of Toronto Press, 1991.

53   Quebec Liberal Party, *A Quebec Free to Choose* (The Alaire Report), Quebec, Quebec Liberal Party, 1991; Commission sur l'Avenir Politique et Costitutionnel du Quebec, *The Political and Constitutional Future of Quebec* (The Boulanger–Campeau Report), Quebec National Assembly, 1991.

54   Special Joint Committee of the Senate and the House of Commons, *The Process for Amending the Constitution of Canada*, (The Baudouin–Edwards Report), Ottawa, Ministry of Supply and Services, 1991; Report of the Special Joint Committee of the Senate and the House of Commons, *A Renewed Canada*, (Baudouin–Dobbie Report), Ottawa, Ministry of Supply and Services, 1992; *Citizens' Forum on Canada's Future* (The Spicer Report), Ottawa, Ministry of Supply and Services, 1991.

55   *Our Future Together*, Ottawa, Ministry of Supply and Services, 1992.

56   The aboriginal organisations participating were: The Assembly of First Nations, Congress of Aboriginal Peoples, The Metis National Council, The Inuit Tapirisat of Canada.

57 Peter Russell, *op. cit.*, pp.224–7; Jeremy Webber, *Re-imagining Canada*, McGill-Queens University Press, 1994, pp.173–5; Kenneth McRoberts and Patrick Monahan, *The Charlottetown Accord, the Referendum and the Future of Canada*, Toronto, University of Toronto Press, 1993, Part 4.

58 *Aboriginal Peoples, Self-Government and Constitutional Reform*, Ottawa, Ministry of Supply and Services, 1991; David C. Hawkes and Bradford W. Morse, 'Alternative Methods for Aboriginal Participation in Processes of Constitutional Reform', in Ronald L. Watts and Douglas M. Brown, *op. cit.*, pp.163–87; Mary Ellen Turpel, 'The Charlottetown Discord and Aboriginal Peoples' Struggle for Fundamental Political Change', in Kenneth McRoberts and Patrick J. Monahan, *op. cit.*, pp. 117–51.

59 Ian Frizzell, Jon H. Pammett, Anthony Westell (eds), *The Canadian General Election of 1993*, Ottawa, Carleton University Press, 1994, Ch. 1 and 10 and *passim.*

60 Editorial, *Montreal Gazette*, 20 September 1995, which continued: 'One of the biggest flaws in the question is that it requires a Yes or No answer on two options that could well be mutually exclusive. The question contains no mention of a unilateral declaration of independence. ... Polls show that many Quebecers believe sovereignty entails continued ties with Canada.'

61 To all Canadians I say that a majority of Quebecers have chosen Canada', Jean Cretien, *Globe and Mail*, 31 October, 1995.

62 The federal government submitted proposals to Parliament in November, 1995, but there was little enthusiasm for further negotiations amongst the provinces. *Montreal Gazette*, 14 November 1995 and *Globe and Mail*, 29 November 1995.

63 Polls by Leger et Leger and Angus Reid during the referendum campaign claimed to reveal extensive misunderstanding in Quebec about the economic issues associated with the 'sovereignty' issue. *Financial Post*, 24 August 1995 and 4 January 1996; *Ottawa Citizen,* 31 October 1995.

64 First Nations Circle on the Constitution, *op. cit.*, p. 40–41.

65 Levels of support for independence varied. In a survey for *Le Soleil* in mid August 1995 40 per cent favoured independence for Quebec; in late September, according to a survey reported in the *Ottawa Citizen*, this had risen to 45 per cent; in a CROP survey for CBC in late March 1996 it had fallen to 30 per cent.

66 This was on the agenda for the federal provincial conference in June 1996 but none of the provinces wished to give it priority.

67   Jean Cretien said he would not accept a narrow majority for separation
     of Quebec, but see *Montreal Gazette*, 20 September 1995.
68   Roger Gibbins, *Speculations on a Canada Without Quebec*, in Kenneth
     McRoberts and Patrick Monahan, *op. cit.*, pp. 264–73; Gordon Gibson,
     The Future of the Rest of Canada, Vancouver, The Fraser Institute, 1994.

10 Spain

A Semi-federal State?

John Gibbons

HISTORICAL OVERVIEW

A combination of geographical, historical and cultural factors, together with a formidable tradition of state centralism, have bequeathed to present-day Spain a highly controversial political environment of multinationalism and regionalism. A mosaic of regions and nationalities, Spain, since the Constitution of 1978, has embraced decentralisation to become a quasi-federation of 17 autonomous regions. One of these regions, Aragón (see map), has slightly more status than an English County Council, while others such as Euskadi (the Basque Country) and Catalunya have just less than a German Land. Also, while the Euskadi authority collects all its own taxes, Catalunya does not, but the Catalans have wider powers to use their language than the Basques.

It is an untidy arrangement, reflecting considerable disparity between the regions: the system includes historic nationalities, with a sizeable electoral support for the right to self-determination, as in the cases of Catalunya, Euskadi and Galicia, historic regions such as Andalusia, as well as other regions where there has not been any strong sense of separate identity such as the region of Madrid, which is largely an administrative creation. Small wonder then that the support provided in the Spanish Cortes (Parliament), after the 1993 general election, by the Catalan party, Convergència i Unió (CIU), to the Socialist (PSOE) minority government of Felipe González, in return for more Catalan autonomy as well as regional financial rewards, brought about a backlash from other regions and nationalities in Spain. They angrily accused Catalunya of a self-interested opportunism which seemed to reap benefits for that region at their expense, but there was at least a hint of envy at the Catalans political guile in Spain's multinational arena. Moreover, following the 1996 general elections, most of the regional and nationalist parties were quite ready to strike a deal that would put more power in their hands and instal the Popular Party (P.P.) leader, José Maria Aznar, as Prime Minister.

ROOTS OF REGIONAL IDENTITIES

Throughout history Spain's geography has conspired against unity: its 500,000 square kilometres crisscrossed by a series of mountain ranges, which have impeded communication between its low-populated communities. Successive governments, despite at times practising a ruthless centralism, have failed to construct communication networks that would serve to successfully overcome such obstacles to their political goal of unity. Such neglect has therefore enhanced the sense of shared identity stored and preserved by members of those separated communities over centuries. A short-lived unity of the Iberian peninsula under the Visigoths, whose language was a variant of Latin and who practised Christianity, was broken by the invasion of the Moslems (Moors), beginning in 710 A.D. Fleeing Visigoth refugees moved to isolated 'safe-areas' of the mountainous north of the peninsula and over the following centuries there evolved out of a Latin linguistic foundation five separate new languages still spoken today in Spain. These are Castellano (Castilian), Catalan, Gallego (Galician), Aragonese and Bable (in Asturias), although the last two are spoken only by a small minority.

When considered together with 'Euskera' (ie. Basque – a pre-indoeuropean language of uncertain origin), spoken in Euskadi, plus a few other linguistic variants dotted here and there in Spain, it is significant that about a quarter of the inhabitants of Spain speak a vernacular language in addition to Castellano which is the official state language as well as the most widely spoken, and what we commonly refer to as 'Spanish'. The reason for the supremacy of Castellano was partly due to its acknowledged flexibility as a means of communication, but also because it was associated with the Christian 'reconquista' (reconquest) which ended with the surrender of the last Moorish stronghold – the kingdom of Granada – in 1492. The victors were Fernando who became King of Aragón in 1479 (the allied territories of which kingdom included Catalunya, Valencia and the Balearic Islands), and

Isabella, Queen of Castilla (with territorial alliances covering large sections of kingdoms and statelets in Andalusia as well as in Asturias, Galicia and Extremadura).

With the 'reconquista' came the spread of the various languages in the Iberian Peninsula as Galician metamorphosed into Portugese and Catalan filtered into Valencia and the Balearic Islands. Castilian meanwhile was spread more widely on the peninsula, sometimes by force; in Andalusia it supplanted Mozarabic, the language of Christians living under Moorish rule, which became extinct.[1]

The unity of Spain is conventionally dated from 1516 when the kingdoms of Castilla and Aragón were joined under King Carlos V, although between 1580 and 1640 Portugal was also under the rule of his son Felipe 11. In reality, far from being centralised and unified, until the end of the eighteenth century Spain was constructed by a series of uneasy alliances between various states under Hapsburg and Bourbon monarchs, who acknowledged this fact by referring to themselves as Rey de las Espanas (King of the Spains). Thus Aragón, for instance, retained its own coinage as well as laws, land tenure and a local parliament with considerable powers. Up until the nineteenth century the Basques also had their own provincial assemblies, to decide what taxes should be paid to Castilla; and, they were exempt from military service.

So, the politics of multinationalism in Spain has been inspired not so much by the history of the emergence of a unified Spain but by the preservation of the memory if not the actual practice of various regional and national privileges. The new Constitution introduced after the death of Franco recognised that even in the late twentieth century a democratised Spain could not take for granted the political traditions of the smaller of Spains nationalities, many of whose members rejected the dominant role played in their lives by the pre-eminent Castilian cultural and political élite. So what are the distinctive features of these smaller nationalities that make their rejection of Castilla so forthright?

Catalunya

Covering an area of 31,929 square kilometres, Catalunya is divided into four provinces: Tarragona, Barcelona, Lerida and Gerona, with a total population of about 6 million inhabitants. When the Generalitat de Catalunya – a governing body-was established in 1289, it protected Catalan liberties and privileges against the ambitions of the centralising Spanish Crown. Between 1410 and the middle of the seventeenth century, Catalunya was under the influence and control of Aragón and the unified Spain. A period of independence from the Spanish Hapsburg monarchy in the seventeenth century ended with a guarantee of its autonomy upon rejoining, a guarantee revoked by royal decree in 1716. Catalan culture, which spread beyond Catalunya to Valencia, the Balearic Islands and some southern provinces of France, was suppressed in Spain during the eighteenth century. However, as part of a cultural renaissance coinciding with a period of prosperity in the nineteenth century, Catalunya experienced a revitalisation of its language and culture which, together with a sense of economic well-being, distinguishing it from the major part of Spain, led to demands for political autonomy. Political movements followed, and in 1932 the Generalitat was restored after a statute of autonomy gave Catalunya control over most of its affairs, except in the areas of external relations. This was a short-lived achievement as the Catalans paid a high price for siding with the Republic in the Civil War in Spain (1936-39): the statute of autonomy was revoked and Catalan culture suppressed.[2]

During the transition to democracy a new autonomy statute was approved by a huge majority in 1979 and the first elections to the Generalitat which had been restored in 1977, took place in 1980. Since those elections the Catalan party, CiU, has been the strongest group, although the socialists (PSOE-PSC) in Catalunya have also done well. Language remains one of the most prominent symbols of Catalan identity, providing a "passport" to the best jobs. As the buoyant Catalan economy has attracted much migrant labour from other parts of Spain, some discrimination against incomers has occurred. During the Franco dictatorship, both Catalans and impoverished immigrants found common cause in their opposition to government policies and so, tensions between them were minimal. Apart from a few bomb explosions in Barcelona in the mid-1980s, political violence has not been forthcoming from Catalan nationalists in the recent phase of its history.

Euskadi (and Navarra)

Comprising an area of approximately 20,000 square kilometres, Euskadi includes the three provinces of Alava, Guipúzocoa and Viscaya (which form the autonomous region of Euskadi (Pais Vasco), established by statute in 1979 and covering only 7,261 square kilometres), the province of Navarra (granted separate autonomous region status in 1982 and 10,421 square kilometres in size) as well as three provinces in south western France. The autonomous region of Euskadi has a population of 5.6 million inhabitants, while Navarra has half a million. Thus the significance of the Basque nationality issue is heightened by the fact that it is crossed by an international border, implying international security co-operation. The Basque language is perhaps its most distinctive symbol. Its antiquity suggests that the Basques have the oldest extant culture on the Iberian peninsula, if not in western Europe as a whole. Political autonomy dates back to the seventh century where each province held legally-binding rights called 'fueros'. Basque separate political identity persisted until the nineteenth century when the fueros were virtually dismantled, culminating in the abolition of symbolically important customs-posts on the Ebro river in 1876. Partly in reaction to encroaching Spanish centralism, Basque nationalism began to emerge, notably in the person of Sabino de Arana who founded the Basque nationalist party (PNV) in 1895 and was responsible for reinvigorating various aspects of its cultural traditions, especially its language. Industrialisation in Euskadi also heightened Basque impatience with the political masters in Castilla and Madrid, although Basque financial capital was more closely linked to Castilla than was that of Catalunya.

During the 1950s, in response to the repression of Basque national identity by the Franco regime, an extreme group within the PNV formed Euskadi ta Askatasuna (ETA), Euskadi and Freedom, which eventually committed itself to armed struggle to achieve its aims. One of the most notorious actions was the killing in 1973 of Francos heir-apparent the Defence Minister, Admiral Carrero Blanco, an action which ironically hastened the emergence of democracy in Spain to fill the political vacuum.

In response to Basque nationalist demands and violence, the post-Franco governments took a number of steps, including, pushing ahead with autonomy for the regions, strengthening the security forces there and increasing security co-operation with France. The statute of autonomy granted to the Basques gave them more control over their own regional government and finances (including tax-raising) than other regions achieved. The Basques also gained the right to set up a police force of their own as well as a radio and T.V. station. These actions failed to stem ETA violence, which has ebbed and flowed over the ensuing years and continued into the 1990s with the killings of two Spanish army generals in 1994 (including one during the European election campaign), and, in 1995, the attempted assassination of José Maria Aznar, leader of the conservative opposition party Partido Popular. The majority of nationalist support has gone to the moderate Basque party PNV rather than to ETA's political-arm, Herri Batasuna (HB), People's Unity.

Navarra was an independent kingdom up until the early sixteenth century after which it was annexed to Castilla and Aragón as part of the unified

Spain. Like the other three Basque provinces it has a tradition of ancient fueros – but unlike the other provinces it retained these rights during the Franco era, including, its tax-raising powers. This was because the province supported Nationalist forces during the Civil War and was allowed this concession by the 'generalissimo' (Franco), in return. In the north of Navarra, the majority of the population speak the Basque language, thus identifying with Euskadi. In the south, Castellano is more widely spoken and the population there identify either with Spain or with a notion of a separate Navarrese identity. Due to the various attitudes to identity in Navarra, the province opted to form its own autonomous region – still maintaining its old tax-raising powers – which was established in 1982. The region does retain the constitutional option of joining the Basque autonomous region some day.

Galicia

Galicia lies on the Atlantic seaboard in the north-eastern corner of Spain. Its four provinces – Lugo, La Coruna, Orense and Pontevedra – cover an area of 29,434 square kilometres populated by 2.8 million inhabitants. It was the area on the Iberian peninsula with the highest concentration of Celtic settlers around 1,000 BC and still retains elements of their culture. The language of Galicia – galego – is Latin based   and is spoken by a higher percentage of the population than either Catalan or Basque in their respective regions.

In the period of the reconquista, Galicia's neighbouring region, Asturias, was politically more significant but Galicia benefited from its proximity to power. One of the Asturian monarchs asserted control over the north and western coasts, so that by the ninth century the area was restored to Christian rule from the Moors. But as the Asturian monarchy created León and Castilla, Galicia was marginalised and discontent became more prevalent amongst its nobility. The fortuitous 'discovery' of the bones of St. James in the region, resulting in the pilgrimage route – El Camino de Santiago – to what became the city of Santiago de Compostela, created some prosperity and defused the sense of neglect in Galicia, for the time being.

In later centuries, Galicia went into economic decline and overpopulation led to the creation of an uneconomic system of agricultural small-holdings (mini-fundia) as well as mass emigration, notable to Latin America. Not until the nineteenth century did Galician nationalism begin to take hold. Cultural awareness and activism preceded political activism, which emerged in the early twentieth century, and, in 1936, autonomy proposals were accepted by the vast majority of the population. Before the autonomy statute could make its way through the Cortes, the Civil War broke out, so killing off the initiative. Unlike in Catalunya and Euskadi, nationalist parties have not had a very significant impact on the post-democratic regional structure in Galicia (ie. the Xunta de Galicia) which was established in 1981. One reason for this lies in the divisions that exist in the Galician nationalist family. The Spanish conservative party, P.P, hold the majority in the regional parliament led by its President, Manuel Fraga, a former information and tourism minister under Franco. The socialists (PSOE-PSG) in Galicia are the second strongest electoral force and, of the nationalist groups, Bloque Nacionalista Galego (BNG), a left-of-centre group, has made the strongest advance since autonomy. In the 1996 general elections, for the first time, BNG won two seats in the Cortes.

Other Nationalities in Spain

Apart from the so called historic nationalities discussed above, the position of other regions with a strong regional consciousness is not so clear. Andalusia is a historic region with a rich culture, extending back to the Moorish period but historically, without a separate national trajectory: since the reconquista it has been populated mainly by Castilians. With autonomy, regional consciousness has actually grown to the point where the Partido Andalucista (Andalusian nationalist party) has developed a significant following, winning a seat in the European Parliament (EP) in 1989, though losing it in 1994.

A look at the other parties contesting elections in post-Franco Spain offers a clue to budding multinationalism in many other areas. These include: Agrupación Independiente Canaria (Canary Independence Association), Partido Aragónes (Aragonese Party), Partiu Asturianista (Asturian Party), Unidad Regionalista de Castilla y León (Regional Unity of Castille and León), Unio Mallorquina (Balearic Island Unity) and Unio Valenciana (Valencian Unity). In considering these smaller groupings, it is relevant also to mention Falange Espanola de las J.O.N.S – the Spanish falangist party committed to extremist Spanish nationalism. It appears that the move to democratic Spain and especially the creation of the autonomous system, which was intended to resolve the issue of multinationalism through a semi-federal Spain, has served to fuel falangist commitment to Spanish unity. However, falangists have very little electoral support.

REGIONALISM AND THE CONSTITUTION

During Spain's transition to democracy between 1976 and 1978 there was an agreement between the main political forces advocating and opposing constitutional change. Part of this agreement, after sixteen months of highly controversial debate, was the insertion of a concept within the Constitution which declared that the different nationalities and regions together, made up what was known as the Spanish Nation. This idea was further developed through the granting of the nationalities and regions their own institutional structures:- presidents, governments, parliaments, high courts and administrations – in regional entities referred to as 'communidades autonomiás' (autonomous communities), a term without precedent in Spanish constitutional law. The seventeen autonomous communities which were established by statute, eventually embraced not just the historic nationalities but those territorial regions with only the barest claim to distinctive and shared affinities. As Moratá notes: 'The Spanish constitution establishes a hybrid system, neither unitary nor federal but based on the "unity of the Spanish nation" and the "autonomy of the nationalities and regions which constitute it" '.[3] This constitutional formula seems to have been a way of appeasing the nervous Spanish military, who suspected that the way was being prepared for the eventual independence of the nationalities and a consequent break-up of Spain.

The historic nationalities were, however, given a head start on this 'home-rule' initiative for example, in the fact that 'pre-autonomous bodies' were established in Euskadi and Catalunya as early as 1977, in anticipation of the new Spanish constitution. Additionally, the Constitution of 1978 contained various distinct processes through which autonomous committees could be set up, one of which, 'the rapid route' related specifically to the historic nationalities (plus the historic region of Andalusia), giving them the right to set up regional structures with full powers, and without delay. This constitutional process was propelled especially by the demands of active nationalist parties and assisted by Spanish opposition parties, the socialists, (PSOE) and the communists, (PCE). Accordingly, the special home-rule status accorded to those 'rapid route' regions was clearly defined in the early years of democracy in post-Franco Spain.

Fuelled by fears arising from threats to the fledgling Spanish democracy, most obviously in the form of a coup attempt in 1981, this special status was quickly watered down later that year as the Spanish state sought, on the one hand, to reassert its own power by placing a ceiling on the autonomy being acquired by those nationalities and, on the other hand, to reassure the military and other opponents of fragmentation, by legislating for more harmonisation across the whole of Spain's seventeen autonomous communities. Reforms to the 1978 Constitution through the controversial harmonisation law, the Ley Orgánica de Armonizacion del Proceso Autonómico (Organic Law on the Harmonisation of the Autonomy Process/LOAPA), revealed the extent of the fears of both government and opposition parties at the Spanish centre, that the autonomous process for the nationalities and regions was getting out of hand and might even be fuelling support for anti-democratic, right-wing elements. Thus, to reassert central government powers, LOAPA indicated that where there was a conflict between state law and regional law, the former should apply. Although judged by the Tribunal Constitucional (Spanish Constitutional Court) in 1983 to be unconstitutional and subsequently repealed, its principles have continued to prevail in state-region relations in the 1980s and early 1990s.

Since 1983, there has been an ongoing political and constitutional debate between central government and the autonomous communities, led especially by the Catalans and Basques, which has focused on the definition of the powers of the autonomous communities accorded by the 1978 Constitutions. This has centred on areas of public policy such as policing, education, health and public administration. As Brasslof has noted, the historic nationalities, especially the Catalans and the Basques have insisted on the 'hechos differenciales' (differential factors) which 'mark them out from others' and their aim has been to maintain the distance between them and the other autonomous communities as they advance their powers.4 Increasingly, the Tribunal Constitucional has become the adjudicator in such disputes as both regional governments and central government have both turned to it to defend their respective interests. By 1989, 800 legal cases had been considered. While the court has supported the right of regional governments to manage the interests of their own communities as provided for constitutionally, and also held that national, regional and local interests are distinctive, nevertheless, it has placed limits on regional autonomy by giving central government the right to promote what are seen as the general interests of Spain. Such a right, the court has held, give central government the responsibility to establish the basic functions and norms of the regional institutions. By attempting to strike such a balance between central and regional power, the Tribunal Constitucional has undermined the *exclusive powers* principle which was invoked in the granting of regional powers (ie. the complete exclusion of central government control from certain designated areas of regional decision-making).

The Spanish system, as increasingly interpreted by the court, reflects

Germany's system of 'executive federalism' where central and regional governments are seen to be connected by their duty to engage in *mutual collaboration* on behalf of the public interest, and so the region has the function not only of making and implementing its own regional laws but also of implementing central government laws.[5] The perceived benefits of invoking the mutual collaboration principle, as opposed to the exclusive powers principle in centre-region relations include the view that it helps in the co-ordination and efficient management of public functions, with little waste or duplication. For the regions, and especially the historic nationalities, who have had governments run by either nationalist parties or the main Spanish opposition parties the principle of mutual collaboration has had little to recommend it. In reality, intergovernmental bargaining between the centre and the region has tended to be characterised by political antagonism oscillating 'between the constitutional management of conflict and hard bargaining until agreement [is] reached'.[6] Regions have argued that this 'mutual collaboration' principle almost invariably results in the reduction of a regional autonomy guaranteed by the 1978 Constitution and the application of central regulations directives and controls, which amount to rolling back the decentralisation inherent in the statutes of autonomy.

The dependence of the PSOE and PP minority government on the votes of the CiU after the general elections of 1993 and 1996, has placed the Catalan nationalists in a unique position to pressurise the government into making concessions to the nationalities and regions and above all, to Catalunya. One of the spin-offs of this has been the activation of reform measures for the upper house of the Spanish Cortes: the Senado (Senate). To hasten reform, a commission, established in 1993 has been undertaking agreed new functions, in advance of full reform of the chamber. Moreover, the autonomous community is likely to be the electoral constituency in the reformed chamber in place of the province.[7] At a symbolic level, the gathering of all the presidents of the autonomous communities to address the Senate in 1994, some in their own language was important, as agreement was reached to change the status of the chamber. The Basque President, however, refused to attend, seeing it as a betrayal of Basque nationalism.

FINANCIAL AUTONOMY AND PUBLIC POLICY

Finance, more than symbolism, have generated some of the most heated debates in the 1990s, between the nationalities, the central government, and, the other regions in Spain.

The Constitution recognised the right of the autonomous communities to financial autonomy. This right had however to be exercised within its overall responsibility to the Spanish state for taxation and for the general interests of all the peoples under its charge. Arising from these constitutional provisions, the Ley Orgánica de Financiación de las Communidades Autonomicas (Organic Law on the Financing of Autonomous Communities/LOFCA) was passed in 1980, which amongst other things established a consultative council composed of the finance ministers of the regional governments and the Spanish government. In this council, issues such as the distribution of resources have been debated intensely. It is a consultative body 'which looks at the co-ordination of policy in regard to public investment, costs of services, public debt and the distribution of resources to the regions'.[8]

Financial autonomy has also involved the rights of regional parliaments to control their own budgets. Apart from Euskadi and Navarra, which for historical reasons won a separate system, the autonomous communities have been paid an annual block-grant in proportion to the services which have been transferred into their charge worked out in complex negotiations in bilateral committees or commissions. Following the 1993 and 1996 elections, after pressure from the Catalan nationalists on the weak PSOE and PD government, regions have also taken responsibility for the retention and disposal of a percentage, currently 30%, of personal income tax, a process called 'fiscal co-responsibility'.

Also arising from the provisions of the Constitution has been the Fondo Compensación Interterritorial (Inter-territorial Compensation Fund/FCI) which has diverted a designated percentage (35% after 1992) of public investment funds into the regions, calculated by reference to a needs-formula reflecting population-density, emigration, unemployment levels and incomes, among other factors, and which, for instance, has favoured areas of manufacturing decline like Euskadi in the 1990s as well as the economically peripheral Galicia. In addition to the central government block-grant and other compensation measures, the regions have been able to raise money by means of some local taxes, service charges, surcharges on state taxes, and borrowing.

Special economic agreements gave the historic nationalities/regions of Euskadi and Navarra the right to collect all taxes, except customs duties and those on petroleum products and tobacco. While they are not permitted to vary the Spanish rates of income, corporation or value added taxes, the fact that they have the power to collect their own taxes has resulted in lower tax evasions in these areas than in the Spanish state generally. As they have to forfeit a 'cupo' (quota) of this tax income to the central treasury, the Basques especially, have complained that they are being penalised for their success in tax-raising. The tax negotiations are carried out for Euskadi by a so-called 'mixed-committee' consisting of six central government representatives, three from the Euskadi government and one each from its three provinces. The reasons for provincial representation is that corresponding to historical precedent it is the provincial administrations not the regional governments which are actually responsible for tax collection in Euskadi, leading to further negotiations between the provinces and the regional government to distribute this income, as it is the latter that actually spends most of it.

Conflict between Euskadi and the Spanish state has also arisen over the system of raising funds by issuing treasury bonds in Euskadi. In 1989 this created a furore when the bonds were offered to investors at a rate which was 1.5 per cent higher than similar bonds offered for sale by the Spanish Central Bank thus threatening an embarrassing if not destabilizing rush of funds from Madrid to Euskadi. Despite claiming that the right to such action derived from the fueros, the government of Euskadi was in due course forced to submit to the Central Bank of Spain on the matter.

The question of financial autonomy for the regions and nationalities, especially in an era of public expenditure cutbacks, continues to be a controversial one. It is made more so by the growing direct links with regions and nationalities outside the Spanish state, other nation states and the European Union.

STATE, REGION AND EXTERNAL RELATIONS

The autonomous communities are constitutionally required to conform to the over-riding rule that the Spanish state is sovereign in the matter of foreign policy. That said, through the statutes of autonomy they are permitted some freedom in the conduct of external relations and in this regard the nationalities have been quite active, not however, without cutting across the bow of central government. Catalunya has been considerably active in projecting itself internationally on a number of fronts: economically (eg. by using its 'consulates' in the major industrialised cities to attract inward investment to the area); culturally (eg. actively promoting Catalan identity overseas) and politically (eg. advancing its interests on the EU Committee of the Regions). Galicia too has incorporated its external relations into day-to-day political realities: culturally (eg. contributing to the development of the pan-Celtic movement and fostering links with other Celtic nations); economically (eg. advocating the case of Galician maritime interests during the tuna fish 'war' with France in 1994 and the halibut 'war' with Canada in 1995); socially (eg. in its contribution to emigrant centres in Latin and Central America); politically (eg. in the 'foreign policy' condemnation of the U.S. blockade of Cuba in September 1994 by the President of the Xunta de Galicia Manuel Fraga, who had earlier hosted a visit of Fidel Castro, also of Galician origin, to the region). The growth of horizontal institutional links between the regions and nationalities of Spain and other European regions, reflect the development of some 'independent' external relations beyond the Spanish multinational state.

Galicia is also a member of the Regional Conference of Peripheral Maritime Regions (Conférence des Regions Peripheriques Maritimes/CRPM) which mostly includes regions of EU member states. The purpose of the organisation of those regions participating in CRPM is to develop inter-regional links to counter handicaps suffered by peripheral maritime regions in Europe. Catalunya belongs to similar organisations concerned with cross-frontier issues such as the Trans Pyrenean Working Group (Communauté de Travail des Pyrenees). The significance of such organisations though, is limited by their comparative lack of direct and specific influence at either central government or supra-national levels.

The autonomous process has also allowed the development of some policy initiatives directed externally. Galicia has developed a number of aid programmes for the Galician emigrant communities in Latin America, for example, pensions.[10] While some superficial freedom of action may be apparent in these external links, the underlying constitutional relationships ensure that such actions take place within the parameters of the 1978 Constitution, the autonomy statutes and the Spanish Treaty of Accession to the European Community. The wide legislative reach of EU and central government policy, limits the actual capacity of those nationalities to develop 'external relations' which lie outside EU and Spanish interests, but the proliferation of such links, albeit under the auspices of EU and Spanish policy initiatives is noteworthy and enhance the nationalities claims to more 'sovereignty' within multinational Spain.

THE EUROPEAN DIMENSION OF MULTINATIONALISM

The argument is commonly voiced that developments in the EC/EU have already, or will, enhance the capacity of the nationalities to pursue, where appropriate, their own separate interests from those of Spain. Indeed, the EU encourages such thinking by employing terms such as 'subsidiarity', 'partnership with the regions' and promoting the idea of a 'Europe of the Regions'. Can we therefore depict the EU as the ally of the nationalities against member-state centralism? Are the nationalities in Spain successfully advancing their interests in the EU? Has the relationship between the regions and central government in respect of European Union matters been resolved? As we will see there are limits to such interpretations of events in multinational Spain.

In some senses it can be argued that the nationalities of Spain are strengthening their position in the EU. A Tribunal Constitucional ruling, which coincided with the 1994 European election campaign, permitted the nationalities to operate their own consulates, for instance, in Brussels where they would have the right of direct negotiation with EU officials in certain areas of exclusive concern. Since the early 1980s, through public organisations like the Patronat Català and Fundación Galicia, various regions have had organisations that serve as information conduits to and from the EC/EU. Also, EU programmes such as that for regional development in the transfrontier-zones between Spain and Portugal allow some room for manoeuvre, for instance, to Galicia, to develop bilateral economic and infrastructural programmes with Portuguese local officials. Representation of the nationalities of Spain on the EU Committee of the Regions also offers the prospect of extra influence over EU decision-making, somewhat counter-balancing member-state level dominance of Council of Ministers decision-making. However, it is worth noting that the Spanish government opposed proposals for the Committee of the Regions which would have given regions and nationalities the sort of policy-influence Belgian and German communities already have in the cultural affairs council meetings, by having official status as participants.[11] There is also evidence of weakness in the nationalities position in Spain within the European Union. As Moratá notes, the transfer of sovereignty from Spain to the EC/EU has affected in a negative way the constitutional position of the nationalities and regions who are not represented in EC/EU decision-making bodies. That this would be the case was evident very early on during Spain's membership of the EC. A proposal in 1986 for an 'Agreement for Co-operation in Community Matters', aimed at the co-ordination of the views of the autonomous communities and the encouragement of co-operation with central government on EC policies, failed to progress very far. The main difficulty was the insistence of the 'historic nationalities', notably the Basques and the Catalans that they should have more autonomy of influence in such policies. Nevertheless, co-operation committees exist to oversee EU policy implementation at a sectoral level involving the representatives of the nationalities and regions, such as in the case of agriculture, and at programme level, for instance, in the case of the Community Support Framework.

Representation in the European Parliament (EP) has also created difficulties for the nationalities. The electoral system adopted in Spain for the 1994 European elections has been heavily criticised, especially by the nationalities, because of the existence of a single country-wide Spanish constituency with members elected through proportional representation from party-lists, rather than multiple constituencies based on the regional autonomies, where nationalist candidates and parties would have a better chance of success in elections. Complex procedural and tactical arrangements have been made necessary by this system, to assist in the attainment of representation from the nationalities to the EP. Many small regional and nationalist parties have found it necessary to join forces in country-wide electoral blocs, so that they might stand a chance of gaining sufficient votes to win seats against the parties with organisational and electoral support structures throughout Spain. One such bloc-Coalicion Nacionalista – consisted of parties from a number of nationalities and regions: the Basque Country (Partido Nacionalista Vasco), Canary Islands (Coalicion Canaria), Valencia (Unio Valenciana), Aragón (Partido Aragónes), Galicia (Coalicion Galega) and Mallorca (Unio Mallorquina). Confusingly for the voters, while some of the Spanish media commentary in the 1994 campaign used the names of such broad blocs, the campaigns at the level of these nationalities and regions with parties in such blocs, was generally conducted by and solely for the benefit of the relevant regional or nationalist party. Additionally, ballot papers in relevant autonomous communities when referring to such blocs carried the names of the local party or parties after the name of the bloc to which they belonged eg. the European Peoples Coalition (Por la Europa de los Pueblos) was named in the Catalan language on the ballot papers in the three regions of Catalunya, Valencia and Aragón as Per L'Europea de les Nacions (Esquerra Republicana de Catalunya – Accio Catalana). Some voter confusion in such circumstances was understandable.

For some nationalist parties however, there was a perceived advantage in belonging to a countrywide constituency, offering the opportunity of attracting the votes of migrants to other regions of Spain. For example, the many natives of Galicia or their families living in Catalunya could, if they so wished, vote for the left-wing Galician nationalist party, BNG, thus boosting the votes of that party from beyond its regional core support. Even so, the Galician party, although certainly boosting its votes, failed to win one of Spain's 64 Euro-seats. However, other nationalities had more success with the electoral system adopted by Spain for the EP elections: the Catalan party, CiU, won 3 seats, while the Basque PNV won 2 (taking a seat from its more militant opponents in HB).

Apart from the question marks surrounding the adequacy of the electoral system used during the Euro-elections, there was also the issue of what, beyond the rhetoric of the euro-idealists at EU level, the nationalist parties in Spain could hope to achieve once their candidates were elected. Certainly, party programmes revealed how wide in scope were their ambitions, if not their expectations at the EU level.

The CiU programme demanded participation for the Generalitat in the EU Council of Ministers. It also called for a strengthening of the powers of the Committee of the Regions and an improvement in the links between Catalonia and European institutions generally. The Catalan language was also promoted, with calls for its recognition as an official language of the EU. CiU emphasised the importance of developing the much-vaunted EU principle of 'subsidiarity', to ensure that powers and competences acceded to the Generalitat by central government in the autonomous process, would be maintained at the regional level and not removed to Brussels.

In Euskadi, the PNV programme, like that of CiU, was also distinctly European in its outlook but its nationalism (with an eye over its shoulder to the more extreme HB) was more vehement than its Catalan counterpart. It emphasised the importance of self-government for the Basques and demanded participation for Basque representatives not only in the EU Council of Ministers but also in other processes such as the Inter-Governmental Conference. Like the CiU, it recommended a more powerful EP, with members elected in Spain from regional constituencies rather than the single countrywide constituency. It also called for the acceptance of the Basque language as an official language of the EU.

Despite such demands, the reality of their representatives position in the new European Parliament made the likelihood of a significant impact for Spain's nationalities in the EP rather remote. Apart from the paucity of numbers which they had in that chamber there was also the question of which party bloc they would join. CiU, which is really a coalition of two Catalan parties, settled the issue for itself by belonging to two different European Parliament groups, the Liberals and the European Peoples Party. The somewhat odd nature of this arrangement becomes more apparent when it is remembered that the CiU was also propping up a minority socialist government in Spain frome 1993 to 1996. All of this has hardly added up to a clear message to European Union decision-makers from the Catalan party, let alone any significant influence. As for the PNV, somewhat oddly, it joined the European Peoples Party, to which the hitherto centralist Spanish party,

P.P., also belonged. Thus, the influence of the parties of the Spanish nationalities in the EP appears very diluted, if not somewhat wayward.

There is also evidence that the interests of the Spanish nationalities have been sacrificed in favour of the broader interests of the state in EU decision-making. For example, the development of the fishing industry in Galicia was considerably curtailed by the outcome of negotiations on fishing quotas for Spain's accession to the EC in 1986. Demands for more quota reductions in the 1990s have led to highly publicised conflicts between Spain and France, Ireland, the U.K. and Canada. The further erosion of the regional fishing industries seem certain, and will profoundly affect the economic and social structures of nationalities like Galicia. EU policies also, in some cases, appear to encourage the exploitation of economically weaker nationalities by stronger ones, adding fuel to the argument of left-wing nationalists that Spain reveals features of 'internal colonialism'. The purchase of a Galician steel plant by a Catalan steel company and its subsequent closure has been cited by Galicia's BNG leader, Xosé Manuel Beiras, as an example of the mechanism by which the stronger economic regions within Spain are better placed to take advantage of EU rules, a factor which sets nationalities in competition with each other.[12] BNG argued that EU production quotas for Spanish steel were, as a consequence of this sale, further concentrated in the stronger region – Catalunya – at the expense of the weaker Galician economy, and, with the full approval and assistance of the EU and the Spanish state.

The optimism evident in the concept of 'Europe of the Regions' may be misplaced when used in the context of the Spanish multinational state. The persistence of inequalities, ambiguities and conflicts of interest in multinational Spain mar the pristine version of relations, between the nationalities, regions and the EU, embodied in such concepts.

THE POLITICS OF MULTINATIONALISM TODAY

If the promise of an active role in a 'Europe of the Regions' has so far failed to quell the demands of Spain's nationalities and to settle their differences with the Spanish government in Madrid, what form are the demands of those nationalities now taking?

The response in Spain to the events of the late 1980s and early 1990s in eastern and central Europe are instructive in relation to this question. Arising from the positive pronouncements of Felipe González towards the end of 1989, on the benefits of self-determination for former republics and satellite states of the USSR, the small radical left-wing Catalan party, Esquerra

Republican de Catalunya (ERC), introduced a motion to the Catalan parliament stating that the Catalan nation 'does not give up its right to self-determination'. With the help of the moderate Catalans of CiU, the motion was passed, followed quickly by a motion passed by members of the Basque parliament (including both PNV and HB) with a more stridently nationalist message. A similar motion to the Galician parliament fell foul of the majority of seats held by PP in that chamber.[13]

The reaction of the Spanish state to these initiatives was extremely vigorous. Army generals based in those nationalities omnimously reminded the public that they were constitutionally bound to protect the territorial integrity of Spain. González strongly echoed their views by rubbishing any talk of self-determination and offering the complete opposition of his government, whatever it took, to any process of self-determination. He also indicated that any further concessions on autonomy would be measured minutely, as though in punishment for those who would dare challenge the unity of the Spanish state. Following much public debate, CiU pronounced, by way of a conciliatory explanation that it was not proposing a move outside existing constitutional principles. PNV, in Euskadi, also clarified its ideas, expressing its views on self-determination in terms of the existing framework of the constitution and the statute of autonomy for Euskadi. Eventually the debate fizzled out but not its significance. It appears that centralism remains the instinctive gut-reaction in Spanish politics, not least of the PSOE in government. Decentralisation, it may be argued, was conceded through the statutes of autonomy less due to the inspiration of the political élite of the transition period by genuinely federalist ideas, and more because of fears of the threat of nationalist violence at a critical time in the transition to and consolidation of democracy.

Despite the 1993 and 1996 election outcomes, there is little evidence, as yet, that government policy on the nationalities question in multinational Spain is based on the principle of partnership. Nor do Spanish governments yet seem to accept the idea that the basis upon which the relationship between the nationalities and Spanish state operates, arises from the consent of the former. This failure to embrace a new conception of the Spanish state which would break from the centralist tradition and which would treat all its nationalities on a partnership basis has resulted in policy initiatives driven by a pluralist free-for-all in which policy is made in reaction to events, most notably in post-election pacts. In such a scenario, the strong regions fare best and are treated with most respect by central government.

In the aftermath of the 1993 general elections, Catalunya emerged as a nationality with a strong card to play: the 17 votes of the CiU members in the lower house of the Cortes which Felipe González needed to stay in government. CiU played that card well from the early days of this government and González became more conciliatory towards it, than he had been in the self-determination debate. CiU support was contingent upon Catalunya gaining a string of concessions, which were never fully publicised and in fact seemed to evolve with events. What was clear was that the price of these concessions was not a low one, a fact verified by the venom poured on Catalunya by politicians and the media in other regions who considered that Catalunya's gain had been at their expense. Having unleashed such uproar by his efforts to stay in power at the centre, González lamely defended his tactics to critics in the opposition, saying that the partnership between the PSOE and CiU was Spanish democracy in practice, with the Catalan party playing its role at the heart of the Spanish state. Ironocally, the pact collapsed under the weight of PSOE 'sleaze'. The PP vowed that it would not be sucked into striking debilitating deals with nationalist parties. But after the 1996 general election Aznar wooed and won the votes, not just of CiU but of PNV and a handful of regional deputies. A symbol of the distrust of PP was their demands for written agreements before they would vote for Aznar's investiture as Prime Minister.

CONCLUSION

It is impossible to understand the nature of political life in Spain without reflecting on its essentially multinational nature and its transformation into a semi-federal state. There are a number of facets that may be readily identified: firstly, the linguistic as well as cultural diversity and richness, evident in the historic nationalities and regions, most clearly in Catalunya, Euskadi and Galicia. This, together with their separate historical experiences, distinguishable in many significant ways from that of Castillian Spain, offers a wealth of evidence of the incontrovertible, multinational essence of Spanish life. Secondly, the recognition and guarantee in Article 2 of the Constitution of 'the right of the nationalities and regions of Spain to autonomy' (which it should be mentioned, also proclaims 'the indissoluble unity of the Spanish nation'), and, the acknowledgement, in Article 3 that the regional languages of Spain are co-official in the regions concerned (alongside castellano), enshrines the legitimacy of multinationalism in Spain, but provokes fierce debates on the whereabouts of the constitutional boundaries – if any – between the nationalities and the nation state in Spain. Thirdly, an inherent feature of the evolution of the public policy process in democratic Spain has been the incorporation of political institutions, organisations and policy actors from the nationalities (and to a lesser extent, other regions) in the decision-making and policy implementation structures of the Spanish state and to a lesser degree in the EC/EU, giving them primary control and autonomy over the distribution of some significant amounts of public resources, albeit with extremely vocal, frequent and unreconciled debates about the imbalance between the relatively weak powers of the nationalities in the autonomous community structure, and those of central government and the EU. Fourthly, there has been a proliferation of external relations between the nationalities of Spain and nation-states as well as other regions outside Spain and supra-national entities like the EU. This phenomenon has taken place within the realms of what is the central government's formal and exclusive jurisdiction in matters of foreign affairs and treaty-making. It also coincides with the transfer to the European Union of powers previously conceded by the Spanish state to the autonomous communities (eg. in aspects of agricultural policy) located in the various nationalities and regions. Nevertheless, despite their sources of limitation on the nationalities, there is growing interaction and participation by them in transnational policy networks that sometimes bypass the Spanish state and thus raise questions about the meaning or relevance of 'state sovereignty' in the fluid political environment of external relations. Finally, the realities of electoral life in Spain have produced political outcomes at central, regional and local levels which have brought together some of the nationalist parties and Spanish parties in various mutually convenient arrangements and 'unholy' alliances for the purpose of political expediency. While such events by no means guarantee that a full political settlement of the Spanish multinational question will be achieved, they do ensure that that question is never far from the top of the various political agendas in Spain.

NOTES

1 J. Hooper *The New Spaniards*, Harmondsworth, Penguin, 1995, p.375; see also P. Heywood, *The Government and Politics of Spain*, London, Macmillan, 1995, Ch. 1, *passim*.

2 E. Moxon-Browne *Political Change in Spain*, London, Routledge, 1989. p.48; see also J.P. Fusi *Autonomias*, Madrid, Espasa-Calpe, 1989, *passim*.

3 F. Moratá 'Spanish Regions and the E.C.' in B. Jones and M. Keating (eds) *The European Union and the Regions*, Oxford, Clarendon Press, 1995, p.116

4 A. Brasslof, 'Spain's Centre and Periphery: Is the tail wagging the dog?',

Political Studies Association (P.S.A) Conference Paper, York, 1995 p.2.
5 J.M.A. Valles and M. Cuchillo Foix 'Decentralisation in Spain: a review' *European Journal of Political Research*, 16, 1988.
6 F. Moratá, *op. cit.*, p.119.
7 A. Brasslof, *op. cit.*, p.8.
8 P.J. Donaghy and M.T. Newton, *Spain: a Guide to Political and Economic Institutions*. Cambridge, Cambridge University Press, 1989, p.105; and 2nd edn, 1997, ch.7, *passim*.
9 *Financial Times*, 30 November 1989, Supplement p.3.
10 Xunta De Galicia 'Planes de Ayuda a la Galicia del Exterior', University of Santiago de Compostela, 1991.
11 F. Moratá, *op.cit.*, p.126.
12 Xosé Manuel Beiras, leader of Galician nationalist party, BNG, interview February, 1991.
13 A.C. Pereira-Menaut, 'The developing debate on self-determination in Spain', Political Studies Association Regional Politics Work Group Meeting, Newcastle, 1991.
14 See M. Guibernan, 'Spain: a Federation in the Making?', in G. Smith (ed) *Federalism: the Multi-ethnic Challenge*, London, Longman, 1995, pp.239–52 for an interesting discussion of the federal question.

Select Bibliography

Abraham, A.J., *Lebanon at Mid–Century: Maronite–Druze relations in Lebanon 1840–1860: A Prelude to Arab Nationalism*, New York, University Press of America, 1981.

AISA, 'Czechs and Slovaks Compared: A Survey of Economic and Political Behaviour', *Studies in Public Policy*, No.198, Glasgow, University of Strathclyde, 1992.

Akarli, Engin, The Long Peace: Ottoman Lebanon 1861–1920, Oxford and London, Centre for Lebanese Studies and I.B. Tauris and Co. Ltd., 1993.

Alatulu, T., 'Tuva – A State Reawakens', *Soviet Studies*, Vol. 44, No.5, 1992, pp.881–95.

Association for Canadian Studies, *Demilinguistic Trends and the Evolution of Canadian Instititions*, Ottawa, Association for Canadian Studies and the Office of the Commissioner for Official Languages, 1990.

Baaklini, Abdo, *Legislative and Political Development in Lebanon, 1842–1972*, Durham, Duke University Press, 1976.

Bakvis, Herman, *Federalism and the Organisation of Political Life: Canada in Comparative Perspective*, Kingston, Queen's University Institute of Intergovernmental Relations, 1981.

Banac, I., *The National Question in Yugoslavia: Origins, History and Politics*, Ithaca, Cornell University Press, 1984.

Barber, Benjamin R., *The Death of Communal Liberty: A History of Freedom in a Swiss Mountain Canton*, Princeton, N.J., Princeton University Press, 1974.

Barsenkov, A., V. Koretsky and A. Ostapenko, 'Inter–Ethnic Relations in Russia in 1992', *Russia and the Successor States Briefing Service*, Vol.1, No.3, June 1993.

Barsenkov, A.S., A.I. Vdovin, V.A. Koretskii, I. S. Kukushin, and A.I. Ostapenko, *Towards a Nationalities Policy in the Russian Federation*, Aberdeen, Centre for Soviet and East European Studies, University of Aberdeen, 1993.

Bell, D. and L. Tepperman, *The Roots of Disunity*, Toronto McClelland & Stewart, 1979.

Bene, V. L, 'Czechoslovak Democracy and its Problems, 1918–1920', in Victor S. Mamatey and Radomír Luŧa (eds), *A History of the Czechoslovak Republic 1918–1948*, Princeton, Princeton University Press, 1973.

Bennett, C., *Yugoslavia's Bloody Collapse*, London, Hurst, 1994.

Bennigsen Broxup, M. (ed.), *The North Caucasus Barrier: The Russian Advance towards the Muslim World*, London, Hurst, 1992.

Bennigsen, A. and C. Lemercier-Quelquejay, *Islam in the Soviet Union*, London, Pall Mall, 1967.

Bennigsen, A. and S.E. Wimbush, *Muslim National Communism in the Soviet Union: A Revolutionary Strategy for the Third World*, Chicago, University of Chicago Press, 1979.

Bercuson, David J. *Canada and the Burden of Unity*, Toronto, Macmillan, 1977.

Birrell. D. and A. Murie, *Policy and Government in Northern Ireland: Lessons of Devolution*, Dublin, Gill and Macmillan, 1980.

Brand, J., J. Mitchell and P. Sturridge, 'Identity and the vote: Class and Nationality in Scotland' in D. Denver (ed), *British Elections and Parties Yearbook*, New York, Harvester Wheatsheaf, 1993.

Brass, P., *Politics of India Since Independence*, Cambridge, Cambridge University Press, 1990.

Bremmer, I. and R. Taras (eds) *Nations and Politics in the Soviet Successor States*, Cambridge, Cambridge University Press, 1993.

Brown A. and G. Wightman, 'Czechoslovakia: Revival and Retreat', in Archie Brown and Jack Gray (eds), *Political Culture and Political Change in Communist States*, 2nd edn, London, Macmillan, 1979.

Brym, Robert J. (ed.), *Regionalism in Canada*, Toronto, Irwin Publishing, 1986.

Bulpitt, J., *Territory and Power in the United Kingdom: An Interpretation*, Manchester, Manchester University Press, 1983.

Burg, S.L., *Conflict and Cohesion in Socialist Yugoslavia: Political Decision Making since 1966*, Princeton, Princeton University Press, 1983.

Carter, S.K., *Russian Nationalism: Yesterday, Today, Tomorrow*, London, Pinter, 1990.

Cohen, L.J., *Broken Bonds – the Disintegration of Yugoslavia*, Boulder and Oxford, Westview Press, 1993.

Coleman, W. D., *The Independence Movement in Quebec 1945–1980*, Toronto, University of Toronto Press, 1984.

Colley, L., *Britons: Forging the Nation 1707–1837*, London, Pimlico, 1992.

Crawshaw, S., *Goodbye to the USSR: The Collapse of Soviet Power*, London, Bloomsbury, 1992.

Crowe, Ralph, 'Parliament in the Lebanese Political System' in A. Kornberg and L. Musolf (eds), *Legislatures in Developmental Perspectives*, Durham, Duke University Press, 1970.

Crowther-Hunt, Lord and A. Peacock, *Royal Commission on the Constitution*, Volume 11, 'Memorandum of Dissent', London, HMSO, 1973.

Denitch, B., *Ethnic Nationalism: the Tragic Death of Yugoslavia*, Minneapolis, University of Minnesota Press, 1994.

Donaghy, P.J. and M.T. Newton, *Spain: a Guide to Political and Economic Institutions*, Cambridge, Cambridge University Press,1989.

Duncan, P.J.S. 'The Party and Russian Nationalism in the USSR: From Brezhnev to Gorbachev', in Peter J. Potichnyj (ed.), *The Soviet Union: Party and Society*, Cambridge, Cambridge University Press. 1988, pp.229–4.

Duncan, W.R., *Ethnic Nationalism and Regional Conflict: the Former Soviet Union and Yugoslavia*, Boulder and Oxford, Westview Press, 1994.

Dunlop J.B., *The Rise of Russia and the Fall of the Soviet State*, Princeton, N.J., Princeton University Press, 1993.

Dunlop, J.B., *The Faces of Contemporary Russian Nationalism*, Princeton, N.J., Princeton University Press, 1983.

Fidler, Richard, *Canada Adieu? Quebec Debates its Future*, Lanzville and Halifax, Oolichan Books and The Institute for Research on Public Policy, 1991.

Finer, S., 'Politics of Great Britain', in R. Macridis (ed), *Modern Political Systems: Europe*, 6th edn, Englewood Cliffs, Prentice Hall, 1987.

Fitzmaurice, J., *The Politics of Belgium: Crisis and Compromise in a Plural Society*, 2nd edn, London, Hurst, 1995.

Flood, J.L. (ed), *Modern Swiss Literature: Unity and Diversity*, London, Oswald Wolff, 1985.

Frankel F. and M.S.A. Rao, *Dominance and State Power in Modern India*. (2 volumes), New Delhi, Oxford University Press, 1990.

Frenkel, Max, *Federal Theory*, Canberra, Australia, NUTECH, 1986.

Fry, M., *Patronage and Principle: A Political History of Modern Scotland*, Aberdeen, Aberdeen University Press, 1987.

Galanter, M., *Law and Society in Modern India*. New Delhi, Oxford University Press, 1984.

Gibson, Ian, *Fire in the Blood*, London, Faber & Faber, 1992.

Glenny, M., *The Fall of Yugoslavia – the Third Balkan War*, rev. edn, Harmondsworth, Penguin, 1994.

Graham, B. *Hindu Nationalism and Indian Politics: The Origins and Development of the Bharatiya Jana Sangh*, Cambridge, Cambridge University Press, 1992.

Harvie, C., *Scotland and Nationalism: Scottish Society and Politics, 1707–1977*, London, Allen and Unwin, 1977.

Hasquin, H., 'Le Français à Bruxelles entre 1740 et 1780', in *Etudes sur le 18ième Siècle*, ULB, VI, 1979.

Hechter, M., *International Colonialism: The Celtic Fringe in British National Development, 1536–1966*, London, Routledge and Kegan Paul, 1975.

Henderson, K, 'Czechoslovakia: Cutting the Gordian Knot', *Coexistence*, Vol. 31, No. 4, 1994.

Henderson, K, 'Czechoslovakia: The Failure of Consensus Politics and the Breakup of the Federation', in *Journal of Regional and Federal Politics*, Vol. 5, No. 2, 1995.

Henderson, K, 'The Slovak Republic', in Bogdan Szajkowski (ed.), *Political Parties of Eastern Europe, Russia & the Successor States*, Harlow, Longman, 1994.

Hettne, B., 'Ethnicity and Development – an Elusive Relationship', in Contemporary South Asia, Vol. 2, No.2, 1993.

Hewitt, V.M. 'The Prime Minister and Parliament', in Manor J. (ed.), *Nehru to the Nineties*, London, Hurst, 1995.

Hewitt, V.M., *Reclaiming the Past? The Search for Political and Cultural Unity in Contemporary Jammu and Kashmir*, London, Portland Books, 1995.

Heywood, Paul, *The Government and Politics of Spain*, London, Macmillan, 1995.

Hitti, Philip, *Lebanon in History*, New York, St. Martin's Press, 1967.

Hooper, J. *The New Spaniards* , Harmondsworth, Penguin, 1995.

Hosking, G.A., J. Aves and P.J.S. Duncan, The Road to Post-Communism: *Independent Political Movements in the Soviet Union, 1985–1991*, London, Pinter, 1992.

Hourani, Albert, 'Ideologies of the Mountain and of the City', in Roger Owen (ed.), *Essays on the Crisis in Lebanon* , London, Ithaca Press, 1976.

Hourani, Albert, *Minorities in the Arab World*, Oxford, Oxford University Press.

Hudson, Michael, 'Democracy and Social Mobilization in Lebanese Politics' in *Comparative Politics*, Vol.1, No.2, 1969.

Hughes, Christopher, *Switzerland*, (Nations of the Modern World Series), Tonbridge, Ernest Benn, 1975.

Irvine, J.A., *State Building and Nationalism in Yugoslavia: the Communist*

Party and the Croat Question, Boulder and Oxford, Westview Press, 1993.

Jalal, A., *Authoritarianism and Democracy in South Asia: A Comparative History*, Cambridge, Cambridge University Press, 1995.

Jones, B. and M. Keating, *Labour and the British State*, Oxford, Oxford University Press, 1985.

Keating, M. and L. Hooghe, 'By–Passing the Nation–State? Regions and the EU Policy Process', in J.J. Richardson (ed.), *Policy Making in the European Union*, London, Routledge, 1995.

Keating, M., *Nations against the State. The new politics of nationalism in Quebec, Catalonia and Scotland*, London, Macmillan, 1995.

Keating, M., *State and Regional Nationalism. Territorial Politics and the European State*, London, Harvester-Wheatsheaf, 1988.

Kerr, Malcolm, 'Political Decision Making in a Confessional Democracy', in Leonard Binder, (ed.), *Politics in Lebanon*, New York, John Wiley and Sons Inc., 1966.

Kesterloot, C., *Mouvement Wallon et Identité Nationale*, Courier Hebdomadaire (CH), No. 1392, 1993, Brussels, CRISP, 1993.

Kirschbaum, S.J., 'Czechoslovakia: The Creation, Federalization and Dissolution of a Nation–State', in *Regional Politics and Policy*, Vol.3, No.1, 1993.

Kisrwani, Maroun, 'Foreign Interference and Religious Animosity in Lebanon' in the *Journal of Contemporary History*, Vol.15, No. 4, October 1980.

Kochan, L. (ed.), *The Jews in Soviet Russia since 1917*, 3rd edn. Oxford, Oxford University Press, 1978.

Kreindler, I., 'The Changing Status of Russian in the Soviet Union', *International Journal of the Sociology of Language*, No.33, 1982.

Krejíí, O, *Kniha o Volbách*, Prague, Victoria Publishing, 1994.

Lagasse, C.E., *Les Nouvelles Institutions Politiques de la Belgique et de l'Europe*.

Lamb, A., *Kashmir 1947: The Birth of a Tragedy*, Herefordshire, Roxford Books, 1994.

Lenin, V.I. *V.I. Lenin on the National Question and Proletarian Internationalism*, Moscow, Novosti, 1970.

Lijphart, A, *Democracies: Patterns of Majoritarian and Consensus Government in Twenty-One Countries*, New Haven and London, Yale University Press, 1984.

Lijphart, A, *Democracy in Plural Societies: A Comparative Exploration*, New Haven, Yale University Press, 1977.

Limaye, M., *Contemporary Indian Politics*, New Delhi, Sangam Books, 1987.

Lipset, S.M., 'The Revolt against Modernity', in *Consensus and Conflict: Essays in Political Sociology*, Ithaca, Cornell University Press, 1985.

Luck, J. Murray, *History of Switzerland*, Palo Alto, Ca, SPOSS Inc., 1985.

Lydall, H., *Yugoslavia in Crisis*, Oxford, The Clarendon Press. 1989.

Mabille, X., *Histoire Politique de la Belgique: Facteurs et Acteurs de Changement*, Brussels, CRISP, 1912.

MacRae K., *Conflicts and Compromise in Multilingual Societies: Belgium*, Waterloo, Ontario, Wilfrid Laurier University Press, 1986.

Madan, S., *Non–Renuciation: Interpreting Hindu Culture*, New Delhi, Oxford University Press, 1987.

Magas, B., *Class and Nation in Yugoslavia*, London, Routledge, 1990.

Magas, B., *The Strange Death of Communist Yugoslavia*, London, Verso, 1993.

Malcolm, Noel, *Bosnia: A Short History,* London Macmillan, 1993.

Malik, Y. and D.K. Vaypeyi, 'The Rise of Hindu Militancy' in *Asian Survey,* Vol.29, No.3, 1989.

Mathernova, K., 'Czecho?Slovakia: Constitutional Disappointments', in A.E. Dick Howard (ed.), *Constitution Making in Eastern Europe*, Washington, Woodrow Wilson Center Press, 1993.

Mathews, Robin, *Canadian Identity*, Ottawa, Steel Rail Publishing, 1988.

McFarlane, B., Yugoslavia: Politics, *Economics and Society*, London, Pinter, 1988.

McPhee, John, *The Swiss Army: La Place de la Concorde Suisse*, London and Boston, Faber and Faber, 1984.

McRoberts, Kenneth and Patrick J. Monahan, *The Charlottetown Accord, the Referendum and the Future of Canada*, University of Toronto Press, 1993.

McRoberts, Kenneth, *Quebec: Social Change and Political Crisis*, Toronto, McClelland & Stewart, 1988.

Meir Zamir, *The Formation of Modern Lebanon*, London and Ithaca, Cornell University Press, 1988.

Midwinter, A., M. Keating and J. Mitchell, *Politics and Public Policy in Scotland*, London, Macmillan, 1991.

Milivojevi, Marko, and Pierre Maurer, (eds), *Swiss Neutrality and Security: Armed Forces, National Defence and Foreign Policy*, NewYork, Oxford and Munich, Berg, 1990.

Milne, David, *The Canadian Constitution*, Toronto, James Lorimer and Co., 1994.

Monahan, Patrick J., *Meech Lake: the Inside Story*, Toronto, University of Toronto Press, 1991.

Morata, F. 'Spanish Regions and the E.C.', in B. Jones and M. Keating (eds) *The European Union and the Regions*, Oxford, The Clarendon Press, 1995..

Morton, G., *Rebirth of a Nation: Wales 1880–1980*, Oxford, Oxford University Press, 1994.

Morton, W.L., *The Canadian Identity*, Toronto, University of Toronto Press, 1972.

Moxon–Browne, E., *Political Change in Spain,* London, Routledge, 1989

Naccache, Georges, 'Deux Negations ne font pas une nation', quoted in David Gilmour, *Lebanon: The Fractured Country*, Oxford, Martin Robertson & Co.

Nagel, G., Comm*unautaire Conflicten in Belgie: Systemen voor Beheersing van Conflicten Tussen de Staat, de Gemeenschappen en de Gewesten: Het Arbitrage–Hof en de Overleg Comité Regering–Executives*, Die Keure, 1984.

Nasrallah, Fida 'The Treaty of Brotherhood, Cooperation and Coordination: An Assessment' in Youssef M. Choueiri (ed.), *State and Society in Syria and Lebanon*, Exeter, University of Exeter Press, 1993.

Oldenburg, V., *The Building of Colonial Lucknow*, Princeton, Princeton University Press, 1984.

Olson, D, 'The Sundered State: Federalism and Parliament in Czechoslovakia', in Thomas F. Remington (ed.), *Parliaments in Transition: The New Legislative Politics in the Former USSR and Eastern Europe*, Boulder, Westview Press, 1994.

Pavlovitch, S.K., *Tito – Yugoslavia's Great Dictator: A Reassessment*, London, Hurst, 1993.

Pinson, M., (ed.), *Muslims of Bosnia–Herzegovina: Their Historic Development from the Middle Ages to the Dissolution of Yugoslavia*, Cambridge, Mass., Harvard University Center for Middle Eastern Studies, 1994.

Pospielovsky, D., *The Russian Church under the Soviet Regime, 1917–1982*, Crestwood, N.Y., St. Vladimir's Seminary Press, 1984.

Puri, B. 'Kashmiriyat: The Vitality of Kashmir Identity', in *Contemporary South Asia*, Vol. 4, No. 1, March 1995.

Quigely, D., *Interpreting Caste*, Cambridge, Cambridge University Press, 1994.

Ramet, P., *Balkan Babel: Politics, Culture and Religion in Yugoslavia*, Boulder, Westview Press, 1992.

Ramet, P., *Nationalism and Federalism in Yugoslavia 1962 – 1991*, Bloomington, Indiana University Press, 1992.

Riggs, A.R. and Tom Velk, *Federalism in Peril: Will Canada Survive?*, Vancouver, The Fraser Institute, 1992.

Robbins, K., 'The United Kingdom as a Multinational State', in J. Beramendi, R. Maiz and X. Nunez (eds), *Nationalism in Europe. Past and Present*, Vol. 11, Santiago de Compostela, University of Santiago de Compostela, 1994.

Rokkan, S. and D. Urwin, *Economy, Territory, Identity: Politics of West European Peripheries*, London, Sage, 1983.

Rothschild, J., *East Central Europe between the Two World Wars*, Seattle and London, University of Washington Press, 1974.

Rudolph, S. and L. Rudolph, *In Pursuit of Lakshmi: State–Society Relations in India.*, Chicago, Chicago University Press, 1987.

Russell, Peter, *Constitutional Odyssey* (2nd edn), Toronto, Toronto University Press, 1993.

Ruys M., *The Flemings: a People on the Move*, Tielt, Lanoo, 1973.

Sakwa, R., *Russian Politics and Society*, London, Routledge, 1993.

Salem, Jean, *Introduction a la pensee politique de Michel Chiha,* Beyrouth, Librairie Samir, 1970.

Salibi, Kamal S., *The Modern History of Lebanon,* New York, Caravan Books, 1977.

Schwarz, Urs, *The Eye of the Hurricane: Switzerland in World War Two*, Boulder, Colorado, Westview Press, 1980.

Scott, F. and M. Oliver, *Quebec States her Case*, Toronto, Macmillan Inc., 1964.

Scowan, Reed *A Different Vision*, Toronto, Maxwell Macmillan, 1991.

Seroka, J. and Pavolic, V. (eds), *The Tragedy of Yugoslavia – The Failure of Democratic Transformation*, Armonk, N.Y. and London, M.E. Sharpe, 1992.

Sheth, D.L. 'The Great Language Debate: Politics of Metropolitan vs Vernacular India', in U. Baxi and P. Parekh, *Crisis and Change in Contemporary India*, New Delhi, Sage, 1995.

Skalnik Leff, C, *National Conflict in Czechoslovakia: The Making and Remaking of a State, 1918–1987*, Guildford, Princeton University Press, 1988.

Smith, A., *National Identity*, Harmondsworth, Penguin, 1992.

Smith, G. (ed.), *The Nationalities Question in the Soviet Union*, London, Longman, 1990.

Sorrell, Walter, *The Swiss: A Cultural Panorama of Switzerland*, London, Oswald Wolff, 1972.

Spillmann, Kurt R. and Rolf Kieser, *The New Switzerland*, Palo Alto, Ca., SPOSS Inc., 1996.

Srinivas. M., *Caste in Modern India*. Bombay, Media Promoters, 1962.
Steinberg, Jonathan, *Why Switzerland?*, (2nd edn) Cambridge, Cambridge University Press, 1996.
Stevenson, G., *Unfulfilled Union*, Toronto, Gage, 1979.
Taylor, Charles, *Reconciling the Solitudes*, Montreal and Kingston, McGill-Queens University Press, 1993.
Teague, E, 'Russia and Tatarstan Sign Power–Sharing Treaty', *RFE/RL Research Report*, Vol.3, No.14, 8 April 1994, pp.19–27.
The Document of National Understanding: An Analysis, Prospects for Lebanon No.4, Oxford, Centre for Lebanese Studies, May 1992.
Thompson, M., *A Paper House – The Ending of Yugoslavia*, London, Vintage, 1992.
Thorer, Georg, *Free and Swiss: The Story of Switzerland*, London, Oswald Wolff, 1970.
Trofimenkoff, Susan Mann, *The Dream of Nation*, Toronto, Gage, 1983.
Tully, M. and S. Jacob, *Amritsar: Mrs Gandhi's Last Battle*, New Delhi, Rupa Books, 1985.
Valles, J.M.A. and M. Cuchillo Foix 'Decentralisation in Spain: A Review' *European Journal of Political Research*, Vol.16, 1988.
Walker, R, *Six Years that Shook the World: Perestroika – The Impossible Project*, Manchester, Manchester University Press, 1993.
Watts, Ronald L. and Douglas M. Brown, *Options for a New Canada*, Toronto, University of Toronto Press, 1991.
Webber, Jeremy, *Re–imagining Canada*, Montreal and Kingston, McGill-Queens University University Press, 1994.
West, R., *Black Lamb and Grey Falcon: Journey Through Yugoslavia*, Edinburgh, Canongate, 1993.
Whittington, Michael S. and Glen Williams, *Canadian Politics in the 1980s*, Toronto, Methuen, 1984.
Whittington, Michael S. and Glen Williams, *Canadian Politics in the 1990s*, Toronto, Nelson, 1995.
Wilson, C., 'Note of Dissent', in *Scotland's Government. The Report of the Scottish Constitutional Committee*, Edinburgh, The Scottish Constitutional Committee, 1970.
Wolchik, S., 'The Politics of Ethnicity in Post–Communist Czechoslovakia', in *East European Politics and Society*, Vol. 8, No. 1, 1994.
Wylie, R. Neville, 'Life between the Volcanoes: Switzerland during the Second World War', *The Historical Journal*, Vol. 38, No. 3, 1995, pp. 759–68.

Xunta De Galicia 'Planes de Ayuda a la Galicia del Exterior', Santiago de
Compostela, University of Santiago de Campostello, 1991.

Zeine, Zeine, *The Emergence of Arab Nationalism*, Beirut, Khayats, 1966.

Zolberg, A.Z., 'Les Origines du Clivage Communautaire en Belgique,
Esquisse d'une Sociologie Historique', *Recherches Sociologiques*, Vol. VII,
No.2, 1976.

Index